MARKETING
An Introductory Text

By the same author

PRODUCT POLICY AND MANAGEMENT (with Ronald McTavish)
(Studies in Marketing Management series)

MARKETING: THEORY AND PRACTICE (*editor*)
(Studies in Marketing Management series)

MARKETING NEW INDUSTRIAL PRODUCTS

MARKETING IN ADVERSITY (*editor*)

INDUSTRIAL INNOVATION (*editor*)

MARKETING
An Introductory Text

Michael J. Baker

B.A., B.Sc. (Econ.), Dip.M., D.B.A.

Professor of Marketing
University of Strathclyde

THIRD EDITION

First edition 1971
Reprinted 1972, 1973
Second edition 1974
Reprinted 1976, 1977, 1978
Third edition 1979
Reprinted 1980, 1981 (twice)

Published by
THE MACMILLAN PRESS LTD
London and Basingstoke
Companies and representatives throughout the world

Printed in Hong Kong

British Library Cataloguing in Publication Data

Baker, Michael John
  Marketing. – 3rd ed.
  1. Marketing
  I. Title
  658.8   HE5415

  ISBN 0–333–23639–4
  ISBN 0–333–23640–8 Pbk

To SHEILA

Contents

Contents

Contents

List of Tables

List of Figures

Preface to the Third Edition

In the Preface to the Second Edition I noted that sufficient changes of substance had occurred to merit an extensive revision of the factual content, together with the addition of some supplementary material reflecting new developments, such as the emergence of Social Marketing. Much the same motives have prompted the preparation of a Third Edition.

However, the author of a marketing text must be conscious not only of the need for accuracy and relevance but also of the needs of his audience. In the eight years which have elapsed since the first publication of this text these needs have altered substantially. Marketing has now found its way into the curriculum of many more courses, all of which require a synoptic overview of both the philosophy and practice. Simultaneously with this wider acceptance has developed a demand for a more rigorous treatment of the theoretical foundation, so that marketing practice may be related more meaningfully to the core disciplines of economics and the behavioural sciences.

To meet these needs the content of this edition has been expanded by almost 50 per cent primarily due to the inclusion of new chapters on:

Market Structure, Conduct and Performance
Consumer Behaviour
Marketing Communications
Marketing and Economic Growth
The Written Analysis of Cases

Additional material has also been included on the definition of marketing (Chapter 1), scaling methods (Chapter 9) budgeting and cost control, margins and discounts, i.e. 'marketing arithmetic'

(Chapter 20). However, to avoid duplication Chapters 2 and 3 have now been combined into a single chapter.

The inclusion of a new chapter on Market Structure reflects two basic trends in the 1970s – a wider acceptance of the role of market forces in centrally planned economies, and the growing involvement of government in the operation of market economies through both regulation and their buying power. Similarly, a brief discussion of marketing's role in promoting economic growth seems called for in view of the growing concern with conspicuous consumption in advanced economies and the accompanying pressures for 'demarketing'. Such pressures tend to ignore the desperate need for many developing countries to improve their standard of living and the role which modern marketing practice and techniques can play in contributing to this goal.

The two, more theoretical chapters on Consumer Behaviour and Marketing Communications reflect the desirability of including an overview of the conceptual foundations upon which much of the practice of 'marketing' rests. They also go some way to reducing the 'economic' bias of the earlier editions.

Chapter 21 'The Written Analysis of Cases' is in fact a reprint of an article which appeared in the *Quarterly Review of Marketing* some years ago in response to student demand for guidelines on how to handle a method of examination which is proving increasingly popular in business courses.

Many of these changes have been prompted by helpful and constructive criticism from colleagues in other countries, especially those whose educational system is similar to that of the United Kingdom. This is particularly true of those developing countries in which the book has been adopted and the need is for a fuller treatment but with a rather different orientation from the major American texts. I hope that this Third Edition will meet these needs, while for those requiring a more detailed treatment the Macmillan Series in Marketing Management will provide the depth of coverage inappropriate for an introductory text.

Similarly, the new edition and specialist texts in the Macmillan series have been designed to meet the syllabus requirements of B.E.C., Scotbec, the Institute of Marketing and C.A.M. and provide a comprehensive coverage of their curricula.

Acknowledgements

The author and publishers wish to thank the following, who have kindly given permission for the use of copyright material:

The Advertising Association, for use of Table 15.6: Total Media Advertising Expenditure.

The American Marketing Association, for use of extracts from an article entitled 'Psychographics: A Critical Review' by William D. Wells published in *Journal of Marketing Research*, vol. XII (May 1975).

The Controller of Her Majesty's Stationery Office, for use of statistical data.

A. C. Nielsen Company Ltd, for use of Table 9.4: Nielsen Food Index.

Martin Simmons, for use of tables from *The Market Research Society Yearbook* (1978).

Every effort has been made to trace all the copyright-holders, but if any have been inadvertently overlooked the publishers will be pleased to make the necessary arrangement at the first opportunity.

Preface to the Second Edition

Although only three years have elapsed since the first publication of this book, sufficient changes of substance have occurred to warrant a revised edition. However, in recognising this need, I have been conscious of the fact that second editions reflect at least modest success of the original. In consequence, one must be careful not to alter the formula unless there are strong indications that such a change is necessary. The many comments I have received from my colleagues do not suggest that wholesale revision is required.

In the Preface to the first edition I made it quite clear that my personal objective was to fill a gap in the marketing literature for a basic introductory text based, as far as possible, on British institutions and practice. I am gratified to learn from both my colleagues and my students that I have been reasonably successful in achieving this objective. Clearly, this is not to say that the text wholly satisfies everyone's needs and I have tried to incorporate some changes prompted by the constructive criticism I have received. However, in doing so, I have been sensitive to the fact that publishing costs are escalating and so have attempted to retain as much of the original text as possible. As a result I am hopeful that costs may be minimised and so permit publication at a reasonable price.

In addition to updating fact and examples I have also made the following changes. First, I have included suggestions for further reading in a number of chapters where I considered insufficient references had been made in the body of the chapter. Second, I have included some examination questions taken from the Papers set by the Institute of Marketing and in my own Department, and gratefully acknowledge permission to reproduce these. Finally, I have added a completely new chapter in which I review briefly what I consider to be the two most significant trends in marketing today.

Preface to the First Edition

In view of the ever-increasing number of books on Marketing one is entitled to question the publication of yet another text on the subject. What claim has it for attention, what differentiates it from all the others?

Few textbooks have the distinction of originality in terms of their content, and the author's justification in writing such a book is that he believes he can present existing knowledge in a more meaningful way, or better suited to a particular purpose. In writing this book I have tried to achieve both of these objectives.

Several years' experience of teaching Marketing to students preparing for H.N.C., H.N.D., D.M.S. and Diploma in Marketing examinations has convinced me of the need for an introductory text which synthesises the basic descriptive material necessary to a broad overview of the subject. Although there are a number of such texts, they suffer from the disadvantage that they are of American origin and so describe American rather than British institutions, added to which they tend to be both verbose and expensive.

From the teacher's point of view this creates a dilemma. He cannot expect his students to buy a series of specialised texts, dealing with various aspects of marketing, written by British authors, and a reading list is of limited use when few libraries possess more than two copies of a given text. Usually this dilemma is resolved by the teacher delivering a series of descriptive lectures to ensure adequate coverage of the basic principles demanded by the syllabus to which he is working. A preferable approach would be to assign readings from a text designed to cover the essential groundwork, and to devote the limited hours of class contact to ensuring that students have understood the subject matter and to reviewing current development and applications. This book represents an attempt to provide such a framework by synthesising the basic principles normally covered in an introductory course in Marketing. Although it is believed that the content is adequate for this purpose it must be emphasised that the author views the text as a foundation for further study. To this end, a list of supplementary readings is included, in addition to specific sources cited in the text, so that the reader may explore specific topics in greater detail. Further, although numerous examples are cited few of these are developed in detail on the grounds that:

(a) The reader should be encouraged to draw on his own knowledge and experience to identify practical implementation of the principles described.

(b) Marketing is a dynamic process and specific examples rapidly become dated. They can also be misleading unless accompanied by a full statement of the actual environmental context which prompted the course of action/outcome described. To have included such extensive descriptions would have greatly increased the length of the text, and consequently its production costs, out of all proportion to their value.

(c) There is an extensive and growing body of case material, together with an increasing number of descriptive articles in the management journals and quality newspapers, which may usefully be used in conjunction with the text.

Clearly, the amount of additional material necessary to ensure adequate coverage will depend upon the specific syllabus which is being followed.

The book itself falls into four parts. Part One is concerned with the concept of marketing and a description of its evolution. Part Two deals with supply and demand, the controlling factors which determine the nature of markets, while Part Three describes extant patterns of distribution within which the firm must operate. Part Four consists of an examination of the various marketing functions and concludes with a brief review of the manner in which they may be combined into a competitive strategy. Essentially, therefore, the book deals with the concept, the environmental constraints and the methodology of marketing.

Part One

Introduction

1 The Marketing Concept

WHAT IS 'MARKETING'?

In Britain recent years have seen a remarkable growth of interest, both public and private, in 'marketing'. The classified columns of the quality papers come out in a daily rash of advertisements seeking to secure the services of 'experienced marketing men', while the editorial columns exhort the industrialist to export more through the adoption of modern marketing practices.

Despite the interest and publicity a cursory sampling of opinion reveals considerable confusion, and not a little scepticism, as to the exact nature of the subject of marketing. The purpose of this chapter is to try and clarify the nature and scope of marketing.

PROBLEMS OF DEFINITION

On first acquaintance with a new subject most of us like to be given a definition which summarises its subject matter as succinctly as possible. Further, we expect this definition to be generally agreed upon by those who profess knowledge of the subject so that whatever personal idiosyncrasies may be demonstrated in the subsequent exposition there will be a common starting-point to which the student can return, and against which he may measure the expositor's interpretation. Herein lies the would-be student of marketing's predicament – virtually every text on marketing starts with a different definition. A selection of the better-known ones in circulation quickly demonstrates this point.

4   *Introduction*

MARKETING DEFINITIONS

1. Marketing is the process of determining consumer demand for a product or service, motivating its sale and distributing it into ultimate consumption at a profit. (E. F. L. Brech, *Principles of Management*: Longmans, 1953)
2. Marketing is selling goods that don't come back to people who do.
3. Marketing is not only much broader than selling, it is not a specialised activity at all. It encompasses the entire business. It is the whole business seen from the point of view of its final result, that is, from the customer's point of view. Concern and responsibility for marketing must therefore permeate all areas of the enterprise.
4. Marketing is the distinguishing, the unique function of the business. ((3) and (4) Peter F. Drucker, *The Practice of Management*: Harper & Row, 1954)
5. Marketing – The performance of business activities that direct the flow of goods and services from producer to consumer or user.

   *Marketing is the creation of time, place and possession utilities.
   *Marketing moves goods from place to place, stores them, and effects changes in ownership by buying and selling them.
   *Marketing consists of the activities of buying, selling, transporting and storing goods.
   *Marketing includes those business activities involved in the flow of goods and services between producers and consumers.

   (Converse, Huegy and Mitchell, *Elements of Marketing*: 7th ed., Prentice-Hall, 1965)

6. Marketing is the set of human activities directed at facilitating and consummating exchanges. (Kotler, *Marketing Management*, 2nd ed., Prentice-Hall Inc., 1972)
7. The delivery of a standard of living.
8. Marketing is – the process whereby society, to supply its consumption needs, evolves distributive systems composed of participants, who, interacting under constraints – technical (economic) and ethical (social) – create the transactions or flows which resolve market separations and result in exchange

and consumption. (Robert Bartels, 'The General Theory of Marketing', *Journal of Marketing*, XXXII (Jan 1968) 29–33)
9. The function of marketing is the establishment of contact. (Paul T. Cherington, *The Elements of Marketing*: Macmillan, 1920)

The proliferation of definitions was the subject of an article entitled 'What Exactly is Marketing' (*Quarterly Review of Marketing*, Winter 1975) in which Keith Crosier reviewed over fifty definitions and which he classified into three major groups:

1. Definitions which conceive of marketing as a *process* 'enacted via the marketing channel connecting the producing company with its market', e.g. 'The primary management function which organises and directs the aggregate of business activities involved in converting customer purchasing power into effective demand for a specific product or service and in moving the product or service to the final customer or user, so as to achieve company-set profit or other objectives' (L. W. Rodger, *Marketing in a Competitive Economy*, 3rd rev. ed., Cassell, 1971)
2. Definitions which see marketing as a *concept* or *philosophy of business* – 'the idea that marketing is a social exchange process involving willing consumers and producers', e.g. 'Selling is preoccupied with the seller's need to convert his product into cash; marketing with the idea of satisfying the needs of the customer by means of the product and the whole cluster of things associated with creating, delivering and finally consuming it' (T. Levitt, 'Marketing Myopia', *Harvard Business Review*, 1960)
3. Definitions which emphasise marketing as an *orientation* – 'present to some degree in both consumers and producers: the phenomenon which makes the concept and the process possible'. Only one example is cited by Crosier (from the philosopher Erich Fromm) and is felt to be an unconvincing argument in favour of a third category beyond the view of marketing as a function or as a concept.

However, one cannot argue with Crosier's final group of definitions, which seem agreed only on the point that marketing is a complex and confusing phenomenon that combines both the philosophy of business and its practice.

There is a general consensus in these definitions *but* there is no single definition. An explanation of this is to be found in *The Meaning and Sources of Marketing Theory* (M. Halbert: McGraw-Hill, Marketing Science Institute series, 1965): 'Marketing, however, has no recognised central theoretical basis such as exists for many other disciplines, notably the physical sciences and, in some cases, the behavioural sciences' (p. 9). (Chapter 17 comments further on the development of theory in marketing in recent years.)

MARKETING: ART OR SCIENCE?

The aim of the book quoted above is 'to explore the possibilities of having a science of marketing. How to put scientific concepts and marketing content together is the subject matter of this report' (preface, p. xiii). Tacitly, the rationale behind the publication of this book is an admission that marketing is *not* a science; it also demonstrates the belief that *it ought to be*.

In examining possible sources of marketing theory Halbert notes that marketing has borrowed heavily from the business disciplines (economics, law, etc), the social and behavioural sciences and the methodological sciences (mathematics, etc.) and that these borrowings have included content, or data, techniques and concepts. As yet this material has not been synthesised into a generally accepted theory and so results in the apparent conflict inherent in the plethora of definitions. Until a general theory is evolved the practitioners' and academics' view of the subject tends to be coloured by an emphasis of the discipline from which they came to marketing. This is certainly true of this book which is biased towards economics but, it is hoped, for reasons other than that the author was trained as an economist.

As indicated by the title, and in the Preface, this book is intended as an introduction to the subject, In view of the fact that many students have studied some economics it seemed logical to build upon this knowledge rather than give a behavioural or quantitative emphasis. Psychology, Sociology and Mathematics are less often found in the curriculum of 'business' courses at the undergraduate level and a 'Primer of Marketing' is an inappropriate place for an introduction of these disciplines. However, some discussion of concepts from the behavioural science is contained in the chapters on Consumer Behaviour (Chapter 4) and Marketing Communications (Chapter 14) and will be sufficient to indicate the relevance of these disciplines to the newcomer to marketing. The student who intends to progress beyond the elementary and descriptive aspects of marketing contained in this book will find sufficient references in the bibliography from which to launch into an investigation of other disciplines and their relevance to marketing.

From a negative point of view, then, marketing is just a hotchpotch of ideas 'borrowed' from other disciplines. More positively it rests on the simple principle that supply must be a function of demand. In the opinion of marketing men this offers the best approach to the solution of the central economic problem – the allocation of scarce resources so as to maximise satisfaction. However, to say that supply must be a function of demand is an oversimplification. Many economists would add that it is a truism which has been in currency since Adam Smith wrote his *Wealth of Nations* in 1775, in which he states that: 'Consumption is the sole end and purpose of production. . . .'

FUNDAMENTAL PROBLEMS OF AN 'ECONOMY'

Essentially an economy is a system by which people earn a living and their standard of living is generally accepted as a reliable indication of the efficiency of the economy. Paul Samuelson states succinctly the three fundamental problems which an economy must grapple with in his standard text *Economics — an Introductory Analysis*, 9th ed. (McGraw-Hill, 1973) pp. 17–18, namely:

1. *What* commodities shall be produced and in what quantities? That is, how much and which of alternative goods and services shall be produced?

2. *How* shall goods be produced? That is, by whom and with what resources and in what technological manner are they to be produced?

3. *For Whom* are goods to be produced? That is, who is to enjoy and get the benefit of the goods and services provided? Or, to put the same thing in another way: How is the total of the national product to be distributed among different individuals and families?

Many solutions have been proposed and some at least have

proved in part successful; others have merely aggravated the situation. At the same time no commonly agreed on solution has been achieved and there is an apocryphal story of a business tycoon who instructed his personnel director to find and employ a one-armed economist. When asked why he replied: 'I'm fed up of "on the one hand this, on the other hand that"!' In reality most economists agree that maximising satisfaction is the problem, but differ only in how this is to be achieved. Those who have accepted the marketing concept believe the real solution may be expressed something like this: 'If economies are comprised of people, and we are endeavouring to allocate scarce resources in order to maximise satisfaction, then it is the satisfaction of people which we are aiming at. This being so it is essential that we determine first what people want and then allocate our resources accordingly.' In other words, we must determine the nature and strength of demand and create supplies of goods and services to satisfy these demands.

In studying how this concept may be related to the solution of the problem two approaches are possible. Firstly, there is the macro approach which treats national economies as the basic unit and then investigates marketing as a part of a bigger whole. Secondly, there is the micro approach which looks at marketing from the point of view of the business organisation and its functioning within the economy. The latter viewpoint is the one adopted for the purpose of this book in the belief that although all of us are members of large groupings, be they national, ethnic or religious, we are more at home in dealing with smaller sub-groups the operation of which it is easier to evaluate and comprehend. If the role and nature of marketing can be understood in these terms its functions in the economy as a whole will be more easily understood.

If the marketing concept is so simple, how is it that only in this century it has gained any credence and support? The answer is to be found in economic history, in which the evolution of economics may be studied, and no apologies are offered for the summary which follows. The objective underlying the inclusion of this summary is the need to put marketing in perspective – to try and explain why it is only in this century that marketing has emerged as a significant concept which is quickly converting many to its tenets.

ECONOMIC EVOLUTION OF A THEORY OF CONSUMPTION

If one examines the development of an advanced industrial economy such as our own, one can clearly distinguish a number of stages through which it has passed, each of which represents a step forward as compared with the preceding stage.

THE DEVELOPMENT OF CRAFT INDUSTRY

From the Norman conquest to the mid-fourteenth century England's economy was organised on a feudal basis in which the Manor represented the major economic unit of production and consumption. The Manorial system was based on an ideal of self-sufficiency under which each self-contained community endeavoured to meet all its own requirements with regard to both production and consumption. Under such a system the variety of goods available for consumption depended directly on the factors of production possessed by the community, and the skill of the individuals comprising it. The limitations imposed by the size of the unit, coupled with similar limitations with regard to the skill and knowledge of its members, effectively reduced it to a subsistence economy concerned primarily with satisfying the essential requirements of life – food, shelter and clothing.

For a variety of reasons the feudal system broke down far earlier in England than was the case in Europe generally. Among the more important reasons may be distinguished the shortage of labour following the Black Death, and the demand for English wool to trade with Europe to secure supplies of commodities not readily available within the economy. This demand encouraged the Manorial lords to free the serfs from their feudal duties in order that the lords might repossess the land they occupied and rear sheep on it. This dispossession of the serfs in turn led to a migration of population from the country to the urban centres in search of employment in the developing craft industries.

Craft industry leads to specialisation in the production of particular goods, units of which can then be sold, enabling the craftsman to satisfy his needs by purchasing the output of other specialist producers. As a result there is an increase in individual skill which leads to greater productivity and output. At this stage of economic development, however, the volume of production is small, the average income is small, and the market is distinctly local with the exception of a very limited range of goods imported and exported to meet the demand of a gentry with sufficient income to afford them.

THE DIVISION OF LABOUR

The next stage of economic development is usually exemplified by Adam Smith's account of the pin-making industry, where an enormous increase in output followed job simplification with the same input of factors of production, excluding raw materials. Smith noted that where men were engaged in all processes involved in the manufacture of pins their average output was twenty pins per day; when the manufacture of pins was broken down into separate processes output for the group rose to four thousand pins per man per day. Two points are of particular significance in this step forward. First, organisation is required to bring together the men, provide a place of work and supply raw materials. Second, the enormous increase in output reduces the price of the commodity, necessitates the development of channels of distribution to make the article available to those with a demand for it, and leads to the exploitation of a much larger market.

THE INDUSTRIAL REVOLUTION

The period when this change occurred coincided with the early stages of the Industrial Revolution, which was to give impetus to the growth of a factory economy, job specialisation and mass production techniques. The nature of the steam engine as a power unit – large, inefficient and expensive – meant that the installation of such a plant was only justified if its power output was fully utilised in driving several smaller machines as, for example, looms. This in turn required the construction of factories in which a number of machines and operatives could be assembled, while the simplification of process meant that unskilled labour could be readily trained to perform simple operations.

Concurrent with the increase in output of both capital and consumer goods, lines of communication were developed (canals, and later railways), as were distributive channels, to cope with the movement and sale of this output. By 1800 we had already become a 'nation of shopkeepers', a derisory epithet used by Napoleon, who later learned to his cost that only a rich and strong nation can support extensive service industries. It is important to remember that at this stage of development the range of consumer goods offered for sale was limited, and that Britain constituted virtually the sole source of supply for a world market hungry for such manufactures. The disposable income of the home consumer was small but a rapid expansion of population due to advances in medicine and public health created a continually expanding demand. The increase in knowledge of the nature and causes of disease in itself would have been of marginal value had not methods of large-scale production permitted the manufacture of the physical goods required in the creation of adequate sewerage and drainage schemes, and created the wealth with which to pay for them.

INTERNATIONAL TRADE AND INDUSTRIALISATION

Throughout the nineteenth century home industry expanded enormously, as did world demand for our products. In 1850 Britain's exports amounted to nearly 40 per cent of all international trade, which, when it is realised that, by definition, the maximum any single nation could achieve is 50 per cent, is an extremely impressive performance and one which has never been surpassed since. This date marks a watershed, however, for it was to see the birth of the United States of America, and later other Western European countries, as competing industrial powers. At first the trend characteristic of the first half of the century continued; namely, the export of capital goods to help establish basic industry in overseas countries in exchange for raw materials and food (coupled with a nearly insatiable demand for consumer goods). The development of industry in other countries resulted in a considerable increase in total output so that although our share of world trade declined, its value and volume continued to increase rapidly as the increase in income in other countries created an ever-growing demand for our products.

Initially, the newly emergent industrial nation must pass through the stages noted in respect of the British economy – namely, the development of basic industries such as iron and steel, which provide the raw materials of manufacturing industry, followed by the development of the latter along with lines of communication, and channels of distribution. However, the process is considerably speeded up for the newcomer as it is able to make use of existing knowledge and skill, and unite all the latest design in plant and equipment pioneered by someone else. As a result the new industrial nations are able to achieve rapid economic growth, e.g. the United States 1870–1900, Japan 1900–13 or 1945–65, creating a growing demand for basic consumer goods which can largely be met by the economy itself. In the meantime, however, the original industrial nations are not standing still but are channelling their skill and knowledge into the production of more sophisticated products which the newer industrial nations are eager, and able, to buy. A good current example of this is the demand for electronic equipment, machine tools and transportation equipment by the developing nations like India or Australia, replacing their former demand for basic products like steel or textiles in which they are now largely self-sufficient.

As a result of this economic development an increasing number of people are earning incomes which enable them to translate their latent demand for consumption goods into an effective demand.

THE CREATION OF 'EXCESS' SUPPLY

However, the market, both nationally and internationally, has changed radically for, despite this growth in demand, increased productivity has resulted in a level of supply which is more than sufficient to cater for effective demand in any specific area. No longer is demand for a product chasing a limited supply of that good so that selling is an automatic result of production. Under present conditions large numbers of producers are competing for the privilege of supplying the consumer with their own output while trying to combat the claims of alternative or substitute goods. It is under these conditions that supply becomes directly controlled by demand, as opposed to demand accepting that which is supplied. Marketing must replace the narrower concept of selling in the sense of merely distributing one's output.

The situation with which we are faced, therefore, is one in which consumer demand dictates that which will be produced. In a sense this has always been the case, in that man has concentrated on producing those items in greatest demand. When the consumer has a limited income the majority of this is expended on essential requirements necessary for the maintenance of life, leaving very little for expenditure on desirable, but less essential, goods and services. This situation is to be found in the underdeveloped countries at the present time. For example in India 85–90 per cent of income is expended on basic essentials, leaving only 10–15 per cent for the purchase of medical services, non-essential foodstuffs, etc. The comparative wealth of some national economies is shown in the table below.

In the eighteenth and nineteenth centuries poverty was prevalent throughout the world for the majority of the population. Production was concentrated in satisfying basic demands, with a

TABLE 1.1 *Gross domestic product per capita U.S. $ (1975)*

$0–200	*$201–400*	*$401–600*
Afghanistan	Bolivia	Jordan
Pakistan	Kenya	Peru
Zaïre	Nigeria	
	Egypt	
$601–800	*$801–1000*	*$801–1700*
Algeria	Turkey	Brazil
Malaysia		Jamaica
Chile		South Africa
		Cyprus
$1701–4000	*$4000+7000*	*$7000+*
Singapore	Australia	Sweden
Venezuela	France	United States
Argentina	West Germany	Denmark
Spain	United Kingdom	Norway
Poland	Canada	Switzerland
	Saudi Arabia	
	Japan	

limited output of luxury goods for a small market comprising the upper classes.

With the rise in real income which accompanied increased productivity and economic growth the proportion of expenditure absorbed by essential purchases is considerably reduced, despite changes in the nature of the demand for these essentials, e.g. less bread and potatoes, more meat and butter, better houses, clothes, etc., so that in an advanced economy only 50 per cent of disposable income is spent on these items, leaving an equal proportion for the purchase of non-essential goods, services and saving.

Within the realm of essential purchases the nature and volume of demand are relatively simple to predict, and patterns of group behaviour are notably marked. With regard to the balance of expenditure on other products determination of demand for a particular item is far more complex.

THE MARKETING CONCEPT IN AN ERA OF ACCELERATING CHANGE

The 'potted history' of the stages through which an advanced economy passes does scant justice to the subject and further reading is essential to a proper and objective understanding of it. As stated initially, the intention underlying its inclusion was to give some perspective to the development of economies to the point at which a need for a new economic concept emerged. A study of economic history develops, above all else, a sense of accelerating change. At the turn of the nineteenth century there were no steam engines or steam ships, large-scale steel production had still to be developed, as had the telephone, electricity, the internal combustion engine and innumerable others that were familiar, though not commonplace, by the end of the century. In this century the tempo has quickened and within fifty years of the first manned flight, man had a satellite in space orbiting the earth. By 1969 he had landed on the moon. Table 1.2 indicates the elapsed time between 'invention' and commercial development of a number of familiar 'products' and emphasises the increase in the tempo of technological advance.

Two points need stessing in this context. First, each new development adds momentum to the process, in that it increases

TABLE 1.2 *Elapsed time, invention to commercial development,*
of a number of familiar products

Product	Time from invention to commercial exploitation
Electric motor	65 years
T.V.	52 years
Vacuum tube	33 years
Zip-fastener	30 years
X-ray tube	18 years
Frozen foods	15 years
Nuclear reactors	10 years
Radar	5 years
Solar batteries	3 years

our ability to produce. This may be immediately discernible, as in the case when automation is introduced, or less directly so, when a computer is installed to permit the solution of complex problems hitherto considered insoluble. These in turn may provide the key to further technological advance. The second point is that increased wealth results in an overall improvement in the standard of living and, consequently, an increase in population.

THE CHALLENGE OF THE POPULATION EXPLOSION

This increase in population is largely attributable to an extension of the expectation of life, due to medical advance, rather than an increase in the crude birth rate, which, on the contrary, has tended to fall with the increase in affluence. More people represents a greater aggregate demand for goods and services. At the same time it represents an increase in a basic factor of production, labour, and thus provides one resource essential to the increase in supply necessary to satisfy this increase in demand.

Many economists have expressed concern over the population explosion, pointing out that whereas population increases in a geometrical progression increases in output, particularly of food-stuffs, tend to follow an arithmetical scale that will soon reach a point where demand will once again outstrip supply, at least in the areas of basic necessities. It would be foolish to deny that there is an element of truth in this contention, just as it would be foolish to adopt a fatalistic approach and accept the situation as inevitable. A superficial examination of the yield of Dutch farms as compared with those in the American Middle West will soon reveal a disparity of 5:1 in favour of the former in terms of yield. In the present situation there is no point in increasing the yield of the wheat farms of the United States as the present supply/demand situation is such that the increased investment necessary to increase yield would not be recoverable in profits owing to low market prices. On the other hand, if demand increases while supply remains static, prices will rise thus making further investments, necessary to increase yield, a profitable exercise. It is realistic to assume that this increased output will be forthcoming. (For an extended discussion of these issues the reader should consult D. Meadows *et al.*, *Limits to Growth* (London: Earth Island, 1972) and the critique of it in H. S. D. Cole *et al.*, *Thinking about the Future* (Chatto & Windus for Sussex University Press, 1973).)

Over a longer time-scale it is possible to envisage a situation where supply created by conventional farming methods, as we know them today, will be insufficient to meet projected demand based on current world population trends. Marketing has no need for Jeremiahs still less for fatalists! Recognising that a need exists or is likely to exist, the role of the marketer is to deploy resources to maximise satisfaction by meeting these needs. If we are to predict the nature of demand in the future it also behoves us to undertake courses of action which will enable us to satisfy this demand. To argue that present methods are insufficient to satisfy a predictable future demand ignores the facts. Icarus failed to master the secret of flight because he lacked a high melting point wax: this is a factor which is virtually irrelevant in terms of aerospace research today. Failures, more often than not, result from the narrow inflexible approach which presumes that no further improvement or advance is possible; that the *status quo* is immutable. The few examples quoted should suffice to show that each breakthrough opens up whole new territories for exploration. 1978 saw the birth of the first 'test-tube' baby and no doubt similar occurrences will attract considerable attention for a year or so. When did you last read a front-page newspaper story about an operation for appendicitis? Other than those performed on notable personalities, or under unusual conditions, no reference is made to the thousands of such operations performed annually. Once they were newsworthy, now they are commonplace. This undoubtedly will be the case with test-tube babies, organ transplantation, bionic men and the like in the years to come – always providing that economies continue to grow and increase wealth so that the physical and human resources are available.

THE ROLE OF MARKETING

Marketing's role is to ensure the continuance in growth of economies, and the individuals' standard of living. In Chapter 2 the nature of demand will be considered in greater detail; at this point it is sufficient to point out that the determination of needs and wants, backed up by purchasing power, must indicate how management is to deploy the resources entrusted to it so as to maximise satisfaction in the total sense. If management succeeds in this, then human welfare will be optimised within the limitations imposed by the then available resources. Not only that; by thinking ahead and predicting the future needs and wants of people, action may be implemented now which will ensure their future satisfaction. (Aspects of welfare economics are largely ignored in this treatment on the basis that if private enterprise concentrates on profit maximisation the State will be able to implement the people's demand for welfare and social services from the taxes levied on these profits, i.e. the bigger the profits the greater the potential revenue from taxation. It is recognised that corporate management frequently abstains from profit maximisation for social and ethical reasons, *inter alia*, but it will be simpler for our purpose here to assume that entrepreneurs seek to maximise consumer satisfaction as a means to maximising profits.)

To conclude this introductory review some reference must be made to the functional aspects of marketing with which the majority of this book is concerned.

MARKETING FUNCTIONS

If we accept the marketing concept, essentially we are agreeing to a simple proposition that supply is a function of demand and, therefore, subservient to it. Demand is the controlling factor, and an analysis and understanding of it must underly all marketing functions. In their excellent book *Business Economics*, Bates and Parkinson distinguish four managerial aspects of demand which for brevity and lucidity would be difficult to better, namely:

1. Analysis and forecasting, i.e. market research.
2. Product development and design.
3. Influencing of demand – design, advertising, etc.
4. Service – distribution, after-sales service, etc.

Much that follows is an examination, in greater depth, of these functions in isolation, but before proceeding to such a consideration, it is necessary to understand that marketing depends on co-ordination of these separate ingredients to achieve a 'mix' suitable to the particular situation in hand.

The idea of a 'mix' of marketing function was conceived by Professor Neil Borden of the Harvard Business School as '. . . a schematic plan to guide analysis of marketing problems through utilisation of

'(*a*) a list of the important forces emanating from the market which bear upon the marketing operations of an enterprise;
'(*b*) a list of the elements (procedures and policies) of marketing programs.

'The marketing mix refers to the apportionment of effort, the combination, the designing, and the integration of the elements of marketing into a program or "mix" which on the basis of an appraisal of the market forces, will best achieve the objectives of an enterprise at a given time.'

Each function is a specialisation in its own right and it is unlikely that any single person could acquire full mastery of them all. Even if one could, it is doubtful whether one would then be able to make an objective assessment of the true relative value of each in any given marketing situation. Similarly, although many very successful marketing men have started life as a specialist in a single function, too high a degree of involvement is bound to bias decisions, albeit subconsciously. At such, the marketer, as a strategist and administrator, should aim at an understanding of the specialisations so that he may select the appropriate tactics to achieve his overall objective.

There is no need for a successful general to be a marksman, a ballistic expert, or expert at any other military skill for that matter. On the other hand, if he is not aware of the possibilities and limitations of the resources at his disposal it is unlikely that he will be able to combine them to achieve the maximum effect. As with the general so with the marketer. It is not necessary to be a clinical psychologist to appreciate the value of motivation research, or a statistician to understand the meaning of significance in relation to sampling results.

At the same time it is essential that the various marketing functions be isolated and examined before returning to the question of their co-ordination into an overall managerial concept. In general terms, the chapters which comprise Part Four concern functional areas within marketing which are specialisations in their own right. At some time or other the aspiring general manager will come into contact with some, or all of them, just as he will endeavour to acquire knowledge and experience of production and financial management. All of us cannot become chief executive and, for most, a particular functional area such as market research may become a job for life from which great satisfaction can be derived. Whatever our ambitions, or our present occupation, it is of paramount importance that one recognises that the mix variables are interdependent and interacting. To view them as if they existed in isolation and in separate watertight compartments is to ignore the true import of the marketing concept. Everyone in a firm or an economy is making a contribution which in the aggregate will determine the material welfare of us all. Co-ordination of individual effort is critical to the overall standard of performance but this cannot be achieved by direction alone. Co-operation is an essential prerequisite, and this can only come from understanding how the separate parts together make a whole greater than the sum of those parts ('Synergy', q.v., H. Igor Ansoff, *Corporate Strategy*: Pelican, 1968).

Before proceeding to an examination of the mix variables:

Marketing research
Product development
Pricing
Packaging
Distribution
Advertising and sales promotion

Selling and merchandising
After-sales service

some consideration has been given to a review of the basic elements – demand, supply, companies – to provide a broad background against which to relate these more specific areas.

Similarly three chapters have been devoted to a description of patterns of distribution as they exist; partly to provide background information and partly to contrast the difference, often more real than imagined, in the markets for raw materials, industrial and consumer goods.

Suggestions for further reading

Bartels, Robert, 'Development of Marketing Thought', in *Science in Marketing*, ed. G. Schwartz (Wiley, 1965)

Borden, Neil H., 'The Concept of the Marketing Mix', in *Science in Marketing*, ed. G. Schwartz (Wiley, 1965).

King, R. L., 'The Marketing Concept', in *Science in Marketing*, ed. G. Schwartz (Wiley, 1965)

Kotler, Philip and Levy, Sidney, J., 'Broadening the Concept of Marketing', *Journal of Marketing* vol. 33 (January 1969)

Lipson, Harry A., and Reynolds, Fred D., 'The Concept of the Marketing Mix: Its Development, Uses, and Applications', *M.S.U. Business Topics* (Winter 1970)

Part Two

The Constituent Elements:

Demand, Supply, Companies

2 Market Structure, Conduct and Performance

In the previous chapter we looked briefly at the stages of economic development which led to the emergence of advanced economies with the potential of creating an excess supply of goods and services. To cope with this change in the traditional balance between supply and demand a new approach to resource allocation became necessary and we termed this the marketing concept because of its emphasis upon the market (demand) as the primary basis for investment and production (supply) decisions.

Of course the marketing concept is not new, for producers have always sought to identify those goods in strongest demand and then set out to supply them. However, under conditions of chronic supply deficiency it requires little expertise or sophistication to identify beforehand the most salient demands. Successful entrepreneurs have always been those who have intuitively identified such unsatisfied demands. But in complex, modern markets this is rarely possible without a sound understanding of market structure and market forces and it is these factors which comprise the subject-matter of Part Two.

In this chapter we look first at the structure of industry before examining the phenomenon of concentration in some detail. Attention is then turned to theories of competition and the interaction of supply and demand at the macro level, and this is followed by a discussion of competition and market structure. Chapters 3 and 4 then explore micro aspects of supply and demand in more detail.

THE STRUCTURE OF INDUSTRY

Any discussion of the role of industry must perforce commence with some definition of what we understand by the term. In everyday usage we are accustomed to refer to industries such as the textile industry, the motor industry or the chemical industry without specifying the basis on which a given firm may be judged to be a member of a particular industry. Essentially, individual firms are categorised as belonging to particular industries by virtue of the nature of their output. Thus most definitions of an industry tend to rest upon the existence of competition between sellers of similar products. However, as we shall see, changes in the nature of industrial organisation have resulted in many firms becoming members of more than one industry. Similarly, changes in a firm's product mix may well lead to a change in its basic industrial classification. We return to some of these distinctions below but first we must consider a more fundamental distinction between types of industry.

Conventionally all industry is divided into three major groupings, which are frequently referred to as the primary, secondary and tertiary sectors. Primary industry is concerned with the production of raw materials and includes agriculture, forestry and fishing. Secondary industry includes mining and quarrying and incorporates all those firms concerned with changing the nature and form of raw materials through some form of manufacturing process to the point where they are suitable for consumption either by other industrial users or by ultimate consumers. Finally, the tertiary sector embodies all those organisations which provide services, such as wholesaling, retailing, transportation, banking, entertainment, and so on.

In the twentieth century, considerable changes have taken place in the relative importance and size of these three sectors. As can be seen from Table 2.1 employment in the primary sector fell from 8.14 per cent in 1911 to 1.91 per cent in 1973. In fact this downward trend has persisted since the industrial revolution and was apparent even before that. At the time of the industrial revolution alternative employment opportunities in manufacturing industry encouraged a migration from the rural areas to the new factory towns and allowed farmers to substitute capital for labour through the employment of more efficient farming

TABLE 2.1. *Industrial analysis of occupied population of the United Kingdom, 1911, 1951, 1973 (per 10,000 occupied persons)*

Industry		1911	1951	1973
A	Agriculture and fishing	814	507	191
B	Mining and quarrying	712	382	160
C	Bricks, pottery and glass	101	142	135
	Chemicals, paints, oils, etc.	85	196	206
	Metals, machines, implements, conveyances	972	1717	1767
	Precious metals, jewellery, plate	40	68	n.a.
	Textiles	741	443	262
	Textile goods and clothing	637	324	194
	Skins, leather and fur	51	36	20
	Food, drink and tobacco	307	336	333
	Woodworking	152	148	129
	Paper, printing and book-binding	186	231	253
	Building and contracting	518	635	609
	Other manufacturing industries	79	119	156
	Gas, water and electricity	64	160	152
	Total of B and C	4645	4937	4376
D	Service industries	4551	4556	5433
		10000	10000	10000
	Total occupied population (in thousands)	18351	22610	22662

n.a. = not available.
Sources: data for 1911 and 1951 based on G. C. Allen, *The Structure of Industry in Britain*, 3rd ed. (Longmans, 1970); for 1973 Ministry of Labour and Ministry of Labour and National Insurance (Northern Ireland) 1974; and the distribution of total manpower statistics from the *Annual Abstract of Statistics for the United Kingdom*.

methods. This trend has continued to the present day with the result that mechanisation, advances in plant and animal breeding, and the development of chemical aids have enabled the primary sector to register a significant improvement in output despite a continually declining work-force.

As can be seen from the table, the decline in numbers employed in the primary sector has been balanced by a significant increase in the numbers employed in both the secondary and tertiary sectors.

The Constituent Elements

TABLE 2.2. *Changes in U.K. industrial output, 1935–71 (£m.)*

Industry	1935		1958		1971	
Food, drink and tobacco	665*	(203)†	3751	(917)	8508	(2556)
Chemicals and allied industries	206	(89)	2197	(736)	5103	(1992)
Metal manufacture	245	(88)	2258	(689)	3820	(1307)
Engineering and allied industries	710	(357)	7022	(3227)	16872	(8045)
Textiles, leather and clothing	656	(249)	2686	(967)	4256	(1883)
Other manufactures	413	(237)	2807	(1313)	7437	(3872)
All manufacturing industry	2895	(1223)	20721	(7849)	45996	(19655)
Mining and quarrying	167	(136)	927	(723)	1103	(793)
Construction	295	(150)	2724	(1245)	n.a.	(n.a.)
Gas, electricity and water	181	(128)	1093	(621)	2994	(1897)

*Gross output.
†Net output.
n.a. = not available.
Note: These output figures include a substantial amount of duplication represented by the total value of partly manufactured goods sold by one industrial establishment to another. The net output figure represents the actual value added by each sector and is given in parentheses. The figures for 1935 are classified according to the 1948 edition of the Standard Industrial Classification (S.I.C.) Those for 1958 are based on the 1958 classification, and the figures for 1971 are based on the 1968 edition of the S.I.C. The figures for 1971 are provisional estimates only.

Source: Business Statistics Office, *Census of Production 1971.*

A closer examination of Table 2.1 quickly reveals that increased employment in manufacturing industry as a whole does not reflect an overall increase in the various constituent industries. The numbers employed in the extractive industries – mining and quarrying – have fallen quite dramatically, as have those in the textile goods and clothing industries. Conversely, chemicals and engineering have shown marked increases.

However, the numbers employed in an industry are only one measure of the level of activity. An equally, if not more significant measure is output, and comparative statistics are given in Table 2.2.

Data such as those presented in Tables 2.1 and 2.2 clearly indicate the marked changes which have taken place in industrial structure during this century. Before examining some of the causes which would seem to account for this change it is important to stress that precise comparisons are difficult due to changes in the definition of industries and in the manner in which data have been collected. It is also important to emphasise that broad categories such as those in the two tables disguise marked changes within the categories themselves. Thus in the engineering industry motor-cars and aircraft have come into existence and exhibited marked growth while more traditional industries such as railway locomotives and shipbuilding have exhibited a decline. Similarly, in the textile industry a chemical revolution has led to the substitution of synthetic fibres for their natural counterparts.

More than anything else change in industrial structure in the twentieth century reflects the application of technology which has led to extensive modification of the traditional craft industries and the birth of completely new industries such as electronics and aviation. The impact of this technological revolution is implicit in the disproportionate increase in productivity *vis-à-vis* employment and other factor inputs. However, technological discovery and advance are only a partial explanation of the radical changes which have taken place during this century.

CAUSES OF STRUCTURAL CHANGE

As noted in the preceding section, changes in industrial structure are not an invention of the twentieth century and are to be discerned from the industrial revolution onwards. As a very broad generalisation it would seem that the catalyst for change has been on the supply side, but that ultimately the nature and extent of change has been determined by demand. In simple terms the industrial revolution was the joint outcome of a mechanical and an organisational revolution, The mechanical revolution is generally attributed to the harnessing of steam-power, which led to an organisational revolution in the setting up of a factory system to replace the cottage industry which had preceded it. The enormous increase in output which accompanied these changes led to a marked improvement in living standards and set in train widespread changes in demand.

It is difficult to generalise about changes in demand as these arise from a number of different yet interrelated causes. The trend towards greater social equality has led to enormous improvements in education as well as to a redistribution of income and it is clear that both education and income have marked effects upon consumption patterns. In turn the move to greater social equality is but one manifestation of a marked political change in which large sectors of the economy have come under public control and the purchasing power possessed by such public corporations as the electricity-supply industry, coal-mining and the railways must have a marked impact upon the nature of demand.

At the same time industry has not been slow to realise the opportunity which is implicit in increased personal disposable incomes. As personal incomes increase the proportion expended upon purchases essential to life diminishes and even allowing for increased saving the individual is able to increase his consumption. The latent demand represented by unexpended personal incomes is one of the major spurs to new-product development whereby manufacturers compete to translate this latent demand into an effective demand for their own output. In their efforts to communicate the availability of their new and improved products the manufacturer is aided by the evolution and growth of new channels of communication.

Demographic changes, too, have their impact upon demand. With an increased expectation of life Britain now has an ageing population with a concomitant increase in the demand for products suited to the older age groups, for increased medical services, etc.

Further changes in the structure of industry can be attributed to the impact of foreign competition. Until the middle of the nineteenth century Britain had few competititors for manufactured goods. However, since that time many other nations have industrialised and our dependency on imported food and raw materials has required that we open our markets to these foreign manufacturers. Certainly the decline of the traditional textile industries owes much to highly competitive imported textiles from countries with lower labour costs than our own.

Collectively all these changes in demand have resulted in a corresponding change in industrial structure. Some firms will decline and disappear while others will adjust to the changed environment within which they operate and continue their existence. Similarly, new technology will spawn new firms and new industries.

In his book *The Structure of Industry in Britain* (Longmans, 1970) G. C. Allen advances six reasons to explain how firms are persuaded to take up new lines of manufacture, namely:

'the movement may occur as a by-product of efforts to solve some problems of production and distribution, or as the result of growth which leads to plant imbalance, or as the consequence of some technical discovery which may have a wider application than the original context, or simply because firms see enlarged opportunities in pressing their existing marketing organisation into new uses. The spreading of risk may provide the motive, or the pressure of adversity may impel firms to try new fields as their only chance of survival as substantial producers.'

The phraseology used by Allen tends to suggest, albeit unintentionally, that firms only embark upon some new form of activity by chance or because they are driven to it. As will become clearer later, in dealing with product policy firms may adopt a more purposive attitude than that implied in the above extract.

Without dwelling on the causes of industrial change, many of which are dealt with in greater detail hereafter, it is appropriate at this juncture to examine an apparent consequence of central interest to any discussion on industrial structure, namely the degree of industrial concentration.

INDUSTRIAL CONCENTRATION

In addition to the changes that have taken place between and within industries in terms of their overall size measured by numbers employed or value of their output there have also been marked changes in the nature of the firms which comprise these industries. A frequently remarked trend has been what J. K. Galbraith in *The New Industrial State* (Penguin, 1974) has termed the rise of the 'super corporation'. In simple terms Galbraith's argument is that an increasing proportion of all output is being concentrated in the hands of a limited number of producers. By virtue of the control which these super corporations exercise over supplies of essential goods and services it is implied that the super corporation may exercise undue influence over the operation of the state. More explicitly it is maintained that supply dominance of this kind eliminates competition to the detriment of the average consumer.

Not all students of industry subscribe to the Galbraithian view, and maintain that the emergence of a limited number of very large firms does not necessarily imply the elimination of competition in the market-place. Clearly, if one is to determine the relative merits of the opposing arguments, some form of measure is required which enables us to make a comparative industry analysis over time. A convenient and widely used measure is the *concentration ratio*.

In fact economists have two concepts of concentration. At the macro, or national level, the concept of concentration is used to define the proportion of total industry output accounted for by some predetermined percentage of all firms. At the micro or industry level the concentration ratio expresses the percentage share of total sales of that industry accounted for by a predetermined percentage of all firms in the industry. It will be noted that both descriptions of concentration ratios state that they are computed by calculating the proportion of all output accounted for by a predetermined number of all firms, and it should be noted that there is no universally agreed convention to state what this number should be. Accordingly, when one is interpreting concentration ratios it is most important to ascertain the basis of the computation. In the United Kingdom the most widely used concentration ratios are based on the proportion of all sales in a given product group accounted for by the five largest firms.

As indicated earlier, there is disagreement between economists as to the degree of concentration in U.K. manufacturing industry and to the extent of change in such concentration over time. Writing in 1969 Allen (in the book referred to earlier) took the view that while the available evidence was fragmentary, such calculations as had been attempted seemed to indicate a stabilisation and possibly a slight decline in the overall concentration in industry since 1930. Further, an examination of the identity of the largest companies shows marked changes in this period, reflecting the changing fortunes of the different industries, with the emergence of new areas of activity such as electronics. However, Allen did not have access to the data from the 1968 Census of Production (which was not published until 1974). A summary of these data was presented in an article entitled 'Concentration in U.K. Manufacturing Industry' by David Elliot (*Trade and Industry*, 1 August 1974) and his findings are reproduced in Tables 2.3–2.7. Like

TABLE 2.3. *Average of five-firm concentration ratios (1958–68)*

1963 and 1968: 295 products		1958 and 1968: 157 products	
Average	Change	Average	Change
1963 = 62.0%		1958 = 56.2%	
1968 = 66.0%	+4.0%	1963 = 59.4%	+3.2%
		1968 = 64.5%	+5.1%

Allen, Elliot points out that the data are incomplete for a number of reasons, among which he cites the following:

(*a*) The Business Statistics Office is bound by disclosure rules and does not publish product groups where individual firms may be identified.
(*b*) Product groups where total sales are less than £10 million are not generally shown.
(*c*) No product groups have been selected covering work-done activities.
(*d*) Products that cannot be identified as being homogeneous have been omitted.

However, despite these deficiencies the evidence contained in the tables clearly contradicts Allen's assertion and confirms the opinions of those who have argued that there has been an increase in concentration over recent years. The overall increase is apparent in Tables 2.3 and 2.7, while the increase in particular industries is shown in Table 2.4.

Increases in concentration arise from two major causes. First, there is the disproportionate growth of certain firms, usually due to the superior nature of their products and management, e.g. Xerox and I.B.M. Second, there is growth through amalgamation by a process of merger and acquisition. As can be seen from Table 2.5, the data indicate that the increase in industrial concentration in the United Kingdom during the 1960s has been due in some part to the higher levels of merger activity during that period. However, data such as these only indicate the broad nature of change and tell us little if anything of how this was brought about.

TABLE 2.4. *Average of five-firm sales concentration ratios of products comprising order*

S.I.C. order	Description	Number of products for which ratios available	1968 sales (£m.) of products for which ratios available	Average concentration ratio (%)			Coverage of ratios for each order (%)
				1963	1968	Change	
II	Mining and quarrying	5	136.8	57.4	65.0	+7.6	15
III	Food manufactured including tea and coffee	33	2420.1	78.1	78.9	+0.8	85
	beer, spirits, etc.	6	1193.7	74.4	77.1	+2.7	98
	Cigarettes, tobacco products	3	1393.0	99.2	99.4	+0.2	100
IV	Coal and petroleum products	6	1010.5	91.5	93.5	+2.0	87
V	Chemical and allied industries	39	1952.4	74.0	75.5	+1.5	78
VI	Metal manufacture	8	975.8	72.9	74.3	+1.4	31
VI	Metal manufacture (including steel)	20	2831.0	70.6	79.8	+9.2	93
VII	Mechanical engineering	35	1521.7	60.3	62.4	+2.1	64
VIII	Instrument engineering	5	109.5	60.1	62.3	+2.2	82
IX	Electrical engineering	27	1546.0	68.1	77.2	+9.1	80
X	Shipbuilding and marine engineering	1	60.1	34.6	57.4	+22.8	14
XI	Vehicles	8	1724.0	85.2	89.1	+3.9	57
XII	Metal goods nes	21	1301.0	55.0	57.6	+2.6	78
XIII	Textiles	28	2040.8	41.5	49.7	+8.2	72
XIV	Leather, leather goods, fur	6	139.0	33.8	37.7	+3.9	90
XV	Clothing and footwear	14	792.1	30.1	37.0	+6.9	91
XVI	Bricks, pottery, glass, cement, etc.	16	662.1	65.6	75.5	+9.9	82
XVII	Timber, furniture, etc.	9	543.5	28.0	28.4	+0.4	87
XVIII	Paper, printing and publishing	10	970.3	54.5	56.2	+1.7	84
XIX	Other manufacturing industries	14	674.7	53.5	57.0	+3.5	88
	Total (excluding steel products)	315	22908.1				

Note: nes = not elsewhere stated.

TABLE 2.5. *Concentration change and uses of company funds*

Industrial group	Change in Concentration 1963–8	Average (1964–8) % of funds used for acquisition of subsidiaries
Food	0.8	12.6
Drink	2.7	17.8
Tobacco	0.2	8.5
Chemical and allied industries	1.6	7.2
Metal manufacture	9.2	8.5
Non-electrical engineering	2.1	9.4
Electrical engineering	9.1	34.7
Shipbuilding and marine	22.8	13.0
Vehicles	3.9	13.5
Metal goods [nes]	2.6	6.8
Textiles	8.2	23.0
Leather, leather goods and fur	3.9	1.7
Clothing and footwear	6.9	20.8
Bricks, pottery, glass, etc.	9.9	16.4
Timber, furniture	0.4	5.6
Paper, printing and publishing	1.7	14.0
Other manufacturing	3.5	7.3

Note. [nes] = not elsewhere stated.

TABLE 2.6. *Frequency distribution of concentration ratios*

Size class of ratio	Number (and %) of product in each class				
	1958	1963	1968	1963	1968
0– 19.9	12 (7.6)	8 (5.1)	3. (1.9)	13 (4.4)	7 (2.4)
20– 29.9	23 (14.6)	19 (12.1)	12 (7.6)	27 9.1)	18 (6.1)
30– 39.9	21 (13.4)	20 (12.7)	17 (10.8)	34 (11.5)	24 (8.1)
40– 49.9	10 (6.4)	13 (8.3)	14 (8.9)	24 (8.1)	28 (9.5)
50– 59.9	16 (10.2)	16 (10.2)	23 (14.8)	36 (12.2)	45 (15.8)
60– 69.9	18 (11.5)	19 (12.1)	12 (7.6)	37 (12.5)	31 (10.5)
70– 79.9	20 (12.7)	19 (12.1)	20 (12.7)	39 (13.2)	35 (11.9)
80– 89.9	15 (9.5)	18 (11.5)	22 (14.0)	29 (9.8)	42 (14.2)
90–100	22 (14.0)	25 (15.9)	34 (21.6)	56 (19.0)	65 (22.0)
Totals	157	157	157	295	295

TABLE 2.7. *Overall concentration share of manufacturing net output by the largest 100 firms (%)*

Year	Per cent
1958	31
1963	37
1968	42
1970	45

For the latter one must consult books such as those by Hart, Utton, and Walshe, *Mergers and Concentration in British Industry* (Cambridge University Press, 1973) or Channon's study, *The Strategy and Structure of British Enterprise* (Macmillan, 1973). The latter book concentrates on the evolution of the 100 largest manufacturing companies in the United Kingdom and traces the development of the strategy and structure of these concerns over the period 1950–70.

CONCENTRATION AND ORGANISATIONAL STRUCTURE

As Channon notes in the introduction to his book the development of the large business organisation is closely associated with the growth of improved communications, and in the case of the United States, where most research has been undertaken, with the development of the railroad in particular. Improvements in communications extend the firm's ability both to obtain supplies of factor inputs and especially raw materials while simultaneously expanding the market for its output. In the early stage of their evolution most large firms concentrated their efforts upon a single product line or functional activity. Similarly, in the early stages of their development the managers of the more successful firms, who are also usually the owners, focus their attention upon expanding through a process of horizontal integration by means of acquisition and merger with other organisations in direct competition with them. Once a firm has attained a certain degree of dominance over one phase in the productive/distributive process the benefits of vertical integration become increasingly attractive. Thus a firm which has become dominant in the extraction or production of a basic raw material may integrate forward into the process of that raw material into a finished product. Conversely, a manufacturing concern may decide to integrate backwards into primary production in order to achieve control over essential factor inputs. Similarly, firms engaged in primary or secondary industries may perceive advantages through integrating forward into the tertiary sector and achieving control of the distributive function. Clearly, dominant retail and wholesaling organisations may see similar advantages to be gained through integrating backwards into manufacturing and primary production.

With increasing size there developed a need for a more specialised organisational structure and for the delegation of authority and responsibility to subordinates. In the early stages of their development most large corporations adopted a functional form of organisation with professional managers appointed to head each of the various functions, e.g. finance, production, sales, etc.

With the transfer of control from owner-entrepreneurs to professional managers it is possible to discern a change in the primary goal of the firm. Thus, while owner-entrepreneurs tend to pursue a primary objective of profit maximisation, professional managers tend to emphasise survival and a satisfactory level of earnings, to be achieved through sales maximisation rather than profit maximisation.

However, as noted earlier when discussing the six causes of change cited by Allen, this view is essentially a negative one. While it is true that most firms adapt themselves to their environment and react to changes in their market, the really dominant firms in any industry appear to have adopted a more positive approach. Thus Channon cites A. C. Chandler's classic study (*Strategy and Structure*, Anchor Books, 1966) in which two alternative strategies to integration are identified. In essence these two alternative strategies are growth through geographical expansion, and diversification. However, as firms pursued either or both of these alternatives it soon became apparent that the traditional functional form of organisation was inappropriate for multi-product firms operating in a number of different markets. Thus in the 1920s Dupont and General Motors began to develop a divisional structure which has now become the dominant form of organisation.

It is not proposed to dwell on such issues here but it it is important to point out that since the 1920s there has been an increasing trend towards diversification. In Channon's study of the 100 largest U.K. companies between 1950 and 1970 it was found that:

> in 1950 the diversified firm represented approximately 24% of the population of the largest 100 firms. This minority was composed essentially of those enterprises engaged in technological or skill related industries where the technology required to compete, naturally led to the evolution of a wide product line. By 1970 the minority had become the majority and no fewer than 60% of the population was relatively highly diversified. This majority included many industries with a wide variety of technological requirements, such as food, chemicals, paper and packaging, textiles, electrical equipment, and electronics and engineering.

As a result of this diversification many of the larger firms operate in several different industries and one must not assume automatically that the very large firms are necessarily dominant in all markets in which they compete.

Interest in the degree of concentration in industry arises largely because of the light which it throws upon market structure and, as Richard Caves notes, in *American Industry: Structure, Conduct and Performance,* 3rd ed. (Englewood Cliffs, N.J.: Prentice-Hall, 1972), 'market structure is important because the structure determines the behaviour of firms in the industry, and that behaviour in turn determines the quality of the industry's performance'. However, as Caves points out, concentration is but one element of market structure, other main elements of which are product differentiation, barriers to the entry of new firms, the growth rate of market demands, the elasticity of market demand, and the ratio of fixed to variable costs in the short run. Collectively all these determine the nature of competition in the market-place and it is to this that we now turn our attention.

THEORIES OF COMPETITION

Current thinking about competition, like many other economic concepts, owes much to the original contribution of Adam Smith, whose *Wealth of Nations* was first published in 1775. As J. M.

Clark (*Competition as a Dynamic Process*, Brookings Institution, 1961) points out, Smith lays the foundation of this thought by defining two competitive states – full and free competition, and complete monopoly – and, in a loose fashion, the contrasting outcomes to be expected of each of these states.

Clark offers a useful summary of the evolution of economic thinking about competition from Smith's original and sometimes rather vague specification through to the contribution of Ricardo, Cournot, and Marshall, in the course of which he points out how theory has changed to reflect reality. At the time when Smith first proposed the two basic competitive states monopoly was essentially a local phenomenon which was to be eroded during the nineteenth century with the development of more efficient lines of communication and transportation, while perfect competition mirrored the bargaining power of people engaged in cottage industries such as weaving. Similarly, as we have noted earlier, agriculture was a much more dominant form of economic activity in terms of employment and the markets in agricultural commodities have traditionally approached most nearly to the model of perfect competition.

Just as the impact of the industrial revolution was to lead to improvements in communication and transportation which diminished local monopolies, so the growth of manufacturing industry diminished the importance of agriculture and led to attention being focused upon intermediate competitive states distinguished as being 'imperfect'.

During the nineteenth century the major emphasis of economic activity was upon supply creation or output and its effect upon price. Together these were seen as the crucial competitive variables. In Clark's view it was the addition of the chemical revolution to the preceding mechanical and electrical revolutions which was to give rise to product proliferation and lead to a situation in which 'automatically, the differentiated product has become an economic variable at least as important as price, along with the methods of selling efforts and demand creation that necessarily go with product differentiation'.

The addition of product and selling efforts as variables alongside the traditional inputs of price and output demanded a radical restructuring of the economist's original model and gave rise to the theories of imperfect competition formulated by Edward Chamberlin and Joan Robinson.

Thus we now recognise that between the polar extremes of monopoly and perfect competitition there exists an almost infinite variety of states of imperfect competition. For purposes of analysis, understanding and prediction it is important that one should be able to distinguish how certain basic elements influence the development of a particular competitive state. It is also important that one should be able to identify the salient facets of each of these states. To this end we are here concerned primarily with the three basic elements of an economic system, supply, demand, and the market, and their interaction, i.e. the state of competitition. (For readers who are pursuing a formal course of study much of the material in this chapter will amount to a review of concepts introduced in a basic course on economics. However, it is anticipated that the treatment here will possibly be more applied than theoretical and its inclusion is predicated on the grounds that it is essential to an understanding of the manner in which real firms behave in the real world.)

Our discussion of supply will concentrate first upon those organisations responsible for its creation, and will then examine the nature of their output. This consideration will be followed by a summary of some of the more salient factors which go together to make up and influence demand. Next we examine the nature of the mechanism through which supply and demand are brought together – the market – and finally we review the basic competitive states to establish the emergence of product differentiation as a major competitive strategy.

SUPPLY: FIRM AND PRODUCT

Although we deliberately referred to 'organisations' in the previous paragraph, thereby implicitly recognising that there are several distinct types of formal association which might be responsible for supply creation, our main concern here is with the form of business organisation which we call the firm.

In economic theory certain simplifying assumptions are made about the firm. It is assumed that a single person, the entrepreneur, is the owner of the individual firm and that he behaves rationally in that his prime objective is to maximise money profits. Further, it is assumed that entrepreneurs will always minimise costs and that the price of all factor inputs are known and fixed and that each firm produces only one product. Now, no sane economist really believes in these assumptions. He merely adopts them in order to simplify his analysis in order to develop explanations of the ways firms will behave given these conditions. In other words the economist is attempting to develop a bench-mark model so that he can then determine how relaxation of the simplifying assumptions might affect real-world behaviour. Unfortunately many students who have only taken an introductory course in economics never proceed to the stage when real-world considerations are introduced into the model. Accordingly such students find it very difficult to relate observed reality, implicit in the earlier discussion concerning changes in firm structure and organisation, and the simplistic descriptions contained in introductory economic texts.

We have already noted that few, if any, firms regard profit maximisation as their primary goal. The reasons why the unbridled pursuit of profit should not be the sole objective of management is apparent in the role of profit itself. Profit is generally regarded as the reward for the assumption of risk and on the whole it is accepted that the greater the risk, the greater should be the reward. It is also accepted that risk is usually measured in terms of the likelihood of loss. Accordingly professional management tends to try and balance its activities in such a manner so as not to put the whole corporation at risk. Clearly by doing so it forgos the possibility of maximising profits. It also avoids the possibility of maximising losses!

One area where the firm does make a conscious decision is in terms of its product mix. Fundamentally there is a basic conflict between the relative merits of specialisation and the attractions of diversification. If one pursues a policy of specialisation, one should be able to benefit from the economies of scale in purchasing and production and so reduce costs to the minimum. At the same time it is clear that any diminution of demand for the single-product firm will result in an immediate loss in earnings and, if continued, this could result in the firm operating at a loss. Diversification offers a firm the opportunity to spread the risk associated with fluctuation in demand for a particular product. At the same time diversification usually requires a firm to duplicate many of the basic business functions, especially in production and marketing, and so increases its cost base. It is clear that if the firm is not operating on a basis of minimum cost, then it will be able to earn less profits than firms which have chosen to specialise in the production of a single product – at least in the short term.

Just as economists make simplifying assumptions about the firm, so too they make simplifying assumptions about the firm's output – its product. The basic assumption which is made is that the output of different firms competing in the same market are viewed as homogeneous by potential consumers. Given this assumption, together with that of a single price, it is clear that users have no rational basis for differentiating between different suppliers of the same product. Accordingly decisions by a consumer to buy a product are perceived as decisions between different categories of products rather than choices between similar products produced by different firms. Thus elementary economic theory proposes that, given a finite disposable income, the consumer will adjust his purchases of different product categories in order to maximise his overall satisfaction. In the sense that all products which the consumer might consider purchasing are competing with one another they are to some degree substitutes for one another.

However, this concept of substitution is too crude to explain the nature of competition between companies like Lever Brothers and Procter & Gamble in the detergent market, Ford and British Leyland in the motor-car market, Hoover, Electrolux and Goblin in the vacuum-cleaner market, and so on. For this purpose we need a clearer definition of possible degrees of difference between products. That proposed by J. M. Clark (*Competition as a Dynamic Process*) provides a useful basic distinction.

Essentially Clark proposes three categories of products. First there are those which 'satisfy the same principal want, and in which the producer is free to imitate others as closely as he wishes, using techniques that are not radically different from theirs and differentiating his product only to the extent that it seems advantageous to him to do so, in order to appeal to some subsidiary want more effectively than other variants do, and thus fit into a gap in the array of variant products'. Clark terms this first category 'differentiated competitition' and it is clear that different brands of detergent, motor-car and vacuum cleaner fall into this category.

Clark's second category, which he terms 'substitution', is defined as including 'products that appeal to the same principal want but which are inherently and inescapably different, due either to different materials or basically different techniques'. Into this category, perhaps, we might put the use of a laundry service in place of the purchase of detergents for home washing, the use of public transport or perhaps bicycle or motor-bicycle in place of a motor-car, or a manual carpet-sweeper, or even a brush, in place of an electric vacuum-cleaner. Clearly in all these instances the substitute product is competing directly with that for which it is a substitute, and seeks to satisfy the same basic want.

In Clark's words 'the third category embraces products that serve independent wants and are substitutes only in the mathematic sense that spending more for one leaves less to spend on others'. We return to issues of product differentiation later in this book. Having briefly considered the supply side of the economic equation, it is now necessary to review some basic concepts of demand.

DEMAND

By and large economists tend to be concerned only with what they term *effective* demand, which is defined as demand backed up by purchasing power. However, most managers are also interested in two other types of demand – which we may describe as 'potential' demand and 'latent' demand.

A latent demand may be thought of as one which the consumer is unable to satisfy, usually for lack of purchasing power. For example, many housewives may have a latent demand for automatic diswashers, but, related to their available disposable income, this want is less strong than their demand for other products and so remains unsatisfied. In other words wants are ranked in order of preference and satisfied to the point where disposable income is exhausted. From the manufacturer's point of view the problem is to translate latent demand into effective demand by increasing the consumer's preference for his particular product *vis-à-vis* all other product offerings.

Latent demand may also be thought of as a vague want in the sense that the consumer feels a need for a product, or service, to fill a particular function but is unable to locate anything suitable. It is clear that latent demand constitutes an important consideration in management planning. In the case of a demand which is latent due to lack of purchasing power a manfacturer may be able to change a consumers' preference through his marketing and promotional activities. Alternatively, if there is a trend towards increasing disposable income, then the producer may be able to project how such increases in purchasing power will enable consumers to translate their latent demand into an effective demand. Given such a forecast he will be able to plan increased production, distribution and sale to keep pace with rising disposable incomes.

In the case of a demand which is latent because the consumer is unaware of the existence of a product or service which would satisfy his ill-defined want, then clearly if the manufacturer produces a product which he feels should satisfy the need, he will wish to bring it to the attention of those with latent demand for it. Alternatively, if a manufacturer does not produce a product which should satisfy a known latent demand but is able to specify what the characteristics of such a product would be, then the latent demand becomes a marketing opportunity which he may wish to exploit.

Potential demand may be said to exist where a consumer possesses purchasing power but is not currently buying. Thus, where a marketer has identified a latent demand and developed a new product to satisfy it, the potential demand consists of all those who can back up their latent want with purchasing power. In another context potential demand may be thought of as that part of the total market or effective demand for an existing product which a firm might anticipate securing through the introduction of a new competitive product.

Once again it must be stressed that while the economists' model serves a useful purpose as a basis for analysing the real world, the assumptions upon which it rests are clearly unrealistic. Thus elementary economic texts usually make assumptions about consumer demand as follows (see A. W. Stonier and D. C. Hague, *A Textbook of Economic Theory*, Longmans, 1953):

1. The consumer's wants remain unchanged throughout.
2. He has a fixed amount of money available.
3. He is one of many buyers.
4. He knows the price of all goods, each of which is homogeneous.
5. He can, if he wishes, spend his money in very small amounts.
6. He acts rationally.

Of these assumptions, only 2 and 3 seem likely to be true with any frequency in the real world. For the rest, as managers are only too aware, consumer demand is fickle and changes frequently. Knowledge of the existence of all those goods which the consumer might buy, let alone their prices, seems unlikely. Further, goods are not infinitely divisible and consumers have to pay the price asked for a product, whether it be 3p for a box of matches or £350 for a colour television set. However, these differences between the model and the real world are fairly obvious, but this is not always true with respect to the correct interpretation of what constitutes rational behaviour.

While the economist talks about rationality in terms of consumers maximising their satisfaction, satisfaction is usually defined in terms of solely objective criteria. Using such an interpretation the price–quantity relationship assumes a distorted level of importance and excludes any concept of subjective satisfaction. That consumers do gain subjective satisfaction is apparent from the existence of brand preference for largely undifferentiated physical products, such as flour, baked beans, detergents, and so on. In fact the creation of subjective differentials in the mind of consumers may be just as important in differentiating a product as the development of real physical differences.

Because consumers take cognisance of subjective values this is not to say that they are behaving irrationally, for clearly it would be irrational to ignore such subjective preferences. It is just because consumers do have different preferences and perceptions that producers have found it necessary to develop differentiated products and sophisticated marketing techniques.

If one traces the development of management thought during this century, one can distinguish three main phases. First, there was a production orientation which mirrored a condition which dates back from before recorded history – namely an excess of demand over available supply. However, because of the technological revolution of the eighteenth, nineteenth and twentieth centuries a position was reached by the 1920s where the advanced economies of the Western world were producing more basic goods than they were able to consume or sell elsewhere.

Faced with a situation in which one is producing more than the market is absorbing the immediate reaction is to try and stimulate consumption further. Such efforts gave rise to the second major managerial orientation, which has been termed the 'sales management orientation'. While it is understandable that producers should increase their efforts to sell what they can currently make, it is also clear that this can be but a short-term remedy if there is a basic imbalance between supply and demand. This in fact was the case with the industrialised economies of the West, but the full implications of such a situation were deferred owing to the outbreak of the Second World War. On the conclusion of the war there was a backlog of unsatisfied consumer demand, with the result that most producers found themselves in a sellers' market until the early 1950s. At this time excess supply once again began to develop and producers began to look for a new managerial philosophy to enable them to earn a satisfactory return on the resources under their control.

The philosophy which emerged and which was to give rise to the third major managerial orientation was that of marketing. As we have seen, in its simplest terms the marketing philosophy postulates that supply is a function of demand and therefore must be subservient to it. To this end producers set out to measure the nature of demand in terms of both objective and subjective influences on consumer buying behaviour. Clearly this is a radically different approach from production orientation, forever immortalised in Henry Ford's famous comment that 'You can have any colour you like so long as it is black.'

COMPETITION AND MARKET STRUCTURE

In essence the nature of competition and of market structure is the outcome of the interaction between supply and demand. As indicated above, it is normal to define two limiting conditions – monopoly and pure competition – and to categorise intermediate forms of competition as 'imperfect'. What, then, are the salient characteristics of these states? Before addressing this issue it is necessary to introduce the concept of *demand elasticity*, for it is this factor which is usually used as the basic indicator of the nature of competition.

Under normal conditions most people anticipate that an increase in the price of a good will result in a decline in the amount demanded, while conversely any fall in price should be accompanied by an increase in the quantity demanded. In simple terms elasticity is a measure of the degree to which a change in price will result in a change in demand. Where a very small change in price is accompanied by a major change in demand, we say that that product has a high elasticity of demand. Conversely, even where significant price changes have only a limited impact upon the quantity demanded, we say that that product has a low elasticity of demand. Thus in order to determine the elasticity of demand for the given good we need to measure the magnitude of changes in the quantity demanded in relation to changes in the unit price. Such information is termed a demand schedule, and is frequently represented graphically as in Fig. 2.1, from which it can be seen that infinitely elastic demand is represented by a horizontal line, infinitely inelastic demand by a vertical line, while varying degrees of elasticity are represented by the angle assumed by the demand curve.

In terms of basic competitive states demand under pure competition is usually represented as being highly, if not infinitely, elastic, while under monopoly conditions demand is considered highly inelastic. However, for a state of pure competition or monopoly to exist certain other conditions must be satisfied.

In the case of pure competition three basic conditions must be satisfied: namely, large numbers of producers, homogeneous output, and freedom of entry. In fact, when talking of a large number of firms it would be more accurate to speak of low levels of concentration, for the basic condition which we are seeking to define

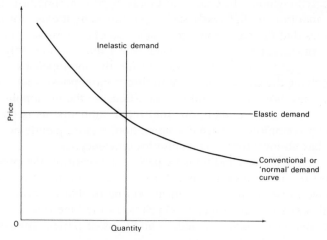

Fig. 2.1. Demand curves

is one in which decisions by any single firm have little or no effect upon the output of the industry as a whole. As we have noted earlier, homogeneity in a product depends upon the perception of a prospective buyer. Only in the case of commodities and raw materials is it usual to find agreement that the output of two different producers which meets a given specification can in fact be treated as identical products. The third condition for the existence of pure competitition is freedom of entry, by which we mean that there are no barriers or artificial restrictions to prevent any individual or firm from setting up in business to produce supplies of the product in question.

It should be noted that pure competition is not synonymous with perfect competition, for the former only describes the competitive state between suppliers, while the latter makes further assumptions about conditions in the market. Essentially these assumptions are that all buyers and sellers have perfect knowledge of the activities of one another, that there are no transportation costs and that there is perfect mobility of factors of production between industries. Under these conditions the market determines the price of a product and effectively the firm has no control over its destiny whatsoever.

The polar extreme to a situation of perfect competition is one of pure monopoly. By definition a monopolist is the sole supplier of a particular product or service, with the result that firm and industry are synonymous. In economic theory a pure monopolist has no competition at all. Clearly such a position cannot exist, for it presumes that the monopolist commands all of a consumer's income. For practical purposes we consider that a state of monopoly exists when there is no close substitute for the monopolist's output. Applying the concept of concentration a monopolist would have a concentration ratio of 100 per cent. Because the monopolist does not face direct competition from other suppliers, as is the case under conditions of perfect competition, it is frequently held that he has no incentive to maximise his efficiency.

Clearly under conditions of perfect competition the producer must maximise his efficiency, for if he does not his costs will rise above those of his rivals, but he will be unable to recoup these higher costs through increased prices. In the long run, therefore, the inefficient producer under conditions of perfect competition will be forced out of business.

From the foregoing descriptions it is clear that conditions of perfect competition and pure monopoly are exceptions rather than the rule. They are the limiting conditions. Under both sets of conditions the seller reacts solely to external environmental forces. However, in intermediate states between the two extremes the factor which really distinguishes imperfect competition is that the firm has to take account not only of the external environment within which it must operate, but also of the action of other suppliers in the market-place. The need, under conditions of imperfect competition, for firms to take into account the actions of their immediate competitors makes for a much more complex situation, and one demanding a far higher level of managerial skill. Under conditions of imperfect competition sellers are mutually interdependent, and so must allow for each other's actions when formulating their plans.

As noted earlier when discussing different managerial orientations during this present century, the growth of imperfect competition is of relatively recent origin. In fact it was not until the early 1930s that Edward Chamberlin and Joan Robinson first put forward their theories of imperfect competition. In time, therefore, the proposal of a theory of imperfect competition coincided with a change from the production to the sales management orientation and the need for companies to compete with one another along dimensions other than cost and price.

Theories of imperfect competition frequently invite an analogy with games in which choices of courses of action are limited not only by the rules of the game but also by the actions of one's competitors. Thus we find that the study of competition places increasing emphasis upon the strategic choices made by participating firms and the impact which these have upon both the fortunes of their competitors and market structure. In making such choices firms have to operate within the environmental constraints – political, legal and social – common to them all. Thus in order to develop a distinctive and, it is hoped, successful strategy they have found it beneficial to give much closer attention to microeconomic aspects of supply and demand – especially the latter. It is these topics which form the subject-matter of the next two chapters.

3 Demand and Supply

INTRODUCTION

Most students of marketing have pursued an introductory course in economics and are familiar with the concept of demand as a function of price. According to this concept, the quantity of a good or service which will be purchased is dependent upon its price, such that the higher the price the less will be demanded, and vice versa. This relationship is frequently expressed in tabular form as a demand schedule, and depicted graphically as a demand curve, as shown below.

In the real world it is clear that many factors other than price affect demand, and the exclusion of such factors is often seen as invalidating

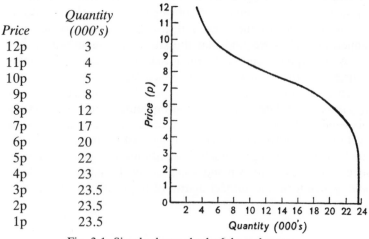

Price	Quantity (000's)
12p	3
11p	4
10p	5
9p	8
8p	12
7p	17
6p	20
5p	22
4p	23
3p	23.5
2p	23.5
1p	23.5

Fig. 3.1. Simple demand schedule and curve

economic price theory. Such an attitude misses the point that the economist is seeking to define an essential functional relationship with which he may then investigate the effect of other independent variables upon the dependent variable, demand. It is not proposed to investigate the sophisticated techniques developed by economists which validate the basic theory, however, and attention here will be concentrated on the nature of these other, independent variables.

NEEDS, WANTS AND CHOICE

Before proceeding to discuss demand variables it will be useful to distinguish between needs, wants and the function of choice.

A *need* is something fundamental to the maintenance of life, such as food, drink, shelter and clothing. Needs are largely physiological in the sense that they are basic and instinctive drives with which we are born. It is clear, however, that a need may be satisfied by any one of a large number of alternatives, e.g. thirst may be assuaged by water, tea, coffee, beer, wine, etc. The availability of alternative means of satisfying a need constitutes *choice*, provision of which is central to the practice of marketing. In the absence of substitute, or alternative, goods there can be no choice, and needs and wants become synonymous.

Where there is more than one way of satisfying a basic need, physiological drives will be modified by economic, sociological and psychological factors. Variations in these factors will predispose individuals to prefer a specific alternative and this preference constitutes a *want*. As will become clear when considering economic and psychological factors in greater detail below, wants are not necessarily synonymous with the concept of demand implicit in a demand schedule. A demand schedule for a specific product may be thought of as expressing effective demand, by which is understood demand backed by the ability to pay a given price. From this it follows that there are two further types of demand – latent and potential.

A latent demand may be thought of as a demand which the consumer is unable to satisfy, usually for lack of purchasing power. For example, many housewives may have a latent demand for automatic dishwashers but, related to their available disposable income, this want is less strong than their demand for other products and so remains unsatisfied. In other words, wants are ranked in order of preference and satisfied to the point where disposable income is exhausted. From the manufacturer's point of view the problem is to translate latent demand into effective demand by increasing the consumer's preference for his particular product *vis-à-vis* all other product offerings. As will be seen, marketing is largely concerned with solving this problem.

Latent demand may also be thought of as a vague want in the sense that the consumer feels a need for a product, or service, to fill a particular function but is unable to locate anything suitable. If such a product exists marketing's role is to bring it to his attention; if it does not exist, then marketing should seek to identify the unfilled need and develop new products to satisfy it.

Potential demand exists where the consumer possesses the necessary purchasing power, but is not currently buying the product under consideration. Thus, where a marketer has identified a latent demand and developed a new product to satisfy it, the potential demand consists of all those who can back up their latent want with purchasing power. In another context, potential demand may be thought of as that part of the total market (effective demand) for an existing product which a firm might anticipate securing through the introduction of a new, competitive brand.

DETERMINANTS OF DEMAND

As implied earlier, basic economic theory is concerned largely with price-quantity relationships, and other demand determinants are invariably excluded for more sophisticated treatment. However, corporate success is very closely related to the manufacturer's ability to predict the strength and nature of demand as a basis for deploying the firm's resources and, consequently, management is deeply concerned with all those variables which condition demand. Broadly speaking, demand determinants may be grouped under two headings – socio-economic and psychological – and the remainder of this chapter will be concerned with identifying the more important factors within these groups.

SOCIO-ECONOMIC FACTORS

Population
People constitute the basic raw material from which markets are

made, for, ultimately, the demand for any given product or service depends upon the aggregate demand of individual consumers, and can never exceed the sum of their numbers. One of the major arguments behind our attempts to gain membership of the European Economic Community was that this would open the door to a market with a population five times as great as that of theUnited Kingdom. Clearly, this represents an enormous potential for increasing sales.

A good example of the limitations imposed by the actual number of people is provided by the 'baby market'. The demand for perambulators, infant feeding formulas, clothes, etc., is obviously dependent upon the birth rate, and the manufacturers of such products will condition their future plans upon the projections of the Registrar of Births, Deaths and Marriages. Since 1965, the absolute birth rate has declined, and this has had a noticeable impact upon the policies of firms specialising in baby products. Johnson & Johnson had an 80 per cent share of the £3.5 million baby toiletries market but their dominant position was little consolation as total sales levelled off and threatened to decline. In order to maintain growth, Johnson's have revitalised Band Aid,developed disposable paper pants, and moved into the disposable paper products market generally with the introduction of J-cloths. Equally significant has been their campaign to extend the use of their Baby Powder into the adult market, in direct competition with the major cosmetic houses. In 1972 the Economic Intelligence Unit estimated the total market size at between £10 million and £12 million, of which 70 per cent was shared between Boots and Johnson & Johnson. (*Retail Business 176*, October 1972 – 'The Nursery Market'.) From this report it is apparent that Johnson & Johnson have achieved considerable success in extending the use of their products into the adult market. It is estimated that currently 14 per cent of the women using cold or cleansing creams, lotions or milk, use Johnson's Baby Lotion, and that no other single product has a larger market share. Similarly Johnson's Baby Powder is used by 14 per cent of women using talcum powder, giving it the second-largest market share. However, until 1973, with the abolition of purchase tax and the introduction of VAT, baby products had a decided price advantage over toiletries in that they carried no tax. It will be interesting to see whether Johnson & Johnson can continue to retain their market share given the erosion of this price advantage.

Absolute numbers are only one aspect of population, however, three other important aspects being age and sex distribution, geo-

graphical distribution and family size. Baby products are associated with a particular stage of the human life cycle, as are many
other products, and recognition of this has led to the adoption of
the life-cycle concept as a useful means of distinguishing the effect
of age on consumption patterns. Although it is increasingly recognised that young children influence purchasing decisions, their lack
of purchasing power usually excludes them from life-cycle classificatory systems which concentrate on decision-making units
(D.M.U.s). A widely accepted system distinguishes the following
eight stages:

1. Young, single.
2. Young, married, no children.
3. Young, married, youngest child under six.
4. Young, married, youngest child over six.
5. Older, married, with children.
6. Older, married, no children under eighteen.
7. Older, single.
8. Other.

Although the distinction between Young and Older is not explicit,
and category 8 is a meaningless 'catchall', the concept provides a
useful basis for breaking down the total population into sub-groups
for more detailed analysis. (A useful exercise is to visualise the
variations that one would anticipate in consumption patterns as
between the different categories in this system.) Life-style analysis is
currently enjoying an enormous wave of popularity amongst marketers and numerous references to its application are to be found in
the management literature.

The physical distribution of the population has a direct bearing
upon the marketer's ability to make his product available to potential
customers at an economic cost. The concentration of population in
Britain, backed by extensive transportation facilities, make this
factor less important than in many other parts of the world, e.g. the
United States, Australia, Africa. In the case of bulky materials of low
unit value, such as cement, or when considering entry into an export
market, it will take on added significance in measuring potential
demand. Physical location also has an important bearing upon the
existence of regional wants and preferences; porridge, tripe and
jellied eels immediately call to mind Scotland, Lancashire and
London respectively. Similarly, woollens are in greater demand in

the north, and cottons in the south. Overall, however, such differences are less marked than in many larger countries.

For planning and administrative purposes, the marketer will often find it convenient to subdivide the country into areas in some systematic way. An obvious approach is to use the Registrar-General's Standard Regions, namely:

North	and the planning sub-regions of
Yorkshire and Humberside	Scotland:
North-west	Highlands
East·Midlands	North-east
West Midlands	Tayside
East Anglia	Edinburgh
South-east	Falkirk/Stirling
South-west	Glasgow
Wales	South-west
	Borders.

The great advantage of using this scheme is that the standard regions are widely used in the collection of Government statistics, and are capable of further subdivision into counties, conurbations, boroughs, etc. On the other hand the standard regions listed above differ from those used prior to the 1971 Census and may be subject to change with Local Government reorganisation. With the ever-growing range of services offered by the independent television companies, many firms now use television areas as a basic unit, although some difficulties arise due to overlap. To some extent this is overcome by the I.T.V. companies distinguishing between primary and secondary areas, i.e. a primary area is unable to receive satisfactory transmissions from adjacent, and competing stations, while a secondary area can.

Several other alternatives are available, including the Nielsen Areas, and 'Geographia's' marketing regions, each of which has its advantages and disadvantages.However, all are to be preferred to a purely arbitrary subdivision which precludes direct use of published data.

Family size has a direct bearing on housing, the size of appliances and cars, container size, etc., etc. In conjunction with income, it also has an important effect on household purchasing patterns for, despite certain economies present in large families, it is clear that for a given income such families will spend more on essentials than small families.

Income

This variable is a major demand determinant and is widely used as a measure of potential demand. With the increase in the number of 'working wives', and recognising that the household is the most common decision-making and purchasing unit, it is more useful to think in terms of aggregate household income than to consider the major wage-earner's income alone.

Two concepts are particularly useful in analysing income levels – net disposable income, and discretionary purchasing power. The former consists of income from all sources including wages, interest on savings and investments, health and welfare benefits, etc., less taxes. It is a measure of the amount available for saving and expenditure. Discretionary purchasing power comprises that amount available after all 'essential' expenditures have been met – it is 'uncommitted' income which the consumer may spend, or save, as he pleases. As noted in Chapter 1, increasing income levels are invariably paralleled by an upgrading in what is considered essential but, overall, Engels's Laws seem to hold, namely: As real income increases the proportion spent on food tends to decline, expenditures on rent, heating, etc., remain constant, while the proportion spent on clothing, education, recreation and travel, etc., tends to increase.

Most incomes are earned in payment for services rendered, and so depend upon the demand for the services in question (as modified by restrictive labour practices). In broad terms, occupation is determined by education, and there exists a strong correlation between the two and income so that, in the absence of income data, many researchers use education/occupation as a surrogate. Incomes vary considerably across occupational categories and the reader should consult the *Department of Employment Gazette* for detailed information on wage rates and earnings. One must be careful not to confuse the two, for wage rates do not necessarily bear any resemblance to the actual wages paid in a particular job or area. Further, the incidence of overtime has a marked effect on earnings, and it is the latter with which the demand analyst is primarily concerned.

Effective demand, as defined earlier, implies that consumption is a function of available income, and this relationship has been the subject of extensive research over a long period. Three separate theories have evolved out of this research in an attempt to explain variations in aggregate consumption functions and may be summarised as:

(a) *The absolute income hypothesis,* which holds that expenditures/savings are a function of income.

(b) *The relative income hypothesis,* which holds that expenditures/saving patterns depend upon the relative position of the spending unit on the income scale, and not on the absolute income earned. This hypothesis recognises the 'keeping up with the Joneses' phenomenon.

(c) *The permanent income hypothesis,* which holds that expenditures are based on average income expectations over time. This hypothesis recognises that consumption patterns are relatively stable over time, which suggests that consumers average out their expenditures, i.e. under inflation they anticipate that they will make good current dissaving, due to price increases, out of future wage increases.

An additional, and complicating, factor in recent years has been the increased availability of credit. Although the amount of credit an institution is prepared to extend to an individual is usually related to his income, there are now so many separate sources that the relationship between credit and income has become tenuous. Clearly, the ready availability of credit has done much to enable the consumer to translate latent demand into an effective demand, and has become an important demand determinant.

Collectively, the factors reviewed above are socio-economic variables, and form the basis of a broad but useful classificatory system. Within the United Kingdom, differences in ethnic origin and religion are usually too slight to merit inclusion in such a system, but they may be relevant in foreign markets. (The upsurge of Welsh and Scottish 'nationalism' and the Protestant-Catholic confrontation in Northern Ireland suggest that greater attention may have to be given to these factors in future.)

PSYCHOLOGICAL FACTORS

When discussing the distinction between needs and wants it was noted that needs are essentially physiological and instinctive, but that such generalised, basic drives are subject to modification by other factors, resulting in specific wants. To a large degree these 'other factors' are psychological. However, men live in social groups, membership of which modifies behavioural response to the extent that it would be more correct to identify these factors as psycho-sociological and/or socio-psychological. Collectively, the study of these influences has created a whole new field of marketing, usually referred to as 'consumer behaviour'. An extended discussion of the more important concepts follows in Chapter 4, but before turning to this it will be helpful to review the other half of the market equation – supply.

SUPPLY: PRODUCTS AND SERVICES

In the preceding section attention was focused on those factors which determine the precise character of demand for specific goods and services. Here, our objective will be to examine how these demand determinants are reflected in the supply of products designed to satisfy particular wants as identified by the marketer.

THE 'PRODUCT' IN THEORY AND PRACTICE

As a subject, economics is largely concerned with maximising satis-faction through the optimum use of scarce resources. Inherent in this construct is tacit acceptance of the fact that available resources are insufficient to satisfy all conceivable demands of mankind, although it is recognised that conditions of over-supply are perfectly possible in the particular.

In theory, production, or the creation of supply, is a function which expresses the relationship between inputs and outputs. Inputs are referred to generically as 'factors of production', and broadly clas-sified as land, labour, capital and management, while outputs are identified as products. (To avoid endless repetition the term 'pro-ducts' will be taken to include both physical goods and services, unless stated to the contrary.)

Given that there is a finite limit to the availability of factors of production, whereas demand is infinite, it follows that we need a criterion which will enable us to determine priorities in the use of these factors in order to maximise satisfaction. Such a criterion is provided by the Law of Variable Proportions or, as it is more usually termed, the Law of Diminishing Returns. This law states that incremental units of a given factor of production, other factors being held constant, will yield increasing returns up to a certain point, beyond which diminishing returns will set in. This point is not fixed, and will vary with changes in technology and the other inputs. However, at any given point in time, it is theoretically possible to determine the optimum allocation of inputs which will maximise total output.

In reality, the multi-dimensional complexity of products precludes viable analysis, and economists have found it necessary to suppress such variables in developing theories of competition. Thus, although more sophisticated treatments recognise product differentiation as a competitive variable, in theory the product is usually viewed as a homogeneous entity. In practice, products may be differentiated by any one of a multiplicity of variables as indicated by the following definition: 'Those aspects of the good or service exchanged whether arising from materials, or ingredients, mechanical construction, design durability, taste, peculiarity of package or container or service . . . all products beyond the raw material stage are highly variable, for the most part on a continuous scale' (E. Chamberlin, *Towards a More General Theory of Value*: Oxford University Press, New York, 1957).

To further complicate the issue, product differences are determined by the perception of the individual consumer, from which it follows that Daz, Tide and Omo are all different products, whereas 'detergent' is a generic name for a group of products possessing similar physical characteristics.

In an article entitled 'What is a Product?' (*British Agents Review*, reprinted in *Marketing Forum* (March/April 1968)) C. P. Stephenson emphasised this point by defining a product as 'Everything the purchaser gets in exchange for his money', and listed the following 'extras' associated with the physical product:

Advisory services
After-sales service
Replacements
Designing and planning services
Deliveries
Guarantees
Credit terms
Reputation
Experience

Individually, and collectively, all these factors will lead consumers to distinguish between the product offerings of competing firms in order to best satisfy their particular wants.

COMPETITION AND THE PROVISION OF CHOICE

As noted, the ability to create excess supplies of basic goods is of relatively recent origin and is largely responsible for the current emphasis on marketing, as opposed to production. This change of emphasis recognises that the competitive 'ground rules' appropriate to conditions of excess demand must be modified under the threat of excess supply.

Maslow's concept of a need hierarchy (discussed at greater length in Chapter 4, pp. 73–4) is reflected in the nature of consumer demand. At the first level, the consumer's prime concern is to satisfy a basic need such as hunger, thirst or shelter, by whatever means are available. Under conditions where there is an insufficiency of supply to satisfy these basic needs, factor inputs are restricted to those alternatives which offer the maximum output consistent with certain minimum levels of satisfaction. In the last century this objective was achieved by product standardisation, which permitted the division of labour and the adoption of mass production techniques. Such conditions prevailed in the United States during the second half of the nineteenth century and, to a lesser degree, in much of Western Europe. Today they are typical of the developing economy.

Once the basic needs have been satisfied, however, consumers advance to a higher and more sophisticated level of demand. Deficiencies in the 'standard' product become apparent, through possession and consumption, and are expressed in the market-place by a preference for differentiated products which more nearly satisfy specific wants. Moreover, the economic growth associated with mass production, and its attendant economies of scale, increases discretionary purchasing power to the point where consumers can afford to pay more for improved, and differentiated, products.

Product homogeneity is fundamental to the existence of perfect competition, under which price is determined solely by market forces and so is beyond the producer's control. In these circumstances a firm's profitability is a direct consequence of its cost structure, and the natural emphasis is on production. The realisation that consumers are both willing and able to pay a premium for products with distinctive attributes offers the firm the opportunity to exercise a degree of control over the market, and escape direct competition with its rivals. Such a position is clearly to be preferred and has led to the present concentration on marketing with its emphasis on the provision of choice to meet varied consumer preferences.

BRANDING

Recognising that homogeneity of product offering precluded identification of a given producer's output at the point of sale, manufacturers 'revived' the practice of branding as a means of distinguishing their product from that of their competitors.

Craftsmen have long been accustomed to identifying their work, either by signature or by the use of a distinctive symbol particular to them. In fact this practice was mandatory under the gild system to protect customers and to ensure that shoddy workmanship could be traced back to its originator. An extant example of this is the 'Hallmark' used on silver as a guarantee of purity and indicator of its origin. Over time, this practice has enabled consumers to form judgements as to the value of given names and symbols as indicators of the quality of the product, and as a guarantee of satisfactory performance.

Clearly, the identification of a product is two-edged in the sense that although it permits satisfied customers to repeat purchase, it also allows them to avoid repetition of an unsatisfactory purchase. None the less, branding is now standard practice for the majority of goods, although it is most frequently associated with products purchased for personal consumption.

From both the consumer's and producer's point of view the brand serves as a useful shorthand expression for a whole collection of attributes and properties associated with a given product. In part these associations are built up by advertising; in part they are the result of the consumer's perception and past experience. Whatever their origin, the brand enables the purchaser to obtain products which satisfy highly specific wants, without having to resort to a detailed description of them.

Brand names may be given to individual products, e.g. Daz, Tide, Surf, Omo, etc.; or a generic, or family, brand may be used for a firm's complete product line, e.g. Heinz, Black & Decker, St Michael. Individual brand names are expensive to establish, and usually require a large investment in advertising and sales promotion. Their use is usually restricted to situations where:

(a) Potential sales of each product are sufficient to justify the necessary expenditures.
(b) The products vary in price, quality, etc., and are designed to appeal to different market segments.
(c) There is a radical innovation with a high risk of failure and the company does not wish to prejudice the success of existing brands.

The U.K. detergent market is a particularly good example of brand competition, with developments regularly documented in *Retail Business*. In recent years new brands tend to have followed developments in washing-machines with the introduction of products such as Lever's Persil Automatic and Proctor & Gamble's Bold. The most recent competitive move is particularly interesting in that it originates from Colgate–a company which has traditionally taken a back seat to the 'big two'. This innovation, reported in *Retail Business* no. 24, March 1978, is the introduction of the first heavy-duty liquid detergent, 'Dynamo'.

Testing began in Scotland and Border television areas in February 1977 with a liquid equivalent of an E3 pack size (this offers retailers a significant product plus as it requires less shelf space). Colgate claim that August 1977 data put Dynamo ahead of Drive or Bold and so would seem to have achieved the target of a market share of 7 per cent. To do so Colgate have had to make a very large investment in advertising and claim to have accounted for 20 per cent of all television detergent advertising in the first ten months of 1977. While pundits may have been initially sceptical about Colgate's chances, the scale of the investment is now so formidable that they may at last have found a niche in the market which they can call their own.

Family brands tend to be preferred in circumstances where physical differentiation between brands is difficult to establish, the potential market is small, and the firm has an established line of complementary products. Hence a firm like Heinz, Max Factor or Marks & Spencer will usually concentrate its effort on the development of an overall image/reputation and rely on this to introduce new products into the market.

Increased competitition at the retail level has prompted many retailers and wholesalers to develop 'own', or 'private', brands which are sold in competition with the manufacturers' brands. (The latter are often termed 'national brands' as they are usually promoted on a national basis.) By avoiding the promotional expenditures necessary to maintain a national brand, private brands can be offered at a lower price, and are widely used in building store 'traffic', i.e. to induce price-conscious shoppers to come into the store in the hope that they will make other purchases.

In many instances private brands are identical with the better-known national brands and, in fact, are produced by the same manufacturers. The use of a second brand allows the manufacturer to sell off his excess production at a lower price than that asked for the major, promoted brand. Naturally, few manufacturers are willing to admit that they are practising this form of price discrimination, and the origin of such private label brands is usually a closely guarded secret. For the price-conscious shopper, private brands offer considerable savings, and are perceived as of equivalent quality to the better-known national brands. However, most consumers prefer the national brands with which they are familiar, and from which they derive additional satisfactions. Whether these arise out of associations built up by advertising, or represent real differences in quality, which is often the case (e.g. washing-up liquids), is largely irrelevant, for the final choice rests with the consumers who will optimise their own choice criterion.

CLASSIFICATION OF PRODUCTS

Given that products may be differentiated in a multiplicity of ways, some form of classification is desirable to simplify discussion and permit the formulation of general principles. Although several bases for classification have been proposed, the most widely adopted system distinguishes two major categories – industrial goods and consumer goods – and is based on the purpose for which the goods are purchased. In the case of industrial goods this same criterion is used to further subdivide the category, but in the case of consumer goods a second criterion, method of purchase, has been found more useful.

It is the author's opinion that little useful purpose can be served by following the example of many writers who attempt to develop their own definitions. Verbal dexterity is rarely mistaken for originality and, in the case of definitions, usually only serves to confuse what it is intended to clarify. Accordingly the definitions used here are those adopted by the American Marketing Association.

CONSUMER GOODS

Goods destined for use by the ultimate household consumer and in such form that they can be used by him without further commercial processing.

Consumer goods are generally divided into three sub-categories according to the method in which they are purchased following the terminology first proposed by Melvin T. Copeland in 1923 – convenience goods, shopping goods and specialty goods ('Relation of Consumers' Buying Habits to Marketing Methods', *Harvard Business Review* (April 1923)).

Convenience goods
Those consumer goods which the customer usually purchases frequently, immediately and with the minimum of effort.

This category encompasses a wide range of household products of low unit value. It is implicit that products in this category have low brand loyalty, as the user is not prepared to go to any effort to secure a supply and will accept a substitute. From this it follows that the producer must secure the widest possible availability if he is to maximise sales.

Shopping goods
Those consumer goods which the customer in the process of selection and purchase characteristically compare on such bases as suitability, quality, price and style.

Products in this group are more complex than convenience goods and exhibit a higher degree of differentiation. Usually they are purchased less frequently and are of higher unit value. Many consumer durables fall into this category.

Specialty goods
Those consumer goods on which a significant group of buyers, characteristically insists and for which they are willing to make a special purchasing effort.

Some critics argue that this is a meaningless category as the 'special purchasing effort' required is due to limited availability and that otherwise such goods would fall into one of the other groups. This argument is rejected on the grounds that brand insistence has a very real bearing on the consumer's patronage of different outlets and therefore on the retailer's stock policy. Thus, although the housewife may be indifferent to the brand of canned peas she buys and will take what is available, she may well change to another store altogether if she cannot find her preferred brand of baby food, cigarette or headache remedy.

INDUSTRIAL GOODS

Goods which are destined for use in producing other goods or rendering services, as contrasted with goods destined to be sold to ultimate consumers.

Certain goods which fall into this category may also be classified as consumer goods, e.g. paper, typewriters, chairs, fuel oil, etc. Where such an overlap exists, the purpose for which the product is bought determines its classification.

Industrial goods fall into four main categories:

Raw materials
Those industrial materials which in part or in whole become a portion of the physical product but which have undergone no more processing than is required for convenience, protection, economy in storage, transportation or handling. Threshed grain, natural rubber and crushed ore fall into this category.

Equipment
Those industrial goods which do not become part of the physical product and which are exhausted only after repeated use, such as major installations or installations equipment, and auxiliary accessories or auxiliary equipment. Installations equipment includes such items as boilers, presses, power lathes, bank vaults, etc., while auxiliary equipment includes trucks, office furniture, hand tools and the like.

Fabricated materials
Those industrial goods which become a part of the finished product and which have undergone processing beyond that required for raw

materials but not so much as finished parts. Steel, plastic moulding powders, cement and flour fit this description.

Supplies
Those industrial goods which do not become a part of the physical product or which are continually exhausted in facilitating the operation of an enterprise. Examples of supplies include fuel, stationery and cleaning materials.

Although few producers give much thought to actually classifying their output along the above lines, this is probably due to the fact that their product line falls within a single category, and not because there is no value in developing such a classification. In fact the product category has a fundamental effect on the firm's marketing strategy as a whole, as well as having far-reaching implications for its internal organisation and operation. This point will be examined in greater detail in Chapter 5.

4 Consumer Behaviour

INTRODUCTION

In *Consumer Behavior*, Engel, Blackwell and Kollat (The Dryden Press, 1978) define consumer behaviour as 'those acts of individuals directly involved in obtaining and using economic goods and services, including the decision processes that precede and determine these acts'. This definition enjoys a very wide measure of support in the majority of texts concerned primarily with consumer behaviour as a field of study in its own right but, in my opinion, it is important to stress that such an emphasis upon *individuals* tends to ignore largely an equally important area of consumption behaviour – that of organisations.

Currently there is a growing interest in what has become to be known as organisational buying behaviour and an American colleague, Arch Woodside, who is a shrewd observer of trends in the United States, has suggested (personal communication) that it is becoming increasingly fashionable among academic researchers on the other side of the Atlantic. Woodside also expressed the view that in this area European and particularly British academics are considerably more advanced than their American colleagues, citing a companion volume *Organisational Buying Behaviour* by Hill and Hillier (Macmillan, 1977) as evidence of this.

However, the existence of separate texts dealing with consumer and organisational buying behaviour is symptomatic of a much larger division within marketing of which new students of the subject should be especially sensitive – namely, the dichotomisation of the subject into industrial marketing and consumer marketing. Ever since the first edition of this book appeared in 1971 I have argued that while there are differences between these two branches of marketing they are a matter of degree only and in essence both rest upon the same foundations, as do new branches such as the marketing of services or marketing by non-profit-making organisations. Accordingly it might be more realistic to classify consumption behaviour as 'individual' or 'collective' depending upon whether such behaviour is undertaken solely in pursuit of one's own satisfaction or is engaged on in conjunction with and/or on the behalf of others.

Such a treatment is more properly the province of an advanced text and in this chapter we will accept the traditional approach in which discussions of consumer behaviour are focused upon individuals or ultimate consumers and their consumption behaviour, i.e. what they consume, how they buy, and why. In doing so it will be necessary to review a number of key concepts and ideas which have been borrowed from other behavioural sciences – notably psychology and sociology – before considering how these ideas have become incorporated in composite models of consumer behaviour. To this end we look first at contributions from psychology: namely, perception, learning, personality, motivation and attitude. Attention is then directed to social influences on consumer behaviour with specific reference to culture, social class, reference groups, role and family influence, with that section concluding with a discussion of life-style as an explanation of how and why people consume, which illustrates how the psychological and sociological foundations have been built upon by marketers. This theme is further developed by a survey of some of the major models of consumer behaviour which illustrate the main schools of thought, concluding with my own composite model of buying behaviour in which I seek to justify my earlier claim that differences between different branches of marketing are a matter of degree and not of principle.

PSYCHOLOGICAL INFLUENCES

Perception
In psychology an important and fine discrimination is made between the concepts of sensation and perception. Sensation occurs when a sense organ receives a stimulus, while perception is the interpretation of that stimulus. The distinction is particularly important for marketers, for in order to initiate an exchange process we must first establish contact through the generation of a stimulus capable of

sensation by the intended recipient. For practical purposes there are five senses – seeing, hearing, touching, smelling and tasting, though experimentation has established eleven sensory mechanisms in all – and it is to one or more of the five basic senses that marketing communications stimuli are directed. However, perception is the critical factor, for this is the interpretation placed upon the stimulus and can vary widely between individuals and even within individuals over time. A frequently used example which makes this point is to compare a photograph – what the eye and the camera physically see – with a painting, which is the receiver's interpretation of that sensation. Clearly Rembrandt and Picasso perceive things rather differently and the critical question must be: 'What factors influence perception?'

In essence, if perception consists of the interpretation of a received stimulus, then, as Sperling (*Psychology*, Made Simple Books, W. H. Allen, 1967) points out, 'What we perceive at any given time, therefore, will depend not only on the nature of the actual stimulus, but also on the background or setting in which it exists – our own previous sensory experiences, our feelings of the moment, our general prejudices, desires, attitudes and goals.' Given that so many forces influence perception it is not surprising that there should frequently occur a mismatch between the interpretation intended by the originator of a stimulus (usually the seller in a marketing context) and the receiver (intended customer). It follows that those responsible for marketing stimuli should pay very careful attention to psychological findings concerning how people perceive things.

A fundamental aspect of perception is that it represents the receiver's effort to organise received stimuli into a meaningful structure. In doing so two major groups of factors are involved – stimulus factors and functional factors. Stimulus factors are neutral in the sense that they are intrinsic to the stimulus and so will be received in exactly the same way by all receivers with normal sensory capabilities. On receipt the brain organises the incoming stimuli into patterns following four basic tendencies: similarity, proximity, continuity and context.

By similarity we understand the tendency of the receiver to group similar things together, while proximity results in the perception that things which are close to one another belong together. In marketing practice similarity is to be seen in the concept of segmentation, while proximity is employed in the use of prominent people to endorse particular products, in the use of generic brands like St Michael, and so on. The need to impose a meaningful structure on stimuli is particularly noticeable in the case of continuity, which is closely associated with closure. The phenomenon of continuity is well illustrated by Sperling with the use of a simple diagram like that below:

In this one sees the dots as straight lines rather than as separate dots, and as two continuous lines rather than four short ones. Closure occurs when one completes an otherwise incomplete diagram, picture, sentence, etc. For example, we all know what 'Beanz meanz'.

Finally, context, or the setting in which a stimulus is received, will have a marked effect upon perception (see any basic book for illustrations of the context influencing perception). In this sense context can have a similar 'halo' influence to proximity and is frequently used by marketers when seeking to develop an image of a product by using media or a setting which conveys the overall impression they wish to create, e.g. use of the Sunday colour supplements to convey a feeling of quality allied to value for money, or young people in leisure situations for Coca Cola.

As noted, stimulus factors are neutral and create sensations which are then interpreted in light of what are generically termed functional factors. Thus individuals have an ability to screen out stimuli which they do not understand or do not wish to recognise, just as they also have an ability to modify stimuli to make them acceptable to us – a phenomenon sometimes termed 'selective perception'.

The classic example of selective perception is that reported by Hastorf and Cantril ('They Saw a Game: A Case History', *Journal of Abnormal and Social Psychology*, vol. 49, 1954) of the perceptions of supporters of two American football teams – Dartmouth and Princeton. The match contained a number of incidents which led to players being injured and penalties being imposed. While most uninvolved viewers felt these were the joint responsibility of both teams, supporters of the two sides were almost unanimous in their view that all the trouble was the fault of the other team.

This tendency to perceive what one wants to 'see' can be traced to several factors. First, there is our ability to screen out or ignore a very large number of stimuli and so enable us to give our full attention to those which have some particular relevance or which strike a discordant note because of the contrast they make with other stimuli. Research has shown that we screen out the vast majority of advertisements to which we are exposed and, in fact, perceive less than 1 per cent of all those we come into contact with. Thus in order to secure our attention advertisers must use contrast, e.g. a colour advertisement in a black-and-white medium, loud noise (or silence) in broadcast media, luxury yacht advertisements in *The Economist*, etc. By the same token we possess perceptual defences which block out stimuli which are offensive, or are otherwise in conflict with our values or attitudes.

The issue of relevance is also important, for clearly we will be more likely to perceive stimuli which cater to our needs, both physiological and emotional, than those which do not. On occasion physical and emotional needs may generate a conflict (termed 'cognitive dissonance') such that acquisition of a physical object to satisfy a need (a car for transportation) may generate uncertainty as to the wisdom of that choice. Under these circumstances it has been shown that purchasers of objects pay more attention to advertising or other stimuli relating to the object than do intending purchasers.

Another perceptual phenomenon of importance to the marketer is that of preparatory set, which, put simply, means that people tend to perceive objects in terms of their expectations (cf. closure, discussed above). A well-known marketing manifestation of the influence of preparatory set is the use of branding and price labelling. Hence, while consumers are unable to distinguish between unbranded products they have no such difficulty when brand names are given. Similarly, Gabor and Grainger, Shapiro and others have clearly demonstrated that we use price as an indicator of quality and will select products with a higher price as 'better' when no differences exist with those carrying a lower price and even when the higher-priced items are objectively inferior.

In recent years marketers have made considerable use of psychological explanations of perception in developing their communications strategies and have developed a number of specific applications of their own. Perhaps the most sophisticated of these applications is known as *perceptual mapping*, which is founded on the premise that individuals will seek to relate new things in terms of their

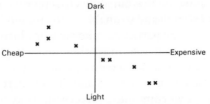

Fig. 4.1. Perception of different brands of whiskey in U.S. market

relationship with or similarity to things with which they are already familiar. By collecting information from consumers of their perceptions of existing brands in a product category one can develop a two-dimensional map (usually by making use of a powerful computer program) which shows the relationships between the various brands in terms of the variables used. In Fig. 4.1 it can be seen that the various brands are clustered in groups, suggesting that they are perceived as very similar. If one were to develop a new brand in this category, then this knowledge would be very valuable – either one has a product with certain characteristics and can identify the immediate opposition, or one can identify 'gaps' which it may be worth filling with a different type of product (cheap and light?). (The example shown is fictitious but it should be stressed that while Americans prefer lighter whiskies and pay a premium for them, the opposite is largely true in Britain).

Learning
Our discussion of perception has made it clear that in every circumstance our perception is conditioned by our prior experience, for it is this which constitutes our preparatory set or expectations and the framework into which we seek to place and organise new stimuli. In other words we have learned from our earlier experience and seek to maintain balance or consistency by relating and interpreting new stimuli in terms of past or learned stimuli.

Learning may have a number of meanings, depending upon the context in which it is used, and Sperling (in *Psychology*) comments that 'the process of learning can consist of all, or some, or one of three steps: INVENTING an original solution to a problem, or THINKING: COMMITTING a solution to memory, or MEMORISING: BECOMING EFFICIENT at applying the solution to a problem, or FORMING A HABIT'.

In essence there are two schools of thought concerning what is learned – the stimulus–response (*S–R*) school, and the cognitive school. Although there are some divisions within the *S–R* camp, the basic theory is that we learn to associate given responses to specific stimuli and these become habitual. One group of *S–R* theorists subscribe to the view that learning occurs only when there are rewards or punishments to *reinforce* the correct response, while others believe that learning is the result of an association between a stimulus and response occuring together, i.e. they are *contiguous*, and that reinforcement is not necessary.

In contrast to the *S–R* theorists the cognitive school argue that we learn cognitive structures, i.e. more broadly based interpretations of the association between stimuli and alternative courses of action.

In a marketing context there would seem to be support for both theories, in that some consumption behaviour is routinised and habitual (*S–R* school), while other purchasing decisions are subject to extensive problem-solving generalising from past experience (cognitive school).

The division of opinion about what we learn also exists in the case of how we learn. *S–R* theorists maintain that learning occurs through a process of trial and error – a view based on extensive experimental evidence using animals. However, some leading members of the cognitive school (notably Wolfgang Kohler) developed what is termed the *Gestalt* explanation of learning as being based on insight.

While it seems likely that the truth is a combination of both schools of thought, in which some actions are learned through direct personal experience based upon trial and error, while others are the product of reasoning, i.e. seeking solutions through symbolic thinking, the *S–R* explanations tend to dominate in consumer-behaviour research in marketing. In turn the most sophisticated statement of *S–R* theory which underlies much of this consumer-behaviour research is that developed by Clark Hull, in *Principles of Behavior: An Introduction to Behavior Theory* (New York, Appleton–Century–Crofts, 1943), whose basic model is

$$E = D \times K \times H \times V$$

where E = behaviour and is a multiplicative function of D = drive, K = incentive potential, H = habit strength, and where V = intensity of the cue.

Drives are discussed at greater length in the section on motivation research which follows, where a distinction is made between a drive which is viewed as the initial stimulus and a motive which is a tendency to activity. It is not felt that this distinction is important in the context of Hull's model. The remaining terms are essentially self-explanatory, and it is clear that in a marketing situation two of the variables – the incentive potential, or satisfaction offered by the product, and the intensity of the cue – are controllable to a considerable degree by the seller. It should also be noted that as the equation is multiplicative no reaction will occur if any of the variable has a zero value. At first sight this would seem to suggest that consumers would never try new products, for if they have not consumed them before, then H (or habit) would be expected to have a zero value. However, this possibility is negated by the principle of *generalisation*, whereby we extrapolate from past experience to a new situation. This potentiality is exploited by companies with generic brand names, where satisfactory experiences with one product group creates a favourable predisposition towards new product groups, e.g. buyers of clothes from Marks & Spencers towards M & S foodstuffs. Of course generalisation is only potential, and past experience soon teaches us that it is not always true that all the products introduced by a company will automatically yield the same level of satisfaction as the one which we originally approved of. In other words we learn to *discriminate* between very similar cues or stimuli.

Before leaving this brief overview of some learning-theory concepts which have been incorporated into studies of consumer behaviour it should be noted that Howard and Sheth's *Theory of Buyer Behavior* (Wiley, 1969) is essentially a learning model. It should also be noted that two important areas of research in marketing draw heavily upon learning theory for their conceptual framework – namely, the study of advertising effectiveness and of brand loyalty.

Motivation

Reference was made in the last section to the distinction between a drive as an initial stimulus, and motive as a tendency to act, though the terms tend to be used interchangeably in everyday speech. However, perhaps a clearer distinction is apparent if one defines drives as physiological stimuli to action, while motives constitute the intervening variable between the stimulus and response. For example, I have a strong drive to smoke a cigarette but my doctor has told me it is bad for my health and will shorten my life. I wish to live to a ripe old age and am strongly motivated to avoid anything which prejudices that goal – result, I stop smoking and resist drive.

Drives and motives are also often called 'needs' and one of the most enduring and widely used classification of needs is that proposed by Abraham Maslow ('A Theory of Human Motivation', *Psychological Review,* vol. 50, 1943). According to Maslow's basic theory we possess five basic needs which can be placed in a hierarchy such that as lower-order needs are satisfied we lose interest in them and concentrate upon satisfying needs at the next higher level which have become the most pressing. The five steps in the hierarchy in ascending order are:

1. Physiological needs
2. Safety needs
3. Love needs
4. Esteem needs
5. Self-actualisation needs.

Physiological needs or basic drives arise mainly from internal stimuli such as hunger or thirst, though some arise from external sources which threaten the individual with pain, injury or death. It is generally believed that satisfaction of these needs is dominant and overrides all other considerations. It is significant that a marketing function as it has developed in advanced economies in the past fifty to sixty years is irrelevant in countries where basic needs are not satisfied.

Safety needs come next in importance and can themselves be ranked into a rough hierarchy – physical security, stable and routine pattern of living, i.e. avoid the risk of the unknown, acquisition of protection against an uncertain future (religion, insurance).

Love needs include the need for affection and the feeling of belonging to a group – family, social group, work group, etc. Much marketing activity seeks to cater for these needs and includes some approaches most criticised by anti-marketers, e.g. advertising which suggests that failure to use a product (toothpaste, shampoo, etc.) will lead to ostracism or exclusion from a group which you aspire to join.

Esteem needs include such things as recognition, status, prestige, reputation, etc. In affluent societies achievement of these needs is often reinforced and made public through the acquisition of physical objects which are felt to be appropriate to a person's position in life.

(Consider the Sunday colour supplements or *Punch* for a sample of such objects.)

Self-actualisation represents the highest level of need to 'do one's own thing'. Relatively few people would seem to achieve this level and when they do they are unlikely to be much influenced by or interested in the market-place!

Maslow's hierarchy of motives constitutes a general statement of behaviour at the macro level – to understand the behaviour of the individual we need a more comprehensive classificatory scheme such as that provided by the concept of personality.

Personality

In his *Introduction to Psychology* (Harcourt Brace, 1967) Ernest Hilgard defines personality as 'The configuration of individual characteristics and ways of behaving which determine an individual's unique adjustment to his environment.' While Hilgard is atypical in offering a definition, as most psychologists fail to do so, his definition reflects the consensus concept of personality as a consistent pattern of response. Because of this overall consistency in an individual's pattern of behaviour it is possible to categorise dominant traits and develop a classification of personality 'types'. In turn such classification provides a valuable working construct for marketers, as it enables them to use personality as a factor in developing marketing strategies and marketing mixes to suit them.

However, if we are to make use of personality as a basis for trying to predict human behaviour, then it follows that we must be able to agree upon what variables we need to measure, and how to measure them, as a basis for classifying individuals. Sperling (in *Psychology*) records that Gordon Allport found 4500 words which designate distinct personal forms of behaviour in the 1925 edition of the unabridged *Webster's New International Dictionary*, and while many of these are no doubt synonyms it underlines the problem of what traits one is to measure to arrive at a personality 'type'. As a result of this extensive range of possibilities, psychologists have devised a battery of personality tests (Allport's being one of the best known and widely used) which reflect different personality theories (Freudian, neo-Freudian, *S–R*/learning theories) and/or the purpose for which the test has been devised. For example, if an employer is looking for persons with a particular and strongly developed personality trait, then they will prefer a test which emphasises identification and measurement of that trait.

Further, although it was stated earlier that personality is a valuable working construct for marketing practitioners, it must be recognised that the research evidence on the relationship between personality variables and consumer behaviour is conflicting. The most widely cited study is that of Franklin B. Evans, 'Psychological and Objective Factors in the Prediction of Brand Choice: Ford versus Chevrolet' (*Journal of Business*, vol. 32, October 1959), in which he used the Edwards Personal Preference Schedule to test for personality differences between owners of the two different makes of car, but concluded that personality is 'of little value in predicting whether an individual owns a Ford or a Chevrolet'. A number of subsequent studies would seem to confirm this conclusion, but at least as many maintain the opposite. Indeed, many writers have criticised Evans's whole approach, but Thomas S. Robertson (*Consumer Behavior*, Glenview, Ill., Scott Foresman, 1970) probably makes the most useful observation when he points out that while personality data only classified correctly 63 per cent of Evans's sample, this is 'some improvement over chance'. For many marketing problems this is all we can expect, and any approach which can reduce uncertainty is to be welcomed.

However, twenty years after Evans's study we are able to take a more balanced view of the value of personality variables as predictors of specific behaviour such as brand choice, and recognise that it is only one of several major influences upon consumer decision-making. Engel, Blackwell & Kollat (*Consumer Behavior*, p. 200) are of the opinion that personality is unlikely to prove a useful segmentation variable, not least because a homogeneous personality profile does not necessaily imply homogeneity in other respects, and most marketing media and channels of distribution tend to be designed to match other forms of homogeneity. None the less Engel *et al*. indicate several ways in which personality theory has considerable promise for marketing applications, particularly in its role as a moderating variable (i.e. where a personality trait can help explain differences in the behaviour of groups which are homogeneous in other respects), or as an intervening variable where primary segmentation is based upon objective factors such as demographics, but intra-group differences can be best explained in terms of motivational attributes.

In some situations individual attributes or traits may prove sufficient, but in others a more generalised statement of personality may be useful. Sperling (in *Psychology*) gives a list of twelve primary dimensions of personality which is based upon extensive measure-

TABLE 4.1. *Primary dimensions of personality*

---

1. Easy-going, generous, genial, warm, versus cold, inflexible
2. Independent, intelligent, reliable versus foolish, frivolous, unreflective
3. Emotionally stable, realistic, steadfast versus emotionally changeable, evasive, neurotic
4. Ascendant, dominant, self-assertive versus self-effacing, submissive
5. Cheerful, placid, sociable, talkative versus agitated, depressed, seclusive, sorrowful
6. Sensitive, sympathetic, tender-hearted versus frank and hard-boiled, poised, unemotional
7. Cultured, aesthetic versus boorish, uncultured
8. Conscientious, painstaking, responsible versus emotionally dependent, impulsive, irresponsible
9. Adventurous, carefree, kind versus cautious, inhibited, reserved, withdrawn
10. Energetic, persistent, quick, vigorous versus day-dreaming, languid, slack, tired
11. Calm, tolerant versus excitable, high-strung, irritable
12. Friendly, trustful versus suspicious, hostile

Source: Sperling, *Psychology Made Simple* (W. H. Allen, 1967) p. 174.

ment of traits which have a very low correlation with one another but whose defining traits have a very high correlation with one another (see Table 4.1).

A more condensed statement of psychographic variables is offered by Kotler (op. cit.) and contains the following seven items:

Compulsiveness: compulsive; non-compulsive
Gregariousness: extrovert; introvert
Autonomy: dependent; independent
Conservatism: conservative; liberal; radical
Authoritarianism: authoritarian, democratic
Leadership: leader; follower
Ambitiousness: high achiever; low achiever

Attitude
Attitude is one of the most frequently invoked behavioural-science concepts in marketing. While its relationship to behaviour is not

entirely clear, the frequent association between attitude and likely future action has resulted in extensive use of attitude surveys in the area of new-product development and in the design and execution of many promotional campaigns. Similarly, public opinion (belief or attitudes) is playing an increasing role in shaping and modifying corporate policy in areas such as consumer protection. It follows that a basic understanding of the current state of knowledge of attitude theory is vital to the student of marketing.

Just as there is no single agreed definition of marketing, so there is a multiplicity of definitions of 'attitude'. In broad terms most of these definitions fall into one of two categories which reflect two basic models in current use, which may be defined as the cognitive–affective–conative (C.A.C.) and expectancy-value (EV.) models. The cognitive–affective–conative model has been traced back to Plato's elements of the human soul – reasonable, spirited, appetitive – which in more modern terms may be defined as the realms of thought, emotions and motives, or knowing, feeling and acting. Marketers have developed a number of variants of their own of the C.A.C. model, some of the better known of which are contained in Table 4.2 under the general heading of hierarchy-of-effects models. In all of the marketing versions, starting with Strong's AIDA (1924) and progressing through Lavidge and Steiner (1961), Rogers (1962) to Engel, Kollat and Blackwell (1968), it is assumed that one proceeds from awareness (cognitive) to preference (affective) to action (conative) – an assumption of the direction of cause and effect for which there is little empirical support. In fact it is widely recognised that frequently one or

TABLE 4.2. *Hierarchy-of-effects models*

	Strong (AIDA)	Lavidge and Steiner	Rogers	Engel, Kollat and Blackwell
CONATIVE (motive)	ACTION	PURCHASE CONVICTION	ADOPTION TRIAL	PURCHASE PROCESSES
AFFECTIVE (emotion)	DESIRE INTEREST	PREFERENCE LIKING	EVALUATION INTEREST	EVALUATION AND SEARCH
COGNITIVE (thought)	AWARENESS	KNOWLEDGE AWARENESS UNAWARENESS	AWARENESS	PROBLEM RECOGNITION

more stages occur simultaneously, e.g. awareness and evaluation, while impulse purchases suggest that the cognitive and affective may occur together, while the conative may, or may not, follow. Despite these deficiencies the C.A.C. model enjoys wide support, and the effectiveness of marketing strategy is often measured in terms of its ability to move consumers up the hierarchy of effects, i.e. from unawareness to awareness, from desire to action – in other words attitude is seen as a predisposition to act.

The expectancy-value model views attitude as comprising two components – beliefs and values – which are broadly equivalent to the cognitive and affective dimensions of the C.A.C. model. It follows that the E.V. model is lacking a behavioural or action element and so is much more limited in its application.

The E.V. model is particularly associated with the work of Martin Fishbein, who built upon the work of Rosenberg, which in turn was developed from Fritz Heider's consistency model. In essence Fishbein argues that an attitude comprises two components – beliefs about the attributes of an object and the *values* ascribed to these beliefs. In order to maintain consistency (or balance, or congruity, as it is sometimes called) consumers need to act in accordance with their beliefs and the values associated with them. Thus, while E.V. models do not seek to establish a link between attitude and behaviour the association between expressed beliefs and action is strong where action occurs, i.e. beliefs experienced about different brands have been found to be good predictors of actual brand preference, where the person expressing a belief about a brand actually consumes an item from that product category. However, there is a world of difference between holding a neutral or positive belief about a product and a willingness to buy it, e.g. ' I believe Romeo and Juliet cigars are of the highest quality, but I would never buy them, because I do not smoke.'

This latter caveat is particularly important and explains why the E.V. model is theoretically more acceptable than the C.A.C. model, which extends the link between an attitude as a *predisposition to act* into *behaviour* without specifying the catalyst which makes action necessary. From a practical point of view it is this missing link which is of crucial importance in converting the results of attitude surveys into realistic sales forecasts. In my own model of buying behaviour I term this motivation to act 'precipitating circumstances', and suggest that the precise nature of these will depend very much upon specific circumstances. Clearly the implication of this is that one must seek to develop one's own check-list of causal factors in the context of one's own marketing problem. In doing so there are a number of other behavioural-science concepts which will prove helpful, including those of change agents, opinion leadership and source credibility. A review of these follows.

While we cannot prove a causal relationship between attitude and behaviour, it is clear that a favourable attitude is more likely to lead to desired action than is an unfavourable attitude. Consequently much marketing activity is devoted to creating a favourable attitude, or climate of opinion, towards an object, or to reinforcing such favourable attitudes if they already exist.

It is generally agreed that attitudes are learned initially from one's family and then from the groups to which one belongs or wishes to belong. From a marketing point of view favourable attitudes to the consumption of particular products and/or services are usually a by-product of more basic group affiliations/aspirations. For example, I wish to be accepted as a student, students wear scarves and jeans, therefore I wear a scarf and jeans. The question is, who sets the group norm which specifies scarf and jeans as the accepted dress of the group?

As in most marketing/behavioural-science issues, there is no single universally accepted answer, but the balance of evidence is that certain individuals take it upon themselves to mould and change attitudes and behaviour by setting themselves up as *opinion leaders*.

The opinion leader achieves his satisfaction through his status as the expert adviser on some aspect of importance to a group of which he or she is a member. This status is often highly specific, e.g. the group expert on hi-fi systems, bargain travel, cheap places to eat, etc., and it is unusual to find an individual who is the opinion leader on all topics of interest to a group. In other words while the existence and role of opinion leaders in influencing attitudes/behaviour is widely accepted, using this idea operationally is restricted, due to the absence, and possibly non-existence, of a profile enabling one to identify the opinion leader.

However, to the extent that opinion leaders act as filters and amplifiers in the communication channel (see Chapter 14, pp. 245–7) their potential role as change agents is particularly significant, as is the concept of source credibility.

Source credibility refers to the confidence we place in the source of information, and has been shown to have an important influence upon the acceptability of new information as a basis for attitude change (as does the presentation of the message itself). Broadly speaking sources may be divided into two categories – personal and impersonal – and may be 'objective' or marketer-dominated ('objective' only in the sense that the source is not paid for by the marketer in the same way as advertisements and salesmen are). The effectiveness of the different sources in the stages of the consumer decision process, which coincide with the stages in the C.A.C. or E.V. models, has been the subject of a great deal of research, and an excellent summary table is to be found on pages 248 and 249 in Engel, Blackwell and Kollat's *Consumer Behavior*.

SOCIAL INFLUENCES

The preceding discussion of psychological influences has concentrated largely upon individual characteristics. In this section we are concerned primarily with people as members of groups, for, as will become clear, group membership has a profound influence upon individual behaviour. The approach followed is to start with macro concepts of culture and social class, and then refine the analysis to look at reference groups, role and family influences, and, finally, the concept of life-style.

Culture
Bennett and Kassarjian (*Consumer Behavior,* Prentice-Hall, 1972) define culture as 'a set of *learned* beliefs, values, attitudes, habits, and forms of behavior that are *shared* by a society and are *transmitted* from generation to generation within that society'.

The emphasis upon *learned, shared* and *transmitted* is important, for it reflects attributes common to a vast multiplicity of definitions of culture. Values and beliefs are *learned*; they are not innate or instinctive in the way in which physiological drives are. Because they are *shared* they become a yardstick for behaviour, departure from which is regarded as deviancy and may be punished with considerable severity. Third, while a culture will evolve over time it possesses an enduring quality which enables it to be *transmitted* from generation to generation.

There are many different cultures, and Robertson (op. cit.) suggests that a structural framework for classifying these may be developed, using three dimensions–distributive, organisational and normative. In his words:

> The *distributive* dimension summarises demographic characteristics, such as income and education levels, and the distribution of the population ecologically (for example, urban, suburban, or rural) and occupationally. The *organisational* dimension summarises participation patterns within the culture, and the structure of cultural institutions. Social class structure and the rigidity or flexibility of this structure, as well as the nature of family relationships, are organisational topics. The *normative* element treats values and norms, including economic or religious philosophy.

While these three dimensions are very useful in drawing broad distinctions between, say, Eastern and Western cultures, it is obvious that they must be used with caution and as a first broad-brush basis for distinguishing between behavioural patterns. Indeed, for most marketers it is *sub-cultures* which are of more direct and immediate interest because they provide a meaningful way of segmenting a society. Sub-cultures usually develop from a basic dimension of race, religion or nationality, and it is these which tend to have most influence upon consumer behaviour. However, age and ecological sub-cultures are also distinguishable and important.

Bennett and Kassarjian (in *Consumer Behavior*) suggest that culture exerts this influence mainly upon consumption *per se* and media image and has greatest relevance in the sphere of international marketing. In the case of consumption differences food preferences are probably the most obvious case in point, followed by clothing and beverages (e.g. Moslem attitudes to alcohol). Sub-cultures have an important influence upon the acceptability of message content, particularly in terms of the cultural expectancies of the audience, e.g. technical information for men, style information for women for consumer durables, and demands careful attention by advertising strategists. (Robertson (op. cit.) gives a number of interesting examples of 'cultural implications for marketing'.)

While it may seem obvious that culture is of most relevance to the international marketer, there is a tendency to exaggerate this. Specifically, the generalisations which are usually cited as dire warnings of the perils of ignoring the cultural differences between different international markets often serve to disguise the fact that there are probably as many different and diverse segments within an overseas market as in the domestic one. Further, given modern communications systems, it is highly likely that very similar segments for particular products may be found in most countries, despite the fact that the commonplace in the United States may be a luxury in Africa or India (or the commonplace in Saudi Arabia a luxury in the United States!). Perhaps the safest policy is to be sensitive to cultural differences but act upon the existence of common sub-cultures.

Social class
A particularly strong and pervasive, indeed universal, sub-cultural division is that of social class, whereby members of a society are stratified into a number of sub-divisions. These sub-divisions or classes are based upon many common characteristics, which usually include income, education, occupation and social status or prestige. These characteristics give rise to similar behavioural patterns and activities which can be differentiated from those of other social classes. This latter point is of particular importance to marketers, for the value of such a classification lies in the ability to discriminate between groupings of people and, it is hoped, to predict their behaviour under given conditions.

Many people find the concept of class offensive, because of the intrinsic implication that people can be ordered according to their worth, and argue that all people are equal. Such an argument would appear to be based largely upon an economic interpretation of equality and leads to attempts to distribute wealth more evenly through society. However, it is clear that the redistribution of wealth has relatively little to do with the value attached to the various roles filled by individuals and it is this which is the essence of social stratification. Thus in most societies teachers and priests are accorded relatively high status and prestige but earn incomes more in keeping with members of a lower class; similarly, pop singers earn more than opera singers but their earnings are probably inversely related to their prestige. Thus, while it is true that the status associated with given roles may change over time, it seems highly improbable that there will ever be a truly classless society.

It follows that if we wish to make use of this universal tendency for societies to 'classify' themselves, then we must identify and measure those factors or criteria upon which such a classification rests. In doing so one must not be surprised if different sets of criteria result in a different number of classes. However, most systems used in Western cultures have a close allegiance to the six-class model proposed by W. Lloyd Warner in his celebrated study of a small New England Town (*Social Class in America*, Harper & Row, 1960).

Social class	Membership
Upper-upper	Aristocracy
Lower-upper	New rich
Upper-middle	Successful business and professional
Lower-middle	White-collar worker
Upper-lower	Blue-collar worker
Lower-lower	Unskilled

While this scheme recognises two more classes than did Centers's 1949 division into upper, middle, working and lower classes, Warner himself saw the issue as a false one in that the number of divisions is

TABLE 4.3. *Socio-economic groupings**

Social grade	Social status	Occupation	% of population (*approx.*)
A	Upper middle class	Higher managerial, administrative or professional	2.6
B	Middle class	Middle managerial, administrative or professional	12.7
C1	Lower middle class	Supervisory or clerical, junior management	22.8
C2	Skilled working class	Skilled manual workers	31.2
D	Working class	Semi- and unskilled manual workers	21.0
E	Those at lowest level of subsistence	Pensioners, casual or lowest-grade worker, unemployed	9.7
			100.0

*The breakdown in the table is derived from data published by JICNARS (Joint Industry Committee for National Readership Surveys) and is not dependent on income, i.e. it is based on the occupation of the head of household with limited exception–when the chief wage-earner is used instead.

relatively arbitrary and dependent upon whose opinion you are seeking. It should also be noted that in many instances one is as much concerned with differences within classes as between them.

The most widely used system in the United Kingdom is that developed for use in the *National Readership Survey* (see Table 4.3).

Just as the concept of culture is useful for classifying people into broadly similar grouping, so social-class concepts help refine the classification into smaller and more specific segments with greater operational potential for practitioners. Engel *et al.* cite a large number of studies which illustrate the application of social class in helping to interpret and predict consumer behaviour – social class has been found to be especially useful in predicting preferences for kind, quality and style of clothing, home furnishings, leisure activities, cars, consumer durables, and use of credit cards. Social class has also been shown to be associated with patterns of media usage, language patterns, source credibility and shopping behaviour. This predictive power is considerably enhanced if one is able to add to it knowledge concerning reference groups, role and family influence.

Reference groups, role and family influence
When discussing psychological influences upon behaviour the emphasis was upon the individual. But 'No man is an island', and all of us are subjected to the influence of others with whom we come into contact. This influence is particularly strong in the case of what are termed *reference groups*.

Social psychologists reserve the description *group* for collections of two or more persons who interact with one another over time. In other words there must be some relationship between the group members which goes beyond collections of persons with common interests such as a theatre audience or passengers in an aeroplane. Bennett and Kassarjian in *Consumer Behavior* cite Krech, Crutch-field and Ballachey's definition from *Individual in Society* (McGraw-Hill, 1962), namely: 'a group is (1) persons who are interdependent upon each other, such that each member's behavior potentially influences the behavior of each of the others, and (2) the sharing of an ideology – a set of beliefs, values, and norms – which regulate their mutual conduct'.

Several different types of reference groups may be distinguished, the most basic distinction being between primary and secondary groups. A primary group is one which is small enough for all of the members to communicate with each other face to face (the family, a seminar group, the area sales team), while a secondary group is one where less continuous interaction takes place (professional societies, trade unions, companies, etc.).

When a group possesses a specified structure and specified functions then it is termed a *formal* group, but where the structure and function are unspecified, as in a circle of friends, we have an *informal* group. Both formal and informal groups have norms which prescribe the pattern of behaviour expected of members and the transmission of these norms to new members is known as *socialisation*. In formal groups the norms are usually much more explicit and readily identified than in informal groups, but the norms of the latter are no less demanding if one wishes to remain in membership of the group. In all cases the influence of the group is towards *conformity*, and the strength of this tendency will depend upon the pressure the group can bring to bear upon the individual, the importance of the group to the individual and the number of groups to which the individual belongs.

In a marketing context perhaps the most important group of all is the family – specifically the *nuclear family* of husband, wife and children (the extended family includes grandparents, aunts, uncles, cousins, etc.). The nuclear family is frequently referred to as 'the household' in consumer studies but such usage is often looser and may include any group of persons occupying the same housing unit, as does the official U.S. Census Bureau definition.

As a primary group the family has great influence upon motives, personality and attitudes and acts as a mediating influence upon external influences which impinge upon it from culture, sub-culture, social class and other reference groups. Because of this mediating influence, and due to the economic interdependence of its members, family (household) decision-making has a profound influence upon purchasing and consumption behaviour. All of the basic disciplines upon which marketing is founded have advanced their own explanation of household decision-making and there is no shortage of theories for the marketer to consider. J. L. Drayton (University of Strathclyde Student Note) has traced the basic themes from these disciplines as follows:

Economics: the household has tended to be viewed as an efficiency unit, using an input/output analysis in which input = time and labour (income) and output = goods and services (wealth). This approach uses a unified demand and preference schedule, i.e. each member of the household views each purchase in the same light in terms of utility gained, maximisation of family satisfaction.

One attempt has been made to derive a household preference theory from Hicks' individual preference schedule (drawn from a marginal rate of substitution of one product for another). Empirical testing of this theory caused it to be abandoned – since no apparent relationship existed between the individually stated preference and actual family choice of products.

Psychology: individuals seeking to meet their own needs; finding a balance between power and harmony; suggests a host of separate utility patterns – but little direct contribution to how these combine (given a limited income).

Sociology: with the sophistication of techniques and theory provided by the study of 'small groups', family sociologists have been the major researchers in the field of how families actually reach a decision. As one would expect, starting from the basis of small group studies, the emphasis has been upon establishing patterns of leadership roles – a dominant partner typology, which might suggest for instance that the U.K. is basically patriarchal in outlook (therefore husbands will dominate decision making); or that the U.S. is matriarchal! Neither typology has been empirically proven. The idea of producing a typology is that this then becomes the 'Family norm' – anything differing from this norm can be analysed to discover why.

Anthropology: concentrates upon the transfer of cultural values from generation to generation; thus decision making here becomes a factor in the socialisation process, with the roles (or status) within a family (and within a society) determined at birth and learned in childhood.

Thus when marketers require information about household consumption there is no shortage of theories to turn to. The problem confronting us is rather 'which one is the most useful in its application to the marketing of goods and services to families?'

The question may well be raised as to how a greater knowledge of the decision-making processes can assist the marketing practitioner.

Three obvious areas spring to mind:

(*a*) Product planning and design
(*b*) Distribution channels
(*c*) Communication strategies

In terms of design factors of household products (e.g. consumer durables) there may be a conflict between the technical perfection the design engineers and production techniques are capable of and the needs of the eventual user. In the trade-off between efficiency and ease of use the marketer needs to know what are the important characteristics of the product as perceived by the product-user/decision-influencer.

A review of empirical studies of family decision-making undertaken throughout the 1960s reveals two major underlying currents:

(*a*) Ideological role theory
(*b*) The resource theory of power

The primary hypothesis in the ideological theory of roles is that household decision-making and activity patterns can be explained in terms of role expectations developed through the pervading culture. Each member of the family has a meaningful set of chores to perform–meaningful in the sense that such chores contribute to family survival and well-being.

The traditional and best-known exposition of family roles is the goal-orientated husband who 'gets things done', complemented by a supportive wife playing a social emotive role of 'keeping the family together'. Division of roles in this way generalises that husbands are responsible for decisions which are essentially concerned with the interface between the household and the external world, while wives take responsibility for activities within the family.

Although role theory has been useful to sociologists in understanding family survival in periods of social change, research into product decisions utilising role theory has been ambiguous and conflicting.

The alternative explanation of household power structure is resource theory. The main thesis is that authority and activity patterns within the family can be analysed in terms of such variables as income, education and social status. The right to make decisions influencing family welfare is related to the comparative resources brought to the marriage.

A resource in this context is defined as 'any special characteristic, skill or competence of one partner that contributes to family goal attainment' and embraces the following:

(*a*) Earning capacity (present and potential)
(*b*) Occupation (both partners)
(*c*) Education level
(*d*) Religion
(*e*) Life-style
(*f*) Age

From a practical point of view it is useful to try and classify the extent and nature of influence in the household decision-making unit and four basic role-structure categories may be distinguished:

(*a*) Husband dominant
(*b*) Wife dominant
(*c*) Autonomic (an equal number of decisions is made by each partner but without consultation)
(*d*) Syncretic (most decisions made jointly)

As suggested earlier, an ability to relate role-structure category and purchase of specific products will be of great value in developing new products and the most effective marketing mix to promote and sell them. A very useful review of research in this area is to be found in Engel *et al*. (*Consumer Behavior*, pp. 152–62).

The physical or demographic composition of the family will also have a significant influence upon its consumption behaviour and the concept of the family life-cycle is a particularly useful framework for analysis. The most extensive model contains six stages (as shown in Table 4.4).

For a very extensive analysis of the relationship between these stages and consumption behaviour the book by Reynolds and Wells contains five chapters dealing specifically with this topic.

Life-style
So far the discussion has focused upon major sociological concepts which have been borrowed and adapted by marketers in seeking to explain and predict consumer behaviour. We now consider a composite concept which has been developed extensively by consumer-behaviour researchers in the past ten years that seeks to synthesise

TABLE 4.4. *Family life-cycles*

Age	Developmental level	Stage in the family life-cycle
18–34	Early adulthood	1 The bachelor stage: young, single people 2 Newly married couples: young, no children 3 The Full Nest I: young married couples with dependent children: (*a*) Youngest child under six (*b*) Youngest child over six
35–54	Middle adulthood	4 The Full Nest II: older married couples with dependent children
55 and older	Later adulthood	5 The Empty Nest: older married couples with no children living with them: (*a*) Head in labour force (*b*) Head retired 6 The Solitary Survivors: the older single people (*a*) In labour force (*b*) Retired

Source: Fred D. Reynolds and William D. Wells, *Consumer Behavior* (McGraw-Hill, 1977).

the economic, psychological and sociological influences, namely 'life-style'.

In essence life-style summarises the way in which we live and is founded upon the observation that people seek consistency or balance in their lives – the old concept of homoeostasis – and so organise their behaviour to try and achieve this state. We have already noticed this tendency in discussing the concepts of perception, personality and motivation and observed how it becomes socialised in cultural traits, norms and values. Given this tendency towards consistency in behavioural response it follows that if we can

TABLE 4.5. *Demographic profile of the heavy user of shotgun ammunition*

	Per cent who spend $11+ per year on shotgun ammunition (141)*	Per cent who do not buy (395)*
Age		
Under 25	9	5
25–34	33	15
35–44	27	22
45–54	18	22
55 +	13	36
Occupation		
Professional	6	15
Managerial	23	23
Clerical/sales	9	17
Craftsman	50	35
Income		
Under $6,000	26	19
$6,000–$10,000	39	36
$10,000–£15,000	24	27
$15,000 +	11	18
Population density		
Rural	34	12
2500–50000	11	11
50000–500000	16	15
500000–2 million	21	27
2 million +	13	19
Geographic division		
New England/Mid Atlantic	21	33
Central (N, W)	22	30
South Atlantic	23	12
E. South Central	10	3
W. South Central	10	5
Mountain	6	3
Pacific	9	13

*Number of respondents in the survey.
Source: W. D. Wells, 'Psychographics: A Critical Review', *Journal of Marketing Research*. vol. XII, May 1975.

identify a consumer life-style in one context, then we should be able to extrapolate from that situation and predict how he will behave in different sets of circumstances.

The measurement of life-style in the subject of an area of research known as *psychographics* is discussed at length in Engel *et al.* (*Consumer Behavior*). An excellent overview of the subject is also to be found in an article by William D. Wells, 'Psychographics: A Critical Review' (*Journal of Marketing Research*, vol. XII, May 1975, pp. 196–213). In this article Wells proposes an operational definition of psychographic research as 'quantitative research intended to place consumers on psychological – as distinguished from demographic – dimensions', a definition which emphasises the distinctive features of the area – it has a quantitative rather than a qualitative orientation and goes beyond demographics. (Engel *et al.* point out that 'psychographics' is often used interchangeably with the mnemonic AIO standing for Activities, Interests and Opinions as a research area.)

In his article Wells discusses a number of case histories of different applications of psychographic research, but the first will be sufficient to indicate how it lends a new dimension to profiling consumers. The example is best illustrated by Tables 4.5 and 4.6, which comprise a demographic and psychographic profile of the heavy user of shotgun ammunition.

As Wells comments:

In spite of this lack of focus, the data [in Table 4.6] show some interesting patterns. First, it is obvious that hunting is not an isolated phenomenon but rather is associated with other rugged outdoor endeavors. Shotgun shell buyers not only like to hunt, they also like to fish and go camping. They even like to work outdoors. These relationships are interesting and useful because they suggest activities and settings, other than hunting scenes, that might be appropriate for shotgun ammunition advertising. They suggest products that might be especially appropriate for joint promotions or other cooperative marketing ventures, such as displaying shotgun ammunition near camping or fishing equipment in retail outlets. [Table 4.6] also shows that ammunition buyers are apt to be do-it-yourselfers, which suggests that hunters are apt to be buyers of hardware and tools.

Items in the third group [in Table 4.6] suggest some

TABLE 4.6. *Psychographic profile of the heavy user of shotgun ammunition*

Base	Per cent who spend $11+ per year on shotgun ammunition (141)*	Per cent who do not buy (395)*
I like hunting	88	7
I like fishing	68	26
I like to go camping	57	21
I love the out of doors	90	65
A cabin by a quiet lake is a great place to spend the summer	49	34
I like to work outdoors	67	40
I am good at fixing mechanical things	47	27
I often do a lot of repair work on my own car	36	12
I like war stories	50	32
I would do better than average in a fist fight	38	16
I would like to be a professional football player	28	18
I would like to be a policeman	22	8
There is too much violence on television	35	45
There should be a gun in every home	56	10
I like danger	19	8
I would like to own my own air-plane	35	13
I like to play poker	50	26
I smoke too much	39	24
I love to eat	49	34
I spend money on myself that I should spend on the family	44	26
If given a chance, most men would cheat on their wives	33	14
I read the newspaper every day	51	72

*Number of respondents in the survey.
Source: As for Table 4.5.

hypotheses about the psychological makeup of the shotgun ammunition buyer. Compared with the non-buyer he is definitely more attracted by violence, suggesting that detective, war, and violent Western TV programs ought to draw audiences with disproportionate numbers of shotgun users, and that action and adventure magazines ought to be considered when placing advertising associated with hunting. Relationships between product use and media exposure are always best documented by direct cross-tabulation, but when these data are not available (and they often are not) relationships suggested by life-style patterns can provide helpful direction.

The relatively high levels of agreement with the fourth section [of Table 4.6] suggest that the hunter is generally less risk-averse than is his nonhunting counterpart. To policy makers charged with keeping hunters from shooting themselves and each other, this willingness to accept risk would suggest that sober warnings about the dangers of firearms may well be ineffective. Lest this conclusion seem hopelessly naive, let it be noted that sober warnings about the dangers of firearms are exactly what some policy makers have attempted.

The relatively high levels of agreement with the fifth section suggest a combination of self-indulgence and lack of internal control that seems congruent with the attitude toward risk just noted. If the hunter is in fact self-indulgent and relatively conscienceless, it would seem unwise to rely on appeals to fair play and conservation to regulate his activities. Again, such appeals have been tried with less success than expected.

The level of agreement with 'I love to eat' and the hunter's professed willingness to spend money on himself suggest markets for premium foods designed to be taken along on hunting expeditions. These two findings also suggest the suitability of game-preparation recipes for hunting magazines, and they indicate that quantity and quality of food should get particular attention from proprietors of hunting lodges. Hunters don't mind roughing it, but they want it to be a well-fed roughness.

Finally, the relatively low level of agreement with 'I read the newspaper every day' should serve as a warning to shotgun ammunition advertisers. This is not to assert that media decisions, positive or negative, should ever be based on responses to a single survey item. Rather, it suggests that any shotgun ammunition advertiser who is spending his budget in newspapers should think twice about alternatives.

Psychographic profiles are usually developed from large-scale surveys (200–300 questions, 1000+ respondents) using self-administered questionnaires covering a wide range of attitudes, opinions, and interests and Likert scales (see Chapter 9, p. 189, for a description). Responses may be analysed by simple cross-classification techniques, but given the wealth of information it is more usual to make use of the powerful multivariate techniques available in packaged computer programs such as S.P.S.S. (Statistical Package for the Social Sciences). Using techniques such as *factor analysis* it becomes possible to reduce the mass of data into a series of principal components which distinguish major groupings within the data. The output of such an analysis is shown in Table 4.7 (again taken from Wells's article).

TABLE 4.7. *Eight male psychographic segments*

Group I 'The Quiet Family Man' (8 per cent of total males)

He is a self-sufficient man who wants to be left alone and is basically shy. Tries to be as little involved with community life as possible. His life revolves around the family, simple work and television viewing. Has a marked fantasy life. As a shopper he is practical, less drawn to consumer goods and pleasures than other men.

Group II 'The Traditionalist' (16 per cent of total males)

A man who feels secure, has self-esteem, follows conventional rules. He is proper and respectable, regards himself as altruistic and interested in the welfare of others. As a shopper he is conservative, likes popular brands and well-known manufacturers. (Low education and low or middle socio-economic status; the oldest age group.)

Group III 'The Discontented Man' (13 per cent of total males)

He is a man who is likely to be dissatisfied with his work. He feels bypassed by life, dreams of better jobs, more money and more security. He tends to be distrustful and socially aloof. As a buyer he is quite price conscious. (Lowest education and lowest socio-economic group, mostly older than average.)

Group IV 'The Ethical Highbrow (14 per cent of total males)

This is a very concerned man, sensitive to people's needs. Basically a puritan, content with family life, friends and work. Interested in culture, religion and social reform. As a consumer he is interested in quality, which may at times justify greater expenditure. (Well-educated, middle or upper socio-economic status, mainly middle-aged or older.)

Group V 'The Pleasure-orientated Man' (9 per cent of total males)

He tends to emphasise his masculinity and rejects whatever appears to be soft or feminine. He views himself a leader among men. Self-centred, dislikes his work or job. Seeks immediate gratification for his needs. He is an impulsive buyer, likely to buy products with a masculine image. (Low education, lower socio-economic class, middle-aged or younger.)

Group VI 'The Achiever' (11 per cent of total males)

This is likely to be a hardworking man, dedicated to success and all that it implies, social prestige, power and money. Is in favour of diversity, is adventurous about leisure-time pursuits. Is stylish, likes good food, music, etc. As a consumer he is status conscious, a thoughtful and discriminating buyer. (Good education, high socio-economic status, young.)

Group VII 'The He-Man' (19 per cent of total males)

He is gregarious, likes action, seeks an exciting and dramatic life. Thinks of himself as capable and dominant. Tends to be more of a bachelor than a family man, even after marriage. Products he buys and brands preferred are likely to have 'Self-expressive value', especially a 'Man of Action' dimension. (Well-educated, mainly middle socio-economic status, the youngest of the male groups.)

Group VIII 'The Sophisticated Man' (10 per cent of total males)

He is likely to be an intellectual, concerned about social issues, admires men with artistic and intellectual achievements. Socially cosmopolitan, broad interests. Wants to be

TABLE 4.7 (*cont.*)

dominant, and a leader. As a consumer he is attracted to the unique and fashionable. (Best educated and highest economic status of all groups, younger than average.)

COMPOSITE MODELS OF CONSUMER BEHAVIOUR

For many years prominent researchers in the consumer-behaviour field have attempted to develop comprehensive theories of consumer behaviour. In *Marketing: Theory and Practice*, ed. Michael J. Baker (Macmillan, 1976), my colleague Jennifer Drayton summarises a number of the more important models – those of Nicosia, Andreasen, Engel, Kollat and Blackwell, Clawson, and Howard and Sheth – as follows:

> These models differ in respect to their complexity and orientation but are nevertheless based upon the same strands of thought. Thus similarities are to be found in the isolation and identification of the relevant variables, and in the perspective of a dynamic decision process, with the actions of the consumer viewed as a movement towards some decision point.

Nicosia
Nicosia uses as a base for his model a computer flow-chart technique, divided into four distinct areas, or 'fields'. The output from each field becomes the input to the succeeding field.

The model depicts a message (for example, an advertisement for a new product) flowing from its source (in this case the business firm) in the direction of an eventual decision outcome by the consumer. In Field 1 the consumer is exposed to and receives the message, with an outcome of the development of some predisposition, or attitude, towards the product, Field 2 is concerned with the search and evaluation process, which has as its output the arousal of the individual's motivation, leading to Field 3, which is defined as 'possible transformation of the motivation into an act of purchase'. If purchase occurs, Field 4 becomes the area of storage and use of the product, with a related output of experience.

In each of the fields the relevant influences upon the eventual outcome are delineated. As the message flows from the business firm to the formation of a consumer attitude, it will be modified or distorted by internal subjective perceptual elements. During the period of 'search and evaluation' (Field 2) the internal and external forces are differentiated in terms of additional information input. Internally initiated data are concerned with the associations, conscious or unconscious, with the firm, the brand of the product, while external data are culled from the environment in the form of word-of-mouth communication, or an increased receptivity to advertising in the product area.

Andreasen

Andreasen has developed the concepts of 'attitude formation' and 'attitude change' contributed by social psychologists to construct a consumer-decision model as an information-processing cycle. This model indicates that attitude change can be achieved via exposure to information. Change of attitude is assumed to be a logical preliminary to a change in behaviour, an assumption which is lacking in verification since the complexity of the attitude–behaviour relationship remains a controversial area in social-psychology studies. It is as yet far from certain that influence in this area is a one-way flow from attitude to behaviour as the model suggests.

Andreasen's model centres upon the individual utilising a message input to reach a decision outcome, with attitude formation and change as the central concepts. The predispositional nature of attitudes (i.e. 'not based on actual experience) is shown to impinge upon the individual's perceptions, which operate as a filter through which the information must pass to reach the cognitive system. Thus attitudes to message source or channel may effectively alter the character of the original communication.

Engel, Kollat and Blackwell

These researchers have produced a sequential approach to the purchase decision which has been described as a complete model of buying behaviour. It is a general model which gives a framework for examining the diverse range of influences to which the buyer is subject as the decision process moves from its initial stage of the beginnings of need awareness through its subsequent steps up to the terminal stage of after-the-event evaluation and rationalisation. The contributions of the three basic internal processes – perception, learning and motivation – represent major steps in the model, while personality and attitudes are seen to exert pressure upon the process. The social and cultural aspects of the possible purchase decision are also shown as influencing the individual's movement through the decision stages.

Clawson

Clawson has extended the views propounded by Lewin in his behavioural studies, with the contribution of *Gestalt* theories clearly in evidence.

The analysis is concentrated in some depth upon the tension element in a purchase decision as the individual assesses the positive and the negative aspects attached to the decision outcome, producing a situation of psychic conflict. The fact that both the positive and the negative features are perceived subjectively by the consumer is also stressed, indicating that the conflict cannot be resolved on the grounds of objective product characteristics or information. These objective criteria may not penetrate the net of selective perception, or may be disorted on the way.

Howard and Sheth

Howard and Sheth have based their approach to the formulation of a general consumer model on the standpoint of the consumer playing an active role in the business transaction. He is not merely exposed to communications but is portrayed as vigorously collecting and processing information.

Fundamentally the model is constructed around a series of stimulus variables passing into the individual's processing system and being acted upon by the internal factors of perception and learning, termed by the researchers 'the hypothetical constructs'. A response variable terminates the process, with the whole being surrounded by the exogenous variables of social class, culture and personality, plus such constraints as time and income availability.

Inputs are separated out into three groups which distinguish source differences. The first group relates to the actual product communications of price, quality, availability, distinctiveness and service. The second group derives from indirect and impersonal sources, such as salesmen or the mass media. The third group of stimulus variables identifies the activity of the consumer collecting data from his social environment via the personal influence of word-of-mouth communication. Thus the interaction between the consumer and his social environment is distinguished and extended, showing the external forces in the decision process not only as a constraint upon behaviour but also as a reference point for the gathering of credible information. Interaction between man and his social environment is seen to be a two-way function.

The hypothetical constructs of perception and learning detail the manipulation of the information gathered from the various sources, affecting the amount and quality of objective information which reaches the system.

Howard and Sheth have acknowledged that these hypothetical constructs and their interrelationships are a consequence of the integration of a number of well-known theories – Hull's learning theory, Osgood's cognitive theory and Berlyne's theory of exploratory behaviour.

In the same book (*Marketing: Theory and Practice*) I propose a composite model of buyer behaviour of my own (pp. 128–31) with a rather different orientation from those outlined above.The essentials of this model are now described.

As noted in the introduction to this chapter there is a tendency to distinguish between individual and organisational buying behaviour by emphasising the qualitative/behavioural nature of the former and the quantitative/rational/economic nature of the latter. In my view this distinction is largely spurious as I believe that all buying decisions are subject to the same economic and behavioural influences and in the majority of cases follow the same basic process. This process is best observed by analysing the purchase of a product of which the user has no prior experience, for otherwise several stages may be omitted, i.e. the purchase of a familiar brand or the automatic re-ordering of an industrial supply.

My basic model may be stated notationally as:

$$P = f[EC, PC, (E_A - E_D), (P_A - P_D), BR]$$

where P = purchase
         f = a function of
         EC = enabling conditions
         PC = precipitating circumstances

E_A = economic advantages
E_D = economic disadvantages
P_A = performance advantages
P_D = performance disadvantages
BR = behavioural response

Enabling conditions is a summary variable comprising a need, awareness of a possible means of satisfying it and the resources necessary to acquire a supply. Precipitating circumstances are those which move the felt need up one's scale of needs/preferences to the point where one will actively consider means of satisfying the need. (E_A-E_D) comprises an economic analysis of the pros and cons associated with purchase of different and competing means of satisfying the need, while (P_A-P_D) constitutes a similar review of the performance characteristics of the object. Together these two sets of analyses may be thought of as a cost–benefit analysis.

Now it should be clear from the content of this chapter that while the stimuli contained within the competing products are objectively the same for all recipients, they will be interpreted subjectively – in other words the *behavioural response* will tend to modify the objective reality. However, it is my opinion that there is a limit to the distortion which normal people will experience. Thus economic rationality is a very compelling norm and likely to dominate purely subjective preferences – 'I would like a Porsche but I need a Mini!' Accordingly I see the purchase decision (individual *or* collective) as a sequential process in which we apply economic and performance criteria to alternatives (with some subjective overtones, of course) in order to arrive at a final choice. If at the end of such an analysis there is no clear-cut preference, and in most competitive markets there rarely is, then behavioural factors will exercise a *determinant* role in guiding our final selection. However, to look at the end-result (Q: 'Why did you buy that Mini?' A: 'I liked its blue and white polka-dot upholstery') would be to misinterpret completely the complexity and thoroughness of the buyer's decision process. Faced with an extensive range of very similar sub-compact cars the colour of the upholstery is a trivial factor but, as stated, could be *determinant* if it is the only way of making a choice. Similarly, when the industrial buyer prefers one supplier of a standardised product to another (e.g. lubricating oil) it would be entirely rational to say that he trusts (a subjective concept) one producer more than the others.

SUMMARY

This chapter has ranged over a very wide area that is the subject of many substantial books in their own right. Its purpose has been to sensitise the reader to factors which influence behaviour in the market-place but a full appreciation must depend upon extensive study of the major sources cited.

5 The Company: Organising for Marketing

The change from a seller's to a buyer's market in the 1950s precipitated a rash of literature promising managerial salvation through adoption of the marketing concept. With the desperation of a drowning man corporations in every field of activity seized the straw, and marketing staff appointments proliferated. As anticipated profits failed to materialise, disillusionment set in and marketing became the scapegoat. Supporters of marketing responded by pointing out that adoption of the marketing concept requires a complete reorientation of the firm's activities which renaming the sales function was unlikely to bring about.

Superficial as this description is, it serves to underline that the firm's organisational structure is critical to marketing success. In the era of excess demand, top management attention was rightly focused on increasing output, and a production orientation was both necessary and understandable. However, a firm is more than a collection of individuals, it is a social system with its own norms, status structure and system of rewards and punishments. It is unrealistic to assume that these can be changed overnight, yet many firms which have rejected the marketing concept have done so because they failed to appreciate the inherent organisational implications, or else instituted extensive changes without full consideration of the possible ramifications. Fortunately, the unhappy experiences of the disillusioned have served to concentrate attention on the organisational implications associated with a marketing orientation.

BASIC ORGANISATIONAL STRUCTURES

Given the possible variations in the extent of corporate resources, the products they manufacture and the markets they serve, it is clear that there can be no single organisational structure of universal applicability. Despite the infinite variations in degree, the fundamental organisational choice revolves around grouping activities by product or by function. This dilemma was the subject of an article by two well-known authorities on organisation behaviour, Arthur H. Walker and Jay W. Lorsch ('Organizational choice: product *vs.* function', *Harvard Business Review*, XLIV, vi (Nov-Dec 1968) 129–38), on which the following discussion draws heavily.

Traditionally, organisational theorists have suggested that the appropriate structure should be decided on the basis of three criteria:

1. Which approach permits the maximum use of special technical knowledge?
2. Which provides the most efficient utilisation of machinery and equipment?
3. Which provides the best hope of obtaining the required control and co-ordination?

Walker and Lorsch feel that these traditional criteria ignore the trade-off between functional specialisation and difficulties of co-ordination, and product specialisation which promotes collaboration between specialists but tends to lose identification with functional goals. To make good this omission the authors propose that three findings from the behavioural sciences should also be taken into account, namely:

1. Functional specialists tend to develop patterns of behaviour and thought that are in tune with the demands of their jobs and their prior training, and as a result these specialists (e.g. industrial engineers and production supervisors) have different ideas and orientation about what is important in getting the job done. This is called *differentiation* and is necessary for functional specialists to perform their jobs effectively.
2. Differentiation is closely related to achievement of co-ordination, or what behavioural scientists call *integration*. This means collaboration between specialised units or individuals. Recent studies have demonstrated that there is an inverse relationship between differentiation and integration: the more two functional specialists (or their units) differ in their patterns of behaviour and thought, the more difficult it is to bring about integration between them.
3. While achievement of both differentiation and integration is

possible, it can only occur when well-developed means of communication among specialists exist in the organisation and when the specialists are effective in resolving the inevitable cross-functional conflicts.

It is suggested that these findings raise three basic questions which must be answered when choosing between a product, or functional, basis of organisation.

(*a*) Does it permit sufficient differentiation for the effective performance of specialised tasks?

(*b*) Is the degree of differentiation consistent with the desired level of integration?

(*c*) How will the structure affect intra-firm channels of communication?

Although the appropriate structure will depend upon external factors, Walker and Lorsch suggest two useful generalisations:

1. The functional type of structure is appropriate where the firm is faced with a routine and repetitive task. Under these circumstances integration can be achieved through plans, and conflict resolved by the hierarchy.
2. Where the task involves problem-solving, i.e. dealing with new situations, then the product organisation is more appropriate.

However, as the authors note, most firms are faced with a combination of both routine tasks and problem-solving, e.g. the marketing of established products and new product development. As a result most firms find it necessary to adopt some form of compromise as is evident from current organisation charts. The question of the most appropriate structure for the firm as a whole will be returned to following a consideration of the organisation of the marketing department *per se*.

ORGANISATION OF THE MARKETING DEPARTMENT

In practice observation suggests that the marketing department may be organised in one of seven basic ways:

1. Functionally oriented.
2. Product oriented.
3. Market/customer oriented.

4. Regionally oriented.
5. Functional/product orientation.
6. Functional/market orientation.
7. Functional/regional orientation.

A marketing department organised on functional lines is illustrated in Fig. 5.1 below.

Under this structure, personnel are grouped by functional specialisation and their activities are co-ordinated by the marketing director or manager. Such a system enjoys the advantages of simplicity and clearly designated areas of responsibility. On the other hand such advantages are often negated by the restricted outlook which such compartmentalisation inevitably breeds. There is a tendency for each department to plough its own furrow, and efforts to co-ordinate the diverse interests of specialists imbued in a specific functional practice can be exceedingly wasteful of managerial time and effort. The larger the company the worse the problem becomes.

Firms with broadly differentiated product lines frequently organise their marketing functions on a product or product group basis. This form of structure, depicted in Fig. 5.2, is only viable where each product/product group generates sufficient sales volume to justify the inevitable duplication of effort. Consequently, this form of structure is usually found in large, decentralised companies, where each division is concerned with the manufacture of a specialised product.

As an alternative to a product orientation, the hypothetical firm illustrated in Fig. 5.2 might prefer to organise on a market or customer basis, when its organisation chart would appear as shown in Fig. 5.3.

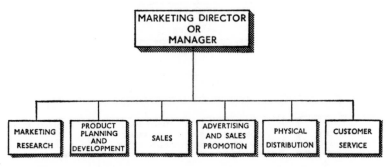

Fig. 5.1. Marketing department organised on a functional basis

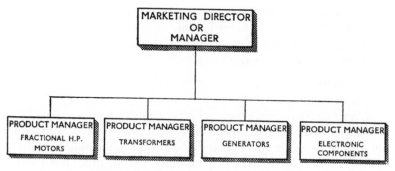

Fig. 5.2. Product-oriented organisation

A regional marketing organisation is most frequently found in the case of a large, decentralised company with extensive markets capable of subdivision into distinct geographical units. It is particularly appropriate to multi-national firms but, in common with the product and market structure, it suffers from duplication of effort, and problems of communication and co-ordination.

In an attempt to overcome these defects, many firms have adopted a line and staff structure which seeks to combine the benefits of functional specialisation with the varying demands of different products and markets. Currently there is considerable debate about the relative merits of organising on a product or market basis and some discussion is appropriate here.

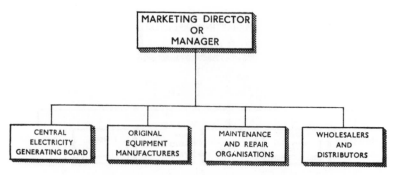

Fig. 5.3. Market-oriented organisation

THE PRODUCT MANAGER CONCEPT

It is often implied that the product manager concept is of recent origin but there is evidence to suggest that General Electric had adopted such a title in the United States as early as 1894, while Libby, McNeil & Libby claim to have appointed product managers in 1919. Generally, however, the introduction of the concept is credited to its leading exponent, Procter & Gamble, who appointed a brand manager for Lava soap in 1928. (Product manager and brand manager are interchangeable terms for the same basic function.)

Essentially, the product manager's function is to co-ordinate all activities associated with the marketing of a given product – a function which became critical with the adoption of product differentiation as a major dimension of competitive strategy. Opinions differ as to the precise responsibilities and authority of the product manager but, in general, it is possible to discern four major activities:

1. *Planning.* At the tactical level the product manager is usually responsible for the preparation of detailed plans for the marketing of his product, e.g. the preparation of budgets and determination of the precise mix of marketing inputs. At the strategic level he is responsible for anticipating change and the preparation of plans to deal effectively with this change, e.g. new product development.
2. *Information seeking and evaluation.* In order to anticipate change it is necessary continually to scan the environment and monitor the strength and direction of relevant trends. Specifically, this involves keeping track of competitors' activities in the widest sense, i.e. one must not only keep informed about directly competing substitutes but also attempt to identify the less immediate threat implicit in new products and processes. Equally, one must be sensitive to marketing innovations such as the development of automatic vending machines, systems selling, etc.
3. *Co-ordination.* As the product 'expert', it is the product manager's responsibility to co-ordinate all those company functions which impinge upon the successful marketing of that product. Of all the functions, this presents the greatest challenge to the product manager as it inevitably requires him to be all things to all men. On the other hand these are the same skills required of top managers, and the product manager position

can prove a valuable training and proving ground for senior appointments.
4. *Control*. This function not only incorporates the familiar price/cost and budgetary dimensions but also includes the introduction of new products and the phasing out of old products.

No valid generalisation can be offered as to the relative importance attached to these four activities in practice as, of necessity, this will vary from firm to firm.

MARKET MANAGERS

As with any organisation innovation, the product manager system has not enjoyed unqualified success and many firms that adopted such a system during the first flush of enthusiasm in the late 1950s have since discarded it. In those instances where the product manager system has 'failed', examination usually reveals that the company was fundamentally unsuited to such an organisational structure. In a company like Procter & Gamble which is producing a group of nearly identical products from the same manufacturing facility, all of which are to be sold through the same distributive outlets, the product manager system ensures that each brand is given the individual attention it needs. On the other hand, where a company is selling the same product into a number of different end-use markets, emphasis on the product will be inappropriate. As noted earlier, the concept of market segmentation rests on the proposition that there are differences in the needs, and buying behaviour, of sub-groups which collectively comprise the aggregate demand for a product. From this it follows that a different marketing strategy will be appropriate to each segment, which, in turn, predicates the appointment of market managers.

In the author's opinion the appointment of a market manager represents the purest implementation of the marketing concept, for it is implicit that consumer requirements will take precedence over all other activities. It is an overt recognition that different market segments represent distinct, and often dissimilar, needs, not only in terms of precise product specification but also in terms of service requirements and buying behaviour. Further, in the case of industrial goods, it recognises that many buyers have a need for a series of related products which may usefully be combined into a 'system', e.g. National Cash Register do not just sell business machines, they sell accounting 'systems' tailor-made to the end-user's specific requirements. Emphasis on the product may well result in the employment of salesmen specialising in given products and thus miss out on such opportunities.

As a broad generalisation it would seem that where customer buying habits are conditioned by the nature of the product and are similar across industry or user categories, then the responsibility for marketing should be vested in a product manager. Conversely, if it is possible to distinguish marked differences in the needs and buying behaviour of separate customer groups, then these should be regarded as different markets and market managers appointed.

THE IMPACT OF MARKETING ON ORGANISATIONAL STRUCTURE

In the organisational context, marketing may be viewed as both a function and a philosophy. All firms have marketing function, even if it only involves selecting an intermediary to sell their output, but few firms have a marketing philosophy as embodied in the marketing concept and described in Chapter 1. Unfortunately, the distinction between the function and the philosophy is rarely stated explicitly, and has resulted in considerable misunderstanding and even acrimony.

As a function, marketing is no more, nor less, important than finance, legal, personnel, production, purchasing, research and development, or any other conceivable area of specialisation. In a given context it is only natural that more emphasis will be accorded to a specific function, which will tend to predominate over the others, but there is nothing to predicate that it will, or should, be marketing. The widely held misconception that marketers are seeking to take over other functional areas is a myth, albeit one fostered by the profession, which largely owes its existence to the high 'visibility' of marketing in the consumer goods field. Even so, firms manufacturing private brands will probably place far greater emphasis on production economies and quality control than on marketing. In the industrial goods field this tendency will be even more pronounced.

As a business philosphy, marketing requires the firm to do what it has always set out to do – combine the resources at its disposal in the manner which will best enable it to achieve its long-run profit goals. What distinguishes it from other business philosophies is that marketing perceives consumption as a democratic process in which consumers have the right to select preferred candidates and elect them by casting their money votes. As the political critics of marketing, and advertising in particular, should appreciate, you may delude the electorate once with spurious campaign promises but you had better not seek re-election. Further, unless you propose policies of which they approve you will have to give way to the candidate who does.

In the democratic environment of a free enterprise economy, success comes to the firm which sets out to discover the nature of human wants and develops products to satisfy such wants in highly specific ways. Satisfying consumers can only be achieved through the concerted efforts of all members of the organisation recognising this as a common goal and working towards it. Thus, the production manager who insists on maximising productivity, in the conventional sense of maximum volume at lowest cost, by excluding non-standard items from his production schedule lacks a marketing orientation. He fails to see that the non-standard item might develop into a market leader, or that the fact that his salesman cannot offer it will predispose the firm's largest customer to switch to the company that can. Conversely, the production manager who balances the conventional criteria against such considerations is marketing oriented, despite his function and job title.

Acceptance of the marketing concept by individuals is insufficient in itself to make the firm marketing oriented – it must also develop an organisational structure that will permit it to translate thought into action. In today's increasingly competitive environment this demands that the firm be more creative and flexible than in the past; specifically, it requires:

(*a*) That the firm continually scan the business environment, i.e. the firm must develop its own early warning system so that it is in a position not only to meet change but also to initiate it.

(*b*) That the firm utilise incoming data to formulate creative plans stating not only what it wishes to achieve, but also how and in what sequence.

(*c*) That these plans be communicated effectively to those

charged with the responsibility for their implementation, and that such responsibility be backed with the necessary resources and authority.

(*d*) That the firm make full use of new managerial techniques developed to assist the decision-maker in arriving at an informed decision, e.g. operations research and Bayesian decision theory.

At a given point in time, however, the firm's immediate success depends on its existing product line. If previous planning has been effective the production and sale of these products should be routine and demand a functional organisation. As noted, however, planning and new product development are problem-solving activities for which a functional structure is unsuited and some form of compromise structure is called for.

One solution is the setting up of project teams comprised of representatives from each of the functional departments (sometimes referred to as a 'matrix' organisation). Such a team may be formed on an *ad hoc* basis to suggest solutions to a particular problem, or to review suggestions from functional departments. Alternatively, the team may be established on a permanent basis and function as a separate department, e.g. many companies have set up Long-range Planning Departments.

Another solution is evident in the trend to what has been termed 'recentralised decentralisation'. During the 1950s concepts such as the 'span of control' predisposed the management of large, diversified companies to decentralise authority on a divisional basis. Under this system each division operates virtually as a separate company, and sets up its own production and marketing organisations. In many instances, however, the benefits of specialisation were negated by diseconomies arising from duplication of effort and poor co-ordination, and prompted top management to recentralise certain functions at corporate headquarters. Foremost among these are purchasing and marketing. Centralised purchasing offers clear benefits due to the economies of bulk buying, while centralised marketing services permit greater specialisation and the development of a consistent marketing approach across the whole field of the firm's activities.

Some indication of the preferred form of marketing organisation is to be found in the British Institute of Management's Information

TABLE 5.1. *Basis for breaking down marketing activities*

Marketing activities broken down by:	Per cent
Products	59
Geographic area	44
Combination of above	39
Customers	32
Others	8

Summary 148, *Marketing Organisation in British Industry* (1970), based on a sample of 553 firms claimed to be representative of present practice in British companies. A question asking the basis on which the company broke down its marketing activities elicited the response indicated in Table 5.1.

Clearly many companies use a combination of methods, the trend being most marked among larger and consumer goods companies.

The extent to which a firm can improve its competitive standing through organisational change is, in the final analysis, conditioned by the resources at its disposal and some reference to this dimension is called for.

CORPORATE RESOURCES

The resources which a company has at its disposal are of two main types – human and physical. Such resources may be internal to the organisation, or they may be external to it in the sense that the firm can gain or exercise control over them, e.g. the distributive channel.

Within the firm, resources, both human and physical, tend to be specific, and so limit the possible range of production/marketing activities which the firm can undertake. In the long run, however, the firm can change its 'resource mix', and the aim of planning is to determine:

(a) What activities will maximise the productivity of existing resources?
(b) What markets offer the greatest potential in future?
(c) What changes need to be made in the present resource mix to enable the firm to exploit these future opportunities?

Clearly, the answers to these questions must be based on an analysis of existing resources, which will be facilitated by the use of a check-list on the following lines:

1. *Physical resources.*
   Land – as a source of raw materials
       – as a location for manufacturing and distributive activities.
   Buildings – general purpose or specific, i.e. designed for light engineering, assembly, storage, etc., or for heavy manufacturing requiring special foundations, services, etc.
   Availability of and access to – power supplies, drainage and waste disposal
         – transportation: road, rail, canal, port facilities, etc.
   Plant and equipment – general purpose, e.g. lathe, press
         – specific, e.g. steel rolling mill, foundry, etc.
2. *Technical resources.* Essentially these reside in the technical expertise of the firm's employees, together with the possession of patents, licences or highly specialised equipment.
3. *Financial resources.* These are comprised of the liquid assets in the firm's balance sheet, the ability to secure loans against fixed assets and the ability to raise capital in the market on the basis of past and anticipated future performance. They also comprise the skill of the firm's financial management.
4. *Purchasing resources.* Managerial expertise backed by any special advantage enjoyed by the firm by virtue of its size or connection e.g. reciprocal trading agreements.
5. *Labour resources.* The skills, experience and adaptability of the work force.
6. *Marketing resources.* The degree of consumer/user acceptance or 'franchise' developed through past performance. Access to and degree of control over distribution; the specialised skills and experiences of its personnel.

The above list is by no means exhaustive but serves to indicate the factors the firm must take into account when appraising its own ability to undertake a given course of action. Clearly, the importance attached to any particular factor will depend upon the unique nature of the problem under consideration. Hopefully, this will become clear when dealing with the separate elements of the marketing mix in subsequent chapters.

However, the firm does not exist in a vacuum and so must condition its policies in the light of environmental constraints. Among these, the existing pattern of distribution will play a major role, and forms the subject matter of the next three chapters.

Part Three

Patterns of Distribution

6 The Distribution of Raw Materials

The term 'raw materials' is often used to describe the physical goods used in manufacturing without distinguishing between natural raw materials and semi-manufactured, or fabricated, materials. For example the raw materials used in the packaging industry – paper, plastics, fibre-board, etc. – are the finished goods of other manufacturers in the chemical industry. To avoid confusion the term will be used here to describe materials in their natural state such as coal, wool, wheat and rubber, which are often termed 'primary commodities'.

A broad distinction may be made between those raw materials which occur in a natural state and those which are the result of man's efforts in developing particular types of natural products through agriculture. The distinction is a logical one, for whereas man cannot alter the absolute supply of 'natural' raw materials, he can increase the supply of crops, both in absolute amount and in terms of specific varieties. Accordingly they merit separate treatment.

'NATURAL' RAW MATERIALS

This category is the one with which the so-called extractive industries are concerned and includes mineral deposits, forest and sea products. It is recognised that it is possible for man to increase the supply of both the latter, just as it may one day be possible to increase the total supply of minerals through deep excavation, or mining them on the moon. In this context, however, they will be treated as being in fixed supply for we have yet to achieve the technological breakthrough which makes such possibilities economically feasible. That this is so is evident in the conservation policies which have been widely adopted.

Another feature which is common to the supply of natural raw materials is that not only is supply fixed in an absolute sense, it is also fixed in the short term if all existing plant is operating at capacity. In other words, supply is not immediately responsive to increases in demand owing to the time-lag between such an increase becoming apparent and resources being diverted to exploit the market opportunity which such excess demand represents. Mines and sawmills cannot be opened overnight, and fishing fleets take time to construct. In the case of minerals the delay is especially protracted as most of the accessible deposits are already being exploited, so that not only do mines have to be opened but road, rail and port facilities also have to be developed. Even reopening disused mines takes time, as is evident from the efforts made in Cornwall during the 1970s to cash in on the world shortage of tin.

Because supply cannot readily be increased in the short term, prices for raw materials react very quickly to variations in demand in the way in which economic theory predicts they will. In fact commodity markets are usually used as examples when studying supply and demand because these factors can be clearly distinguished in operation, free from the complications which advertising, sales promotion and the like introduce into consumer goods markets. Owing to the tendency for raw material prices to fluctuate widely with variations in both demand and supply, many attempts have been made to stabilise the functioning of commodity markets – usually with little success as will be seen below.

SALIENT FEATURES OF THE EXTRACTIVE INDUSTRIES

The extraction of raw materials is usually expensive, and involves considerable capital investment even in the case of the more common materials such as coal, iron ore, basic chemicals and mineral oil. As a result, production of these materials is usually concentrated in the hands of a limited number of firms with the necessary capital and technical resources. From the point of view of the basic industries which process and refine these raw materials, the uncertainties associated with a free market represent a considerable threat to their own security and stability, and predispose them to secure control over a substantial part of their raw material requirements. This is not always possible, however, as many countries limit, or forbid, foreign participation, particularly where they have a monopoly over available supplies. In these circumstances the firm has no option but to buy in the world's commodity markets, the operation of which is very similar to the wheat market described in detail later in this chapter. In an introductory text of this nature it is not possible to consider political interference in the operation of free markets, e.g. the Arab countries' restriction of oil supplies following the Arab–Israeli conflict in 1973.

The position with regard to the less common raw materials differs in that although production tends to be concentrated for the reasons outlined above, demand is made up of a large number of consumers with limited individual requirements. To satisfy these demands, specialist markets have been developed wherein the processes of concentration, equalisation and dispersion can take place, e.g. the London Metal Exchange.

In addition to what might be termed the basic raw materials of industry such as oil, chemicals, iron ore, etc., and the rare materials such as gold, silver, tin and diamonds, there is a wide range of materials which occur regularly in nature, and are relatively easy to extract with limited capital equipment. Like many other raw materials they are usually bulky, and the cost of transportation plays a significant role in their marketing. Extraction is closely governed by the proximity of the market to the source of supply and distribution is strictly local, precluding the need for the central markets associated with less common materials. Sand and gravel are examples of such locally distributed materials.

PRODUCER-USER AGREEMENTS

As noted earlier, the inherent instability of commodity markets has stimulated both producers and users to seek some form of agreement to minimise the impact of fluctuations in supply and demand. Under normal conditions the establishment of an agreement is beneficial to both buyer and seller, as it invariably fixes a price bracket for the commodity. Thus, producers can treat the lower limit of the bracket as a guaranteed selling price and plan their output accordingly. Similarly, the buyer can cost his own output in the knowledge that the price of the raw material content cannot exceed the upper limit set by the bracket. However, if supply and demand should get in serious imbalance such agreements are put to a test which few are capable of surviving.

The classic example of the validity of this statement must be the Tin Council, which was long quoted as the model for such agreements. For many years the Council successfully held prices within the limits agreed on by producers and users, through the maintenance of a buffer stock. As soon as the price of tin fell to the lower limit prescribed by the agreement the Council entered the market, and supported it by buying at that price until sufficient excess supply had been removed for the price to rise above the 'floor'. (These are identical to the tactics of the Bank of England in the foreign exchange market.) Similarly, at the other end of the scale, as soon as excess demand or a decline in supply resulted in the price reaching the agreed ceiling, the Council would release stocks until the price fell within the bracket. A particularly attractive feature of the scheme was that it was self-financing, as the margin between the upper and lower limits was sufficient to cover the stockholding and administrative costs involved. The Tin Council functioned perfectly on this basis until the early 1960s, when demand began to outstrip supply with the result that the market price was invariably near its upper limit. In order to keep the price within the prescribed limits the Council was increasingly called upon to release its stocks, but was never able to replenish them at the lower price. Eventually the inevitable happened and the stocks were exhausted, leaving a free market in which prices spiralled rapidly before stabilising at a more realistic level some £500 above the old limit. It is possible that the market free-for-all might have been avoided if the Council had had more funds at its disposal with which to build up stocks in time of excess supply, or had appreciated the fundamental disequilibrium earlier and raised the market price sooner. As it was, the Council's operations masked the development of imbalance between supply and demand and gave the market a false appearance of stability.

It is pertinent to note however that the Council survived this crisis and currently enjoys a membership of 27 member countries.

AGRICULTURAL PRODUCTS

Agricultural products may properly be regarded both as industrial raw materials and as consumer goods. In that there are significant differences in distribution, depending upon whether crops are sold direct into consumption or to manufacturers for processing, it will be convenient to deal separately with these two categories. At the same time there are certain features common to both which deserve consideration prior to a discussion of the salient differences in distribution.

Probably the most striking feature of agriculture is the smallness of the average production unit. Although there has been a consistent trend towards larger unit size in nearly every industrialised country as alternative employment opportunities have become available, this is still true today. In the author's opinion there is unlikely to be a significant decline in the number of small farms and, in fact, it seems reasonable to anticipate that their numbers will increase. As the world's population continues to expand geometrically so will the demand for food increase. At present the economists' calculations are based on average income per acre, from which it is argued that farms are too small to enable the average farmer to attain an adequate standard of living. Further, it is true that increased unit size would permit more extensive use of labour-saving equipment and improve the marginal productivity of capital by comparison with investment in a small farm. These arguments neglect the fact that the small, intensively farmed unit has a significantly higher yield per acre than the large, mechanised unit – a comparison of average wheat yields as between the United States and Holland reveals that the latter are some 400–500 per cent greater than the former. In the future, as demand outstrips supply, prices will rise and thus make intensive farming not only necessary but also more profitable. If the argument is valid, it would seem that the supply of agricultural products will continue to flow from a large number of small producers albeit of a more sophisticated kind.

Although agricultural products are usually thought of as being homogeneous, in fact there are considerable variations in quality, and some form of grading process is necessary before they can be offered for sale. Further, crops are perishable and need careful handling and storage to prevent deterioration. Neither of these operations can be performed economically on a small scale, nor with the limited resources at the small farmer's disposal, and a complex distributive network has been developed to facilitate the marketing of crops and foodstuffs.

THE CAUSES OF MARKET DISEQUILIBRIUM

A commonly observed feature of agricultural markets is the erratic fluctuation of price, particularly in the short term. This instability is essentially attributable to variations in supply, as the demand for most agricultural products is fairly stable and predictable in advance. Obviously, climate is a major cause of supply instability, but its effects are compounded by the behaviour of producers in the manner outlined below.

In the case of many products such as wheat, cotton, rubber and livestock, a high proportion of the total supply is accounted for by large, specialist producers. Allowing for the vagaries of climate, their output tends to be fairly constant and calculable in advance, from which it follows that the major variations in supply must be attributed to the output of the small farmers.

Most land may be used to grow a variety of crops, and the major decision facing the small producer is which crop to plant in order to gain the greatest return; a decision that must be made several months before the crop will be ready for sale. In assessing market opportunity it is natural that the farmer should be influenced by current prices, and there is a strong probability that a large number will independently decide to plant those crops which are currently fetching the best prices. The reason certain crops are fetching above average prices is clearly due to the fact that the existing supply is insufficient to satisfy the total demand, and thus the price mechanism is having the desired effect of encouraging an increase in supply. However, it would be purely fortuitous if the separate decision of thousands of producers to increase planting of a specific crop resulted in an exact balancing of supply and demand. It is nearly certain that the increased supply will depress price and fail to meet the farmer's expectations. Further, the decision to switch from, say, wheat to barley will reduce the supply of wheat and its price will go up, thus encouraging the farmer to increase his acreage under wheat and to decrease planting of barley.

It is the time-lag between the decision to sow a particular crop and its reaching fruition, the inability to go back on the decision once it is made, and the farmer's imperfect knowledge of others' sowing decisions which create fluctuations in supply that disturb market equilibrium.

THE IMPACT OF THE MARGINAL PRODUCER

A good example of the manner in which the small farmer determines the final level of supply is afforded by the market for natural rubber.

Between the two World Wars the leading rubber-producing countries agreed to limit supply in order to ensure a fair market price for their output, e.g. the Stephenson scheme in South-east Asia. The restriction in supply forced prices up and encouraged the peasant farmers in the Dutch East Indies to clear land, which they would otherwise have been unable to cultivate, to plant rubber trees. These trees were not given the same careful attention as is typical of the commercial plantation, and which accounts for the major production costs, they were simply left to grow for the eight to ten years necessary to achieve maturity. As soon as the trees were big enough to tap, native rubber flooded on to the market, causing prices to plummet and the producer agreements to collapse.

The native product is only slightly inferior in quality to the plantation product, and now accounts for about 30 per cent of total supply. The commercial grower's position is aggravated by the fact that although he is committed to the high fixed costs of maintaining his plantation, the native grower is not, and only taps his trees when the market price justifies the effort. Thus, whenever the market price becomes favourable from the plantation owner's point of view the marginal producers enter the market and force the price down.

Given the possible variations in supply and its diverse origins, it is not surprising that man has developed elaborate marketing systems to permit concentration of output so that it may be made available to those with a demand for it. Such marketing systems possess many features in common and the discussion of the market for a single product will help to clarify these. The wheat market in the United States is particularly well documented and will be used as an example here.

THE MARKETING OF WHEAT

The first stage in the marketing of wheat is concentration at the local elevator by individual farmers. The elevator may be owned by an independent wholesaler, or by the farmers themselves as a co-operative. In either case the elevator will usually offer to purchase the grain outright at central market price, less the cost of freight to the central market and the elevator owner's commission, or, alternatively, to store the grain for a fixed charge. The farmer's decision to sell or store is based on the current price, and expectations as to its future movements, as against the cost of warehousing. (Note: there is an absolute floor to market price determined by Federal Government subsidy. This subsidy is analogous to the guaranteed farm prices offered by the British Government to ensure a minimum level of domestic production prior to entry to the E.E.C. when the Common Agricultural Policy came into force.)

Most of the grain in local elevators is resold to manufacturers in the same area, but the balance is sold either to wholesalers in the 'terminal' markets, e.g. the 'Wheat Pit' in Chicago, or else sent to commission agents in such centres for sale at the best price available. Dealers at the central market frequently combine the functions of merchants, agents and brokers, unlike other markets where dealers tend to specialise in only one of these functions.

The merchant is usually in business for himself and buys stocks with the intention of reselling them at a higher price, so that his income is determined both by the size of the margin and by the volume of business transacted. By contrast, agents usually act on behalf of a client for a fixed commission, and so may find it more profitable to achieve a high turnover than to withhold supplies until the price rises; similarly, they lack the merchant's incentive to buy at the lowest price. Brokers occupy an intermediate position between merchants and agents as they buy and sell both for clients and on their own behalf. Unlike merchants, however, they rarely take physical delivery or hold stocks.

In order to bring buyers and sellers into physical contact and facilitate the exchange of title to goods, it is usual to find a place specifically designated for this purpose. Usually the dealers who comprise the 'exchange' or 'market' draw up rules to regulate the transaction of business, and to exclude non-members from participation in its operation. Within the market transactions fall into two main categories – spot and futures trading. Spot, or cash, transactions concern existing or readily available goods, on which immediate delivery can be effected, while the futures market is concerned with contracts for sale and delivery at some future, and usually specified, time.

In fact the futures contract is not a contract to buy or sell at all, but is an option to buy at an agreed price, at a stated time. From the buyer's point of view an option ensures the future availability of supplies at a fixed, maximum price. If, when the option matures, the market price is less than that negotiated, the option is not taken up, for the commodity can be obtained for less in the open market. Conversely, if the price in the market is higher, the option will be exercised and the seller will have to bear the loss. Naturally, the dealer's success depends on his being able to predict accurately the future level of supply, and setting a price which will be attractive to the potential purchaser while exposing the dealer to the minimum of risk. To achieve this the dealer must secure a continuous supply of accurate market data as the basis for forecasting future price levels. Although some dealing in futures is purely speculative, the majority of dealers depend on it for their livelihood and so base their forecasts on facts rather than hunches, In doing so they perform a valuable service, for they reduce uncertainty concerning both demand and supply in the markets in which they operate.

'CONSUMER' CROPS

Although there is a fairly clear-cut distinction between crops which comprise the raw materials of industry and those which are consumed in their natural state, it is difficult to maintain the distinction if processing is used as the delineating factor. Nowadays the distinction would seem to rest on the necessity for processing as a prerequisite of consumption, rather than the existence or absence of processing. In the case of crops which are usually classified as 'industrial', the common denominator is the fact that they must undergo some physical change before they can be consumed. This change may be relatively minor, as is the case with flour milling, or extensive – if, say, one is converting wool into a suit of clothes. By contrast 'consumer' crops may be used immediately in their natural state but in advanced economies an increasing proportion are now processed in some way or other prior to consumption.

FACTORS UNDERLYING THE GROWTH OF PROCESSING

The volume of agricultural output is ultimately determined by the length of the growing season. Assuming an adequate water supply, temperature is a critical variable. Plants will not grow at or below freezing, and make very little progress until the temperature rises above 40° F. Thereafter, the rate of growth doubles approximately for every 18° increase in temperature, so that the farther one moves away from the equator the shorter the length of the growing season. Thus, from early times, man has been preoccupied with methods of preserving and storing food for out-of-season use.

The slow growth of population until recent times is at least partly attributable to lack of success in balancing excess with famine. The growth of international trade partially alleviated the problem but had to await the development of the steam ship and refrigeration to make any real impact. Similarly, a revolution in farming techniques has greatly increased our ability to increase crop yields and prolong the growing season, but the problems of preservation and storage still exist, and command ever-increasing attention.

Refrigeration is expensive in terms of capital installation, and suffers from the same basic disadvantage as canning and similar methods of preservation – the majority of the good stored is water. Although dehydration eliminates this diseconomy, traditional methods tended to so change the nature of the food that they were largely unacceptable. The development of freeze drying overcame most of the problems associated with satisfactory reconstitution, but the expense was too great to justify general commercial usage. However, research sponsored by the Ministry of Agriculture came up with a method of speeding up the process, and Accelerated Freeze Drying (A.F.D.) was born. The improved process is less costly and has been widely adopted e.g. Batchelor's Vesta range and Surprise peas, Nestlés Gold Blend instant coffee, Dornay Food's Wonder-mash, etc.

Thus we now have a situation in which the consumer is able to buy highly perishable foodstuffs at any time of the year. Not only that, as methods of preservation have improved costs have fallen, and many 'processed' foods now possess distinct advantages over 'fresh' products. Two obvious advantages are the reduction in waste and the added convenience. Canned, frozen or A.F.D. peas are invariably of uniform quality, which is not the case with peas bought in the pod, and require the minimum of preparation.

The advantages offered by processed foods have had a marked impact on purchasing patterns, and many items traditionally associated with the fresh produce market are now sold through dry-goods outlets, i.e. supermarkets and grocery shops, as distinct from green-grocers. Retailing forms the subject matter of a later chapter and will not be discussed here, but a brief description of the traditional channels is called for.

THE DISTRIBUTION OF FRESH PRODUCE

Essentially, fresh produce reaches the ultimate consumer by one of the four channels illustrated in the diagram below:

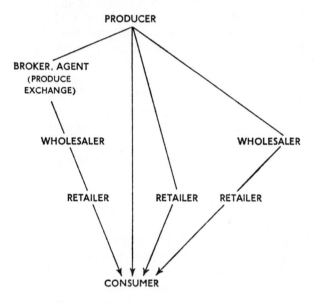

Fig. 6.1 Channels used in the distribution of fresh produce

    The functions of broker, agent and produce exchange are identical with those discussed earlier in connection with the marketing of wheat. The term wholesaler is synonymous with merchant, and is increasingly preferred to the latter designation.

    The most direct channel, producer–consumer, is usually only encountered on a limited and local scale, e.g. door-to-door sales or the stall in the local market, and most growers prefer to sell through conventional retail outlets. Sales direct to retailer fall into three categories:

1. The producer acts as his own wholesaler and establishes direct contact with local outlets.
2. The producer sets up his own retail outlets or, conversely, the retailer with a chain of outlets integrates backwards into production.
3. The producer sells under contract to large retailers, e.g. the major supermarket chains, Woolworth's, Marks & Spencer.

Few growers are able to dispose of their total output in this way, however, and most sales are made initially to the wholesaler, either direct or through the medium of a broker or agent. Most urban centres of any consequence have wholesalers who specialise in breaking down bulk supplies into small quantities for resale to the multitude of small retailers in their area. These wholesalers obtain supplies direct on a local basis, but also buy in the central markets from brokers and other wholesalers, e.g. Covent Garden for fruit, vegetables and flowers, Smithfield for meat, Billingsgate for fish. There can be little doubt that the degree of control exercised by some of the central markets results in diseconomies of which the producer rightly disapproves. Despite the perishability of, say, lettuce, it is difficult to account for the services which increase their value from a farm-gate price of 5p per dozen to a shop price of 15p each. Such excesses go apparently unnoticed by comparison with the criticism levelled at the promotional expenditures of the manufacturer of branded goods.

In order to ensure an adequate supply of certain basic foodstuffs the Government has seen fit to provide incentives for farmers by guaranteeing payment of a minimum price for their output. There are several methods by which this may be achieved, but the most overt and controversial method is through the establishment of a marketing board.

AGRICULTURAL MARKETING BOARDS

The agricultural marketing boards operating in the United Kingdom at the present time were set up under the Agricultural Marketing Acts, 1931–58. The basic features which they have in common are:

(a) They are producer-controlled.
(b) They can only come into existence at the request of the

majority of producers involved with the production of the commodity concerned, e.g. milk, hops.

(c) Their declared object is to secure the best possible return for their members.

(d) They are committed to improving quality, output, distribution and management within their own field of activity.

Space does not permit detailed consideration of the organisation and operation of the various boards, which may be obtained from their offices on request, but in view of the fact that the boards are run by producers for producers, some comment seems called for.

In essence the constitution of marketing boards results in the creation of producer-controlled monopolies and, while it is accepted that all monopolies are not necessarily harmful, they do create supply-controlled markets which are the antithesis of the marketing concept. Either the consumer must accept what the producer is prepared to offer, or he must do without. This is tolerable if there are acceptable substitutes for the monopolist's output, e.g. butter/margarine, or where the product is non-essential, but this is not the case with fresh milk, eggs, potatoes, etc.

Only if there is a free market where the volume and quality of the supply offered reflect consumers' preferences can we be sure that we are maximising the satisfaction to be derived from the resources employed. The fact that unstamped eggs used to sell at a premium before the Egg Marketing Board was disbanded in the spring of 1970 is a clear indication that consumer preference was not being satisfied. In fact the disbandment of the Board was the direct result of the dissatisfaction of producer and consumer with its operation. Further, the marketing boards pay a standard price to producers for equivalent grades of produce, irrespective of the fact that some are remote from the market and so are being subsidised by those in more economic locations. Similarly, consumers in rural areas tend to subsidise those in urban areas, particularly London, through the adoption of near-standard retail prices. It seems unlikely that maximum efficiency will be achieved so long as all farmers are treated alike and there is little incentive to concentrate on the production of those products which the consumer prefers. (Students who seek a more detailed analysis of the operation of agricultural marketing boards are recommended to *Farming for Consumers*, by Graham Hallett and Gwyn James: Hobart Paper 22, Institute of Economic Affairs.)

At the time of writing the following agricultural marketing boards were still operating:

Hops Marketing Board
Milk Marketing Board (various)
Pig Marketing Board (Northern Ireland)
Potato Marketing Board
British Wool Marketing Board

For information on these readers should make direct contact, while for the latest information on E.E.C. Regulations they should consult *A Report on Agricultural Marketing Schemes* (H.M.S.O., 1978).

7 The Distribution of Industrial Goods

By contrast with the clearly defined patterns associated with the distribution of raw materials, it is difficult to generalise with regard to the channels of distribution associated with the three main categories of industrial goods – equipment, fabricated materials and supplies. Observation suggests that a number of different channels are used, and that selection is conditioned by a host of factors which are summarised in the following check-list:

CUSTOMER CHARACTERISTICS

Number of potential users.
Geographical distribution of potential users.
Frequency of purchase.
Average order size.
Distribution of users on the basis of consumption.
Relative importance of product to user, i.e. is the product an essential input from the user's point of view, or may its purchase be postponed or delayed?
Degree of user sophistication *vis-à-vis* product characteristics, i.e. does the user need technical service, if so, what type?
Credit standing.
Preferred purchasing pattern – a single preference is unlikely to emerge owing to variations in the above factors, e.g. need for after-sales service.
Degree of associated service requirements – both before and after sale.

MIDDLEMAN CHARACTERISTICS

Market coverage.
Gross margin.
Proportion of salesmen's time available for selling product.
Degree of technical expertise.
Financial strength and stability.
Stock carrying capacity.
Servicing capability.
Number of substitute products carried.

COMPANY CHARACTERISTICS

Size – both absolute, and relative to the industry/market of which it is a member.
Financial strength.
Industry position – leader or follower?
Spatial relationship between plant(s) and major users.
Degree of technical competence.
Degree of specialisation.
Breadth of product line.
Ability to provide desired services.

ENVIRONMENTAL AND COMPETITIVE CHARACTERISTICS

The nature of seasonal, cyclical and secular trends in demand.
Degree of concentration in user industry(ies).
Nature and usage of existing distributive channels.
Extent and nature of legal restrictions and regulations.
The impact of taxation, e.g. on leasing.
Government procurement policy.
Consumer needs – in so far as the demand for industrial goods is derived from consumer demand shifts in the latter will have an impact on the former.

As will be seen in a later chapter, consideration of all these factors plays an important role in determining a firm's distribution policy and results in many diverse alternatives. On the other hand, it is possible to distinguish broadly similar channels operating across the whole field of industrial goods, which suggests that the most useful approach will be to identify the basic structures and illustrate them with actual examples.

SALIENT FEATURES OF INDUSTRIAL MARKETING

Before proceeding to make such a review, however, it will be useful to state some of the salient features which differentiate the marketing of industrial and consumer goods implicit in the 'check-list' outlined above.

Although the basic marketing principles described in this book are felt to be equally applicable to the marketing of all types of goods and services, there are certain differences in degree that condition their relative importance. In the case of industrial goods these differences may be summarised as:

1. *Derived demand.* The demand for industrial goods, and raw materials, is derived from the demand for consumer goods in the sense that any expansion or contraction in the latter will be reflected by a corresponding shift in the former. The more distant the manufacturer is from the production of a specific consumption good, the less direct will be the impact of a change in demand for that good.

2. *Rational buying motives dominate the industrial market.* This is frequently misinterpreted in one of two ways: (*a*) there is an absence of emotional motives in the industrial purchasing situation, or, (*b*) consumer purchasing behaviour is irrational. Neither of the above statements is correct: consumers are rational and industrial buyers are influenced by emotional factors, but there is a difference in degree, i.e. the industrial buyer will emphasise objective criteria to a greater degree than the average consumer.

3. *Concentration of buyers.* The number of potential buyers for an industrial good is generally far smaller than is the case with consumer goods. Further, industrial buyers tend to be concentrated geographically, e.g. the cotton and woollen industries. One must be careful not to overstate the importance of this distinction for, clearly, its validity depends upon the precise nature of the product. For example the market for office supplies is both large and dispersed, whereas the

market for some consumer goods may be both small and concentrated, e.g. speciality goods produced on a purely local basis. It is also important to remember that although a national brand may have millions of users, the producer may concentrate his direct sales and distribution efforts upon a limited number of major buyers, e.g. wholesalers and grocery chains.

4. *The scale of industrial purchasing is greater.* In absolute money terms this is generally, but not always, true. In a proportionate sense, i.e. size of purchase, *vis-à-vis* disposable assets, the reverse may often be true.

5. *Industrial products are technically more complex.* Again this is true absolutely but not relatively. The purchaser of a car or television set is faced with a similar degree of technical complexity as the buyer of a computer–in both instances the buyer evaluates performance rather than construction, and is dependent upon the seller for both advice and service.

6. *Industrial buying is a group process.* The same might also be said of the household as a decision-making unit for consumer purchases. It is unlikely that the latter will have formalised evaluation and decision procedures, however, both of which are common in the industrial buying context.

7. *The role of service is greater.* Again this depends upon the nature of the product and the type of service. Immediate availability is a prerequisite for sale of a convenience good – this is rarely the case with even the most common of industrial goods – and consumer durables need after-sales service just as much as many industrial goods.

8. *Leasing, renting, and the extension of credit are important.* This is increasingly true of consumer goods.

From the comments made in respect of the 'distinguishing' factors it is clear that although industrial marketing may differ in degree, there are sufficient points of similarity to permit the transfer of principles and techniques from one to the other. As such, undue emphasis of differences may be harmful if it induces practitioners in either field to neglect thought and practice in the other. In particular, it will become apparent that marketing tactics are largely a function of product and market, irrespective of whether the specific product be designated 'consumer' or 'industrial', so that a given mix may be equally appropriate to products in either category.

DISTRIBUTIVE CHANNELS

As noted earlier, distributive channels tend to cut across arbitrary product/industry boundaries and attention here will be concentrated on major variations in structure.

Essentially, the same three basic alternatives are open to manufacturers of both industrial and consumer goods, namely:

1. Direct sale to user/consumer.
2. Indirect sale through the medium of a third party.
3. A combination of both direct and indirect sale.

For the most part manufacturers adopt some combination of both direct and indirect sale and, as will be seen in the chapter on channel policy, the precise mix will depend upon two basic criteria – cost and control.

Direct sale offers the greatest degree of control, but can be uneconomic where there is a large number of customers for the product in question. Under these circumstances some form of intermediary may be able to operate at a lower cost by combining the disparate, but complementary, outputs of several manufacturers for resale to small users of such products. Distribution through an intermediary, or wholesaler, offers the manufacturer the opportunity to improve his overall profitability, albeit at the sacrifice of some measure of control, and so is frequently used to extend the coverage of the producer's own sales force.

Wholesalers vary considerably in terms of both the nature and extent of the services which they provide, and it is common to draw a broad distinction between 'full' and 'limited' service organisations. The full-service wholesaler usually employs his own sales force, holds stocks from which to make immediate delivery, provides information, advice and technical service, and is usually prepared to extend credit. As the name implies, limited-service wholesalers generally perform a restricted function, and often confine themselves solely to stockholding and delivery. In the latter case the manufacturer is responsible for stimulating demand and the provision of technical services.

THE DISTRIBUTION OF STEEL

Although the manufacture of steel is largely concentrated in the hands of a state-owned monopoly, which excludes competition

between separate production facilities, it provides a good example of
the need for a complex distributive structure.

Steel is frequently thought of as an essentially homogeneous
product when, in reality, it is highly complex and produced in an
enormous variety of shapes and to very different specifications, to
meet widely disparate end-use requirements. For example mild steel
sheet, used in the fabrication of consumer durables such as cars and
washing machines, is very different from electrical steels used in
transformers and generators, and from high carbon steels used in the
machine-tool industry. To simplify matters discussion here will be
confined to flat-rolled mild steel producers.

In order to meet specific end-use requirements, an order for
flat-rolled mild steel may vary according to any one of the following
factors:

> Hot-rolled or cold-reduced
> Quality
> Quantity
> Thickness
> Sheet or coil
> Width (and length in the case of sheets)
> Coated or uncoated – if coated, type and thickness of coating and
> method of application of coating

From the user's point of view, each of these factors is highly important and will be specified precisely to meet his exact needs. From the
producer's point of view, however, such variants create diseconomies as they interrupt the smooth flow of production and
reduce the mill throughput. In turn, the diseconomies created by
operating the mill at less than optimum efficiency to meet customer
needs are reflected in the producer's price structure. However,
beyond a certain point the diseconomies involved in meeting a
precise specification become so great that the producer must refuse
to accept less than a minimum order quantity (M.O.Q.). The M.O.Q.
is determined by a number of complex factors which cannot be
discussed here but, over the years, increasing automation has
resulted in a gradual increase in the size of the minimum acceptable
order. This increase has had little impact on the large-scale user,
whose minimum requirements for a given specification are normally
far in excess of the M.O.Q., but could have been a major threat to the
user with a limited demand had it not been for the existence of steel
wholesalers, or 'stockholders'.

Although some stockholders are subsidiaries of the steel producers, the majority are independent organisations. Given the enormous variety of steel products, all but the largest stockholders find it necessary to specialise in some category, e.g. tinplate, sheet and plate, structural steels, etc. In essence, the stockholder functions by anticipating the likely needs of small users, which he combines into an acceptable mill order, normally for a 'standard' size. In fact there are no 'standard' sizes, but certain combinations of width and length have been widely adopted as they offer the maximum benefits within the mills' price structure, and so reduce the scrap loss when cutting to the exact size required. To meet the precise size requirements specified by their customers, most stockholders install shearing, slitting and shaping machines and, increasingly, are ordering in coil form, which permits them to cut to any length without loss.

In addition to breaking bulk to meet small users' requirements, the stockholder also helps to even out fluctuations in supply and demand. Steel-making is a complex, multi-stage process in which an order may be 'lost' at any stage of manufacture, necessitating a 'remake'. If an order is rejected at final inspection it can take three to four weeks to replace, assuming that it can be fitted into the mill schedule immediately. Further, production of an exact quantity is a virtual impossibility, so that most orders turn out less than, or in excess of, the specified amount. Steel buyers are familiar with the technological constraints involved in steel production and adjust their buying policies accordingly.

Where a specification is known to be difficult to produce, buyers maintain sufficient stocks to cover the possibility of late or partial deliveries. However, the maintenance of stocks ties up capital, and most buyers reduce their stock levels to the minimum consistent with normal deliveries in the knowledge that temporary shortages may be made good by buying from stockholders. From the producer's point of view the stockholder performs an equally valuable service in absorbing excess supply in the short term. In addition to buying excess production against mill orders that the customer is unprepared to accept, the stockholder provides an outlet for cancelled orders and reject materials which the mill would find it uneconomic to reclaim. Thus, through specialisation and local knowledge the stockholder performs a number of valuable functions for both producer and user, at a lower cost than would be possible if they performed these functions themselves.

CONCENTRATION RATIOS AS A CRITERION (see Chapter 2 for an extended discussion of *industrial concentration*)

The factors which predispose the steel producer to adopt both a direct and indirect approach are typical of many industries with high concentration ratios. (The concentration ratio is an economic concept that is widely used in comparative industry analyses in preference to the less precise distinction between perfect and imperfect competition.) Concentration ratios take into account both the size and number of firms in a market, and are computed by summing the percentage of total sales accounted for by a given number of firms – thus a true monopoly would have a concentration ratio of 100 per cent, while a highly oligopolistic industry might be defined as one in which the four largest firms account for more than 50 per cent of total sales.

For the marketer faced with the decision of selling direct or through an intermediary, the concentration concept provides a useful rule of thumb when applied to purchases by users, as opposed to sales by producers. By ranking firms in terms of their consumption of the product concerned, it is relatively simple to arrive at a measure of concentration and decide whether direct sale is economically feasible and, if so, to what extent. Many analyses of this kind have revealed what has been termed the 'heavy half' phenomenon, i.e. 50 per cent of total purchases are accounted for by a small percentage of buyers.

As a generalisation, it is reasonable to state that the higher the concentration ratio the more direct sale is to be preferred, but this does not necessarily mean that the producer will attempt to make *all* sales direct. Consider, for example, the suppliers of the motor-car assembly industry, where a small number of buyers account for a very high percentage of total demand. Irrespective of the producer's size, or the nature of his product, he will deal direct with Ford, British Leyland, etc. Over time, however, the cars produced by these companies will require replacement parts, but it is unlikely that many components manufacturers will attempt to sell them to every garage and repair shop in the United Kingdom with an uncertain demand for such parts. In consequence, the component manufacturer must decide whether to set up his own regional warehouses, to have distribution to the car manufacturer, or to use the services of motor accessory and parts wholesalers.

Similarly, the manufacturers of standardised parts such as bearings, industrial fasteners or electrical components, and the producers of general-purpose equipment such as bulldozers, fork-lift trucks or lathes will find that a high percentage of sales are accounted for by a limited number of customers. However, unless the producer has a very strong franchise with such major users and can depend upon them consistently to absorb his output, he cannot afford to ignore the multiplicity of small users that make up the balance of the market. The more numerous and geographically segregated the latter are, the less economic direct sale becomes, so that in markets with a very low degree of concentration the producer may well find it necessary to channel his total output through an intermediary. Many operating supplies produced by small, specialised producers fall into this category, e.g. stationery, hand tools, cleaning materials.

MANUFACTURERS' AGENTS

Although attention has been focused on wholeslers as a link between producer and user, many firms prefer to employ agents, either in addition to, or in place of, a sales force of their own.

From the manufacturer's viewpoint, the major advantage of employing agents is that he only pays commission on actual sales and so avoids the fixed costs associated with the maintenance of a sales force. Further, agents enter into a contractual agreement with their principal and so are subject to a greater degree of control than is usually possible when selling through an independent wholesaler.

Most agents handle a line of complementary but non-competing products, and operate within a clearly defined territory. The successful agent depends heavily upon his established contacts, and so offers the manufacturer a 'ready-made' salesman when introducing a new product or extending his geographical coverage. On the other hand, agents are not without disadvantage for, as noted when discussing the wheat market, the agent rarely has a complete identity of interest with his principal. This is particularly so when the agent is selling several different products, when he is likely to take the line of least resistance and sell what is in greatest demand, rather than devote his time to missionary selling, i.e. making cold calls to stimulate demand. Also, unlike wholesalers, the agent does not take delivery of goods, and the manufacturer must maintain and finance a larger inventory than would be necessary if he sold through a wholesaler. Hence, where there are seasonal fluctuations in demand, or the manufacturer is short of working capital, the wholesaler will usually be preferred to the agent.

From the foregoing description it is clear that there is frequently a conflict between the desire for the most economic method of distribution and management's wish to retain control over the marketing of the firm's output. This conflict will be examined in greater detail in Chapter 13, but attention now must be turned to the distribution of consumer goods, or retailing.

Suggestions for further reading.

Hill, Roy W., *Marketing Technological Products to Industry* (Pergamon Press, Oxford, 1973)

Rowe, D., and Alexander, L., *Selling Industrial Products* (Hutchinson, 1968)

8 The Distribution of Consumer Goods

As noted in the previous chapter, the demand for industrial goods is derived from the demand for consumer goods. Although this link may sometimes appear tenuous, it is clear that all other productive activities finally depend upon selling goods and services into ultimate consumption. Although several distributive options are open to the consumer-good manufacturer, almost all eventually involve a retail outlet of some type or other, and this chapter will be largely concerned with the function and operation of such outlets.

RETAILING FUNCTIONS

Most dictionaries define retailing as 'the sale of goods in small quantities to ultimate consumers'. As such, the retail outlet constitutes the final link in the distributive chain, and is responsible for the performance of several important marketing functions, namely:

1. The physical movement and storage of goods.
2. The transfer of title to goods.
3. The provision of information concerning the nature and use of goods.
4. The standardisation, grading and final processing of goods.
5. The provision of ready availability.
6. The assumption of risk concerning the precise nature and extent of demand.
7. The financing of inventory and the extension of credit to consumers.

In many instances it is difficult to distinguish exactly where manufacturing ends and retailing begins, owing to the assumption of some of these functions by organisations that are not usually considered to be retailers or, conversely, by the assumption of functions by the retailer which are more often associated with manufacturers. Thus, in recent years there has been an increasing tendency for manufacturers to assume responsibility for the provision of information through extensive advertising and sales promotion campaigns, while many retailers have integrated backwards into wholesaling and even manufacturing activities. In the opinion of one authority, Professor W. G. McClelland (*Costs and Competition in Retailing:* Macmillan, London, 1966), the distinction must rest on the performance of those functions inherent in the very nature of retailing – the physical movement of goods and arrangement of transfer of title. To a lesser extent, functions (3), (4) and (5) in the above list also serve to distinguish retailing from other forms of manufacturing and distributive activity, and an examination of these five functions follows.

PHYSICAL MOVEMENT AND STORAGE

As one would expect, there is an enormous variation in the cost of transporting and storing goods depending upon the method of transport used, the length and complexity of the journey, the amount of handling and protection required, etc. In the case of bulk cargoes for transport by sea, the cost may be as low as £0.01 per ton mile while, at the other extreme, door-to-door delivery of groceries may cost as much as £20 per ton mile. Clearly, the more homogeneous the cargo and the larger the bulk for delivery at one point, the lower the unit cost incurred. The potential savings inherent in such economies have led in recent years to the growth of larger retail units and the virtual elimination of door-to-door delivery.

Within the retail outlet, recognition of the high costs arising from counter service, both in terms of the duplication of effort in putting goods on display and then fetching them for customers on request, as well as the waste of valuable selling space, have led to widespread adoption of self-service. Competitive pressures, and the ever-growing variety of goods available for sale have also encouraged the retailer to keep the majority of his stock on display and to depend upon rapid delivery from central warehouses for replenishing his supplies. As a result there has been a strong trend towards the concentration of stocks at the wholesale level, leaving the retailer to stock only those goods for which he feels there is an immediate demand.

TRANSFER OF OWNERSHIP

When one considers the degree of concentration usually associated with the production of goods and the widely dispersed nature of the consumer market, it is clear that few manufacturers will be in the position to undertake direct sale. Thus the need arises for an intermediary to perform this function and effect a transfer of ownership.

In the case of shopping and specialty goods, e.g. Singer sewing machines, the customer may be prepared to make a special purchasing effort and seek out the nearest distribution point. However, in the case of many convenience goods brand loyalty tends to be low, and maximum distribution is essential to high volume sales. Like the steel stockholder, the retail outlet offers the manufacturer the opportunity to make contact with the consumer at an economic cost. By stocking a line of complementary products the retailer is able to spread the overheads involved in personal selling. Also, by catering to the separate demands of a large number of individual consumers, he is able to buy in economic quantities from the producer and still further reduce the costs of effecting a transfer of ownership.

From the consumer's point of view, retail outlets greatly facilitate the purchasing decision as they provide the opportunity to inspect and compare both the prices and quality of competing products. The location of retail outlets, and the nature of the goods in which they deal are readily ascertained, whereas the manufacturer's identity and location are not so easy to determine. Similarly, although many manufacturers publicise a recommended selling price, increased competition and the abolition of Resale Price Maintenance have resulted in a situation where the retailer is often the sole reliable source of this information on which so many buying decisions depend. Finally, the retailer often has to break bulk and the price, which represents the consideration given in exchange for ownership of the goods, cannot be determined until the consumer has specified the quantity which he wishes to purchase.

READY AVAILABILITY

Depending upon the nature of the product, consumers are prepared to go to varying lengths to obtain goods to meet their specific needs. Given the number of competing products and outlets, both retailers and manufacturers are highly sensitive to this aspect of consumer behaviour, and adjust their stockholding policies accordingly to offer the desired level of availability.

By definition, a convenience good must be immediately available as the consumer is not prepared to wait to take delivery. From the retailer's point of view the problem is less critical than it is for the manufacturer, as he will usually stock several brands which are acceptable substitutes for one another. However, although convenience goods were defined earlier as those which the consumer buys frequently and with the minimum of effort, the ultimate distinction lies not in the product itself but in the consumer's perception of it, and what may be a convenience good for some may be a specialty good for others. Thus if the housewife is unable to find her preferred brand in one outlet she may well transfer all her custom to another where she can. In that the overall level of brand preference is reflected by the brand's share of the total market, most retailers will stock competing products in the same ratio to one another in the hope of maintaining store loyalty.

In the case of shopping goods, demand is neither so regular nor so predictable as is the case with convenience goods, and the retailer's stock policy, and ultimately his success are based on his judgement of the precise nature of consumer demand. Such decisions invariably create a conflict between the desire to offer a sufficiently wide selection to cater to variations in consumer preference, and the need to hold a sufficient stock of given products to meet the demand for them. A good example of this conflict, shared by both producer and retailer, is the demand for knee-length women's boots in relation to the demand for more conservative forms of winter footwear. In the past two or three years the demand for such boots has been consistently underestimated, and represents a lost profit opportunity of considerable dimensions. On the other hand, if the retailer overestimates likely demand he will incur additional inventory costs, and may have to sell at a loss to recover his working capital. Although such miscalculations ultimately have an effect on producers' sales, the majority of the risk is carried by the retailer.

THE PROVISION OF INFORMATION

Retailers supply information to both consumer and manufacturer. In the latter case, the most important information supplied by the retailer is the actual order which he places with the producer, in that it reflects future expectations concerning consumer demand by those in most direct contact with it. However, orders are subject to influence by the manufacturer's salesmen, and may represent wishful thinking rather than informed and objective opinion. Also, in the absence of information concerning stock levels, it is difficult to say whether orders are placed in anticipation of an upswing in demand, or merely to replenish stocks depleted by past demand. Even if the order does accurately reflect changing consumer preferences, it does not give the manufacturer an explanation as to the causes – to obtain such information the manufacturer will have to undertake research.

The provision of information to consumers varies considerably in terms of both amount and quality. Often the most meaningful information provided is the opportunity to examine competing products in close juxtaposition to one another. Price is a more concrete piece of information but, as the advent of the discount house has proved, it is frequently a measure of the retailer's efficiency rather than the value of the product.

Spoken information is still provided by retail sales assistants in many outlets, but consumers would seem to regard much of this information as emanating from a low credibility source, i.e. they place little reliance on its accuracy or objectivity. The adoption of this attitude is unsurprising in view of the low status and pay attached to retail selling in general, which is hardly conducive to the recruitment of highly motivated personnel. Hopefully, more retailers will follow the example of pioneers like Boots and Marks & Spencer in upgrading the quality of their employees through the provision of adequate training and incentives. (The establishment of an Industrial Training Board for the Distributive Trades has done much to accelerate this trend.) As things stand at present, however, manufacturers are likely to fill the information gap by the continued use of advertising and sales promotion.

PROCESSING

The increase of prepacked goods on display in retail outlets is an outward manifestation of the reduced importance of this traditional retailing function. In part this may be attributed to consumer preference, but it is equally due to the manufacturer's desire to make his product identifiable at the point of sale.

In general, it is more economic to pack at the factory than at the point of sale, as the volume of output permits the use of the most productive machines. However, there are a number of important exceptions to this generalisation:

1. Some products may be transported more economically in a completely knocked-down state ('C.K.D.') e.g. beds, wardrobes, bicycles.
2. Some commodities may be preserved more easily in bulk form, e.g. bacon, cheese.
3. In some cases the consumer's exact requirements can only be met by processing at the point of sale, e.g. 'three lamb chops', 'a pint of mild and bitter'.
4. Packaging can only occur after the customer is satisfied that the goods meet his requirements, e.g. clothing, fresh produce.

THE STRUCTURE OF THE RETAIL TRADE

At a given point in time it is impossible to derive an exact measure of the size and structure of the retail trade in Britain owing to the rapid changes which are taking place. For the purpose of this book the 1971 Census of Distribution is used although later estimates are incorporated where possible. Readers must be warned however that such estimates are subject to revision and cannot be taken as definitive. For estimates of changes which have occurred since the Census was taken, the student should consult the *Department of Employment Gazette*, the *Annual Abstract of Statistics* or *Retail Business*, published monthly by the Economist Intelligence Unit. Several other sources are also available, including the trade press and the publications of independent research organisations, e.g. the *Nielsen Researcher*.

The size and changing nature of the retail trades are best conveyed by reference to Table 8.1 overleaf.

As can be seen from Table 8.1, considerable changes have taken place within the past two decades. Whereas the volume of business has more than doubled (ignoring the decline in the value of money), there has been only a slight increase in the number of outlets. More detailed examination reveals that these general trends vary considerably in magnitude depending upon the type of outlet. For comparative purposes it is often helpful to convert raw data such as those in Table 8.1 into percentages, and this has been done for the period 1961–66 in Table 8.2 on pp. 150–1.

Table 8.3 contains more recent index numbers for the main types of outlet and confirms the trends apparent in the Census data.

Although Tables 8.2 and 8.3 clarify the general trends and indicate that growth has been greatest in the non-food sector, they fail to reveal the impact of important changes in the particular; for example, during this period many specialised outlets introduced totally new merchandise into their product line which has had a marked impact on their overall performance, e.g. Marks & Spencer's now have an extensive food operation and have recently started to sell selected household textiles. Similarly, many supermarkets have added soft goods, hardware, and alcoholic beverages to their traditional food lines. One must also remember that direct comparisons of the type made in Table 8.2 are misleading unless it is clearly understood that they are based on nominal money terms and make no allowance for price increases.

TYPES OF RETAIL OUTLET

For descriptive purposes, British retail outlets are usually grouped into three main categories:

1. Independent retailers, including small chain stores with nine or fewer branches.
2. Multiple retailers with ten or more branches, but excluding retail co-operative societies.
3. Retail co-operative societies.

The main retail outlets excluded from this classification are department stores, gas and electricity showrooms, and mail order houses.

TABLE 8.1. *Retail and allied service trade estab*

	1950[1]			
	Number	Turnover (£ thousand)	Number of persons engaged	Number
Total retail trade[2]		5,084,847		
Retail shops[3] [4]	583,132	5,000,130	2,392,226	542,301
Co-operative societies	25,544	571,488	179,181	29,396
Multiples[5]	53,949	1,093,178	401,665	66,701
Independents[6]	503,639	3,335,464	1,811,380	446,204
Grocers and provision dealers	145,709	1,228,797	522,683	146,777
Other food retailers	137,867	991,331	534,710	114,655
Dairymen	10,231	195,382	78,593	6,573
Butchers	41,799	287,693	137,757	42,419
Fishmongers, poulterers	9,511	61,244	30,221	6,330
Greengrocers, fruiterers (including those selling fish)	43,948	193,133	114,943	33,073
Bread and flour confectioners	24,181	178,476	152,992	17,260
Off-licences	8,197	75,403	20,204	9,000
Confectioners, tobacconists, newsagents	74,606	502,661	254,266	70,108
Clothing and footwear shops	100,011	966.336	427,885	86,555
Footwear shops	14,870	138,283	57,501	14,104
Men's and boys' wear shops	15,581	199,903	71,413	13,577
Women's and girls' wear, household textiles and general clothing shops	69,560	628,151	298,971	58,874
Household goods shops	54,081	454,299	206,017	60,343
Furniture and allied shops	16,104	232,473	81,653	16,498
Radio and electrical goods shops (excluding hire)	11,761	93,003	50,256	16,517
Radio and television hire shops	168	1,678	492	2,225
Hardware, china, wallpaper and paint shops	26,048	127,145	73,616	25,103
Other non-food retailers	69,217	420,591	256,087	60,113
Bookshops and stationers	10,388	67,359	53,462	5,967
Chemists, photographic dealers	18,205	167,037	86,894	18,097
Cycle and perambulator shops	8,865	46,178	25,068	5,630
Jewellery, leather and sports goods shops	18,896	87,914	51,579	17,506
Other non-food shops	12,863	52,103	39,084	12,913
General stores	1,641	436,115	190,578	3,750
Department stores	529	308,339	129,304	784
Variety and other general stores	1,112	127,776	61,274	2,966
Market stalls and mobile shops[7]	–	–	–	35,006
Electricity board showrooms[8]	1,107	15,963	–	1,333
Gas board showrooms[8]	1,347	22,875	–	1,458
Mail order businesses[9]	434	45,879	13,238	556
Automatic vending machine operators[9]	–	–	–	26
Service trades				
Footwear repairers	18,467	18,983	34,199	11,154
Hairdressers	33,113	38,153	84,232	40,152
Laundries, launderettes and dry cleaners[9] [10]	–	–	–	4,573

[1]The figures for 1950, 1961 and 1966 may differ from those previously published. They have been adjusted to correspond as fa possible with the 1971 figures. Differences arise from changes in presentation and classification. Detailed notes on the kinds of busine which shops are classified appear in Appendix B of the *Report on the Census of Distribution and Other Services 1971* (H.M.S.O.).

[2]As defined in the table except for 1950 when sales through automatic vending machines were not covered in the census.

[3]Retail shops include fixed lockable premises in permanent markets, mobile shops and non-lockable market stalls belonging to operative societies and multiple, distributing depots from which roundsmen operate and premises used as a base by credit traders w trade is done by calling on customers. The figures for 1950, however, include all market stalls and mobile shops.

[4]Excluding electricity and gas board showrooms.

[5]Organisations, other than co-operative societies, with 10 or more branches.

[6]Organisations, other than co-operative societies, with less than 10 branches.

1961¹		1966¹			1971		
Turnover (£ thousand)	Number of persons engaged	Number	Turnover (£ thousand)	Number of persons engaged	Number	Turnover (£ thousand)	Number of persons engaged
3,779			11,757,314			16,685,462	
8,111	2,484,622	504,412	11,131,816	2,555,737	472,991	15,610,730	2,541,430
9,339	195,144	26,684	1,015,938	173,458	15,413	1,107,999	132,204
8,898	632,661	73,852	3,837,244	741,833	66,785	6,083,560	814,666
9,875	1,656,817	403,876	6,278,634	1,640,446	390,793	8,419,171	1,594,560
0,711	551,601	123,385	2,907,655	522,343	105,283	4,156,487	542,676
7,896	471,533	104,359	2,081,314	459,358	92,524	2,614,683	418,437
3,739	73,600	4,456	442,342	67,320	3,853	563,190	59,287
5,156	150,815	38,351	727,972	139,073	33,939	894,174	123,614
5,838	21,462	5,466	80,402	20,331	4,678	82,456	15,481
9,598	98,409	27,172	314,180	89,195	23,318	383,058	85,917
3,025	102,768	18,099	292,629	114,778	17,299	332,598	106,421
0,539	24,479	10,815	223,789	28,661	9,437	359,207	27,717
7,832,	249,853	63,333	1,045,572	297,762	52,064	1,305,875	275,458
6,737	396,996	83,095	1,719,336	410,503	81,279	2,371,766	403,744
9,621	62,796	13,519	258,909	65,229	13,445	349,347	68,661
0,022,	63,488	15,099	350,246	72,153	14,619	482,527	71,046
7,094	270,712	54,477	1,110,181	273,121	53,215	1,539,891	264,037
8,335	264,586	65,850	1,292,186	289,549	70,342	2,006,634	289,691
1,346	90,974	19,469	526,244	103,527	22,131	725,932	92,759
9,942	76,039	16,691	327,674	77,253	17,942	572,511	76,610
1,350	15,829	3,881	131,786	23,424	3,808	225,396	28,196
5,696	81,844	25,809	306,481	85,345	26,461	482,795	92,126
6,913	237,208	61,381	1,019,225	269,738	66,724	1,568,726	298.043
3,721	28,713	5,841	122,150	33,801	6,001	189,089	36,255
6,504	102,173	17,959	501,325	114,901	16,670	728,966	116.382
8,509	13,805	3,841	31,094	9,490	2,793	38,791	7,372
2,745	55,572	19,086	255,292	66,469	21,786	404,338	76,404
5,433	36,945	14,654	109,364	45,077	19,474	207,543	61,630
9,687	312,745	3,009	1,066,529	306,484	4,775	1,586,559	313,381
5,421	181,757	760	652,849	178,914	818	950,030	181,567
4,266	130,988	2,249	413,680	127,570	3,957	636,529	131,814
0,749	39,462	–	–	–	31,790	146,965	37,829
5,029	–	1,332	83,850	–	1,218	144,118	6,752
9,145	–	1,680	101,930	–	1,141	139,182	3,827
6,673	40,589	495	428,834	54,787	771	632,585	59,816
4,072	992	56	10,884	2,156	65	11,882	1,787
5,436	24,183	8,769	26,039	19,154	5,494	22,412	10,996
7,267	139,175	47,632	135,823	163,298	47,191	166,158	154,950
2,483	136,819	5,621	172,287	141,329	8,405	212,349	115,488

Excluding fixed lockable stalls in permanent markets and non-lockable stalls and mobile shops belonging to co-operative societies and
tiple retailers. Non-lockable stalls and mobile shops other than those belonging to co-operative societies and multiple retailers were not
ered in the Census for 1966. The figures given are for returns received only, no estimates having been made for non-response.
In 1950 and 1961 charges for the installation, maintenance and repair of appliances are excluded from figures of turnover but included
966 and 1971.
Numbers of organisations are given; separate figures are not collected for the individual establishments of these types of retail and
ice trade organisations.
In 1961 excluding firms engaged in the hire of linen and industrial clothing which are included for 1966 and 1971.

rce: Business Statistics Office, *Annual Abstract of Statistics 1976*.

TABLE 8.2. *Retail trade; index numbers of value and volume*[1,2]

	Sales in 1966 £ million	Weekly average (1971 = 100)				Sales in 1971 £ million	Weekly average (1971 = 100)			
		1967	1968	1969	1970		1972	1973	1974	1975
Value										
All kinds of business: total all retailers	11,549	75.3	80.4	84.9	91.4	15,895	112.0	126.9	146.7	174.5
Independent retailers	5,802	79	83	86	92	7,530	109	121	138	161
Multiple retailers	3,784	69	76	82	90	5,831	115	133	156	188
Co-operative societies	1,000	87	88	92	94	1,134	108	120	140	172
Department stores	535	72	78	83	90	781	116	131	147	175
Mail order businesses	429	75	82	88	99	619	124	149	180	211
Food shops: total all retailers	5,016	77.2	81.2	87.0	92.1	6,693	108.9	122.8	144.5	174.6
Independent retailers	2,596	81	84	88	93	3,247	107	119	138	164
Multiple retailers	1,641	69	76	84	90	2,548	113	130	155	190
Co-operative societies	779	86	87	92	94	898	107	118	138	172
Grocers[3]	2,957	76	80	87	92	4,062	110	124	149	180
Butchers	736	82	85	89	93	905	108	127	147	170
Greengrocers, fruiterers	320	85	85	90	94	381	105	116	133	161
Fishmongers, poulterers	82	94	92	93	95	84	110	125	142	161
Bread and flour confectioners[4]	256	81	85	88	92	323	109	119	144	167
Off-licences	219	64	70	79	91	355	113	131	159	201
Dairymen	447	79	82	85	91	584	105	112	106	142
Non-food shops: total all retailers	6,533	73.8	79.9	83.3	90.9	9,202	114.2	129.9	148.2	174.4
Clothing and footwear shops: total all retailers	1,771	78	82	85	92	2,314	112	128	149	172
Independent retailers	777	84	87	88	93	920	109	119	132	147
Multiple retailers	886	71	77	82	91	1,290	115	136	162	191
Co-operative societies	109	99	99	97	96	104	106	115	134	148
Footwear shops	269	78	81	85	92	349	112	126	144	165
Men's wear shops	366	76	81	84	92	487	111	126	143	156
Women's wear shops	1,137	78	82	86	92	1,479	112	130	152	178
Durable goods shops: total all retailers	1,229	72	79	79	87	1,801	118	136	143	166
Independent retailers	650	75	81	81	88	886	115	128	137	156

Other durable goods shops[5]									
total	638	68	75	77	86	1,027	121	141	151	173
Radio, electrical, cycle and perambulator shops	350	63	71	72	84	600	120	141	149	169
Electricity showrooms	65	57	68	72	84	131	115	126	109	125
Gas showrooms	92	85	92	90	92	117	124	113	128	156
Radio and television rental specialists	131	78	83	85	91	179	130	173	202	240
Department stores	535	72	78	83	90	781	116	131	147	175
Mail-order businesses	429	75	82	88	99	619	124	149	180	211
Miscellaneous non-food shops	2,570	73	79	84	91	3,687	111	125	145	174
Confectioners, tobacconists, newsagents	1,040	83	87	89	95	1,293	108	117	138	171
Booksellers, stationers[6]	80	58	66	75	86	153	112	127	146	173
Chemists, photographic goods dealers[7]	353	70	76	80	87	520	114	132	153	182
Jewellers	124	69	81	83	91	196	121	145	178	202
Leather goods, sports goods, toys and fancy-goods shops	130	68	76	81	90	199	114	131	153	179
Ironmongers and hardware shops[5]	300	63	71	77	87	512	114	128	145	166
Variety and other general stores	397	70	78	84	92	580	112	124	142	177
Other miscellaneous non-food shops[8]	104	65	74	80	88	178	106	118	133	144
Volume									
All kinds of business	11,549	94.6	97.2	97.3	99.0	15,895	105.8	110.7	109.9	107.9
Food shops	5,016	99.5	100.5	101.6	101.7	6,693	101.5	101.0	101.8	99.3
Non-food shops	6,533	91.1	94.8	94.2	97.1	9,202	109.0	117.7	115.9	114.2
Clothing and footwear shops	1,771	93	96	96	98	2,314	105	109	107	108
Durable goods shops	1,229	87	92	89	92	1,801	115	127	123	121
Other non-food shops	3,533	92	96	96	99	5,087	109	118	117	115

[1] A description of the series was published in *Trade and Industry*, 5 October 1972.

[2] The series are based on the provisional results of the Census of Distribution for 1971 (see *Trade and Industry*, 8 November 1973).

[3] Including the bakery departments of co-operative societies.

[4] Excluding the bakery departments of co-operative societies.

[5] Excluding co-operative societies.

[6] Independent retailers only.

[7] Excluding receipts under the National Health Service.

[8] Including florists, nurserymen and garden seedsmen, pet shops, pawnbrokers and general second-hand dealers.

Source: Department of Industry, Annual Abstract of Statistics 1976.

the comparative performance of these categories of outlet may be judged from Table 8.3, which gives index numbers for the period 1973 to 1977.

Although the 1971 Census of Distribution is still the primary source of data it is now considerably out of date. (See, for example, *Retail Business 176 — Shop Numbers in the U.K.*, Oct 1972, Economic Intelligence Unit.) Accordingly, one must be very careful in the generalisations which one makes concerning the nature and extent of change in the retail trade. There is a large measure of agreement, however, in the observation that independent retailers have declined in both their numbers and share of total trade in recent years. This decline is largely attributable to the aggressive price competition which has paralleled the rise of the supermarket and discount houses operating on small margins, rapid turnover and minimal services. It is clear, however, that the independents are not prepared to yield without a fight and it is significant that the average turnover of such shops has increased in real terms over the past decade.

Multiple retailers have exhibited the fastest rate of growth in the post-war period, especially in the food trades, where their turnover increased by almost 60 per cent in the period 1961–6, by comparison with an increase of 6.5 per cent for independent outlets and a mere 2.8 per cent for co-operative retail societies. The continuation of these trends is reflected clearly in Table 8.3. The multiples' scale of operation enables them to employ functional specialists, to enjoy the benefits of bulk buying, and to use their more extensive financial resources to acquire the best sites. Multiple organisations

TABLE 8.3. *Index of retail sales by type of outlet (1971 = 100)*

	Independents	Multiples	Co-operatives	Mail order	Department
1973	121	133	120	149	131
1974	138	156	140	179	147
1975	161	189	173	209	175
1976	181	220	203	239	203
1977	201	256	229	285	229
% change 1976–7	+11	+17	+13	+19	+13

Source: Department of Industry, *Retail Business*, August 1978.

may conveniently be subdivided into three groups:

(*a*) Food chain stores such as Tesco, Sainsburys and Mac Fisheries.
(*b*) Variety chain stores such as British Home Stores, Littlewoods, Marks & Spencer and Woolworths.
(*c*) Speciality chain stores such as Boots, Burtons, Dolcis and Times furniture stores.

Co-operative retail societies, taken together, have a turnover greater than the next four largest multiples combined. Despite its size, however, the Co-op has failed to exploit fully the economies of scale open to it and has consistently lost ground to multiple and independent alike over the past quarter of a century. Retail co-operative societies are voluntary, non-profit-making organisations which are controlled by committees elected by customers who are members of the society. In the opinion of many it is this factor more than any other which has slowed the growth of the movement by delaying the adoption of modern retailing techniques. As long ago as 1958, the Gaitskell Commission recommended that the Co-op should adopt a new management structure, in addition to the setting up of more specialised shops and a reduction in the number of societies. By the end of 1966 the number of societies had been reduced from 1015 in 1958 to 762, through a process of amalgamation into more viable groupings. This policy would appear to be bearing some fruit, for, as Table 8.3 shows, the co-operatives have performed much better than the independents and are not far from matching the multiples' rate of growth.

An important type of outlet which is found in all three of the major groups is the department store – in 1966 there were 778 such stores, of which 238 were owned by the Co-op and 213 by multiples. For the purpose of the Census, department stores are defined as establishments with 24 or more employees engaged in selling clothing and at least four other major commodity groups. Within the category size varies considerably – in 1961, 53 stores had a turnover in excess of £2 million and accounted for nearly 40 per cent of all department store turnover, while the nine largest each had sales in excess of £5 million. From Table 8.3 it can be seen that in value terms department stores have performed less well than mail-order houses and the multiples in recent years – a continuation of their performance in the 1960s.

THE 'WHEEL OF RETAILING'

The 'wheel of retailing' is a major hypothesis concerning patterns of retail development. Advanced by Malcolm P. McNair, a professor at the Harvard Business School, the hypothesis holds that new types of retailers usually enter the market as low-status, low-margin, low-price operators, and gradually acquire more elaborate establishments and facilities involving increased investment and higher operating costs. Finally, they mature as high-cost, high-price outlets, vulnerable to new competitors, and the 'wheel' goes round again.

Although there are a number of exceptions which suggest that the hypothesis is not universally valid, the general pattern of British retail development conforms with it remarkably closely. As a result of wartime restrictions and controls between 1939 and 1952, the normal evolution of the retail trade was brought to a virtual standstill, but with the removal of restrictions, it would seem that it is now making every effort to make up for lost ground. In fact the scale of innovation and the changes in retail structure which have resulted are often referred to as the 'Retail Revolution'. Some of the major changes associated with this revolution are outlined below, but for a comprehensive review the reader is recommended to consult Christina Fulop, *Competition for Consumers*, published by André Deutsch for the Institute of Economic Affairs (London, 1964).

MAJOR RETAILING INNOVATIONS SINCE 1950

Self-service. Although the first self-service shop in Britain was opened in 1942, the war-time restrictions referred to above delayed its development and these controls were removed, e.g. there were 10 outlets operating on self-service principles in 1947, less than 500 in 1950, 4000 in 1957 and nearly 9500 in 1961. There can be no doubt that self-service has been a major factor in improving the productivity of retail distribution, by increasing the utilisation of the available floor area, the carrying of stock on open shelves where it can be selected, rather than in a stock-room, and the reduction in personal service.

Self-service is particularly suited to the sale of branded convenience goods, and thus has had the greatest impact on the food sector, where it has led to the development of supermarkets. Supermarkets are defined as 'self-service shops with a minimum sales area of 2000 square feet and at least three check-outs'. Multiple traders such as Tesco and Sainsbury's have been most aggressive in the development of supermarkets and have gradually expanded their product lines from foodstuffs and household requisites such as soap and cleaning materials to include hardware, paint, toiletries and cosmetics and selected soft goods. The supermarkets' scale of operations has permitted them to adopt aggressive pricing policies, and the 'battle of the high street' has forced the independent retailer and wholesaler to join forces to meet the threat through the formation of voluntary chains.

Voluntary chains. The growing success of the multiple outlet rests largely on the integration of both wholesaling and retailing activities. Independent wholesalers had long realised that the growing power of the multiples would place the independent retailer at a competitive disadvantage and that it was only a matter of time before this group, which comprised their chief customers, would seek to take collective action and set up their own wholesale co-operatives. To forestall such a possibility, the more astute wholesalers took the initiative and organised voluntary chains of independent retailers. Essentially, such chains are based on an agreement whereby the retailer agrees to place a minimum weekly order with the wholesaler, to submit orders by a specified time, often on specially designed forms, and to accept delivery at a prescribed time. In addition many chains, or Symbol grocers as they are often called, agree to undertake co-operative advertising campaigns, to adopt a distinctive and uniform décor or 'house style', and to carry 'own brands'. In return for these promises, the wholesaler passes on economies in storage and transportation costs in the form of lower prices, organises joint promotional activities, advises on shop layout and management, and often lends capital for store modification and improvement.

While voluntary chains are most active in food retailing they are also to be found in a generally less sophisticated form in other sectors, e.g. Unichem serving the needs of chemists, Jen in the footwear trade, as well as a number of associations in the tobacco, confectionery and hardware trades. However, as the multiples continue to expand their share of the total retail trade one may anticipate further groupings developing among the independents. For example, pressure upon independent chemists has led to the setting up of a second voluntary trading group known as Care Chemists. This group has been founded by an amalgamation between the old-established National Pharmaceutical Union and 15 major wholesalers who between them have a turnover of over £50 million in non-ethical products. By the end of its first year of operation Care expects to have increased its sales through the member wholesalers by at least £20 million, and to have attracted some 5,000 independent chemists as members. Members will pay a £100 membership fee and a £50 contribution to the advertising budget which is anticipated to be around £1 million in the first year of operation. (*Financial Times* report, 31 October 1973.)

Mail order. Although accounting for a relatively small percentage of total retail sales, mail order has exhibited the highest and most sustained growth in recent years. In 1950 sales amounted to £46 million, by 1961 they had increased fivefold to £227 million, and by 1966 they had reached £431 million. Despite a setback in 1971 attributable to the effects of the postal strike, mail order sales have continued to grow spectacularly and totalled £1805 million in 1977. 1978 sales are projected at £2075 million, an increase of 15 per cent over 1977, with a similar increase forecast for 1979.

Mail-order houses fall into two basic categories – general and specialist. The latter usually concentrate on a single product group and are particularly active in the market for seeds, bulbs, plants and small horticultural items. At the other end of the scale, mail order is dominated by the general-line firms with sales well in excess of £5 million per annum, and including household names such as Littlewood's, Great Universal Stores, Grattans and Freemans. Nearly half the goods sold by mail order are clothing, and another quarter is accounted for by household goods.

Given the extensive network of retail outlets throughout the country, the growth of mail order appears at first sight to be an enigma. In fact, it reflects the marketing skills of the operators who have consistently pursued a policy of high quality, backed by a guarantee of satisfaction that is scrupulously honoured with none of the unpleasantry found in some retail establishments. Add to this the convenience of shopping in the comfort of one's home, and generous credit and repayment terms, and the combination becomes virtually irresistible.

Discount houses. The development of discount houses in Britain was delayed for some years, following their introduction in the United States, owing to the existence of Resale Price Maintenance. Since the abolition of this practice, however, they have become a growing force in the field of retailing.

In the simplest terms a discount house may be defined as a non-food supermarket, and operates on the same principle of low mark-up and rapid turnover. Recently, however, firms such as Kwiksave Discount and Asda have extended discounting principles into the food sector. In the first stage of their evolution they have tended to concentrate on shopping goods and particularly on consumer durables with a high average margin, which permits the discounter to offer savings of as much as 50 per cent on recommended retail prices, e.g. Comet Radio Vision Services, Status Discount, Kettering Motor Services. In the future we may anticipate that the 'wheel' will turn, as it has in the United States, and that the discounters will upgrade their image by improving the amenities, range of goods and service offered, to the extent that they will resemble cut-price department stores. The move towards the establishment of out-of-town shopping centres and/or hypermarkets may be viewed as a step in this direction.

Automatic vending. According to the 1971 Census returns there were sixty-five organisations specialising in automatic vending machines, with sales of over £11 million derived from the 300,000 machines estimated to be in use. Machines selling sweets, cigarettes and postage stamps have long been familiar, but there has been rapid expansion into other product areas in the past decade and one may now obtain hot and cold drinks, foodstuffs, stockings and paperback books to mention only a few. Automatic vending machines have become increasingly popular in factories and offices, and it is estimated that over 7000 organisations now have such facilities. The future of automatic vending is difficult to predict as it is largely dependent upon the convenience it offers outside of normal shop hours, any extension of which is bound to reduce growth.

Franchising. Franchising has yet to catch on in the same way that it has in the United States, but the Wimpy Bar and self-service launderette are an indication of a trend in this direction. In essence a franchise agreement allows an individual to set up in an established business by adopting the name and practices of its originator, e.g. Wimpy Bars have a more or less standardised layout and menu. Franchisors exercise varying degrees of control over the operation of franchisees, and provide varying levels of support which preclude generalisation. Given the attraction of running one's own business under the protective umbrella of a franchise offering specialised retailing skills and experience normally accessible only to the large organisation, one may anticipate considerable growth for franchising, particularly in the catering and service sectors.

In December 1977 *Retail Business* reported continued progress by Kentucky Fried Chicken, which is mainly operated on multiple franchises by large operators contributing to a central fund for promotional purposes. The Wimpy Bar operation built up by Lyons over many years was eventually sold to United Biscuits as part of the reorganisation of the Lyons interests. The group comprises 620 Wimpy Bars, 120 Golden Egg restaurants and nearly 100 Bake'n Take units.

CHANNELS OF DISTRIBUTION

In broad terms the same channels of distribution noted in respect of the manufacturer of industrial goods are also open to the consumer goods manufacturer, namely:

1. Direct to the ultimate consumer.
2. Direct to the retailer for resale to the ultimate consumer, i.e. the retail outlet is regarded as the customer.
3. Indirect sale through the medium of a wholesaler or agent.
4. A combination of any or all of these alternatives.

Direct sale to ultimate consumers
Direct sale to the consumer may be achieved by the manufacturer/seller of services in one of three ways:

1. Forward integration into retailing and the establishment of one's own outlets. (Usually it is the retailer who integrates backwards, however.)
2. Mail order selling.
3. Door-to-door selling.

The advantages and disadvantages of each of these alternatives may be summarised as:

1. *Own retail outlets*
Advantages:

(a) Complete control over the selling function, e.g. price setting, terms of trade, provision of services, sales training, etc.
(b) Economies of scale in storage, transportation and administration.
(c) The ability to co-ordinate in-store promotion with advertising and other promotional activities.
(d) Closer contact with the consumers and therefore a better understanding of their needs and preferences.

Disadvantages:

(a) Limited access to the market.
(b) The assumption of all risks.
(c) The need for extensive financial resources to cover both fixed investment and working capital needs.

Examples: Boots, British Shoe Corporation, Burtons, Singer.

2. *Mail order*
Advantages:

(a) Complete control.
(b) Economies of scale.
(c) Access to the whole market, including areas with insufficient population to support conventional outlets.
(d) Consumer convenience.

Disadvantages:

(a) High delivery costs.
(b) High promotional costs.
(c) High costs of building and maintaining an up-to-date mailing list.
(d) Costs of financing credit sales.

Examples: Lowland Bulb Company, SCOTCADE. (Note: although many of the general-line mail-order houses have their own production facilities a large part of their merchandise represents the output of other manufacturers.)

3. *Door-to-door*
Advantages:

(*a*) Complete control.
(*b*) Most effective method of selling certain goods and services where demonstration or complex explanation is necessary, e.g. vacuum cleaners, insurance policies.

Disadvantages:

(*b*) Unsolicited calls are viewed with suspicion.
(*b*) High cost – usually offset by paying low basic salary and high commission.
(*c*) Difficult to recruit and retain suitable salesmen owing to unattractive working conditions.

Examples: Avon Cosmetics, Kleen-Eze, Prudential Insurance, various publishing houses.

Direct sale to retail outlets
In view of the high costs associated with direct sales to the consumer, most consumer-goods manufacturers prefer to sell through some form of independent retail outlet. Given the number of retail outlets, direct sale might appear totally uneconomic at first sight. On reflection, however, it is clear that a very large percentage of sales are channelled through a very limited number of buying points, e.g. in 1965 Nielsen's estimated that it was theoretically possible to gain access to 76 per cent of the retail grocery trade through 1588 buying points, by contrast with 2800 buying points necessary to reach 43 per cent of the total business in 1950. In view of the amalgamations and acquisitions which have taken place since, it is clear that the manufacturer can gain direct access to the market through relatively few centralised purchasing agencies. On the other hand, to reach the remaining 24 per cent of the grocery market in 1965 the manufacturer would have found it necessary to call on approximately 74,000 additional outlets. According to the *Nielsen Researcher* between 1976 and 1977 the number of co-operative societies was reduced to 206. Adding to the six major multiples' head offices, fifty-two other multiple head offices and forty-four major Symbol wholesalers gave a total of 308 'buying points' controlling or influencing 77 per cent of grocers sales in 1977 – a staggering increase in concentration from that

reported in 1965. Whether such an operation is economically feasible requires consideration of the cost and control factors mentioned in the previous chapter, and usually resolves itself into a policy decision on the relative merits of selective, *versus* extensive, distribution. If the latter is chosen, as it invariably is with mass consumption, widely advertised convenience goods, most manufacturers find it necessary to sell at least part of their output through an intermediary.

Selling through wholesalers
The advantages of selling through a wholesaler have already been examined when discussing the distribution of industrial goods, and will not be pursued further here. In general, manufacturers of consumer goods will find it appropriate to make use of the wholesaler's services under the following circumstances:

1. Where a large number of small, widely dispersed outlets account for a significant share of total sales.
2. Where the manufacturer has limited working capital and is unable to bear the costs of direct selling.
3. Where the manufacturer is new to the market and seeking to gain retail acceptance.
4. Where the manufacturer has an excess supply which could be sold under a wholesaler brand, or where he has no brand of his own.
5. Where demand is irregular and/or seasonal, e.g. fireworks!
6. Where trade custom has resulted in channel control becoming vested in the wholesaler.

FUTURE TRENDS

A number of likely future trends have already been touched upon in passing, which reflect growing competition at the retail level. Three other trends deserve mention here.

First, there is a growing interest in consumer protection, as evident in recent legislation and the activities of independent consumer organisations. The Weights and Measures Act 1963, the Hire Purchase Act 1965, the Trades Descriptions Act 1968, the Fair Trading Act 1973 fall into the first category while the Consumers' Association and its publication *Which?* is an example of the latter. The marketing oriented firm has little to fear from this growing interest in 'consumerism', but it must be considered a warning to the non-marketer to put his house in order. Some of the implications of the consumerist movement are examined at greater length in Chapter 22.

Second we may anticipate greater pressure from the distributive trades to modify extant legislation governing hours of business.

Third, as car ownership increases, the development of more suburban and out-of-town shopping centres, on the pattern of Woolco's Oadby development, seems likely. It is clear, however, that such development will not proceed at the same pace as in the United States or possibly France. Planning permission for out-of-town developments is notoriously difficult to get and reflects the Department of the Environment's concern to restrict urban sprawl and ribbon development which encroach upon the greenbelt areas surrounding our major conurbations. Further, experience in the United States of the decay of the urban core and the associated social problems which follow in its wake have caused many planners to have second thoughts about the real benefits accruing from apparently low cost out-of-town shopping operations.

A fourth development which merits comment is the growth of cash-and-carry wholesaling. It has been estimated that the turnover in cash-and-carry wholesale operations in 1973 would approximate £700 million showing a 10 per cent growth on the 1972 figures.

Cash-and-carry wholesaling developed out of the independent wholesaler and retailers' desire to remain competitive with the multiple sector. As such it represented an alternative to the formation of voluntary chains which have already been referred to. While the setting up of a voluntary chain resulted in formal relationship being entered into between retailer and wholesaler, cash-and-carry operations place no such restrictions on either party. While it is apparent that the very large wholesaler voluntary groups such as Mace, VG and Spar/Vivo have maintained growth over the last decade into the 1970s there is evidence that the symbol trade group as a whole is stagnating. One consequence of this is that many of the smaller wholesalers have lost patience with the standard of retail efficiency and co-operation and so are increasingly turning their efforts to a cash-and-carry operation where no formal relationship is entered into.

Suggestions for further reading.

An invaluable source of information on retailing is the Economic Intelligence Unit's publication *Retail Buiness*, recent issues of which have contained the following articles:

November 1977	'Grocers and supermarkets'
December 1977	'Annual Review of the Catering Trade'
April 1978	'Annual Review of Retailing'
May 1978	'Co-operatives'
July 1978	'Department Stores'
August 1978	'Mail order'

Other recommended publications are *Retail and Distribution Management, Nielsen Reporter,* and *Group Grocer.* For future trends, reference should be made to 'The Future Pattern of Shopping' Distributive Trades EDC (1971) and *People, Shops and the Seventies* by Jennifer Canburn, published by Retail Audits (1970).

Part Four

Marketing Functions: The Mix Elements

9 Marketing Research

It is not without significance that this chapter is entitled 'Marketing Research' as opposed to the more familiar title 'Market Research', although some might consider it pedantic that a distinction be drawn between the two. It is reasonable to say that most of the published literature on market research is, in fact, concerned with marketing research in that it deals with the question of research in relation to marketing on a much broader front than is implied by the former description. By definition, market research is concerned with measurement and analysis of markets, whereas marketing research is concerned with all those factors which impinge upon the marketing of goods and services, and so includes the study of advertising effectiveness, distributive channels, competitive products and marketing policies and the whole field of consumer behaviour.

DEFINITIONS

In his *Principles of Management* (second edition), E. F. L. Brech defines market research as: The study of all problems relating to the transfer of goods and services from producer to consumer with the aim of producing practical answers consistent with accepted theoretical principles. At a later point the objective of undertaking research is stated as: To reduce the areas of uncertainty surrounding business decisions. Both these definitions indicate a function of much greater scope than is inherent in the more limited concept of the market and analysis of it.

The British Institute of Management has adopted a slightly modified version of the original definition (now superseded) of the

American Marketing Association, namely: The objective gathering, recording and analysing of all facts about problems relating to the transfer and sale of goods and services from producer to consumer or user.

The last word in this definition is important for it emphasises that marketing research is equally concerned with industrial goods – a point which is frequently overlooked in definitions which refer solely to consumers, as the latter are usually interpreted as 'ultimate' consumers.

THE SCOPE OF MARKETING RESEARCH

Explicit in the introduction to this chapter is recognition of the fact that marketing research is concerned with the scientific investigation of *all* factors which impinge upon the marketing of goods and services. It follows, therefore, that the scope of this function is virtually limitless, and discussion here will have to be confined to those types of research most frequently undertaken in practice.

Essentially, marketing research seeks to provide answers to five basic questions: Who? What? When? Where? and How? The associated question Why? extends inquiry into the area of socio-psychology and is sometimes distinguished as a separate field known as motivation research. (Unfortunately, this title has developed certain undesirable connotations due to the dubious activities of some practitioners.) In practice, marketing research is usually concentrated on a limited number of recurrent problems, often on a continuous basis, which may be classified as follows:

Market research
The size and nature of the market in terms of the age, sex, income, occupation and social status of consumers.
The geographical location of potential consumers.
The market shares of major competitors, i.e. brand share analysis.
The structure, composition and organisation of distributive channels serving the market.
The nature of economic and other environmental trends affecting the structure of the market.

Sales research
Determination of territorial variations in sales yield.
The establishment and revision of sales territories.
Sales call planning.
Measurement of the effectiveness of salesmen.
Evaluation of sales methods and incentives.
Cost-benefit analysis of physical distribution systems.
Retail audits.

Product research
Analysis of the competitive strengths and weaknesses of existing products, i.e. both one's own and one's competitors'.
Investigation of new uses for existing products.
Product concept testing.
Product testing.
Packaging research.
Variety reduction.

Advertising research
Copy research.
Media research.
Measurement of advertising effectiveness.

Business economics
Input–output analysis
Short- and long-range forecasting, i.e. based on trend analysis.
Price and profit analysis.

Export marketing research
Any or all of the above where relevant.

Motivation research
This check-list is by no means comprehensive but serves as an outline of the possible scope of research activities. Although research in most of the above areas is concerned with the recording of fact, qualitative research into the nature of attitudes and opinions is also appropriate in a number of instances, e.g. product concept testing.

ORGANISING FOR MARKETING RESEARCH

In view of the frequent references to the increasingly competitive nature of the business environment one might expect that the majority of firms would have a marketing research department – in fact, remarkably few do. Recent data are hard to come by but a survey by the B.I.M. in 1966 achieved only a 40 per cent response from the 265 companies contacted – presumably because the majority had no research department as such. However, it would be erroneous to assume that this implies a correspondingly low usage of research findings, as a large part of marketing research is carried out by specialist organisations. It is also true that many companies have departments which are performing a marketing research function although identified by some other title such as Economic Intelligence. The more recent B.I.M. survey, *Marketing Organisation in British Industry* (1970), would seem to confirm this view in that it indicated that 74 per cent of the respondents undertake marketing research but only 38 per cent of the respondents have appointed somebody full time to this activity. Some indication of the magnitude of expenditure on marketing research is provided by Table 9.1, while Tables 9.2 and 9.3 contain data on users of market research and number of research agencies.

The decision to set up one's own marketing research department clearly depends upon an evaluation of its potential contribution to

TABLE 9.1. *Value of commissioned research in Great Britain*

	£m.	% increase on previous year	Index*
1969	14–17	—	100
1973	31	—	200
1974	34	10	219
1975	36	7	232
1976	43	19	277
1977	55	27	355

*1969 (£15.5m.) = 100, based on Wills' estimate.
Source: M. Simmons, 'The British Market Research Industry' *Journal of the Market Research Society*, vol. 20, no. 3, July 1978.

TABLE 9.2. *Users of market research 1966—76*

Organisation	1966 1100 (%)	1974 *Total user members* 1400 (%)	1976 1400 (%)
Food, drink and tobacco	19	19	22
Other manufacturing	32	28	28
Service trades	3	7	6
Advertising agencies	30	19	15
Media	8	9	8
Academic institutions	4	9	10
Public sector	4	9	11

Source: *Market Research Society Yearbook*, July 1978.

TABLE 9.3. *Number of research agencies 1963—76*

	No.	*Index*
1963	48	100
1965	67	140
1966	78	163
1968	88	183
1969	108	225
1970	120	250
1971	122	254
1972	143	298
1973	154	321
1974	175	365
1976	174	363

Source: *Market Research Society Yearbook*, July 1978.

the firm's overall operation. Such an evaluation is essentially qualitative, and will vary from firm to firm, precluding the statement of
hard-and-fast rules. For our purpose it will suffice if it is assumed a
decision has been made to establish such a department and attention concentrated on the factors which must then be taken into
account. These may be summarised as:

1. The role and function of the department.
2. Its position within the organisation structure.
3. The role and function of the department manager.

ROLE AND FUNCTION OF THE DEPARTMENT

From the check-list covering the scope of marketing research it is
apparent that a very large department would be necessary to cover
all the areas mentioned. If a firm is undertaking research for the
first time it would be well advised to draw up a list of priorities and
content itself with attempting to achieve only the more important
in the first instance. This does not mean that all other research
must be discouraged absolutely, as too rigid lines of demarcation
can only lead to an inflexible approach and the neglect of lines of
inquiry complementary to the main purpose of the research.

All too often firms make the mistake of handing over responsibility for the maintenance of routine records to the newly formed
marketing research department. The transfer of such records
invariably creates both friction and inefficiency – it hinders the
operation of the department which depends upon such records for
its routine operation, e.g. sales, and diverts the marketing research
department from its main function – research. In that much
routine work involved in the compilation and maintenance of
records will have preceded the setting up of a specialist research
department it is best if the various divisions retain this function,
making the data available as and when required. In order to avoid
both duplication and fragmentation of effort, each department's
responsibility should be clearly stated, and only those returns
essential to the marketing research department's internal research
efforts should be submitted.

ORGANISATIONAL POSITIONING

The positioning of the marketing research department within the
organisation depends very largely on the existing structure. As a
generalisation, the department should have direct access to the
managing director, as it is performing a staff function and, in many
instances, is providing the chief executive with the raw material
upon which policy, as opposed to operating decisions, will be
made. In the larger organisation, with executive directors in functional appointments, the marketing director may well be delegated
responsibility for directing the efforts of the research department
and deciding which reports should be submitted to the chief executive. Even so there is a strong case for a 'dotted line' relationship
between the managing director and the department to ensure that
reports that are critical of a particular aspect of the firm's activities
are given a hearing, and to avoid straining relationships between
the marketing and other functional directors. Further, the managing director is concerned with the overall effectiveness of the firm
and so is in a better position to see the implications of research
findings without becoming subjectively involved with the possible
effect on an individual department.

Some writers recommend that the manager of the marketing
research department should be of equivalent status to the managers of the major operating divisions, but it is felt that this is
unrealistic in view of the discrepancy in size and responsibility that
usually exists. Provided the manager has access to the board of
directors his status should be directly related to the importance
accorded the department within the organisation as a whole.

THE ROLE AND FUNCTION OF THE MARKETING RESEARCH
MANAGER

The job specification of the marketing research manager will vary,
depending upon the size and function of the department and the
degree of external control and direction. In all cases, however, the
manager must be technically competent and possess personal
integrity. Technical competence includes not only experience and
skill in marketing and analytical techniques but also the ability to
translate management problems into viable research projects cap-

able of implementation within the constraints imposed by time, and the available budget.

Personal integrity requires that the marketing research manager interpret findings objectively in accordance with generally accepted principles of scientific inquiry. 'Lies, damned lies and statistics' can only enjoy currency so long as the unscrupulous use 'facts' to support preconceived conclusions by judicious selection, manipulation and presentation – 'massaging the data', in research jargon.

In addition to these essential requirements the manager should also possess those skills common to all managerial positions – administrative ability, an understanding of human behaviour and the ability to communicate effectively.

THE PLANNING AND EXECUTION OF RESEARCH

Marketing research activity falls into two main categories – continuous and *ad hoc*. Marketing is an on-going process in a dynamic environment, and continuous research is essential if the firm is to remain informed of changes in the demand determinants outlined in Chapter 3 and be able to modify its policies accordingly. Much data of this type is collated by specialist organisations and government departments, but is often too generalised to meet the individual firm's specific requirements and needs to be supplemented by 'in-house' research.

However, many marketing situations are unique, e.g. the introduction of a new product, and demand a specific or *ad hoc* investigation. Such research invariably follows a clearly defined sequence which includes the following stages:

1. Recognition of the need for research.
2. Analysis of the parameters which predicate this need – problem definition.
3. Exact statement of the objective of the research.
4. Formulation of an experimental or survey design based on the analysis of stage 2.
5. Data collection.
6. Tabulation and analysis of data.
7. Interpretation of results and the formulation of conclusions and recommendations.

8. Preparation and presentation of a report containing the findings.
9. Evaluation of results of action initiated on basis of research findings, i.e. 'feedback'.

Clearly, continuous research must follow the same procedure in the first instance, but the first four stages will be omitted subsequently.

PRIMARY AND SECONDARY DATA

The data collection phase of a research investigation draws on two main sources of information, which are distinguished as primary and secondary sources. Secondary sources consist of existing data and should always be examined first. Frequently, however, such data have been collected for purposes peripheral to the researcher's main line of inquiry and so need to be supplemented by the collection of new, or primary, data. These differences in the source of data are recognised in the distinction between Desk Research and Original, or Field, Research.

DESK RESEARCH

Desk research into secondary data sources is a common-sense preliminary to any field research. Not only is it possible that the required information is already available, albeit in a form which requires retabulation, but also such research is essential to indicate the precise nature of the data to be obtained by survey or experimentation. Further, published sources are more accessible and offer savings in time and money if properly used.

Logically, desk research should begin with the firm's own records. It was argued earlier that the responsibility for maintaining records should be left in the hands of the individual departments, but it is the marketing research department's responsibility to ensure a sufficient degree of uniformity to permit collation of these records into a common data base for the firm as a whole. The area in which records are usually maintained from which to compile such a data base normally include:

1. Purchasing – stock levels, unit costs, usage rates, etc.

2. Production – output, material, labour, inventory, physical distribution and overhead costs, machine utilisation, etc.
3. Personnel – wage costs, turnover, efficiency levels, absenteeism, etc.
4. Marketing – promotional and administrative expenditures, market and brand data, etc.
5. Sales – by product volume, value, contribution to, profit, order size
   – by type of outlet/customer
   – by area and by salesman.
6. Finance – all cost and accounting data.

In addition to these internal data, the researcher also has access to a large number of external sources, which may be conveniently grouped into five main categories:

1. Government – domestic and foreign.
2. Universities and non-profit research organisations, e.g. *Oxford Bulletin of Statistics*.
3. Trade associations, e.g. British Institute of Management.
4. Academic and professional journals, the trade press.
5. Commercial research organisations, e.g. Attwood Statistics, Economist Intelligence Unit, Gallup, Nielsen, etc.

The publications of government departments are far too extensive to permit full documentation, and only a few may be detailed here. A comprehensive list is contained in the *List of Principal Statistical Series and Publications* which is number 20 in the *Studies in Official Statistics* published by H.M.S.O. The more important Government sources are:

Abstract of Regional Statistics (1975)
Annual Abstract of Statistics
Blue Book on National Income and Expenditure
British Labour Statistics Year Book
Business Monitor
Censuses of Distribution, Population, and Production
Department of Employment Gazette
Economic Trends
Financial Statistics

Guide to Official Statistics
Monthly Digest of Statistics
Overseas Trade Statistics
Report on Censuses of Production
Report on Censuses of Distribution
Social Trends
Statistical News
Trade and Industry
U.K. Balance of Payments

Commonly used international sources include:

Balance of Payments Year Book (I.M.F.)
E.E.C. and E.C.S.C. publications
International Financial Statistics (I.M.F.)
International Labour Review
International Travel Statistics
International Reports on Cotton, Sugar, Tea, Tin, etc.
U.N. Year Book of National Accounts Statistics
U.N. Year Book of International Trade Statistics
U.N. Demographic Year Book
U.N. Direction of International Trade
U.N. National Statistical Yearbook
U.N. Statistical Papers
Yearbook of International Trade Statistics
Yearbook of Fisheries
Yearbook of Forest Product Statistics
Yearbook of Food and Agricultural Statistics
Yearbook of Labour Statistics

An extensive listing of foreign sources is to be found in the Stationery Office publication *International Organisations and Overseas Agencies Publications.*

When using published sources it is important to ascertain the method employed in the compilation and tabulation of the data, and to avoid direct comparative analysis where this differs. Further, such data should only be used when the researcher has satisfied himself as to their validity, reliability and homogeneity.

FIELD RESEARCH

When all published sources have been evaluated, the research issue may still remain unanswered, although much more clearly defined. As noted earlier, desk research is often incapable of providing answers to highly specific problems, but it will often indicate factors which have proved important in similar situations in the past. None the less, there are a number of areas in which field research is usually necessary, and these may be summarised as:

Advertising research – the effectiveness of advertisements *per se*, i.e. copy testing, and media research – usage, coverage, etc.

Consumer research – investigation of the factors underlying consumer choice and preference.

Distribution research – effectiveness of alternative channel structures, methods of handling, etc.

Packaging research – colour, design, size, shape, informational content, etc.

Product research – concept testing, acceptability of new product offerings, development of user and non-user profiles, etc.

THE COLLECTION OF PRIMARY DATA

Original data may be collected by one, or a combination, of three methods – observation, experimentation and sample survey. Observation is the simplest, but usually least satisfactory, alternative and consists essentially of observing the processes associated with the factor under investigation. A good example of this approach is the measurement of customer flow patterns within retail outlets, from which many principles of store layout have been derived.

Observational techniques depend heavily on the skill and objectivity of the observer, and suffer from the need for secrecy if behavioural patterns are not to be disturbed as a result of the subject's awareness that he is under scrutiny. Further, overt behaviour rarely throws much light on the subject's motivation and decision processes, and it is these that one is usually trying to determine.

Experimentation avoids the lack of control common to observational methods and is usually less expensive to undertake than a sample survey. Several examples of experimental method are contained in the section on 'Laboratory Techniques' in Chapter 15 and make it clear that the major drawback lies in the difficulty of replicating normal behaviour in the laboratory setting. In part this may be overcome by conducting such experiments in their normal context, e.g. testing pack design by putting the test item(s) on display in a shop. However, if the results of such tests are to be taken as valid it is necessary to hold constant all variables other than that which is actually under test. Difficulties in identifying both the nature and effect of other variables may be largely overcome by repeating the experiment a sufficient number of times to permit the derivation of an average or representative results, and through the use of controls. A control often consists of running an experiment identical with the test situation with the exception of the test variable, on the assumption that any differences which arise are due to this variable.

Measurement of a single variable can be both expensive and time-consuming, in view of the large number of variables which may require testing. For example in the case of a new pack one may wish to isolate the separate effect of name, colour, size, shape, information value, etc., as well as the total effect. Techniques such as Latin Square and Factorial Design have now been developed which permit multiple variable analysis of this sort, and most modern statistics texts detail their use, e.g. M. J. Moroney, *Facts from Figures* (Pelican A236, 1956). A more specific treatment is to be found in Cox and Enis's *Experimentation for Marketing Decisions* (Intext, 1973).

Probably the most familiar method used in the collection of primary data is the sample survey. Survey method and sampling are both subjects on which a number of specialised texts have been written, and only the briefest coverage can be attempted here.

CENSUS *VERSUS* SAMPLE

As will be seen, marketing researchers have access to a wide selection of survey methods and, subject to time and financial constraints, their choice will be dictated by three separate considerations:

1. Respondent selection.

2. The means of establishing contact with respondents.
3. The information required and the means of obtaining it.

Theoretically, the ideal method of collecting primary data is to undertake a census of the whole population possessing the attribute to be investigated. In practice such an exercise is near impossible and only practicable where the population, in the statistical sense of all units belonging to a clearly defined group, is both small and readily accessible. Thus, although one might successfully conduct a census of a narrowly defined population such as 'all students registered in the first year marketing course at X college', if one were to extend the population to all students in the college, or 'all students of marketing', it is almost certain that one would be unable to establish contact with some members of the population.

Even assuming one could complete a census of a large population, the cost would be enormous and the data so extensive that it would be out of date before it could be collated and analysed, e.g. the 1960 Census of Population was not published until 1964 and the 1970 Census until 1973. For these reasons most researchers content themselves with a representative sample of the population which they wish to study.

Once the marketer has precisely identified the population to be studied, e.g. 'the market for instant cake mixes', the researcher can set about the construction of a sample design which will yield the desired information within the ever-present time and budgetary constraints.

SAMPLING

Sampling is based on two fundamental principles of statistical theory which are usually termed 'The Law of Statistical Regularity', and 'The Law of Inertia of Large Numbers'. The first law holds that any group of objects taken from a larger group of such objects will tend to possess the same characteristics as the larger group. The second law holds that large groups are more stable than small groups owing to the compensating effect of deviation in opposite directions.

On the basis of these and similar principles, one can determine the size and composition of a sample which will yield a desired level of accuracy while allowing for, and eliminating, possible sources of error. In fact, a properly designed and executed sample may prove to be more accurate than a poorly conducted census.

In most instances, the researcher wants some measure of the reliability of the data he has collected, and so will select a sample design based on probability theory such that the chance that any given unit will be selected may be assigned a definite, non-zero probability. There are many types of probability-based sample design, including simple random sampling, stratified samples, cluster samples and multi-stage samples, and the interested student should consult Moser and Kalton's *Survey Methods in Social Investigation*, 2nd ed. (Heinemann Educational Books, 1971) for a clear and concise exposition of their nature, usage, etc.

Although some form of probability sample is essential if the results are to be used for predictive purposes, there is often a need for a 'quick and dirty' survey as a preliminary to such a sample, to clarify basic issues, or to provide generalised information required in a hurry. To this end three types of non-probability sample are sometimes used – the convenience sample, the judgement sample and the quota sample.

Convenience sampling consists of soliciting information from any convenient group whose views may be relevant to the subject of inquiry. Thus, one might stop passers-by on the street to ask their views on parking meters and off-street parking to get a feel for the subject, and as a basis for formulating more precise questions to be asked of a representative sample.

Judgement sampling is a slightly more refined technique in that respondents are selected on the basis of the interviewer's subjective opinion that they constitute a representative cross-section of the population to be investigated.

Quota sampling represents a distinct improvement on both these approaches in that the respondent 'type' is specified on the basis of characteristics of the population at large. Each interviewer is then assigned a quota and solicits information from people who meet the specification. Clearly, the more detailed the latter is, the more representative will be the data, e.g. if the quota calls for ten middle-class housewives between twenty and thirty-five years old, with at least one child under school age, there is a precise specification that can easily be met by visiting a residential suburb and interviewing young women pushing prams or push-chairs. In a number of cases, well-designed and well-executed quota samples have achieved results comparable to much more expensive probability samples. However, such verification can only be established in retrospect and is no basis for accurate prediction.

ESTABLISHING CONTACT WITH RESPONDENTS

Once respondents have been identified from the sampling frame, i.e. list of all members of a given population, the researcher may establish contact by one of three methods – personal interview, mail questionnaire or telephone interview.

Taking these in reverse, it is clear that the telephone possesses the major disadvantage that private subscribers represent only a proportion of all households and tend to be concentrated in the higher socio-economic groups. These factors can be overemphasised, however, and researchers are becoming increasingly aware of the advantages of the telephone for quick, low-cost interviews. This is particularly true in the field of industrial market research, where the compulsion to answer the phone can often secure an otherwise unobtainable interview, or where one wishes to limit investigation to members of the higher socio-economic groupings.

To be effective telephone interviews should be both short and explicit. If they are not the interviewer runs the risks of respondent confusion and of having the interview terminated before it is complete. In the United States, where a higher proportion of households have telephones, this method is widely used to monitor reaction to radio and television programmes and to measure advertising recall.

The mail survey possesses the advantage that it enables the researcher to reach any household or business establishment in the United Kingdom at very low cost. It also avoids the problem of interviewer bias. Unfortunately, the ability to contact an individual does not ensure his co-operation, and mail questionnaires suffer from very high refusal rates – a 50 per cent response would be considered excellent. In part this may be overcome by increasing the number of potential respondents, but one cannot escape the possibility of bias which arises from respondent self-selection, i.e. it is reasonable to argue that people who do complete mail questionnaires are different from those who will not. As with the telephone interview, there is also the possibility of misinterpretation of the actual questions asked, and although this may be reduced by using short, simple questions, the value of the information obtained is correspondingly reduced.

It is because of the disadvantages associated with telephone and mail questionnaires that the personal interview remains the most popular survey technique, despite its high cost. The use of trained interviewers invariably produces a high percentage of acceptable returns with a low refusal rate. The ability of the interviewer to clarify ambiguities improves accuracy, permits the use of longer and more complex questionnaires, and greatly reduces the problem of respondent self-selection. Further, the interviewer may be able to obtain additional information from observations, e.g. type of housing, possession of durables, etc. The major disadvantages of personal interviewing are high cost, and the shortage of trained interviewers, which increase the possibility of interviewer bias, e.g. the interviewer may 'lead' the respondent, or simply record the answers inaccurately. However, many of the problems involved in data collection may be minimised through good questionnaire design. (A full treatment of the above issue is to be found in Joan McFarlane-Smith's *Interviewing in Market and Social Research* (Routledge & Kegan Paul, 1972).)

QUESTIONNAIRES

Most formal questionnaires are structured so that they may be administered easily to a large number of respondents, and to simplify subsequent analysis. Conversely, unstructured questionnaires are of great value when one is seeking to get the feel of a problem, but they are difficult to interpret owing to the differences in emphasis and meaning which arise when respondents are allowed free choice of vocabulary. In either case, the questionnaire may conveniently be considered to consist of four basic elements.

First, all questionnaires must be identifiable and so must be given a title and a distinctive number. Further, where the questionnaire is to be administered by an interviewer, provision should be made for recording the date and time of the interview, the place where the interview took place, and the interviewer's number and signature.

Second, all questionnaires should make provision for the recording of basic respondent data as a basis for subsequent classification, and to permit comparative analysis with other surveys. These data may be obtained partly by questioning and partly by observations, and should include: age, sex, social class, occupation of head of household, marital status, family size and composition, level and type of education. Optional, but useful, data are: name and address, owner or tenant of property, type of property, ownership of consumer durables. Income is obviously a desirable piece of information, but many respondents consider such questions too much of an intrusion on their privacy and either refuse to answer or exaggerate. If personal questions of this type are to be asked, it is best to leave them until the end of the interview to avoid antagonising the respondent and possibly securing an incomplete interview.

Third, the questionnaire should contain control questions to check on respondent consistency and to ensure that it has been administered or completed in accordance with the instructions given. The form of such questions depends on the nature and subject matter of the survey.

Finally, the questionnaire must contain questions that will elicit the information required to provide answers to the problem under investigation.

QUESTION DESIGN

Questions may be dichotomous, multiple choice or open-ended. Dichotomous questions require a straight yes or no answer and are easy to ask, understand, record and analyse. On the other hand a large number of questions will be necessary if detailed information is required, and the responses will not reveal possible shades of meaning. Thus, although they are useful for securing factual data, e.g. 'Do you have a refrigerator?', they are of limited value when seeking opinions or attitudes, when multiple choice questions are to be preferred. As the name implies, multiple choice questions offer the respondent a number of alternatives and so permit the collection of more detailed and accurate data, e.g. 'How often do you use Whizzo?'

At least once a week . . .
Once a fortnight . . .
Once a month . . .
Less than once a month . . .
Never . . .

Similarly, one can obtain a measure of the strength of opinions or attitudes, e.g. 'Old age pensions should be increased.'

Strongly agree . . .
Agree . . .
Disagree . . .
Strongly disagree . . .
No opinion . . .

Some form of pilot survey is usually necessary to ensure that an adequate list of alternatives is offered, and 'All', 'None', or 'Don't know' should be included if the alternatives are not mutually exclusive. In recent years a number of sophisticated techniques, such as multi-dimensional scaling, have been developed to improve the quality of the data obtained through the use of multiple choice questions.

Open-ended questions give the respondent complete freedom in answering and so yield the maximum information, as well as eliminating interviewer bias. They are very useful in situations where it is impossible to formulate all possible alternatives, or shades of opinion, and reveal many facets of the respondent's attitudes and behaviour beyond the scope of dichotomous or multiple choice questions. On the other hand there are several disadvantages. The answers have to be recorded verbatim, for subsequent editing and analysis, to avoid the possibility that the interviewer is only recording what he considers significant. In addition, much of the data may be irrelevant, or become so, through the need to group it into categories for purposes of analysis.

In so far as is possible, all questions should be clear and unbiased, and phrased in terms which are meaningful to the likely respondent. To meet these requirements each question should be formulated in the light of the information which it is hoped to elicit. For example if one is investigating smoking habits there are a number of possible dimensions along which data may be secured, and it is pointless to ask a multiple-dimensional question, 'What kind of cigarettes do you smoke?', which may be answered in terms of brand, price range, whether tipped or not, etc. Similarly, the question 'Why do you smoke brand X?' may be answered in terms of quality, price or satisfaction, all of which are interrelated and so give no clear indication of the salience of such factors taken in isolation.

The sequence in which questions are asked also has an important bearing on the value of the data obtained. Most respondents are nervous or suspicious initially, and so should be asked simple questions of a non-personal nature. Conversational questions, e.g. 'Have you lived here long?', and those which seek the interviewee's preference, e.g. 'Do you like making cakes?', often help to break the ice, as well as leading naturally into more specific questions. Sequence is also important, in that each answer inclines the respondent to make use of the same ideas in answering subsequent questions, e.g. if you ask questions about price, followed by questions on reasons for brand preference, price will usually be stated as a major reason. Similarly, if you ask women questions about fashions, followed by questions on their attitude to advertising, you will get many more favourable responses than you would if you had omitted the questions on fashions.

Questionnaires should always be field tested before use to ensure that they meet the criteria outlined above.

The standard reference on questionnaire design are A. N. Oppenheim, *Questionnaire Design and Attitude Measurement* (Heinemann, 1967), and S. Payne, *The Art of Asking Questions* (Princeton, 1951).

ATTITUDE SCALES

While the precise nature of the link between attitudes and behaviour is subject to debate there can be no argument that attitude is one of the most important and pervasive concepts in marketing. This concept has been discussed earlier (Chapter 4) and the purpose here is to review some problems associated with the measurement of attitudes.

Many of the problems of measuring attitudes are inherent in the concept itself and in the varying interpretations of it by different theorists. However, as Gilbert A. Churchill Jr observes (*Marketing*

Research: Methodological Foundations, Dryden Press, 1976, pp. 206–7) there is substantial agreement on the following:

1. Attitude represents a predisposition to respond to an object, and not the actual behavior toward the object. Attitude thus possesses the quality of readiness.
2. Attitude is persistent over time. It can change to be sure, but the alteration of an attitude, which is strongly held, requires substantial pressures.
3. Attitude produces consistency in behavior outcroppings. Attitude is a latent variable that produces consistency in behavior when manifested. This consistency occurs whether the manifestations are in the form of verbalizations about the object, or approach or avoidance of the object.
4. Attitude has a directional quality. It connotes a preference regarding the outcomes involving the object, evaluation of the object, or positive–neutral–negative affectations for the object.

Of these four clusters of attributes it is the latter which poses the strongest need for measurement through the assignment of some form of number which reflects the directional nature of an attitude. This object is achieved through scaling but one must be careful to determine the nature of a scale before jumping to too hasty a conclusion of the interpretation to be placed upon it.

In brief there are four types of scale, nominal, ordinal, interval and ratio, and their properties may be summarised as:

1. *Nominal scales.* This is the weakest form of scale in which the number assigned serves only to identify the objects under consideration. Library classification schemes employ nominal scales, as does the Standard Industrial Classification (S.I.C.) such that members of the same class will be assigned the same number but each class will have a different number. By extending the number it is possible to achieve finer and finer distinctions until a unique number is assigned to a specific object, e.g. a telephone number.
2. *Ordinal scales* seek to impose more structure on objects by rank ordering them in terms of some property which they possess such as height or weight. As with nominal scales

identical objects are given the same number but the ordinal scale has the added property that it can tell us something about the *direction* or relative standing of one object to another, e.g. 1 may represent the smallest member of a group such that we can safely say that 2 is bigger than 1, 5 is bigger than 2 and 17 is bigger than 5. However, this is all we can say (other than reversing the scale) and in order to be able to draw conclusions about differences between the numbers we must know something about the interval between the numbers.

3. *Interval scales* have this property in that they are founded on the assumption of equal intervals between numbers, i.e. the space between 5 and 10 is the same as the space between 45 and 50 and in both cases this distance is five times as great as that between 1 and 2 or 11 and 12, etc. However, it must be stressed that while we may compare the magnitude of the differences between numbers we cannot make statements about them unless the scale possesses an absolute zero, in which case we would have a ratio scale.

4. *Ratio scales*. Ratio scales are the most powerful and possess all the properties of nominal, ordinal and interval scales, while in addition they permit absolute comparisons of the objects, e.g. 6 feet is twice as high as 3 feet and six times as high as 1 foot.

The above discussion is essentially descriptive – for a discussion of the mathematical properties of the various scales one should consult *Research for Marketing Decisions*, by Paul E. Green and Donald S. Tull (Prentice-Hall, 1966) pp. 183 ff.

SCALING METHODS IN MARKETING

Marketing researchers have borrowed a number of different scaling techniques from the behavioural sciences, among which the most important are:

Thurstone's comparative judgement technique
Likert scales
Guttman Scales
The Semantic Differential
Q-sort technique

Thurstone scales were first introduced by L. L. Thurstone in 1928 and have been very widely used ever since. In essence a Thurstone scale is an attempt to construct an interval scale by selecting a set of statements about a subject which range from very favourable to very unfavourable expressions of attitude towards the subject with each statement appearing to be equidistant from those on either side of it. Scales may contain eleven, nine or seven statements, which are chosen by a panel of judges from a pool so as to achieve the property of equal-appearing intervals, and respondents are asked to select the statement which most accurately reflects their attitude. A score is assigned to each statement and is used, often in conjunction with scores for other sets of statements, in order to provide a summary statement of attitude towards the object of inquiry.

Likert scales differ from Thurstone scales in that respondents are presented with a series of statements and asked to indicate their degree of agreement/disagreement with each. Respondents are usually offered five categories – Strongly Agree, Agree, Uncertain, Disagree, Strongly Disagree, though three or seven divisions are used by some researchers – and are asked to select the position corresponding most closely with their opinion. By scoring a series of statements on a given subject, e.g. qualities of a brand, content of an advertisement, it is possible to construct a generalised attitude towards the object with an indication of the *intensity* with which the attitude is held.

Guttmann scaling represents an attempt to ensure a highly desirable property of an attitude scale which is only partially achieved by the Thurstone and Likert methods – the property of unidimensionality, i.e. all the statements used belong to the same dimension. The construction of Guttmann scales is more complex and laborious than for Thurstone and Likert scales and is described at some length by Moser and Kalton (*Survey Methods in Social Investigation*, 2nd ed., Heinemann, 1971) – as are all the other methods referred to here. However, relatively little use is made of the method in marketing research.

In contrast the Semantic Differential technique developed by Osgood *et al.* (*Method and Theory in Experimental Psychology*, New York, Oxford University Press, 1952) is very widely used, largely because it is much simpler to construct than any of the scales discussed so far and yet yields a very high measure of agreement with these more elaborate measures. The method consists of a series of bipolar adjectives (strong–weak, good–bad, etc.)

Marketing Functions

separated usually by between five to nine points. The respondent is asked to check-mark the point which best indicates their attitude. Scale positions are sometimes qualified, for example:

Extremely good. Very good. Fairly good. Neither good nor bad. Fairly bad. Very bad. Extremely bad.

However, such qualification tends to discourage selection of the extreme positions.

MULTIDIMENSIONAL SCALING

All the scales discussed so far use a single number to represent a person's attitude – or, as Churchill puts it, 'a linear compensatory model' (*Marketing Research: Methodological Foundations,* Holt–Saunders, 1976). Such a model rests upon the basic assumption that attitude is unidimensional such that we balance negative and positive factors in arriving at a single summary statistic.

In recent years marketing researchers have challenged this basic model and have argued that attitude is multidimensional. In turn this requires a concept of a multidimensional space rather than a unidimensional scale and considerable effort and ingenuity has been devoted to developing measures of this space.

The basic characteristic of multidimensional scaling is that respondents are asked to make judgements concerning the degree of similarity/distance between pairs of stimuli using a scale which may be either *metric* (interval or ratio scale) or *non-metric* (ordinal scale). A particularly attractive feature of non-metric multidimensional scaling is that it converts an ordinal input into an interval scale or metric output. Thus as long as the respondent can rank order all the stimulus pairs it is possible to convert such 'greater than', 'less than' statements into absolute statements concerning the status of all the objects.

Multidimensional scaling is based upon sophisticated mathematical techniques, a full discussion of which is to be found in Paul E. Green and Frank J. Carmone, *Multidimensional Scaling and Related Techniques in Marketing Analysis* (Allyn & Bacon, 1970), or *Theory and Methods of Scaling* by Warren Torgenson (Wiley, 1955). However, for normal use packaged computer programs such as M–D–SCAL are available which require only basic mathematical skills.

PRESENTATION OF FINDINGS

Space limitations preclude consideration of field interviewing procedures, and the techniques used in collating, tabulating and analysing the data collected. Once these steps have been completed, the findings, and recommendations based on them, must be presented in the form of a report.

Most research findings have to be presented to two distinct groups – general management and research specialists – and the different needs and orientation of these groups usually requires the preparation of two separate reports. The first of these consists of a fully documented technical report, while the second consists of a short but detailed account of the major findings, conclusions and recommendations abstracted from the first.

The Market Research Society has adopted the following standards as constituting the minimum acceptable content of a survey report:

1. The purpose of the survey.
2. For whom and by whom the survey was undertaken.
3. General description of the universe covered.
4. Size and nature of the sample, including a description of any weighting methods used.
5. The time when the field work was carried out.
6. The method of interviewing employed.
7. Adequate description of field staff and any control methods used.
8. A copy of the questionnaire.
9. The factual findings.
10. Bases of percentages.
11. Geographical distribution of the interviews.

In order to ensure that a technical report satisfies these minimum requirements and presents the material in a logical sequence, many organisations have adopted a formal layout on the following lines:

1. *Introduction*.
   Title of the report.
   Name of sponsor.
   Title of research organisation.
   Date of publication.
2. *Table of Contents*.

3. *Preface* stating terms of reference, and acknowledgements where appropriate.
4. *Statement of purpose*. This generally consists of an elaboration of the terms of reference contained in the preface. It should outline the general nature of the problem to be investigated and the specific hypotheses on which the research was based.
5. *Methodology*. This section should outline the stages through which the project passed, step by step, and include a statement of the definitions adopted, the research techniques employed, the sources of data used, details of sample size and composition, a description of the methods of analysis employed, and any explanatory observations deemed necessary by the researcher.
6. *The findings*. This section consists of an abstract of those data considered relevant to the problem under investigation.
7. *Conclusions* drawn from the findings.
8. *Recommendations* based on the conclusions.
9. *The appendices*. These should include a detailed account of the sample design and its theoretical reliability; a copy of the questionnaire and instructions to interviewers; detailed statistical tables; the bibliography and glossary of terms if appropriate; details of any tests of reliability, theoretical proofs, etc.

In reports intended for line management as opposed to other researchers it is common to find that the conclusions and recommendations follow immediately after the statement of purpose or terms of reference, and the description of the methodology is consigned to the appendixes. Reports of this nature usually also include a single-page statement of the basic purpose and findings entitled Management or Executive Summary.

THE ROLE OF MARKETING RESEARCH AGENCIES

It was stated earlier that many companies utilise the services of independent marketing research agencies, either to supplement their own research effort or as a substitute for a research department of their own. To provide these services, most independent agencies are capable of undertaking all aspects of the research process described above, and act in both an advisory and executive capacity.

In addition to undertaking *ad hoc* research on behalf of client firms, some of the bigger organisations specialise in documenting a particular area of marketing on a continuous basis. The findings from such research are usually incorporated in standardised reports which are circulated to subscribers at regular intervals. A well-known example of such a service is the Inventory Audit of Retail Sales, which is often referred to as the Nielsen Index, after its originator.

Once the manufacturer's products leave his factory there is invariably a time-lag before they are purchased and consumed. The longer this time-lag, the more difficult it becomes for the producer to exercise control over supply to meet variations in demand and modify his production to maximise profit. The Inventory Audit helps reduce these uncertainties by monitoring both sales and stock levels for three major product groups – food, drugs and pharmaceuticals. The actual audit is made in a representative sample of outlets, carefully selected from the population of all retail outlets stocking the three product groups. Each outlet enters into an agreement with Nielsen's under which all invoices are retained for inspection and auditors are permitted to take physical stock on the premises. By the simple process of adding goods invoiced to opening stock and deducting closing stock, sales of each item may be determined. These data are then circulated to subscribers, together with information covering the number of outlets stocking given brands, prices, average order sizes, merchandising schemes, etc. A fact sheet issued by Nielsen for their Food Index is reprinted as Table 9.4.

The Television Consumer Audit is sponsored by the six major ITV Programme Companies, ATV Network Limited, Granada Television Limited, London Weekend Television Limited, Southern Television Limited, Thames Television Limited and Trident Management Limited. It is based on a panel of 6000 households who regularly record purchase data on a wider range of packaged grocery household and toiletry products. The panel is representative of Great Britain (soon to be extended to Northern Ireland), with regional samples sufficiently large to permit separate reporting on nine separate ITV regions, and is run by Audits of Great Britain Limited.

TABLE 9.4. *Nielsen Food Index*

Scope	Since 1939 the Nielsen Food Index has measured the performance of product categories sold in grocers. At the last government census (1971) there were 105,283 grocers in Great Britain.
Sample size	857 grocers, carefully selected to allow analysis of type and nine areas.
Audit frequency	Audits are conducted on a bi-monthly frequency on a Jan–Feb, Mar–Apr cycle or Feb–Mar, Apr–May, etc. Monthly audits can also be arranged.
Report contents	For each brand, size, flavour, etc. specified by the client and an 'All other' section.

CONSUMER SALES and Shares	Units Sterling Average/shop handling
RETAILER PURCHASES and Shares	Units
SOURCE OF DELIVERY	Co-ops (*ex depot vs other*) Multiples (*ex* depot *vs* other) Independents (direct *vs* other)
RETAILER STOCKS and Shares	Units Average/Shop handling
STOCK COVER	Days/weeks/months
PRICES	Average retail selling prices
DISTRIBUTION Shop and £ weighted	Handling Total out-of-stock Out-of-stock in selling area Purchasing Displaying*
ADVERTISING	Press, magazine and TV expenditure*

Sub-divisions in the Report		
	SHOP TYPES All grocers Co-operatives Multiples Major multiples*	REGIONS London TV Anglia TV Southern TV Wales, West and Westward TV

TABLE 9.4. (*contd*)

Total independents	Midlands TV
Major symbols	Lancashire TV
Other independents	Yorkshire TV
	Tyne-Tees TV
	Scotland

Additional data   The free special analyses in the Nielsen report are shown above by an asterisk. Many other special analyses are available to help solve unusual problems.

Interpretation   All clients are assigned a team of Nielsen executives who make six charted presentations a year, and are available at all times for consultation.

The research technique, unique amongst consumer panels of this type, involves a weekly audit of purchases by 400 investigators. This physical pantry check reduces reliances on memory of the panel housewife to a minimum, improves accuracy of data selection and contributes substantially to the continuity of the panel.

The following data are obtained about each panel home and each purchase made by these households.

The home	*The purchase*
1 Age of Housewife	1 Brand Name
2 Size of Household	2 Size
3 Social Class	3 Flavour–Variety
4 With or without Children	4 Actual Price Paid
5 Television Viewing	5 Weight of purchase
6 Cat–Dog Ownership	6 Quantity Bought
7 Ownership of Refrigerator	7 Special Offers
8 Ownership of Washing Machine	8 Name of Shop
9 Ownership of Freezer	9 Type of Shop

Subscribers to the TCA service receive standard four-weekly

reports on their selected product fields, for the country as a whole and each ITV region separately. They include the following information.

1. Total Consumer Expenditure – market/brand/size within brand – at actual prices.
2. Total Consumer Expenditure by weight or by unit measurement.
3. Market share by brands.
4. Product penetration.
5. Special offers and percentage sold on offer.
6. Average prices by brand and size of brand.
7. Analysis of consumer purchases by intensity of ITV viewing.
8. Trend charts of the total market and of major brands.

Manufacturers using television as their primary advertising medium, and satisfying minimum annual expenditure qualifications in each area, can receive separate four-weekly reports in selected product fields at special rates for the London, Midlands, Yorkshire, Lancashire, Southern and North Eastern ITV areas and/or the country as a whole.

All data relating to each household's weekly purchasing are retained by TCA and can be provided in various forms according to the particular marketing situation which needs to be analysed.

The principal types of special analysis are weekly purchasing, brand profiles, repeat purchasing, brand share predictions, brand switching, and source of purchase.

Other forms of analysis relating to test marketing, product usage, television viewing, effectiveness of coupons, samples and special offers and cross matching of purchasing and media data can be provided.

Further information about the Television Consumer Audit may

be obtained from

The Controller
Television Consumer Audit
Knighton House
52–66 Mortimer Street
London W1N 8AN
Telephone: 01 636 6866

Other well-known sources of continuous research data are the Attwood Consumer Panel, the British Market Research Bureau's Target Panel, and Audits of Great Britain Ltd (A.G.B.) Home Audit. Further details of these panels are to be found in Peter M. Chisnall's book *Marketing Research* (McGraw-Hill, 1973).

THE APPLICATION OF BAYESIAN TECHNIQUES TO MARKETING RESEARCH

Traditionally, marketing research has employed a methodology based on classical statistics as exemplified by the principles stated in the section on sampling. In recent years, however, increasing attention has been given to the Bayesian, or subjective, approach to probability which incorporates the decision-maker's personal feelings regarding the likely occurrence of specified events.

The aim of marketing research is to reduce uncertainty concerning the outcome of future events or a given course of action. It is clear, however, that even the most extensive research is unlikely to result in perfect information and that even if it did, the value would not be justified by the cost. Thus, even when the results of research are available to him, the decision-maker will still be faced with some degree of uncertainty and the value of the Bayesian approach lies in its ability to quantify such uncertainties and incorporate them in an analysis of the problem. In practice, many managers make use of subjective probabilities in an informal way and always have, e.g. the sales manager forecasting next year's sales adjusts the individual salesman's estimates on the basis of his own opinion of their likely accuracy; the production manager decides to use a substitute material to meet an urgent order because he feels the chances are eight out of ten it will work.

Although the Bayesian approach is rejected by many classical statisticians, it is the author's opinion that it is a valuable technique when properly applied. While it is beyond the scope of this book, the student is recommended to consult one, or all, of the following:

1. 'Better Decisions with Preference Theory', John S. Hammond III, *Harvard Business Review* (Nov–Dec 1967) 123–41. The 'best' short introduction to the use of subjective probabilities in analysing real-world problems.
2. *Analysis of Decisions Under Uncertainty*, Robert Schlaifer (McGraw-Hill, 1969). An introductory text by one of the pioneers in the field. It is difficult to follow, but involves no sophisticated mathematics. Well worth the effort of the several readings usually necessary to achieve understanding.
3. *Research for Marketing Decisions*, Paul E. Green and Donald S. Tull (Prentice-Hall, 1966). Integrates both traditional and Bayesian approaches, as well as covering most of the new research techniques. Strongly recommended to the student who wishes to specialise in marketing research.
4. 'Making Decisions in Marketing', T. Cass, *Marketing Forum* (May–June 1968) 15–24. A 'home-grown' review article based largely on Schlaifer's book.

Suggestions for further reading
In addition to the books already cited in the main body of this chapter students may wish to consult: Anthony Davis, *The Practice of Marketing Research* (Heinemann, 1973); Benn M. Enis and Charles L. Broome, *Marketing Decisions: A Bayesian Approach* (Intertext Books, 1973); D. S. Tull, and G. S. Albaum, *Survey Research* (Intertext 'books, 1973).

10 Product Policy, Planning and Development

A cardinal principle of marketing is that firms should seek to determine the multi-dimensional nature of consumer demand, and then deploy their resources in the creation of products which will satisfy these demands. Acceptance of this principle recognises that the firm's ultimate success, whether measured by total profits, return on investment, market share or any other criterion, is largely dependent upon its product policy.

PRODUCT POLICY

A firm's product policy is fundamental to the whole operation of the business. Most new companies are conceived to produce a specific product or group of products, and it is this decision which dictates the industry to which they will belong, the markets they will serve, and the nature and extent of the resources, methods and techniques they will employ. These factors often tend to be overlooked, however, for most companies are long-established members of a given industry and inextricably linked with their product line. Similarly, it is often erroneously assumed that companies are irrevocably committed to their current product mix, which ignores the fact that apart from certain highly specific capital equipment, most corporate resources may be put to other uses.

The latter assumption may be attributed to the fact that companies rarely do undertake a radical change in product policy, even when environmental changes indicate that they should – a fact which prompted Theodore Levitt to write the now classic 'Marketing Myopia' (*Harvard Business Review* (July–Aug 1960)).

Levitt's thesis is that companies take too narrow a view of their market because they think in terms of their product offering, rather than in terms of the fundamental needs which these products satisfy. Thus the American railroads thought of themselves as the ultimate development in overland transportation, and failed to respond to the invention of the internal combustion engine which gave us the car, lorry and aeroplane. If the management of the railroads had thought of themselves as being in the 'transportation business', then doubtless they would have integrated these new methods of moving goods and people into their existing network. As it was, the expanding demand of a rapidly growing economy masked the impact of the new competition and lulled the railroads into the complacent belief that they could look forward to continued and uninterrupted growth. Even when the threat was appreciated the railroads chose to compete head-on, failing to realise that they could not hope to duplicate the speed and convenience offered by their rivals, with the result that they are now members of a dying industry.

The writings of Levitt and Peter Drucker, among others, have given us the concept of corporate strategy which, in essence, consists of a statement of the firm's objective, and the mix of policies to be used in the attainment of that objective. A first step in the formulation of a corporate strategy is to answer the questions 'What business are we in?' and 'What business do we want to be in?' Declining industries have invariably failed to define their business in sufficiently broad terms. Had the railroads thought of themselves as being in the 'transportation business' it is reasonable to assume that they would have been responsive to the development and introduction of new methods of transport, irrespective of whether they involved rails and locomotives.

Gulf Oil exemplifies the broad viewpoint in that it has defined its role as 'Servicing the travelling public'. Although the company's past growth has depended largely upon the refining and sale of petroleum products to motorists, Gulf has recognised that developments in fuel cell technology and growing concern over air pollution may be sounding the death-knell of the petrol engine. The motor car represents only one stage in the evolution of personal transport, however, and it is clear that people will continue to travel even though we may not be able to predict the exact nature of the next development. While travelling, people have a need for both rest and refreshment, and to meet this continuing need Gulf has developed a nation-wide network of Holiday Inns.

Hopefully, this example makes it clear that by defining the business they are in, and want to be in, Gulf have not committed themselves irrevocably to a given product mix, but will modify their product offering in the light of changes in consumer demand – this is their product policy.

THE CONCEPT OF THE PRODUCT LIFE CYCLE

The above examples clearly indicate that, over time, man develops new and better ways of satisfying basic needs, with the result that as new products are introduced, established products become obsolescent and eventually pass into oblivion. In time the cycle repeats itself, and the once new product suffers the fate of the product which it originally replaced. In many ways this process resembles the human life cycle, with its phases of birth, growth, maturity, senility and death, and has given rise to the concept of the product life cycle.

The first stage in the product life cycle is represented by its introduction into the market. As with human beings, this is a critical stage, for the product has little to protect it from the hostile environment into which it is introduced. (Fortunately, medical science has been more successful in protecting new-born offspring than has the marketer!) Assuming survival, new products enjoy a period of increasing demand and rapid growth, but as most innovations are merely substitutes for existing products, other manufacturers will react strongly to the newcomer, and their own decline in market share, eventually stemming the newcomer's growth. The levelling out of demand for the new product represents the onset of maturity.

In time, other new products will enter the market offering advantages over the now mature product, which will experience a decline in demand as consumers switch their allegiance. This phase has been characterised as senility or decay.

Unlike the human life cycle, however, one cannot predict the length of any of the phases of the product life cycle – certainly there are not the equivalent of actuarial tables for new products. Further, marketers have the option to practise euthanasia and quietly dispose of products which fail to live up to expectations, or, alternatively, to prolong the life cycle through a rejuvenation process. The analogy is a useful one, provided that one bears in mind that it is a generalisation and says nothing specific about the duration of any given phase. However, by monitoring changes in demand, one can predict the onset of growth, maturity and senility, and vary one's marketing inputs accordingly, e.g. reduce the level of advertising expenditures during growth and emphasise production and physical distribution; step up the amount of sales promotion at the onset of maturity; retire the product when senility sets in.

WHAT IS A 'NEW' PRODUCT?

The first stage in the product life cycle posits the introduction of a new product – the question is, 'What constitutes a *new* product?' There can be no hard-and-fast answer, for newness is essentially a subjective concept that depends upon one's state of knowledge or, in the case of a firm, its current range of activity. It is possible to distinguish a spectrum of newness ranging from an invention, which Mansfield has defined as '. . . a prescription for a new product or process that was not obvious to one skilled in the relevant art at the time the idea was generated' (Edwin Mansfield, *The Economics of Technological Change* (W. W. Norton & Co., New York, 1968) 50), to a minor change in an existing, widely known product, e.g. the addition of a new blue whitener to a detergent.

For the purpose of this book a new product will be considered anything which is perceived as such by the consumer, or with which the firm has no previous experience. The former permits the inclusion of variants in existing products, and their packaging, as well as totally new products such as A.F.D. foods. The latter acknowledges that production of an existing product with which the firm has no previous experience raises the same marketing problems as does a totally new product. Further, it may also be perceived by consumers as a new product, e.g. the sale of foods under the 'St Michael' brand by Marks & Spencer.

THE ROLE OF THE NEW PRODUCT DEVELOPMENT

Although it is impossible to predict the life span of a given product, there is an inevitable certainty that it will eventually be replaced by the introduction of a new substitute or even made totally obsolete as the result of technological innovation.

In Chapter 2 it was stated that branding developed in its present form as a result of the realisation that many mass markets were faced with the possibility of over-supply, such that the individual manufacturer could only protect his position by distinguishing his output from that of his competitors. Many critics of advertising would argue that the claimed differences between brands are more a figment of the copywriter's imagination than a reality, and still view products such as detergents and canned peas as homogeneous. This view is admissible if one adopts a narrow definition of a product, based solely on the function that it performs in terms of objective and quantifiable criteria. However, from the arguments advanced concerning newness, it is clear that the consumer's perception is modified by subjective considerations which are not amenable to quantification. Thus a relatively minor change in a product's composition or marketing may assume major significance in the user's eyes and result in a marked shift in demand for that product. It is argued, therefore, that branding can only succeed as a competitive strategy given the existence of perceived differences.

If this is so it follows that a competitive market will be characterised by a continual effort to develop such differences. Clearly, the producer who succeeds in distinguishing his product from that of his competitors, through the creation of a new and desirable attribute, will enjoy an advantage which will enable him to expand his sales and share of market. Such an advantage is in the nature of a monopoly, which may last for years if protected by a patent, e.g. the Polaroid camera and film, or be eroded overnight by imitative innovation, e.g. enzyme active detergents.

The role of new product development is the creation of such competitive advantages.

THE IMPORTANCE OF NEW PRODUCTS

Any attempt to measure the contribution of new products to a firm or industry's growth and profitability is bedevilled by a lack of consensus as to what constitutes a new product. Similar difficulties also exist when one seeks to measure the failure rate of new product introductions.

Ignoring the problems of data comparability for the present, two

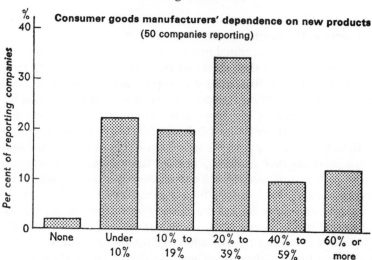

Fig. 10.1. Consumer goods manufacturers' dependence on new products

Fig. 10.2. Industrial goods manufacturers' dependence on new products

(From *The Marketing Executive Looks Ahead*: 'Experiences in Marketing Management' 13, National Industrial Conference Board, 1967.)

valid generalisations may be advanced:

1. Firms are increasingly dependent upon new products for the maintenance and expansion of sales.
2. A large proportion of new product introductions are failures in the sense that they do not achieve the expected sales level, and are withdrawn from the market.

The first generalisation is supported by Figs 10.1 and 10.2 reproduced opposite. More recent data are reported in Table 10.1, based on a survey of a representative cross-section of U.K. industry in 1974.

Estimates of new product failure rates vary enormously from the oft-quoted level of 80 per cent (Ross Federal Research Corporation, quoted in the *Wall Street Journal*, 5 April, 1961), to an absolute low of 7 per cent (A. C. Nielsen Company, *How to Strengthen Your Product Plan*, 1966) if the firm makes full use of the screening and testing procedures described below.

ALTERNATIVE NEW PRODUCT STRATEGIES

Relatively few new products emanate from totally new companies, and attention here will be focused on the established firm with an existing product line. Such firms vary in their willingness to innovate and develop new products, and are usually categorised as 'leaders' and 'followers'.

Many industries which are highly concentrated or oligopolistic in structure are dominated by one or a small number of firms which determine the competitive character of the market along such dimensions as price, quality, distribution policy and innovation. These firms are the leaders. The remaining firms are thought of as followers in that they imitate the policies of the leaders and rarely possess a sufficient market share to affect industry practice through independent action. (Although this is not the place to enter into a discussion of the evils of monopoly/oligopoly, there is a considerable body of evidence which suggests that small firms in an industry are the most innovative, and it would be wrong to assume that it is always the industry leader who stimulates innovation.)

Whether a firm is a leader or follower, there are several distinct

TABLE 10.1. *Inter-industry variations in dependence on new products*

Where does the largest proportion of your own sales come from?

Industry	Products launched within the last five years		Products launched more than five years ago		Totals	
	%	n	%	n	%	n
Building and construction	45	13	55	16	100	29
Chemicals/allied products	29	12	71	30	100	42
Clothing	67	19	33	9	100	28
Electrical machinery	38	13	62	21	100	34
Engineering/general machinery	41	71	59	102	100	173
Fabricated metal	21	8	79	30	100	38
Food, drink, tobacco	11	6	89	49	100	55
Furniture and fixtures	57	8	43	6	100	14
Iron and steel	21	6	79	22	100	28
Leather	54	7	46	6	100	13
Paper	24	5	76	16	100	21
Plastics	50	9	50	9	100	18
Printing and publishing	38	8	62	13	100	21
Textiles	50	33	50	33	100	66
Miscellaneous	64	9	36	5	100	14
Stone, glass, clay	24	5	76	16	100	21
Total	38%	232	62%	383	100%	N = 615

Source: M. J. Baker and S. T. Parkinson, 'An Analysis of the Significance of Innovation', Appendix to *S.S.R.C. Report 1974*.

ways in which it can add to its product line which may be summarised as:

1. Modification of an existing product, e.g. addition of a new ingredient in a detergent, toothpaste or cake mix; increase in the cubic capacity of a car engine, adoption of disc brakes, etc.
2. Addition of a complementary product, e.g. a new brand of cigarette, a new flavour in a food or beverage; the development of a new model of car.
3. Entry into an existing market new to the firm, e.g. Cadbury's entry into the cake market; Rank Organisation's entry into the office-equipment market.
4. Development of a new market through the introduction of a totally new product, e.g. Polaroid camera, television, computers.

These alternatives are listed in ascending order of risk. The first strategy usually entails a low level of risk, and is frequently in response to overt public demand. Thus, offering a 1300 c.c. engine in place of the original '1100' extended the competitive positioning of this car, but required little additional investment by British Leyland.

The second strategy involves a greater degree of risk, as the firm has no previous direct experience of the production and marketing of the new item. However, in so far as it is a complementary product, previous experience with similar products and markets will be almost directly relevant and reduce the risk accordingly.

Entry into an existing market of which the firm has no previous experience is unlikely to be viewed favourably by the companies currently sharing that market. Thus the new entrant's inexperience is compounded by the aggressive reaction of competitors, and involves a still higher level of risk.

The fourth alternative exposes the firm to a completely unknown situation, added to which the value of fundamentally new products may take years to establish owing to the innate conservatism of the potential user. Further, it is only when a product achieves wide-scale trial that many of its limitations become apparent, which may involve the innovator in many years of adjustment and modification. At the end of this time another firm may well enter the market which the innovator has developed and deprive him of the fruits of his labours, e.g. I.B.M. in the computer market.

NEW PRODUCT DEVELOPMENT

Despite the risks involved, new product development is a competitive necessity and has prompted many companies to evolve formalised procedures for dealing with the complexities and uncertainties inherent in the process. Such procedures will normally include:

1. Location and screening of new product ideas.
2. Evaluation of market potential and possible contribution to the firm's overall objectives.
3. Prototype development and product testing.
4. Test marketing.

Many new product development procedures distinguish additional stages, but these tend to be a more detailed statement of the basic steps outlined above.

THE LOCATION AND SCREENING OF NEW PRODUCT IDEAS

To be effective, any search for new product ideas should be structured, in the sense that efforts should be directed towards a specific area and pursued systematically. Most firms possess some special skill or 'distinctive competence', and it is this which they should seek to exploit in developing new products. Thus, if a firm has developed a reputation for precision engineering it should seek to build on this strength, rather than branch out into mass-produced, fabricated products. Although there are cases of firms which have achieved success following a radical departure from their original product policy, the author would argue that this is attributable to their developing a distinctive competence they previously lacked or had failed to exploit.

The adoption of search criteria is essential if the firm is to avoid wasteful exploration of the multiplicity of sources open to it. Such sources may be internal or external to the firm.

Internally, every member of the company is a potential source of new product ideas, and company suggestion schemes have thrown up many more valuable suggestions than they are generally credited with. Many companies now have their own Research and Development Department, specifically charged with developing in-house projects, in addition to which Sales, Marketing and Production usually have distinct ideas of how the current product line could be improved or extended.

Externally, the firm's distributors and customers are frequently a fruitful source of ideas, as are the product offerings of one's competitors. Another major source is the published literature of the universities and professional bodies, the technical and trade press, and the various government research departments. Much of the information to be gleaned from these sources is incapable of immediate application but is sufficient to stimulate further investigation – the A.F.D. process described earlier is a clear exception to this generalisation.

The major source of ideas for radical innovations is undoubtedly the private inventor, whose work may be reviewed by consulting the Patent Office files or the weekly *Official Journal*. (Few inventors appreciate the commercial potential of their ideas, and those that do frequently meet with a cool reception from potential manufacturers, e.g. Xerography, the Hovercraft, but nearly all patent their ideas.)

In drawing up a short-list of product ideas for detailed investigation the search criteria mentioned earlier will also help reduce the need for subsequent screening, i.e. weeding out of marginal ideas. Such criteria usually require that:

(a) The product will meet a clearly defined consumer need.
(b) The product is consistent with the firm's production and marketing policies.
(c) The product will utilise the firm's existing skills and resources.
(d) The product will contribute to the firm's long-run profitability.

Once a short-list has been compiled, the next step is to evaluate each product's potential. To ensure consistency, many firms make use of a factor rating table similar to that reproduced in Fig. 10.3,

	Very good	Good	Average	Poor	Very Poor
I. MARKETABILITY **A. Relation to present distribution channels**	Can reach major markets by distributing through present channels	Can reach major markets mostly by distributing through present channels, partly through new channels	Will have to distribute equally between new and present channels, in order to reach major markets	Will have to distribute mostly through new channels in order to reach major markets	Will have to distribute entirely through new channels in order to reach major markets
B. Relation to present product lines	Complements a present line which needs more products to fill it	Complements a present line that does not need, but can handle, another product	Can be fitted into a present line	Can be fitted into a present line but does not fit entirely	Does not fit in with any present product line
C. Quality/price relationship	Priced below all competing products of similar quality	Priced below most competing products of similar quality	Approximately the same price as competing products of similar quality	Priced above many competing products of similar quality	Priced above all competing products of similar quality
D. Number of sizes and grades	Few staple sizes and grades	Several sizes and grades, but customers will be satisfied with few staples	Several sizes and grades, but can satisfy customer wants with small inventory of non-staples	Several sizes and grades, each of which will have to be stocked in equal amounts	Many sizes and grades which will necessitate heavy inventories
E. Merchandisability	Has product characteristics over and above those of competing products that lend themselves to the kind of promotion, advertising, and display that the given company does best	Has promotable characteristics that will compare favourably with the characteristics of competing products	Has promotable characteristics that are equal to those of other products	Has a few characteristics that are promotable, but generally does not measure up to characteristics of competing products	Has no characteristics at all that are equal to competitors' or that lend themselves to imaginative promotion
F. Effects on sales of present products	Should aid in sales of present products	May help sales of present products; definitely will not be harmful to present sales	Should have no effect on present sales	May hinder present sales some; definitely will not aid present sales	Will reduce sales of presently profitable products
II. DURABILITY **A. Stability**	Basic product which can always expect to have uses	Product which will have uses long enough to earn back initial investment, plus several (from five to ten) years of additional profits	Product which will have uses long enough to earn back initial investment, plus several (from five to ten) years of additional profits	Product which will have uses long enough to earn back initial investment, plus one to five years of additional profits	Product which will probably be obsolete in near future
B. Breadth of market	A national market, a wide variety of consumers and a potential foreign market	A national market and a wide variety of consumers	Either a national market or a wide variety of consumers	A regional market and a restricted variety of consumers	A specialised market in a small marketing area
C. Resistance to cyclical fluctuations	Will sell readily in inflation or depression	Effects of cyclical changes will be moderate, and will be felt after changes in economic out-	Sales will rise and fall with the economy	Effects of cyclical changes will be heavy, and will be felt before changes in economic out-	Cyclical changes will cause extreme fluctuations in demand

D. *Resistance to seasonal fluctuations*	steady sales throughout the year	Steady sales except under unusual circumstances	Seasonal fluctuations in inventory and personnel problems can be absorbed	...ations that will cause considerable inventory and personnel problems	...ations that will necessitate lay-offs and heavy inventories
E. *Exclusiveness of design*	Can be protected by a patent with no loopholes	Can be patented, but the patent might be circumvented	Cannot be patented, but has certain salient characteristics that cannot be copied very well	Cannot be patented, and can be copied by larger more knowledgeable companies	Cannot be patented, and can be copied by anyone
III. PRODUCTIVE ABILITY					
A. *Equipment necessary*	Can be produced with equipment that is presently idle	Can be produced with present equipment, but production will have to be scheduled with other products	Can be produced largely with present equipment, but the company will have to purchase some additional equipment	Company will have to buy a good deal of new equipment, but some present equipment can be used	Company will have to buy all new equipment
B. *Production knowledge and personnel necessary*	Present knowledge and personnel will be able to produce new product	With very few minor exceptions, present knowledge and personnel will be able to produce new product	With some exceptions, present knowledge and personnel will be able to produce new product	A ratio of approximately 50-50 will prevail between the needs for new knowledge and personnel and for present knowledge and personnel	Mostly new knowledge and personnel are needed to produce the new product
C. *Raw materials' availability*	Company can purchase raw materials from its best supplier(s) exclusively	Company can purchase major portion of raw materials from its best supplier(s), and remainder from any one of a number of companies	Company can purchase approximately half of raw materials from its best supplier(s), and other half from any one of a number of companies	Company must purchase most of raw materials from any one of a number of companies other than its best supplier(s)	Company must purchase most or all of raw materials from a certain few companies other than its best supplier(s)
IV. GROWTH POTENTIAL					
A. *Place in market*	New type of product that will fill a need presently not being filled	Product that will substantially improve on products presently on the market	Product that will have certain new characteristics that will appeal to a substantial segment of the market	Product that will have minor improvements over products presently on the market	Product similar to those presently on the market and which adds nothing new
B. *Expected competitive situation – value added*	Very high value added so as to substantially restrict number of competitors	High enough value added so that, unless product is extremely well suited to other firms, they will not want to invest in additional facilities	High enough value added so that, unless other companies are as strong in market as this firm, it will not be profitable for them to compete	Lower value added so as to allow large, medium and some smaller companies to compete	Very low value added so that all companies can profitably enter market
C. *Expected availability of end users*	Number of end users will increase substantially	Number of end users will increase moderately	Number of end users will increase slightly, if at all	Number of end users will decrease moderately	Number of end users will decrease substantially

Source: John T. O'Meara, Jr, 'Selecting Profitable Products', *Harvard Business Review* (Jan–Feb 1961) 83–9.

Fig. 10.3. Factor and subfactor ratings for a new product

which suggests the use of five ratings, ranging from Very Good to Very Poor, for seventeen different factors. By assigning a value, e.g. 10, 8, 6, 4 and 2, to the rating, and by weighting the factors in terms of their relative importance to the firm, it is possible to compute a score for each product idea and limit further investigation to the highest scoring ideas.

Once management is satisfied that the basic idea is indeed consistent with its policies, and within its engineering and production capabilities, it should formulate a product concept, i.e. a precise statement of the need the product will fill and the form it will take. Based on this statement the marketing research department can develop a profile of the potential market and the production department can estimate unit cost at various levels of output. (The latter may necessitate the construction of a prototype(s).) Utilising these data, the marketing department can then develop its own estimate of the costs associated with varying levels of market penetration.

FINANCIAL CONSIDERATIONS

New product introductions represent an investment opportunity for the firm, and it is essential that such opportunities be evaluated in the light of all other possible uses of the firm's resources. In the normal course of events a company is faced with a disparate collection of investment opportunities, and so must develop a common denominator with which it may rank dissimilar projects in order of preference. The discounted cash flow (D.C.F.) technique has been widely adopted for this purpose.

The basic principle upon which the D.C.F. technique is based is recognition of the fact that a currently available sum of money can be invested to generate a stream of future earnings. Thus £1 invested today will be worth £1.10 a year hence if the return on investment is 10 per cent per annum. Conversely, £1 received a year hence is only worth £0.909 today if it could be invested at 10 per cent. By applying the D.C.F. technique one can make direct comparisons of investment opportunities with very dissimilar future cash flows and select the one with the highest net present value. Naturally, the method is not infallible, as it is very dependent upon the accuracy of the predicted future cash flows. The more distant these are the less accurate they become – a factor which partially accounts for the popularity of payback and similar methods which emphasise the time in which the original investment will be recovered. Many students will be familiar with these techniques already; those that are not are recommended to refer to *Discounted Cash Flow* by M. G. Wright (McGraw-Hill, London, 1967).

At this stage of the new product evaluation procedure it is unlikely that sufficient information exists to permit a detailed comparison of proposals, but even a rough computation will help reduce the list.

TESTING THE PRODUCT CONCEPT

Given the revised short-list, the next step is a detailed feasibility study based on tests of the product concept. Such tests may have been made already, but if not, it is essential that they be undertaken prior to detailed market studies and the finalisation of prototypes. In its original form the product concept represents the marketer's perception of a product which will satisfy a specific consumer want, and may differ considerably from the consumer's own perception of what is required. As it is the latter who ultimately decides whether the product will be a success, reconciliation of any discrepancy is vital. Further, outlining the broad characteristics of a new product to a potential consumer may well stimulate the latter to suggest specific attributes previously unthought of.

In some instances the product concept is too complex to be tested verbally, and some form of mock-up or prototype must be used to communicate the idea and gain consumer reaction. For example the concept of the Deltaphone, a new lightweight phone with a distinctive and variable pitch 'ring', is difficult to convey in words but eminently simple to demonstrate.

Once the product concept has been validated, a detailed market study should be undertaken. If it is subsequently decided to market the product this study will form the basis of the marketing plan. Concurrently the engineering and production departments will develop final prototypes, and decide on the production techniques to be used if the project is adopted.

PRODUCT TESTING

In view of the high risks associated with new product introductions, field testing should logically precede firm commitment to large-scale production and marketing. Product testing consists of an objective appraisal of the product's performance, free of subjective associations created by other elements of the marketing mix, e.g. price, packaging, brand image, etc. It should not be confused with test marketing, which includes consideration of these factors.

The precise nature of a product test obviously depends upon the product itself but, essentially, all seek to determine how well it will perform in actual use. Certain product attributes are capable of precise measurement, e.g. the efficiency of an engine, the life of an electric light bulb, whereas others depend upon consumer preference and defy exact quantification, e.g. the taste of a food or beverage. Recognised tests exist for the measurement of most items included in the product specification and subsequently incorporated in the description of the goods as offered for sale. With the passing of the Trade Descriptions Act, 1968, which came into force on 30 November of that year, the importance of ensuring the accuracy of such quantitative statements became a matter of law rather than conscience. This Act makes it an offence to use a false trade description, which is defined as covering:

(*a*) The composition, quality, quantity, and size of goods.
(*b*) Their suitability and fitness for any particular purpose.
(*c*) Their testing or approval by any person.
(*d*) The method, origin, date of manufacture, production or processing.
(*e*) Their history and previous ownership.

Under the provisions of the Act, the use of a false description becomes a criminal offence punishable by fine and/or imprisonment, whereas previously misrepresentation was only actionable in a civil action.

As noted, however, many product qualities are a matter of individual perception and preference, the incidence of which can only be established through actual trial. In practice a number of experimental methods have been developed, some of which will already be familiar to the reader as a result of their incorporation in television commercials.

In that the manufacturer is seeking to establish how his new offering will be perceived by the consumer, a commonly used test involves comparison with a leading competitive product. The detergent advertisement which shows two halves of a badly stained article washed in an identical manner, except for the fact that one powder is Spotto and the other Brand X, is an example of such a paired comparison. Although scientifically valid, a successful rating on a blind test in which the new product is identified solely by a code number is no guarantee of market acceptance. The purpose of such tests is to test a specific variable such as taste, texture, washing power, etc., and thus requires that all other variables be held constant. In the real world the consumer does not normally select a product along one dimension alone, even though a single factor such as washing power may predominate. Products are bundles of attributes which are viewed collectively and which create their own associations in the mind of the potential user, so that a preference for A over B based on a single variable may be reversed when all the variables are taken into account. Thus, although a successful product test is an essential preliminary to continued development, it is not conclusive evidence of market success, and many producers will only make a final decision on the product's future after large-scale market testing.

TEST MARKETING

Basically, test marketing consists of launching the product on a limited scale in a representative market, thus avoiding the costs of a full-scale launch while permitting the collection of market data which may subsequently be used for predictive purposes.

In practice the term 'test marketing' tends to be used loosely, and it is important to distinguish the original concept, as outlined above, from two associated techniques commonly confused with it. The first of these is often referred to as pilot marketing, and fulfils the same function for the marketer as the pilot plant does for the production engineer, i.e. it tests the feasibility of the proposed course of action. In many instances companies become so involved with the development of a new product that by the time successful product tests have been completed they feel irrevocably committed, and any course of action other than full-scale marketing is unthinkable. However, companies of this type are usually aware of the critical importance of a well-designed and co-ordinated marketing plan, and so test its feasibility in practice prior to full-scale operations. Pilot marketing on a regional basis may also serve to give the firm valuable marketing experience while commissioning new plant to meet the anticipated demands of a national market.

The other practice often confused with test marketing is the testing of mix variables, i.e. measuring the effect of changes in the test variable, all other variables being held constant, e.g. copy testing. Such tests are often used to improve the marketing of existing products, and should not be confused with the true test market in which the collective impact of all variables is being tested simultaneously.

It is clear that if test market results are to be used to predict the likely outcome of a full-scale national launch, then the test market must constitute a representative sample of the national market. Despite the claims of various media owners it is equally clear that no such perfect microcosm exists and that test marketing is of dubious value if undertaken for predictive purposes alone. In addition to the dangers inherent in scaling up atypical test market results to derive national sales forecasts, many marketers feel that test marketing increases the risks of aggressive competitive reaction in an attempt to nip the new product in the bud. Test market validity depends heavily on the assumption that trading conditions in the market are 'normal', and it follows that any departure from such conditions will bias the results. Competitors learn quickly of test marketing operations and typically react in one of two ways. If the new product closely resembles existing brands, the manufacturers of these brands will usually step up their advertising and sales promotion in the test market to maintain existing brand loyalties and prevent the new entrant getting a foothold. These tactics also ensure the existence of 'abnormal' trading conditions during the test period. Alternatively, if the new product represents a radical departure from existing products, competitors can easily monitor its test market performance while developing their own substitutes. If the test results seem promising the imitative innovator may well enter the national market at the same time as the originator of the idea – if not before!

For these reasons many manufacturers now undertake more exhaustive tests of the mix variables and omit the test market stage altogether. If the new product is launched on a limited scale initially, more often than not it is in the nature of a feasibility study rather than in the hope of obtaining hard data from which to predict the outcome of a national launch.

Suggestions for further reading

Baker, Michael J., and McTavish, Ronald, *Product Policy and Management* (Macmillan, 1976).

Constandse, William J., 'How to Launch New Products', *M.S.U. Business Topics* (Winter 1971); Rothe, James T., 'The Product Elimination Decision', *M.S.U. Business Topics* (Autumn 1970); Horwood, William, 'Test Marketing on Trial', *Marketing* (July 1973); 'Test Marketing in the 1970s' (Southern Independent Television)

Kline, Charles H., 'The Strategy of Product Policy' *Harvard Business Review* (July/August 1965)

11 Packaging

Surprisingly few introductory marketing texts devote much attention to the role of packaging as an element in the marketing mix.
When one considers that total packaging industry sales amounted
to over £3,500 million in 1977, and have risen steadily since, it is
clear that packaging costs are a major marketing expenditure and
deserve fuller treatment.

The present lack of attention is partially attributable to the tendency to classify packaging as a production cost, so that it is seldom isolated in the way that expenditures on advertising and
promotion are. In part it is also attributable to the practical function which the pack performs, which tends to shield it from public
scrutiny of the type directed at promotional expenditures whose
practical virtues are less easily discernible. In reality packaging
costs often exceed all other marketing costs and, in some instances,
constitute the major element of total cost, e.g. cosmetics. These
facts were emphasised by a cost analysis of the items in a
'household food basket' with a retail value of £6, in which it was
found that advertising costs amounted to £0.125 while packaging
costs totalled £1.375. In the same vein the Chairman of Teachers
the whisky producers was quoted in the *Financial Times* in June
1973 as stating 'In spite of stringent control in purchasing
materials at the lowest possible cost consistent with quality, the
value of the packaging material in a standard case now exceeds
that of the whisky.'

Although more recent data are hard to come by, it is clear that
the trend for packaging to comprise an increasing proportion of
the total cost of convenience goods continues. In an article in
Retail and Distribution Management (Mar–Apr 1974) reference
was made to the rapidly increasing costs of packaging raw materials, together with the observation that 'We may soon reach the

situation where the plastic and cardboard wrapper around four tomatoes or half a dozen nails costs more than the goods involved.' In absolute terms it is quite clear that packaging costs have increased significantly in recent years, as can be seen from Table 11.1.

TABLE 11.1   *Manufacturers' sales of packaging products: summary (£000)*

	1974	1975	1976	1977
Paper and board	1,096,919	1,119,466	1,396,347	1,613,085
Plastic	349,087	341,558	504,665	623,163
Laminates	74,113	71,681	117,785	159,039
Metal	434,079	478,177	630,227	788,119
Glass	144,082	178,118	225,076	272,023
Wood, etc.	75,406	70,965	72,037	89,892*
Canvas	10,394	10,377	10,951	11,133
Total	2,184,080	2,270,342	2,957,088	3,556,454

*Excluding sales of baskets, etc., of natural fibre from third quarter 1977.
Sources: *Business Monitor* (1974–8)

BASIC PACKAGING FUNCTIONS

The basic function of any pack is to protect its contents in transit, in storage and in use. This criterion will play a major role in determining the shape, size and materials used, but in recent years there has been a tendency to subordinate such practical aspects to design and promotional considerations. In most cases there will be little or no conflict between the physical characteristics considered desirable by manufacturers and distributors and the promotional and design elements demanded by consumers. However, it will be useful to consider the requirements of these two groups separately to emphasise the varying nature of their needs.

DISTRIBUTOR REQUIREMENTS

As noted, the prime function of any pack is to protect the contents. From this it follows that pack design will depend very largely on the nature of the contents in terms of their value, physical composition and durability. In addition one must also take into account the length of the distribution channel, the amount of handling which the container will receive, and variations in climatic conditions which may be encountered between the point of manufacture and sale.

Most small items are bulk-packed in some type of outer container capable of withstanding the anticipated degree of rough handling. However, such containers can only reduce the shock of mishandling, so that the individual packs must also be capable of resisting such punishment. An example of the degree of protection necessary is provided by the findings of the Printing, Packaging and Allied Trades Research Association that containers which one man is just capable of handling are likely to be dropped from a height of three feet somewhere in transit. This distance corresponds to waist height, or the level of a lorry tailboard, and requires that containers should be able to withstand an equivalent shock. It was also found that heavier packages tended to receive more careful handling as two men were needed to lift them, or else mechanical handling methods were used e.g. fork-lift trucks. Such methods are widely used now, and it is in the packer's interest to determine the capacity of such equipment and take it into account in establishing bulk pack size and weight. Modifications to containers to satisfy mechanical handling requirements may well increase their intrinsic cost, but such costs are invariably more than recouped through a reduction in the amount of handling required.

Breakage in transit due to rough handling is only one aspect of protection, and equal attention must be given to spoilage from other causes. Foremost among these are moisture, fungus, insects and exposure to sunlight.

Transportation and storage costs are usually computed on the basis of weight and/or volume, and it is clearly in the manufacturer's interest to use packages which make maximum use of a given space. At the retail level the space/volume factor takes on added importance, as it directly affects the number of different items which can be put on display. Sales per square foot, or per linear foot of shelf, are frequently used measures of retail productivity, and it is clear that retailers will avoid packs which occupy a disproportionate amount of space in relation to their value. However, the retailer, like the manufacturer, recognises that purely physical properties must be modified in the light of consumer preferences, and so may be prepared to subordinate these in favour of packs with greater promotional appeal.

CONSUMER REQUIREMENTS

Reference has already been made to the fact that the packaging of consumer goods was originally a retailing function but that competitive pressures, and the growth of branding, resulted in the manufacturer assuming responsibility for it. Through the adoption of a distinctive pack and brand name, the manufacturer is able to differentiate his product at the point of sale and to develop advertising and promotional strategies designed to create consumer preference for his output. Further, by packaging the product himself the manufacturer is able to exercise much greater control over the condition in which the ultimate consumer will receive it, and so avoid dissatisfaction arising from poor storage and packing at the retail level.

Essentially, consumers want products, and have little direct interest in their packaging *per se*. In many instances, however, the satisfaction to be derived from a product is dependent upon its packaging, and consumers are receptive to both technical and aesthetic improvements in pack design. Many competing products are incapable of differentiation on the basis of objective criteria, and in these instances packaging and promotion often constitute the sole distinguishing features upon which the product's success or failure depends.

A clear example of this is the United Kingdom sardine market. Some years ago a number of fish packers in Britain offered a variety of brands of sardines in competition with Scandinavian and Portuguese imports. Although sardines tend to be associated with the latter countries, the domestic product was competitively priced and secured a strong following among those who could perceive no difference in product quality – real or imagined. As a group, however, sardine eaters became increasingly frustrated by the difficulties associated with opening the conventional pack, as the tag frequently broke when the key was turned, facing them with the almost impossible task of opening the tin with an ordinary tin-opener. In part the trouble was due to the fact that few people used the key correctly, but it was also due to the lock-seamed construction of the can which required that the tag be sufficiently strong to tear open a double thickness of material at the seam. The Scandinavians overcame this problem by adopting aluminium lids, while the Portuguese soldered the lid to the body, leaving a line of weakness which opened easily. Neither course was open to the British packers – aluminium is much more expensive than in Scandinavia, and high labour costs precluded following the Portuguese practice. Consumers responded enthusiastically to the new pack and the domestic share of market sagged dismally owing to the inability of the United Kingdom packers to duplicate the improved container at a competitive price. Ease of opening is clearly a significant consumer 'plus'.

Conventional demand curves indicate that as price falls the volume demanded will increase. In theory this relationship is continuous and we can establish the volume which will be demanded at any given 'price'. In practice prices are discrete and should properly be represented by a 'stepped' demand curve. However, theory suggests that if the manufacturer can offer his product at a lower price he will be able to increase demand, and this is frequently achieved by offering the consumer a variety of different sizes. In addition to catering for variations in household size and usage rates, a range of pack sizes enables the manufacturer to reach consumers with limited purchasing power. As the retired population expands less perceptive marketers will increasingly come to appreciate that lifelong consumption patterns may well have to be modified as inflation reduces the purchasing power of fixed retirement incomes. It would be naïve to expect manufacturers to offer small packs at a price proportionate to the 'standard' size in view of the high proportion of fixed costs incurred irrespective of unit size. None the less, the provision of non-standard pack sizes is not only good marketing, it is a socially desirable activity.

Many products are not consumed immediately the package is opened but are used over varying periods of time. To prevent spoilage such products must be packed in resealable containers, the most familiar of which are the screw-top bottle and jar, and the lever-lid can. Screw-top jars have long been in use for the packaging of products containing sugar, such as jam, which are susceptible to mould when exposed to the atmosphere. However, cheap metal screw caps have only recently come into their own as bottle closures as an alternative to the crown cork. The latter suffers from the disadvantage that it is difficult to remove without an opener and cannot be reused unless fitted with a plastic insert, which greatly reduces it cost advantage as a closure. Lever-lid cans are widely used for packaging hygroscopic materials such as dried milk, instant coffee, cocoa and health salts, but are losing ground to plastics for certain applications. Although ease of opening and reclosure are desirable, many mothers want a pack to be stable and 'child-proof', to prevent accidents to young children, and will show a preference for packs with the latter attributes.

Visual appeal is also an important aspect of pack design, particularly in the case of products of a luxury or semi-luxury nature where the pack itself may add to the image of product quality which the manufacturer is seeking to create. Some critics have argued that elaborate and expensive packaging is used to disguise inferior products, or to permit the seller to inflate the true worth of the product. Neither claim will sustain much examination, for poor packaging is almost always a good indicator of a poor product, and no amount of packaging can disguise a poor product for long. Similarly, few consumers are prepared to pay more for a product solely on account of its packaging unless such packaging will add to their enjoyment of the product itself – After Eight Mints are a classic example, and it is irrelevant if the added satisfaction is purely subjective to the consumer and incapable of objective measurement.

Finally, consumers demand packages which satisfy their information needs. Certain information is required by law, e.g. statement of weight and composition of product, although frequently the latter is expressed in language incomprehensible to the average consumer. In addition to this basic information, consumers favour a clearly marked price (now largely a retailer responsibility since the abolition of Resale Price Maintenance), information on how the product should or may be used, and, preferably, some view of the contents themselves.

THE RESOLUTION OF CONFLICT BETWEEN DISTRIBUTOR/
USER REQUIREMENTS

Such conflict as does exist between user and distributor requirements is almost invariably resolved in favour of the user. Diseconomies in weight/volume relationships due to the use of odd-shaped containers, and losses due to breakages can often be minimised through the use of standardised outer containers. However, the manufacturer can only afford to incur such additional costs if the consumer is prepared to pay a premium for the added benefits received.

Similarly, retailers are more concerned with turnover and gross margins than with the actual number of units on display. If it can be shown that although a promotional pack may occupy twice the space of a conventional container, it will generate increased demand or help build store traffic, then the retailer will usually co-operate in the promotion, e.g. Pyrex coffee jugs filled with instant coffee.

However, manufacturers are not unresponsive to retailer demands and many new packs have been developed as a result of pressure from the big food chains, especially those employing self-service. Self-service has largely replaced counter service owing to the lower operating costs possible through the elimination of sales assistants. This in turn has stimulated manufacturers to develop new packaging materials to help the product sell itself and lead to the elimination of many traditional practices.

In the former category may be included plastic bottles, first introduced in 1964 by I.C.I., aluminium foil, bubble-packs, and shrink-wrapping for prepackaged meats, etc. In the latter category the one-trip bottle was developed to encourage supermarkets to carry carbonated beverages, which they had virtually dropped owing to the diseconomies associated with returning deposits and handling empty bottles. Innovation has not been confined to the development of new materials alone, and many improvements have been made in the use of traditional materials. Lightweight tinplate has reduced both the cost and weight of cans and closures, while increased strength has permitted the development of the aerosol, sales of which now amount to hundreds of millions every year. The difficulties described earlier in connection with sardine cans have now been overcome with the development of the Ziehfix can in which the lid is attached to the body by a rubber sealing ring and is easily stripped off. (It is doubtful if this innovation would have saved the sardine packer, for such cans cost more to manufacture than a conventional can. For a distinctive product such as John West's kipper fillets the added cost would appear to justify the convenience, however.) Similarly, the strip-top beer can has combined the advantages of two competing materials – aluminium and tinplate.

THE PACKAGE AS A MARKETING VARIABLE: A CASE HISTORY

In recent years a number of articles have appeared describing how manufacturers have used packaging as a competitive weapon in their marketing strategy. The one-trip bottle was adopted by Schweppes in an attempt to recapture the market share lost to Beechams, who had capitalised on the supermarkets' unwillingness to handle returnable bottles by introducing the Hunt range of 'mixers' in cans. After Eight Mints' luxury image was born out of careful pack design backed up by an effective advertising campaign. Van den Bergh commissioned Rockwell glass to design a streamlined, lightweight bottle for their Tree Top line of fruit squashes to give it added appeal at the point of sale. One of the classic cases is provided by Gerber's entry into the United Kingdom babyfood market, which was the subject of an article in the *Financial Times* by Patrick Coldstream (25 November 1965, 'Building a Market Round a Glass Jar').

In 1964 Heinz dominated the United Kingdom market for preserved babyfoods with a 95 per cent share of total sales. At this time Gerber, the brand leader in the United States, was looking around for new markets and decided that Britain offered considerable potential for development as per capita consumption was only half that achieved in the United States. Gerber realised that if it was to successfully enter the market it needed an established distributive network and so linked up with Corn Products so that it could make use of the sales force of the latter's wholly owned subsidiary, Brown & Polson.

Although this move assured Gerber of wide distribution it was clear that they needed some distinctive or unique selling point (U.S.P.) if they were to break Heinz's stranglehold on the market. Motivation research indicated that mothers were mainly concerned with hygiene and purity when evaluating babyfoods, and that they associated these attributes with glass containers. A glass container would certainly differentiate Gerber from Heinz, for the latter's products were packed exclusively in cans. On the other hand packing in glass would increase unit cost by 20 per cent over the price of an equivalent sized can.

Despite the additional cost of glass, Gerber decided to pack in jars and stress hygiene and purity in their promotional campaign, although this meant asking a higher price than for an equivalent Heinz product. Despite the higher price, the unit margin was less than that for Heinz, and made it clear that Gerber could not 'buy' distribution by offering incentives to retailers. In the event Gerber adopted an aggressive approach and stipulated that retailers must take a minimum of one case of each variety, or none at all. Some of the larger outlets baulked at the idea of adopting a new product line of forty different items and reached a compromise with Gerber. However, the majority of retailers must have felt that the new line offered considerable potential for they acceded to these terms.

Within a year of entering the market Gerber had justified both its own and the retailers' belief in the product's potential by securing a 15 per cent market share. As predicted, housewives perceived the glass jar as a symbol of purity and Heinz were forced to respond by introducing a selection of their more popular items in glass containers. Clearly, in this market there was nothing to be gained by emphasising that the Heinz product in a can was cheaper owing to the tendency to use price as an indicator of quality, i.e. to associate higher price with a better quality product.

A report in the October 1972 issue of Retail Business shows that Gerber's initial success was rapidly eroded and their market share fell to just under 7 per cent in 1968 and 1969. However in 1970 Heinz's market share had been reduced to just under 82 per cent due to competition from other new entrants into the market, which undoubtedly helped Gerber to increase its share of market to 8.5 per cent. By 1971 Heinz's market share had fallen still further to 79 per cent while Gerber's had increased to 11.7 per cent. In 1972 Gerber recorded still further increases and it was estimated that their share had increased to 13 per cent. It is interesting to note that part of this increase was attributed to adverse publicity on the use of cans for baby food in which it was claimed that canned foods contained twice as much lead as the average national diet. Clearly Gerber's use of the packaging variable has enabled them to break into a monopolistic market and forced Heinz to up-date their own packaging and adopt a more competitive posture.

At the time of writing the most recent information available is for 1975 when Heinz's market share had been reduced to 75 per cent and Gerber had climbed to 18 per cent. Cow & Gate (Unigate) accounted for the remaining 7 per cent of the strained and junior-foods market, with a company spokesman reported as saying 'Glass jars are used as they are considered by this company to have the selling edge on cans.'

However, the battle between cans and jars continues. It is claimed that jars also have disadvantages: exposure to light causes the vitamin content to diminish; it is often difficult to lever off the lid (Gerber introduced twist-off caps to counter this claim); fragments of glass can get into the jar on the production line (new manufacturing techniques have been developed to make sure this cannot happen); but, despite these claims, plus cost and weight disadvantages, the appeal of glass remains strong.

FUTURE TRENDS

In the future we may anticipate greater use of the pack as a competitive weapon. In terms of cost the cheapest form of packaging is the 'bag in a box', e.g. Kellogg's Cornflakes; next comes the tinplate container, followed, in ascending order, by aluminium, glass, polythene and P.V.C. Despite their higher cost, increased use is being made of the latter materials because of the added convenience and improved performance which they offer consumers, for which they are clearly prepared to pay. At the same time, manufacturers of 'traditional' materials are responding to the threat by continually upgrading their product and through the introduction of improved fabricating techniques, e.g. Metal Box has more than doubled the speed of its production lines by the simple expedient of forming a cylinder equivalent to the size of two cans and then cutting it in half.

In addition to new and improved materials, and the development of new containers like the aerosol can and plastic bottle, we may also anticipate a continued increase in the range of products available in packaged form. This trend will be emphasised as more and more women return to work once their children are of school age, which will stimulate the demand for convenience products as well as generating the purchasing power to cover their increased cost. Concurrently we may anticipate further strides in food processing technology similar to that achieved by the A.F.D. process.

A third trend which has assumed increasing importance in the 1970s has been concern over waste resulting from the enormous expansion in the use of packaging materials. In 1973 this concern was underlined by a general shortage of packaging materials throughout the United Kingdom. In part this situation was blamed upon above average consumption of canned and bottled beverages due to a prolonged period of fine summer weather. On balance, however, it is believed to reflect an overall increase in the consumption of packaging by consumers. At the same time it is clear that all consumers do not welcome the prodigal waste of resources associated with much of today's non-returnable packaging. This concern is to be seen in the pressure for returnable containers or else the use of materials which may be reused through recycling.

Taken together, these trends predicate that packaging will play an increasingly important role in the marketing mix. At the same time they also suggest that the marketer must be sensitive to the increasing concern for the quality of the environment and the need for conservation of scarce resources when making packaging decisions.

12 Pricing and Price Policy

Given the central role played by price in economic theory one might expect a similar emphasis in marketing. In fact price policy tends to be relegated to a secondary role and much more attention is devoted to other dimensions of competitive strategy, as is borne out by the findings of Udell and Pass reproduced as Table 12.1 overleaf.

Among the possible explanations of the low rating accorded pricing may be included:

1. Perfect competition prevails. Under these circumstances the firm cannot have a 'price policy', it must accept the market price.
2. Under conditions of imperfect competition there is a tendency towards 'rigid prices', and for competition to be concentrated on non-price elements such as product differentiation, advertising, service, etc. Thus competitors prefer to avoid direct price competition, which could lead to a price war, and adopt the price level of the industry leader.
3. The construction of a demand schedule is considered impossible owing to the enormous number of interacting variables which condition consumer preference. Even if it were possible to quantify demand at various price levels the value of the information would not justify its cost, thus a trial and error approach, or acceptance of the 'going rate', is to be preferred.
4. Marketers lack an adequate understanding of the theoretical concepts and so avoid the complexities involved in developing a 'scientific' price policy.

TABLE 12.1. *Policy areas selected by industrial producers as vital to successful operation.* (After Udell and Pass.)

	Udell		Pass		
Policy areas	Percentage of 68 firms selecting the policy area	Policy areas	Percentage of 40 firms selecting the policy area	No of firms selecting the policy area as being of primary importance
Product		**Product**		
Product research and development	79	Product research and development	85	20
Product service	79	Product service	80	4
Average product-selection ratio	79	Product quality	75	5
		Average product-selection ratio	80	–
Sales efforts		*Sales efforts*		
Sales research and sales planning	63	Market research and sales planning	62	6
Advertising and sales promotion	37	Advertising and sales promotion	62	–
Management of sales personnel	49	Management of sales personnel	35	–
Average sales-effort selection ratio	50	Average sales efforts selection ratio	41	–
Pricing	47	*Pricing*	35	2
Other areas		*Other areas*		
Organisational structure	50	Organisational structure	28	2
Distribution channels and their control	34	Distribution channels and channel management	20	1
Financing and credit	18	Financing and credit	8	–
Marketing cost budgeting and control	12	Marketing cost budgeting and control	10	–
Transportation and storage	9	Physical distribution management	40	–
Public relations	7	Public relations	5	–

Source: Roy W. Hill: *Marketing technological products to industry* (Pergamon Press, 1973).

The prevalence of rigid prices has led to much adverse comment in recent years, and is frequently quoted as evidence of a lack of competition in a given market. It is felt that this contention ignores the intense competition generated by non-price elements, but none the less it does highlight the lack of attention given to creative pricing policy. The pricing decision cannot be made in a vacuum, however, and it is important to take both internal and external variables into account in order to formulate a policy consistent with the firm's overall objectives.

EXTERNAL PRICE DETERMINANTS

A major determinant of price policy is the structure of the market in which the firm is selling its output. Many authors tend to confuse industry structure with market structure, and limit their attention to the size and number of firms engaged in creating perfect substitutes. Thus it is common to find references to monopolistic and oligopolistic industries when the total output of a given product is concentrated in the hands of one, or a few, firms. Although it is acknowledged that the true monopolist is a price-maker, and that oligopolistic industries frequently exhibit price rigidity owing to the price leadership of a dominant firm, it is felt that the industry view oversimplifies the true situation.

Conventionally, the industry approach would distinguish the manufacture of aluminium, steel, glass, paper and plastics on the basis that their output possesses different physical properties and is the result of distinctive production processes. Each would be classified as a separate industry, yet all compete with one another for the packaging market. This suggests that one must take into account not only the prices of perfect substitutes but also the prices of all goods which compete for the same market and can be used to satisfy the same basic wants. Certainly no self-respecting buyer is going to confine his attention to a single material when several acceptable alternatives are available, and the technique of value analysis has been developed largely to permit comparative cost analysis of competing substitutes.

If the above arguments are accepted, then it follows that the firm must look beyond the narrowly defined industry of which it considers itself a member, and should evaluate the price structure of its end market and the policies of all firms/industries operating in that market. (In the language of the economist, one must analyse the cross-elasticity of demand.)

The second major external price determinant is best summarised by the economist's concept of elasticity. Essentially elasticity measures the responsiveness of demand to changes in price, i.e. it is a measure of price sensitivity. Thus if a 1 per cent change in price results in a change in the amount demanded of more than 1 per cent demand is said to be elastic, if less than 1 per cent then demand is inelastic, and a directly proportionate change indicates unitary elasticity. Elasticity of demand is conditioned by the importance of the product in the consumer's scale of preferences, by the disposable income of existing and potential consumers, by the existence of substitutes and a number of other, lesser factors. As a summary measure it is of great value in determining the firm's basic attitude to price – if demand is elastic pricing will be a major policy area, if inelastic it will be of secondary consequence.

Thirdly, the firm's pricing policy will be influenced by government policy as expressed in the extant and proposed legislation in such areas as price maintenance, monopolistic practices, minimum performance standards for products, etc., e.g. the introduction of cut-price detergents by Procter & Gamble and Lever Brothers following the Monopolies Commission recommendation to this effect.

INTERNAL PRICE DETERMINANTS

The major factor conditioning the firm's price policy is its own definition of the business it is in, for this will determine the products it will produce and the nature of the markets it will seek to exploit. The product mix identifies the firm with an industry, while its market specifies the firms, industries and products with which it will compete, and the dimensions along which it will compete.

Traditionally, the firm's success has been measured by its profitability, which is simply a measure of the amount by which income exceeds expenditures. If, as implied earlier, the majority of firms accept the going market price, it is evident that profits will depend very largely on the firm's ability to minimise expenditures or costs. To this end considerable effort has been devoted to the development of sophisticated cost measurement and control systems, and management is often happier to immerse itself in the tangible realities of such systems than grapple with the complexities of price determination. Further, both shareholders and the Government require the firm to account for the way in which it spends its income, and so emphasise the need for detailed cost analyses and statements. As will be seen below, such data are widely used in the formulation of prices.

The third internal constraint on the firm's price policy is the nature and extent of its corporate resources, which were discussed in Chapter 5 and will not be reiterated here.

It follows from the brief outline above that the price-setter's discretion is circumscribed by a number of factors, admirably summarised by Joel Dean as:

1. The number, relative sizes and product lines of competitors who sell products to do the same job.
2. The likelihood of potential competition.
3. The stage of consumer acceptance of the product.
4. The degree of potential market segmentation and price discrimination.
5. The degree of physical difference between the seller's product and those of other companies.
6. The opportunities for variation in the product–service bundle.
7. The richness of the mixture of service and reputation in the product bundle.

(Joel Dean, *Managerial Economics* (Prentice-Hall, New York, 1951) p. 402.)

PRICING OBJECTIVES

In an article entitled 'How to Price for Maximum Profits' (*Management Methods* (November 1958)), Jules E. Anderson quotes a survey by the National Industrial Conference Board which revealed that only 4 out of 155 leading U.S. manufacturers used a clear-cut, written procedure in setting prices. Although dated, these findings tend to confirm a widely held belief that most firms lack clearly defined, explicit pricing objectives and formalised pricing procedures. It is the author's opinion that this belief is erroneous, and based upon faulty data derived from poorly designed surveys. This opinion tends to be supported by the findings of more sophisticated researchers, in particular those of Robert Lanzillotti ('Pricing Objectives in Large Companies', *American Economic Review*, XLVIII (Dec 1958) 921–40) and W. Warren Haynes (*Pricing Decisions in Small Business*: University of Kentucky Press, Lexington, 1962) both of whom have undertaken extensive field research into the firm's pricing objectives.

Lanzillotti's findings were: 'The most typical pricing objectives cited were: (1) pricing to achieve a target return on investment; (2) stabilisation of price and margin; (3) pricing to realise a target market share; and (4) pricing to meet or prevent competition.' The main conclusions drawn from this study are considered sufficiently significant to be quoted verbatim, namely:

> The general hypothesis which emerges is that (*a*) the large company has a fairly well-defined pricing goal that is related to a long-range profit horizon; (*b*) its management seeks – especially in multiproduct multimarket operations – a simultaneous decision with respect to price, cost, and product characteristics; and (*c*) its pricing formulas are handy devices for checking the internal consistency of the separate decisions as against the general company objective. Under this hypothesis no single theory of the firm – and certainly no single motivational hypothesis such as profit maximisation – is likely to impose an unambiguous course of action for the firm for any given situation; nor will it provide a satisfactory basis for valid and useful predictions of price behaviour (pp. 938–9).

2. It seems reasonable to conclude that the pricing policies are in almost every case equivalent to a company policy that represents an order of priorities and choice among competing objectives rather than policies tested by any simple concept of profit maximisation (p. 939).

3. Another relevant aspect of the data for theoretical analysis is the conception of the market held by managements of large corporations. Individual products, markets, and pricing are not considered in isolation; the unit of decision-making is the enterprise, and pricing and marketing strategies are viewed in this global context. Because of the tremendously complex joint-cost problems and lack of knowledge of actual relationships between cost and output or sales, on the one hand, and the joint-revenue aspects of multiproduct companies, on the other, pricing is frequently done for product groups with an eye to the over-all profit position of the company. This means that costing of products ends up as a result of price policy rather than the reverse. In view of the various external pressures on the company and the nature of the strategy of the enterprise, it is doubtful if price would have any closer relationship to actual costs were detailed

cost data available to management. The incentive to realise target rates of profit for the long haul better suits the objectives of management-controlled companies than any desire to profiteer or seek windfall profits (p. 940).

From these conclusions it is clear that firms do establish pricing objectives, even though they may not be stated explicitly. Frequently such objectives are implicit in the company's overall objective, in other cases they may take the form of a generalised statement such as:

'All prices must cover fully allocated costs.'
'Prices will not exceed those asked by immediate competitors.'
'Prices will be set which will discourage the entry of new firms into the market.'
'All prices must yield a return of investment not less than X per cent.'

PRICING 'FORMULAS'

Even though the firm may not have committed itself to a formal statement of price policy, in practice its pricing behaviour is usually sufficiently consistent to permit identification and classification. Observation indicates that there are a limited number of pricing formulas, or methods, in general use, and these may be classified as:

Full-cost or cost-plus pricing. In simple terms, all this involves is the addition of a predetermined margin to the full unit cost of production and distribution, without reference to prevailing demand conditions. In practice, it is doubtful if the firm can establish its true unit cost in advance, owing to uncertainty as to the volume it can make/sell. Broadly speaking, all costs may be classified as fixed or variable. Fixed costs are incurred irrespective of the volume of output and are the result of management policy, e.g. the depreciation of fixed assets, the level of selling, general and administrative overheads, while variable costs fluctuate more or less directly with the volume of output, e.g. raw material and labour costs. In that unit cost is computed by dividing total cost by output in units, it is clear that this can only be established when the two quantities are known. The price-setter may forecast sales volume and compute unit cost on the basis of this estimate, adding the predetermined margin in order to arrive at a price. It would be purely fortuitous if demand at this price were to coincide exactly with the available supply, with the result that the seller will either be left with unsold units or else will sell his total output at a lesser profit than could have been obtained. Further, as Lanzillotti implies, the allocation of fixed costs to given products tends to be arbitrary, so that the unit cost used as the basis for a price may bear no relation to true cost at all.

Although cost plus a fixed margin may be a valid method to adopt when deciding whether to enter a new market, most sellers would be prepared to vary this price in the light of potential consumer reaction to it, implicit in current market prices. If this is so, then the price-setter's decision rule is rather different from that generally associated with full-cost pricing – cost plus a predetermined margin is not *the* price, it is a minimum acceptable price and the actual price adopted may be any amount greater than this. This being so, it is erroneous to contend that prices based on cost take no account of consumer demand.

Break-even analysis. Break-even analysis utilises the concepts of fixed and variable costs, and enables the price-setter to investigate the implications of any number of price–volume alternatives.

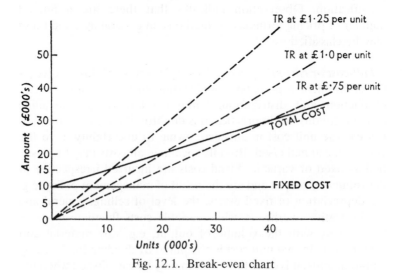

Fig. 12.1. Break-even chart

The first step in a break-even analysis is to compute the firm's total cost curve by adding the variable costs incurred at different levels of output to the fixed costs, e.g. if fixed costs (FC) = £10,000, and unit variable cost (VC) = £0.25, then total cost (TC) = £10,000 + 0.25x where x = the number of units produced. The next step is to compute total revenue (TR) curves for the range of prices under consideration and plot these graphically as shown in Fig. 12.1.

Clearly the 'break-even' point for a given price lies at the intersection of the total revenue curve for that price and the total cost curve, e.g. with a price of £0.75 the firm will break even at a sales volume of 40,000 units. On its own, this information is of little value to the price-setter, unless he has some feeling for the likely volume of demand over the range of prices for which he has calculated break-even points. In reality, the price-setter will usually have at least a preliminary analysis of the potential market for the product, from which he may derive a hypothetical demand curve as shown in Fig. 12.2.

By reference to the demand curve it can be seen that at a price of £0.75, 36,250 units will be demanded and the firm would incur a loss. Closer inspection would seem to indicate that the best price is £1.05, at which 20,000 units will be sold.

Marginal costing/contribution analysis. Break-even analysis

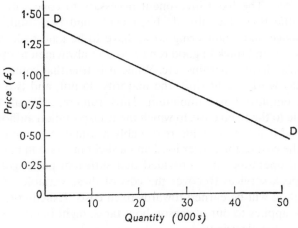

Fig. 12.2. Hypothetical demand curve

allocates fixed costs to a product at a predetermined rate in such a way that, collectively, the firm's products will absorb the firm's total fixed costs. Many price theorists contend that this conventional accounting approach can lead to incorrect decisions, and advocate the adoption of techniques based on marginal analysis as developed by economists.

In essence the marginal approach states that one should ignore fixed costs and concentrate on the relationship between variable cost and revenue, usually termed the 'contribution'. For example, if the variable cost of producing a unit is £0.25 and this unit may be sold for £0.50, then the contribution is +£0.25. It is understood that contribution means 'contribution to fixed costs, variable marketing costs, and profits', and the firm's objective in setting price should be to maximise the total contribution. If average unit cost is used as a criterion, then it is likely that the firm will reject any price less than average cost, and so forego the contribution which sale at such a price would generate. A simplified example will help clarify this point.

During the day many trains in the London area carry only a few passengers, and it seems clear that the revenues earned must be less than the average cost of running a train. Ignoring the social responsibilities of a public transportation authority, such a practice seems economically suicidal. However, marginal analysis reveals that elimination of these services would lead to lower profits (bigger losses!), in that the incremental cost incurred in running a train is negligible. The fixed investment necessary to cope with rush-hour traffic flows has already been made and is a 'sunk' cost; maintenance and engineering crews have to be paid to keep the rolling stock and track in good repair, as do railwaymen to operate the signals, drive the trains, etc. While it is true that some of the latter may work a split shift, the majority do not, and two shifts must be employed as a minimum. Thus, running off-peak trains adds little to the fixed costs to which the transportation authority is committed if it is to provide reasonably adequate commuter services – the cost of the power used and a slight increase in maintenance and operating cost. Provided that sufficient passengers use the off-peak services to cover the cost of these variables, then a contribution will be earned towards fixed costs. Exactly the same principle applies to out-of-season boat fares, night flights and off-peak rates for electricity.

Many managers find it difficult to ignore fixed costs and so make incorrect decisions. The argument that a firm has spent £x million in developing a product, and so must continue with its production and sale in the face of unfavourable user reactions, is a classic example. The best advice in such a situation might well be 'Don't throw good money after bad.'

Contribution analysis does not simplify the problems inherent in forecasting demand and costs, but it does ensure that management does not reject projects which would improve the firm's overall profitability solely because they are not self-supporting on an average cost basis.

Other techniques. The pricing formulas described above are the best known, and most extensively used, techniques at the present time. As a basis for 'scientific' decision-making, they are beset with faults and difficulties, and a number of new techniques have been evolved in recent years in an attempt to remedy these defects. It is impossible to do justice to these in an introductory text and the student should refer to the following sources for detailed coverage: Robert D. Buzzell, *Mathematical Models and Marketing Management* (Graduate School of Business Administration, Harvard University, Boston, 1964); Ronald E. Frank, Alfred E. Kuehn and William F. Massey, *Quantitative Techniques in Marketing Analysis* (Irwin, Homewood, Ill., 1962); Paul E. Green, 'Bayesian Decision Theory in Pricing Strategy', *Journal of Marketing*, XXVII i (Jan 1963) 5–14; Alfred Oxenfeldt, David Miller, Abraham Shuchman and Charles Winick, *Insights into Pricing* (Wadsworth, Belmont, California, 1961).

Some insight into the current practice of British companies is to be found in the B.I.M. survey *Marketing Organisation in British Industry* (Information Summary 148). Respondents were asked the question 'On what basis do you generally fix your prices?' and were offered four alternatives

'Cost plus'
'Cost plus' modified by market conditions
Market conditions
Any other (please specify)

From the 553 usable replies the following picture emerged.

Basis	*Per cent*
Cost plus modified by market conditions	59
Market conditions	26

| Cost plus | 10 |
| Others | 3 |

PRICING STRATEGIES

So far, attention has been focused on quantitative aspects of price determination and little consideration given to the qualitative factors which shape the final pricing decision. Given the difficulties involved in constructing a demand schedule, pricing formulas can only give a broad indication of the range within which the desired sales volume might be achieved. Hence, the final price decision must depend upon a judgemental assessment of the impact of a given price strategy. In broad terms there are two alternatives open to the marketer – a high price approach aimed at 'skimming the cream' off the market, and a low price strategy aimed at pre-empting a significant share of the total market.

High price strategies are appropriate to mature or saturated markets, which show a degree of segmentation on the basis of quality, design features, etc., or to the introduction of a product which differs significantly from anything currently available. In the case of existing markets, consumers in the higher income groups are often prepared to pay a premium for products which are differentiated from those appealing to the mass market, e.g. a Rolls-Royce or Rover 3500 compared with a British Leyland Marina or a Ford Cortina. Owing to the limited demand at the higher prices, a small, high-quality producer can maintain a profitable level of sales without building up a sufficiently large market share to attract the competition of firms catering to the mass market. This does not mean that the latter type of firm will not diversify into the high price segment to make fuller use of its resources, but the established reputation of the quality producer will provide a high degree of protection against such competition.

Skimming the market is also attractive to the firm with a new and unique product. As noted earlier, new product development invariably represents a considerable investment on the part of the innovator, and a high initial price offers the opportunity to limit the costs of launching the product into the market while earning monopoly profits. A good example of such a strategy is the launching of the Polaroid Land camera, which was originally put on the market at a price of around £100, with very limited distribution and promotion. The novelty of a camera which could produce a finished print within a matter of seconds attracted a lot of free publicity, as well as being something of a status symbol because of its price. As demand at the initial high price was exhausted, Polaroid lowered prices and 'slid down the demand curve', with the result that a basic camera is now available at around £10. It is interesting to note that in the United States, where the camera was developed and first put on sale, a rather different strategy was adopted and the camera offered originally at a relatively low price. The reasoning in this instance was that the purchase of a camera tends to be once and for all, whereas there is a continuing market for film, thus the more cameras that were sold the greater would be the demand for film. As the film was unique, and protected by patents, competition from other manufacturers such as Eastman–Kodak was precluded and offered greater long-run profitability, provided sufficient cameras could be sold.

When adopting a skimming strategy, with the intention of subsequently reducing price to appeal to a wider market, it is important not to create ill will by reducing price too quickly. This danger may be reduced by differentiating the appearance of the product and offering it as a 'stripped-down', or economy model. The use of this strategy is to be seen in the marketing of both desk and pocket electronic calculators and may be anticipated very shortly in the market for colour television sets.

A low price policy recommends itself in a number of circumstances pre-eminent among which is entering a market with a high price-elasticity of demand. The newcomer will have to achieve a certain level of sales in order to break even, and in the short run may only be able to wrest sales from existing products through the medium of an attractive discount on current prices. Penetration pricing, as this strategy is sometimes termed, usually involves the firm in accepting a loss initially, while achieving sampling of the product and the development of brand loyalty. As suggested earlier, however, few firms are willing to buy market share openly for fear of setting off a price war, and a penetration policy is usually disguised as some form of sales promotion, e.g. price-off labels, coupons, etc. Where the firm possesses a cost advantage it has little to fear from a low price strategy, but it is rare that a new entrant into a market can undercut the existing brand leaders owing to the economies of scale open to them. In fact, contrary to popular belief, oligopolists often practise a low price policy to discourage the entry of new competitors into the market.

In 1954 E. R. Hawkins elaborated on these two basic strategies when he listed the pricing policies described by 'marketing specialists' (Edward R. Hawkins, 'Price Policies and Theories', *Journal of Marketing*, XVIII (Jan 1954) 233–40). These policies may be summarised as:

1. *Odd pricing* – i.e. the adoption of prices ending in odd numbers. This policy is notably prevalent in food retailing, and is also used extensively on low ticket items in general. The adoption of such prices implies the existence of a stepped or discontinuous demand curve, i.e. avoidance of intermediate prices ending in round numbers suggests that the price-setter believes that demand is totally inelastic at that price, e.g. reducing an item from 1s 11d to 1s 10d in pre-decimal currency would not increase demand so price was reduced to 1s 9d. The logic of this is doubted by the author.

2. *Psychological pricing*. This differs from odd pricing in that the price need not be an odd number but merely one that has an apparent psychological significance for the buyer, e.g. 19s 6d instead of £1, or a price in guineas in pre-decimal currency.

3. *Customary prices*. Such prices are fixed by custom, e.g. the old 6d bar of chocolate. Like the first two strategies the adoption of such prices assumes a kink in the demand curve. (Between them, decimalisation, the abolition of resale price maintenance and inflation seem to have seen the demise of customary prices for products like shoes and confectionery where they were formerly commonplace. However, 'psychological' prices still prevail, and 99p seems to have assumed a particular significance in this context.)

4. *Pricing at the market/meeting the competition*. This strategy presumes a marked inelasticity of demand below the current market price, such that a price reduction would not be justified by increased sales revenues. This approach is frequently adopted to avoid price wars.

5. *Prestige pricing*. This strategy implies a skimming approach in which the seller gives prestige to his product by asking a price well in excess of those asked for near perfect substitutes, e.g. Estee Lauder cosmetics, After Eight Mints.

6. *Price lining.* This policy of adopting specific prices for certain types of merchandise is common among retailers and is closely related to both psychological and customary prices, e.g. women's dresses, nylon stockings.
7. *Geographic pricing.* This policy is sometimes used where the marketer serves a number of distinct regional markets and can adopt different prices in each without creating consumer or distributor ill will. Petrol is priced in this way, depending on the distance of the garage from the nearest bulk terminal.
8. *Dual pricing strategy.* The marketer sells the same product at two or more different prices. Within the same market it is necessary to use different brands, but in distinct regional markets it may be possible to justify price differentials on the grounds of varying distribution costs, cf. petrol.

In the introduction to this chapter it was noted that pricing tends to be relegated to a secondary role in the formulation of competitive strategies. To a large degree this is due to the fact that price is highly visible and readily understood by consumers and competitors alike, whereas other elements of the marketing mix are less capable of direct and objective assessment. It is hoped, however, that the material in this chapter will sensitise the student to the large number of alternatives open to the marketer, and encourage a more creative and open-minded approach to pricing than has been characteristic of marketing practice in the past.

Suggestions for further reading
Hague, D. C., *Pricing in Business* (Allen & Unwin Ltd, London, 1971).
Livesey, Frank, *Pricing* (Macmillan, 1976).
Scherer, F. M., *Industrial Pricing* (Rand McNally, 1970).

13 Distribution Policy and the Selection of Marketing Channels

In that three chapters have already been devoted to 'Patterns of Distribution', this chapter may well appear superfluous at first sight. However, the earlier chapters were essentially descriptive, and it now remains to investigate *how* the marketer selects the most appropriate distribution channel.

DISTRIBUTION: A NEGLECTED SUBJECT

It is generally agreed that the subject of marketing owes its origin to economists' inquiries into the nature of the distributive process at the end of the last century. However, despite this early interest, it is only in recent years that the firm has turned its attention to the role which distribution has to play as an element of competitive strategy.

In a review of the current status of distribution, Donald Bowersox advances two reasons which he feels account for the delay in the development of this area of marketing: (*a*) the lack of computers and applied analytical tools sufficient to deal with the complexities of the problem; (*b*) the absence of adequate motivation (Donald J. Bowersox, 'Physical Distribution Development, Current Status and Potential', *Journal of Marketing*, XXXIII (Jan 1969) 63–70). Of these it is felt that the latter is the more important, and two main factors may be distinguished which were to provide the necessary motivation – technological innovation and increased competition.

Increased competition is apparent across the whole range of marketing activities, both domestic and international, and stems from the profits squeeze of the late 1950s and early 1960s. Of late this squeeze has been further exaggerated by inflationary trends in the economy and, in particular, by the pressures exerted by the wages spiral. Outwardly increased competition is manifest in the rash of mergers and acquisitions, as manufacturers seek to protect their market position through integration and/or diversification, and in the growing number of new product introductions.

Writing in the April 1962 issue of *Fortune*, Peter Drucker characterised distribution as the 'Economy's Dark Continent' and noted that whereas the cost of physical distribution accounted for as much as half of the total cost of finished goods, it had received relatively little attention by comparison with managements' cost reduction efforts in other directions. Since the publication of this article there has been an enormous expansion in the literature of physical distribution, but it is significant that little of the research represented by this literature has been concerned with the strategic implications of channel policy. As Bowersox notes, extant concepts assume vertical integration or, alternatively, take the viewpoint that physical distribution operations and responsibilities cease where a transfer of ownership occurs. The latter ignores the fact that many manufacturers sell at least part of their output through intermediaries, and implies that they take no further interest in the sales process once their output has passed into the wholesaler's inventory. Similarly, vertical integration is atypical of present distributive structure.

Given the competitive pressures attributable to escalating costs, increased industrial concentration as the result of acquisitions and mergers, and the threat of product obsolescence inherent in accelerating technological innovation, it is clear that distribution policy has become a question of acute importance to the marketer.

THE FUNCTION OF THE DISTRIBUTIVE CHANNEL

Although the functions performed by distributive channels have already been described in respect of various types of goods, it will be useful at this point to synthesise common features into a series of empirically valid generalisations. In order to avoid misunderstanding, a channel of distribution is here defined as: The structure of intra-company organisation units and extra-company agents and dealers, wholesale and retail, through which a commodity, product or service is marketed. This definition was designed to be broad

enough to include: (*a*) both a firm's internal marketing organisation units and the outside business units it uses in its marketing
work and (*b*) both the channel structure of the individual firm and
the entire complex available to all firms (*Marketing Definitions:*
American Marketing Association, 1962).

As economies develop there is an increasing emphasis on specialisation and the division of labour, as a result of which a 'gap'
develops between producer and user. The primary purpose of a
distributive channel is to bridge this gap by resolving spatial and
temporal discrepancies in supply and demand. Irrespective of the
extent of these discrepancies, certain essential functions need to be
performed which may be summarised as:

1. Transfer of title to the goods involved.
2. Physical movement from the point of production to the point
   of consumption.
3. Storage functions.
4. Communication of information concerning the availability,
   characteristics and price of the goods.
5. The financing of goods in transit, inventory and on purchase.

The importance of these functions varies, depending upon the
nature of the goods themselves. Physical movement and storage
tend to predominate in the case of bulky raw or part-processed
materials such as basic chemicals, petroleum products and steel,
where price and specification are standardised and the market is
comprised of a limited number of buyers and sellers. As the complexity of the product increases the provision of information and
product service becomes predominant. In the case of consumer
goods, advertising and sales promotion constitute the major communication channel, but industrial goods depend more on personal
selling owing to the more heterogeneous nature of the goods
involved and the possibility of modifying them to meet end-user
requirements.

In essence, then, the functions are common to all distributive
channels, but in the particular it is necessary to consider the precise nature of the product, and seller–buyer relationships, to
determine their relative importance.

As noted previously, the manufacturer is faced with three basic
alternatives when deciding upon a distribution policy:

(*a*) Direct sale.
(*b*) Sale through an intermediary.

(*c*) A 'dual' policy combining direct sale with the use of an intermediary.

The advantages and disadvantages commonly associated with these alternatives may be summarised as:

Direct sale
The major advantage associated with direct sale is that it permits the seller to retain full control over the total marketing process. Its usage is favoured by the existence of:

A limited number of potential buyers.
A high degree of geographical concentration of potential buyers.
A high degree of technical complexity requiring extensive service.
A high level of technological innovation.
Stable demand conditions, i.e. the absence of seasonal and cyclical trends which necessitate stockholding.

Any of these factors in itself may be sufficient to predicate adoption of a policy of direct selling; in combination they are virtually irresistible. Conversely, a conflict between, say, the number of buyers and their geographic dispersion may make direct selling a totally uneconomic proposition – the major disadvantage linked with this approach.

Sale through an intermediary
When cost considerations militate against the adoption of direct selling, manufacturers frequently make use of an intermediary who, by acting on behalf of a number of buyers and sellers, is able to perform the necessary functions more economically, i.e. the gross margin demanded by the intermediary is less than the on-cost which would be incurred through providing the same services oneself. The advantages and disadvantages of using an intermediary may be summarised as:

Advantages:
  1. Cost advantages: use of an intermediary
     – Minimises the cost of a field sales organisation.
     – Eliminates warehousing costs.
     – Minimises inventory financing charges.
     – Minimises sales costs – invoicing, financing of accounts, etc.
     – Minimises the risk of loss through inventory obsolescence.

– Minimises loss through bad debts and reduces the cost of credit control.
– Eliminates local delivery costs.
– Reduces the costs of processing to meet non-standard orders.

2. Coverage. The use of intermediaries allows the producer to reach all potential users without having to incur the fixed costs which would arise if direct selling were used.
3. Provision of service. Intermediaries can provide immediate availability and necessary pre- and after-sales service on a local basis more effectively than many producers.

Disadvantages:
The major disadvantage associated with the use of an intermediary is the loss of direct control over any, or all, of the following:

Selling effort – Customer selection
          – Call frequency
          – Product emphasis
          – Promotion and missionary selling effort.

Pricing.
Delivery.
Service – Standard and availability.

Clearly, the importance attached to retaining control over these functions will vary from product to product and manufacturer to manufacturer.

Dual distribution
In order to try and reconcile the conflict between the desirability of direct contact and the economies offered by selling through an intermediary, many manufacturers have adopted a compromise solution, usually referred to as 'dual' distribution. Under this alternative the manufacturer sells part of his output direct but entrusts the balance of his sales effort to an intermediary. As noted elsewhere, this policy is favoured by the existence of the 'heavy half' phenomenon, where a limited number of users constitute the major demand with the balance fragmented among a large number of small or irregular users.

The major disadvantage associated with dual distribution is the

difficulty intrinsic in determining a fair division of the market between producer and intermediary.

The B.I.M. survey referred to elsewhere revealed the following
in response to the question 'Which of the following distribution
channels do you use?'

	per cent
Direct to users	41
Wholesalers and retailers	26
Wholesalers only	13
Retailers only	11
Others	4

N = 553 Source: B.I.M. Information Summary 148.

MAJOR DETERMINANTS OF CHANNEL POLICY

Fundamentally, the channel decision requires resolution of the
often conflicting forces of cost and control.

Cost is readily understood even if it is sometimes difficult to
quantify, and several aspects of control have already been stated.
However, the concept of control must be broadened to recognise
the fact that a firm's ability to exercise control is a function of its
competitive strength *vis-à-vis* other channel members. Thus it is
usual to find that one member of the distributive channel dominates its practices and is regarded as the 'locus of channel control'
(see Louis P. Bucklin, 'The Locus of Channel Control', *Proceed-
ings of the Fall, 1968, Conference of the American Marketing
Association*, pp. 142–7). In general the dominant members are
either producers or users/consumers, but there are situations
where a channel intermediary may be dominant and so condition
the structure and operation of the channel. The latter situation is
most likely to occur where both producers and users are small and
the market is geographically dispersed, and is equally true of
retailer/wholesalers in the consumer goods market as it is of the
industrial goods wholesaler. Overall, dominance or control is
determined by a number of factors which may be summarised as:

Buyer/seller concentration ratios in terms of production/
consumption, and spatial relationships.

Technical complexity. In the case of technically complex products, dominance will be conditioned by the relative sophistication of the producer *vis-à-vis* the intermediary and/or user. Thus a small firm may exercise considerable influence over much larger users or intermediaries.

Service requirements – the more complex these are the more likely it is that the producer will exercise control.

In the final analysis, however, the determining factor is economic advantage, i.e. which channel member can perform the necessary channel functions at the lowest cost consistent with the required degree of efficiency. At a given point in time the structure of a trade channel serves as a rough and ready guide as to the relative efficiency of its members, but it is clear that over time environmental changes may predicate the adoption of an alternative structure to better meet the needs of users/consumers. Similarly, lack of control may persuade a channel member to modify his policies in order to protect his position – a tendency which is implicit in Galbraith's concept of 'countervailing power'.

Examples of competitive reaction within the distributive channel are well documented in the field of consumer goods but less so in the industrial sphere. The growth of dominant retailing institutions was noted in Chapter 8, together with the response of the independent wholesaler whose livelihood was threatened, and similar trends are to be observed in industrial markets.

Among the latter may be noted the adoption of contract purchasing, also known as systems contracting, stockless purchasing and automatic ordering. Under this sytem, buyers negotiate contracts for the continued supply of standard requirements from a single source at a fixed price. Effectively, this reduces the actual stock of parts, supplies or components to the absolute minimum consistent with day-to-day operations, and transfers the inventory costs and risks of obsolescence to the supplier. Such contracts are invariably based upon a total cost analysis rather than on a basis of minimum price. Associated with contract purchasing there is a growing trend in the United States towards computerised ordering systems in which standardised and routine orders are placed direct with the supplier (producer or wholesaler) through the medium of electronic data processing equipment, e.g. Data Phone, WATS-line and Flexowriter. In that these practices not only result in operating economies but also free the purchasing agent to devote more time to non-routine buying decisions, they are resulting in a fuller and more sophisticated evaluation of competitive offerings.

To counteract the growing sophistication of buyers, many sellers have switched to systems selling, in which they offer a complete 'package' of related products and services which would formerly have been purchased from a variety of different sources. Similarly, the appointment of market managers, as opposed to product managers, recognises the need to adapt marketing practice to the specific needs of different end-use markets.

THE CHANNEL DECISION

Whether one accepts profit maximisation as the basic corporate objective or not, it seems reasonable to affirm that uncertainty about the future business environment and the competitive activity of other firms will predispose the firm to reduce costs to the minimum level consistent with achievement of its own stated objective. If this is so, then the channel decision may be viewed as a three-stage process. The first stage consists of a qualitative assessment of the environmental opportunity which the firm is best suited to exploit, conditioned by less tangible objectives such as 'To build the best product', 'To provide the best after-sales service'.

Once the broad strategy has been determined, management must decide which mix of policies offers the optimum probability of attaining the desired result. Such decisions cannot be made in isolation, for the success of a strategy demands that the separate marketing policies in respect of price, distribution, promotion, etc., be synthesised into a consistent and cohesive whole. Usually, however, one variable will take pre-eminence over the others by virtue of the basic strategy decided upon – the 'strategic variable'. For example, if the basic strategy is to sell mass consumption convenience goods, extensive or mass distribution may well be considered the key or strategic variable, and will condition policies adopted in respect of other mix elements. Similarly, if the basic strategy is to build a reputation for high product quality the product itself will become the strategic variable, and probably result in a high price, selective distribution policy.

In order to decide which distribution channel or combination of channels is to be preferred the marketer should then quantify the costs associated with the available alternatives. This analysis should be based initially on a check-list similar to that in Chapter 8, followed by a detailed cost breakdown for direct sale to the number of accounts thought to be necessary to achieve the desired sales volume. Such a breakdown would normally include consideration of the following:

Number and geographical distribution of accounts.
Number of calls per account adjusted to allow for potential order size.
Average sales per call.
Average time per call.
Number of salesmen necessary to achieve the optimal call pattern.
Saleries and commission payable.
Travelling and administrative costs incurred.
Costs of holding inventory.
Costs of financing receivables.
Costs of extending credit.
Costs arising out of bad debts.
Costs of providing necessary services.
Costs of invoicing, order processing, expediting, etc.
Transportation costs.

On the basis of such a cost analysis one may then compute the average selling, general and administrative costs per unit sold, and compare this with the gross margin asked by intermediaries for providing the same services and market coverage. Obviously, if the margin asked is greater than the average unit cost, direct sale will appear more attractive, and vice versa. The outcome of such an analysis is rarely clear-cut, however, and even when it does appear so it does not necessarily represent the optimal strategy. The latter may only be determined effectively on a marginal or contribution basis, which in turn will usually require the use of a computer to cope with the enormous number of possible combinations and permutations.

As inferred earlier, the selection of a strategy is basically a judgemental process. Only under certain limited circumstances will the decision-maker be without prior information, and in most cases his evaluation will be based upon a consideration of alternatives related to current practice. Although he will still be faced with considerable uncertainty, the existence of prior information suggests that the channel decision should be amenable to analysis using a Bayesian approach.

The application of Bayesian methodology to the channel selection decision is discussed in *Planning and Problem Solving in Marketing* by Wroe Alderson and Paul E. Green (Richard D. Irwin, Homewood, Illinois, 1964) pp. 311–17. The example used is highly simplified, and ignores the difficulties associated with quantifying the cash flows attributable to different courses of action and the complexities inherent in different channel combinations. None the less, it does demonstrate that if the decision-maker can quantify his expectation as to the probability of the occurrence of basic events, he will be better able to select the policy which will maximise profits or other preferred criterion.

Once the optimum distribution policy has been quantified, the final step in the analysis should be to review the original qualitative assessment in the light of the quantitative data and to eliminate any inconsistencies, e.g. the quantitative analysis may suggest that the original decision would not optimise the opportunities open to the firm.

Suggestions for further reading

Bucklin, Louis, P., 'A Theory of Channel Control', *Journal of Marketing*, XXXVII (Jan 1973) 39–47.

Rosenberg, Larry J., and Stern, Lewis W., 'Conflict Measurement in the Distribution Channel', *Journal of Marketing Research*, VIII (Nov 1971).

14 Marketing Communications

INTRODUCTION

In the view of some authors (e.g. M. Wayne Delozier, *The Marketing Communications Process*, McGraw-Hill, 1976) all the marketing-mix variables and indeed all company activities may be regarded as marketing communication variables. Conversely, E. J. McArthy (*Basic Marketing*, 6th ed., Irwin, 1978) takes a more narrow approach and defines marketing communications as the *promotional* activities of advertising, personal selling, sales promotion and public relations. Our own discussion will incline towards the latter, narrower, functional treatment as it is felt to be more appropriate to an introductory text. However, an attempt will be made in this chapter to put this basically factual and descriptive treatment into a theoretical perspective by reviewing some of the major concepts and ideas which have found their way into the marketing literature in recent years.

To this end the chapter begins with a definition of communication and proceeds to examine some of the basic models of the communication process in current circulation. References will be made to the role of attention and perception as prerequisites of action by the receiver – usually in the form of some attitudinal or behavioural change, or both – as well as to the relevance of learning theory to the propagation and understanding of marketing communication. Both these topics were introduced in Chapter 4 ('Consumer Behaviour').

The remainder of the chapter looks more closely at some of the major components of any marketing communication – the source, the message and the medium – and concludes with a discussion of the role of communication in the marketing mix.

COMMUNICATION DEFINED

Wilbur Schramm defined communication as 'the process of establishing a commonness or oneness of thought between a sender and a receiver' (*The Process and Effects of Mass Communications*, University of Illinois Press, 1955, p. 3). Central to this definition is the concept that for communication to occur there must be a transfer of information from one party – the sender – which is received and understood by the other party – the receiver. In other words both receiver and sender play an active role in establishing communication – a fact which is given particular point when one considers that the average consumer is estimated to be exposed to approximately 1500 promotional messages a day but only receives nine of these messages.

Pictorially the simplest model of the communications process is shown in Fig. 14.1. However, this simple model ignores the fact that it is necessary to convert ideas into a symbolic medium to enable them to be transmitted via a communication channel. To allow for this we must introduce two more elements into the model – encoding and decoding – as shown in Fig. 14.2.

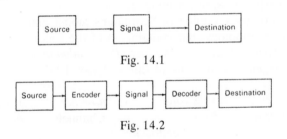

Fig. 14.1

Fig. 14.2

As Schramm points out, this model can accommodate all types of communication so that in the case of electronic communication the encoder becomes a transmitting device – microphone, teletype, etc – and the decoder a receiver – radio or television set, telephone, etc. In the case of direct personal (face-to-face) communication then one person is both source and encoder while the other is decoder and destination and the signal is language. It follows that if an exchange of meaning is to take place, then both source and destination must be tuned in to each other and share the same language. Put another way, there must be an overlap in the field of experience of source and destination – which Schramm illustrates as follows:

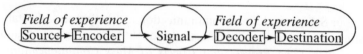

We must also recognise that all communication is intended to have an effect and introduce the notion of *feedback* into our model of communication, for it is through feedback that the source learns how its signals are being interpreted. In personal communication feedback is often instantaneous through verbal acknowledgement or gesture but in impersonal communication through the mass media it may have to be inferred from other indicators, e.g. audience size, circulation, readership, or monitored by sampling opinion.

The final element in Schramm's model is the *channel* or, more correctly, channel*s*, for messages are rarely transmitted through a single channel. Thus in personal communications it is not merely the words which convey the message but the intonation of our voice and the gestures which accompany them. Similarly, in the print media we lend emphasis by *italicising* key words, by use of different type faces, underlining, etc.

The marketer's version of Schramm's model employs slightly different terminology, but contains all of the following elements (see C. Shannon and W. Weaver, *The Mathematical Theory of Communication*, University of Illinois Press, 1962):

Who . . .	*says what* . . .	*how* . . .	*to whom* . . .
Communicator	Message	Channels	Audience
	Feedback		
	with what effect		

Kotler (op. cit.) defines these basic elements as follows:

Communicator: the sender or sources of the message

Message: the set of meanings being sent and/or received by the audience

Channels: the ways in which the message can be carried or delivered to the audience

Audience: the receiver or destination of the message

From his model Schramm derives four basic 'conditions of success in communication . . . which must be fulfilled if the message is to arouse its intended response'. These are:

1. The message must be so designed and delivered as to gain the attention of the intended destination.
2. The message must employ signs which refer to experience common to source and destination, so as to 'get the meaning across'.
3. The message must arouse personality needs in the destination and suggest some ways to meet those needs.
4. The message must suggest a way to meet those needs which is appropriate to the group situation in which the destination finds himself at the time when he is moved to make the desired response.

Consideration of these four requirements should strike a receptive chord in the memory of the reader who is methodically working his way through the book, for they echo closely points discussed in Chapter 4 concerning hierarchy-of-effects models in consumer behaviour. In fact Schramm's four conditions are very similar to Strong's basic AIDA model – *A*ttention, *I*nterest, *D*esire and *A*ction. It will be useful, therefore, to recapitulate on this earlier discussion but specifically in the context of marketing communications. In doing so we will first provide a broad overview and then pick out certain key concepts for a fuller discussion, namely diffusion theories, opinion leadership and the two-step flow of communication, source credibility and cognitiveconsonance and dissonance.

HOW ADVERTISING WORKS

One of the earliest explanations of how advertising works is based upon the stimulus–response theory of learning in which advertising is perceived as a stimulus and purchasing behaviour the intended and desired response. However, it is clear that advertising, even when very intense does not lead automatically to purchase and it was postulated that the act of purchase is the culmination of a whole sequence of events. If this is so then it is argued that advertising's role is to move people up the steps from a state of unawareness to purchase and a number of models of varying levels of sophistication have been put forward including Strong's AIDA model (Attention, Interest, Desire, Action) Lavidge and Steiner's 'Hierarchy of Effects' Model (Awareness, Knowledge, Liking, Preference, Conviction, Purchase), and Rogers's 'Innovation Adoption' Model (Awareness, Interest, Evaluation, Trial, Adoption). (See pp. 77–8.)

An important feature of all these models is that they start with the audience and are concerned with their response to the message transmitted from a given source via various channels. On the other hand, the models suggest a sequence of events which observation and experience often contradict, especially in the case of impulse purchases. Notwithstanding this deficiency it is clear that most advertisers find the learning model intuitively appealing and often set objectives in terms of moving potential customers up the various steps from unawareness to purchase.

Two basic problems may be identified immediately: first, audiences are comprised of persons who differ from each other in many demographic and psycho-social respects; second, there is likely to be considerable variation in the levels of knowledge and awareness of different members of the audience at any given point in time. As a consequence individuals will vary in their response to the advertisers' message and the channels through which it is communicated. It follows that insight into and understanding of how such variance occurs is of vital importance in designing marketing communications.

Many communication experts subscribe to McLuhan's thesis that 'the medium is the message' and so would argue that once a target audience has been identified the primary decision is selection of the medium or channel to be used. Conversely others point out that media planning is a complex activity only because there are so many similar media that choice between them is difficult. This being so, then it is the message which must be selected first and this will help identify the most appropriate medium to reach the target audience. In reality, however, it seems that both approaches are used and that preference is situation-specific. But on balance the channel seems to exercise the greater influence and will be dealt with first.

In general channels may be divided into two major categories: *personal* and *non-personal*. As the name implies personal channels embrace all those situations in which a direct, face-to-face communication takes place, while non-personal channels comprise all media through which messages are transmitted *without* face-to-face communication, e.g. press, television, exhibitions, etc. The available evidence suggests that both types of channel have a role to play and it is usually held that non-personal media are most effective in establishing awareness and interest, while personal influence is necessary to move the members of an audience up the hierarchy through desire to action. Further, it has been found that personal influence is most effective in high-risk purchase situations, i.e. where the consumer is expending relatively large amounts and purchases infrequently (shopping goods) or where the product/service has social connotations which link brands with social groups (specialty goods). (The obverse of this is that mass communication is most appropriate for convenience goods.)

As indicated, however, it is usual to find a combination of both personal and non-personal channels used in a given campaign. Research by Lazarsfeld (*The People's Choice*, Sloan & Pearce, 1944) showed that impersonal channels are often mediated in their effect by personal channels – the so-called 'Two-step flow of communication'. According to this model certain members of the population act as filters and amplifiers for messages and these persons have been designated *opinion leaders*. It follows that if the two-step model applies then the communicator should identify the opinion leaders and transmit his messages through them. Often opinion leaders are best reached via impersonal channels and themselves become a personal channel performing the role of unpaid salesmen.

Clearly, the achievement of direct face-to-face communication could be expensive and impersonal channels help reduce the cost of conveying messages to consumers. However, many messages transmitted through the mass media compete for our attention and most of these are screened out by the psychological defence mechanism of selective *perception, distortion* and *retention*. As a result the power of mass communication as a persuasive influence is largely discounted nowadays and the mass media are seen primarily as leading to learning and reinforcement over time. Further, different media act in different ways and the skill of the media planner lies in selection of the medium or combination of media best suited to the audience he is seeking to reach.

Reference has been made to the message on several occasions and its importance is obvious, for, as Kotler (op. cit.) says, it is the means 'by which the communicator attempts to make the product meaningful and desirable to the buyer'. Perhaps the most important point about the message is that it should be designed so that it is meaningful to the recipient after the distortion which will inevitably occur on transmission through the chosen channel or channels and its selective screening by the audience. It follows that the message is an infinitely variable element in the communication process, as it must be tailored to the differing needs and levels of knowledge/experience of a constantly changing audience. However, two broad schools of thought exist concerning message structure and content, one favouring *consonance* (i.e. conforming with held beliefs, aspirations, etc. – 'pleasant' messages), the other dissonance (i.e. contrary to held beliefs and so creating discomfort or dissonance).

The final element is the communicator himself. His influence is both direct – identification of audience, selection of channel, choice of message – and indirect – the way he is perceived by the audience as the source of the message (the 'source effect'). Again, it is important to stress that the source is not necessarily the communicator himself but rather the origin of the message as perceived by the audience (cf. the testimonial advertisement). In turn the audience's perception of the message will be governed by its interpretation of the *source credibility* – a concept developed by Kelman and Hovland and seen as comprising two elements – expertness and trustworthiness. Fundamentally the precept is 'the higher the source credibility the greater the effectiveness of the communication'. However, source effect decays over time and must be reinforced through repetition.

DIFFUSION THEORIES

In discussing hierarchy-of-effects models in Chapter 4 reference was made to Everett Rogers's five-step adoption model – awareness, interest, evaluation, trial, adoption – which has been used extensively in many studies of new product marketing and marketing communications. However, Rogers's basic model has been subject to a number of criticisms. Specifically, it suggests that adoption is a consequence of the process when in fact the decision might be to reject the innovation, or even to 'wait and see', i.e.

deferred rejection/adoption. Second, the five stages need not occur in the sequence proposed (cf. impulse purchasing) and it seems likely that evaluation is not a discrete phase but takes place throughout the process. Further, in many instances the trial phase may be omitted. Finally, some critics have pointed out that adoption (purchase of a product) is not the final stage in the process, as post-adoption activity will occur leading to feedback which will influence subsequent behaviour.

To meet these criticisms Rogers joined forces with Floyd Shoemaker and proposed a revised 'paradigm of the innovation – decision process' containing four stages (see *Communications of Innovation*, 2nd ed., Free Press, 1971):

1. *Knowledge*. The individual is aware of the innovation and has acquired some information about it.
2. *Persuasion*. The individual forms an attitude, pro or con, towards the innovation.
3. *Decisions*. The individual performs activities which lead to an adopt–reject decision about the innovation.
4. *Confirmation*. The individual looks for reinforcement regarding his decision and may change his earlier decision if exposed to counter-reinforcing messages.

Clearly this model is more flexible and less mechanistic than the original and permits the accommodation of the criticisms outlined earlier. Diagrammatically the model appears as shown in Fig. 14.3. The reader will be familiar with the antecedent variables, for these were reviewed in Chapter 4, so attention will be focused on the process itself. However, before doing so it will be useful to introduce the concepts of *adopter categories* and *diffusion*.

Under another name (the concept of the product life cycle, P.L.C. – see pp. 201 ff.) the diffusion process is one of the most familiar and fundamental of marketing ideas. In essence the P.L.C. and cumulative adoption curves are the same and show that after a slow initial start sales grow rapidly and then begin to level off until saturation is achieved. If these sales are plotted against elapsed time from introduction of an innovation, then a normal distribution results and this has lead to attempts to analyse and classify the adoption/buying behaviour of individuals in terms of the properties of the normal distribution. Fig. 14.4 illustrates this.

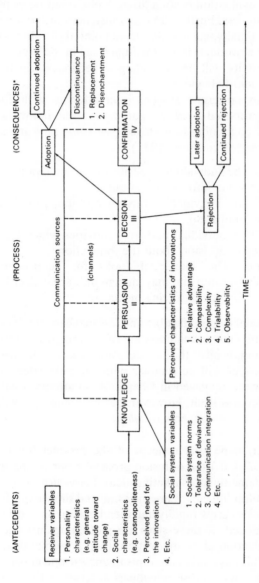

Source: Everett M. Rogers with Floyd Shoemaker, *Communication of Innovations*, 2nd ed., New York, Free Press, 1971.

Fig. 14.3. Paradigm of the innovation decision process

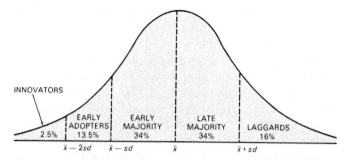

Source: Rogers and Shoemaker, op. cit.

Fig. 14.4. Adopter categorisation on the basis of innovativeness. The innovativeness dimension, as measured by the time at which an individual adopts an innovation or innovations, is continuous. However, this variable may be partitioned into five adopter categories by laying off standard deviations from the average time of adoption.

It follows that if we are able to identify beforehand certain individuals as being more receptive to a given innovation, then we should be able to accelerate adoption by focusing our initial marketing efforts upon them. In turn, because the diffusion process is probabilistic, this will accelerate the whole diffusion process and result in enhanced profitability.

Returning to the process of adoption it has been determined that certain communication mixes are more appropriate than others at different stages and this knowledge is of great value in planning a communications strategy.

The *knowledge* stage is one of awareness and preliminary information-seeking in which impersonal sources tend to dominate. Other things being equal one could conceive of a situation in which all potential buyers of a new product were exposed to information about it simultaneously but because of selective perception and distortion relatively few would react to the information. Ealy adopters are those who do react quickly and they have been found to possess a number of characteristics which distinguish them from later adopters. Specifically, they make it their business to be well-informed and so make greater use of mass media and personal sources of information – both social and professional (i.e. sales personnel or 'change agents') – and they also tend to be better-educated, extrovert and more cosmopolitan than later adopters.

The second stage in the process is that of *persuasion*, in which the potential user moves from a state of neutral awareness to the development of an attitude towards the new object. In my model (pp. 99 ff.) this change is initiated by 'precipitating circumstances' and leads to formal evaluation of possible solutions to the felt need. In the Rogers and Shoemaker model this evaluation is based upon the perceived characteristics of the innovation – relative advantage, compatibility, complexity, trialability and observability. At this stage prospective users will seek to extend their information base and make greater use of personal sources. It is at this juncture that opinion leadership assumes great importance as the potential user will seek the advice of those he sees as knowledgeable about the item under consideration.

Relative advantage is defined as 'the degree to which an innovation is perceived as better' than an existing idea or object and it is stated that the higher the relative advantage the greater the likelihood of adoption. Compatibility and complexity are self-explanatory and tend to vary inversely with one another, i.e. the more compatible an object is with one's field of experience, attitudes and value structure, etc., the less complex it is likely to seem and vice versa. Trialability, or the extent to which an individual can try out an innovation before coming to a decision, is an important factor in reducing perceived risk and an aid to speeding up decision-making (it works both ways!) Finally, observability refers to the visible effectiveness of the innovation.

While these perceived characteristics enjoy wide currency I am not overly fond of them myself. For example, relative advantage is really a catch-all for all the other characteristics and it is tautologous to state that the greater the perceived advantage the faster adoption – even the clinically insane act in the manner which maximises their own perceived self-interest however misguided some people may regard it. Accordingly the reader is warned that while the concept is appealing one must beware that it is not meaningless due to circularity of definitions, e.g. the greater the relative advantage the faster adoption but the faster the adoption the greater the perceived advantage. Certainly it is difficult to operationalise the concept, for the perception of characteristics tends to be individual-specific.

Following his evaluation the potential user will make a decision to adopt or reject which, as the model shows, is open to subsequent modification, i.e. an adopter may continue in use or reject and vice versa for a rejecter. Once made the decision is subject to *confirmation*, in which the person seeks to validate the rightness of his decision and therefore alleviate any post-decision cognitive dissonance (discussed below). This being the case it might be more accurate to show confirmation following the actual decision: 'Adoption' or 'Rejection'.

Like many marketing concepts Rogers's diffusion model is most valuable for the insights which it gives rather than in providing direct practical applications. Thus it provides a framework for organising one's thinking about the decision process and the stages which the individual goes through which can be related to the specific features which distinguish a particular marketing problem.

OPINION LEADERSHIP AND THE TWO-STEP FLOW OF COMMUNICATION

Early models of communication regarded both impersonal sources (the mass media) and personal sources as establishing direct contact with an audience – the so-called 'hypodermic effect'. Belief in this model leads to speculation concerning the influence of the mass media upon voting behaviour – thus the undertaking of one of the most celebrated pieces of communication research, reported in Paul F. Lazarsfeld *et al., The People's Choice* (Sloan & Pearce, 1944).

Lazarsfeld and his colleagues set out to study the influence of the mass media on individual voting behaviour in the 1940 presidential election in the United States. Contrary to expectations it was found that influence did not flow directly from a medium (press, radio, etc.) to an audience but was channelled through an intermediary who was designated the 'opinion leader'. It was this finding which gave rise to the two-step model which has had a significant influence on communication research and practice ever since. However, it must be emphasised that the two-step hypothesis does not exclude the possibility of a direct flow (one step) and its main contribution is in introducing the mediating effect of personal influence on impersonal communications. Thus nowadays the mass media are regarded primarily as *information* sources and considerable attention is focused upon the nature and behaviour of opinion leaders – how to identify them and how to communicate effectively with them.

In simple terms an opinion leader is one to whom others turn for information and advice. However, it must be emphasised that in the usual marketing context opinion leaders are not a distinct and easily classified group in the sense in which Cabinet Ministers or Managing Directors of major companies are. More often than not opinion leaders are people just like you and me, for if they are to be effective at a personal-influence level they must be accessible, which implies that they are members of reference groups with which people have contact. In fact most reference groups develop around shared interests and some members will be seen as more influential than others in the context of that interest. But we belong to many reference groups, leader and follower roles may be reversed, e.g. the captain of the football team may well seek the first reserve's opinion on the merits of hi-fi systems. It is this tendency which makes identification of opinion leaders difficult but, despite this, a number of studies have been completed which permit some generalisations to be made. Writing in 1971 Thomas S. Robertson (*Innovative Behavior and Communication*, Holt, Rinehart & Winston) offered those shown in Table 14.1.

TABLE 14.1. Summary profile of opinion-leader traits

Characteristics	Findings
Age	Varies by product category
Social status	Generally same as advisee
Gregariousness	High
Cosmopolitanism	Limited evidence that higher than advisee's
Knowledge	Generally greater for area of influence
Personality	No major distinguishing traits
Norm adherence	Generally greater than advisee's
Innovativeness	Higher than advisee's

Source: T. S. Robertson, *Innovative Behavior and Communication* (Holt, Rinehart & Winston, 1971) p. 179.

Research in the past decade has done nothing to modify significantly these generalisations and Elihu Katz's summary (cited by Robertson, *Innovative Behavior*, p. 180), made in 1957, would still seem to be valid.

> influence is related to (1) *the personification of certain values* (who one is), (2) *competence* (what one knows), and (3) *strategic social location* (whom one knows). To the extent that an individual represents or personifies group values, he stands a better chance of leadership. Thus if the group emphasises an 'in' manner of dress, the person who dressed most accordingly may well be influential. Again, to the extent that an individual is highly knowledgeable, he stands a better chance of leadership. Finally, to the extent that an individual is available and active in the everyday interpersonal communication process, the better his chance of leadership.

Engel *et al.* (*Consumer Behavior*, p. 289) conclude from their survey of the available evidence that opinion leaders gain satisfaction from one or more of five basic motivations – product involvement, self-involvement, concern for others, message involvement, and dissonance reduction. Conversely people accept opinion leadership where there is limited alternative information available, where their own knowledge is inadequate, where there is a high degree of perceived risk and, of course, because there is little or no cost to such information.

From the above summary it follows that marketers must identify the opinion leaders for their own product/service category. Certain of the generalised traits outlined above will assist in this identification, as will the trait of innovativeness. It is also clear that opinion leaders maintain their status, which gives them satisfaction, from being well-informed and so are likely to make greater use of both personal and non-personal sources of information.

SOURCE EFFECT

As the basic model of communication makes clear, all communication originates from a source and this source has a marked bearing upon the subsequent interpretation of the message. In a marketing context it is important to distinguish between the true source – the organisation which is responsible for the generation of the message and pays for its communication in promotional channels – and the perceived source, which is the consumer perception of its origin. This distinction is important because we (consumers) often identify messages with the communicator (sales agent, personality in the television commercial) or the channel (*Good Housekeeping*, *Reader's Digest*, Radio Clyde) rather than the company 'behind' the message.

A great deal of attention has been given to source effect and extended discussions are to be found in several of the texts cited. Probably the best of these is to be found in M. Wayne Delozier, *The Marketing Communications Process* (McGraw-Hill, 1976) and is summarised below. (This book is highly recommended to students requiring an extensive, thorough and up-to-date treatment of the subject.)

1. In general, a source is more persuasive when his audience perceives him high, rather than low, in credibility.
2. A source's credibility, and thus his persuasiveness, is reduced when his audience perceives that the source has something to gain from his persuasive attempts (intention to manipulate).
3. Over time the opinion change attributed to a high-credibility source decreases, whereas the opinion change induced by a low-credibility source increases, resulting in about the same level of retained opinion change for both low- and high-credibility sources.
4. Reinstatement of a high-credibility source some time after his initial message presentation results in higher opinion change retention than if no reinstatement occurs; whereas reinstatement of a low-credibility source some time after his message presentation results in lower opinion change retention than if no reinstatement occurs.
5. The low-credibility source can increase his influence by arguing for a position which is against his own self-interest.
6. A communicator increases his influence if at first he expresses some views already held by his audience, followed by his intended persuasive communication.
7. A communicator increases his persuasiveness if at the beginning of his message he states that his position on the topic is the same as that of his audience, even though he may argue against that position.

8. The more similar members of an audience perceive the source to be *themselves*, the more persuasive the communicator will be.
9. What people think of a communicator's message affects what they think of him (his image).
10. A source is more persuasive when he holds a positive, rather than a negative, attitude toward himself, his message and his receiver.
11. The more powerful and attractive a source is perceived to be, the more influence he has on a receiver's behaviour.

CONSONANCE AND DISSONANCE

At various places in the text reference has been made to dissonance and it will be useful to indicate the role this concept has to play in marketing communications.

In the discussion of perception (pp. 66–70) it was indicated that we seek to organise perceived stimuli (cognitions) into coherent and consistent patterns which are in accord with our knowledge, beliefs and attitudes – in other words we are seeking a state of *consonance*. If two cognitions are not consonant, they may be either irrelevant, i.e. they have no relationship to one another, or dissonant, i.e. in conflict with each other. Clearly dissonant cognitions create a state of psychological tension which the individual will seek to avoid, reduce or eliminate. It is also clear that in any choice situation there is a potential for dissonance, as the recognition of choice implies alternative solutions to a perceived need. In many consumer purchasing situations these alternatives are very similar and the propensity for dissonance is correspondingly greater.

Attention was first focused upon this phenomenon by the publication of Leon A. Festinger's *A Theory of Cognitive Dissonance* (Row & Peterson, 1957) and has been the subject of much interest ever since. It is generally agreed that dissonance can arise from one of three basic causes – logical inconsistency, a conflict between attitude and behaviour or two behaviours, and when a strongly held belief is contravened or negated. Faced with a state of dissonance we tend to use a number of approaches to remove the state, and all these contain elements of selectivity. *Avoidance* is a clear example in which we screen out stimuli which conflict with our preferred interpretation (this can occur both before a decision and after and may be subconscious), while in the case of *rationalisation* we interpret the stimuli to suit our preferred belief (cf. the example of the American football match on p. 68). Alternatively we can *seek additional information* which supports our choice – again on a selective basis – or *forget* or *suppress* the inconsistent information we have. It follows that dissonance can occur at any stage of the purchase decision, though most interest has been shown in the post-purchase phase when commitment has been made to a particular choice, and is likely to be most acute in the case of major purchase decisions.

In a paper given at the 1970 Market Research Society Annual Conference ('The Complementary Benefit Principle of How Advertising Works in Relation to the Product') Peter Hutchinson suggested that the existence of cognitive dissonance has two basic lessons for practitioners:

1. Perfect in manufacture those product benefits which are readily available.
2. Advertise those attributes which are not immediately observable or easily learned.

The first recommendation underlines the importance of ensuring that those dimensions on which direct comparisons can be made are highly developed in one's product, while the second emphasises the need to provide the potential user with additional reasons for preferring your alternative to all the others.

THE MESSAGE AND THE MEDIUM

Earlier in the chapter reference was made to Schramm's four basic conditions for successful communication, all of which involved the basic element of communication – the message. The message is the subject of a separate chapter in *Delozier* (*The Marketing Communications Process*) and this source should be consulted for a full discussion of the topic. Only a brief overview can be presented here.

There are three dimensions of messages which demand particular attention – structure, appeal or content, and the symbolic code (words, music, gesture, etc.) in which the message is couched.

The structure of a message embraces three main considerations

– whether it should be a one-sided or two-sided presentation, the sequence in which information should be presented, and whether a conclusion should be offered. In fact there is no single preferred structure, for this will vary according to the audience. For example, one-sided messages are most effective with people who agree with the source, are poorly educated and unlikely to be exposed to any counter-arguments, while a two-sided message is better suited to convert persons inclining to an opposite opinion, better educated and likely to be exposed to counter-arguments. Similarly, in the case of sequence some messages are more effective when they build up to a climax (high audience interest), others to an anti-climax (low audience interest), while in the case of two-sided arguments controversial material is most effective when presented first (the *primacy* effect) and bland or uninteresting information is favoured by *recency*, i.e. the material presented last is more effective. Finally, while messages are in general more effective if a conclusion is presented, this applies more to persons of low intelligence than persons of high intelligence and is less so in all cases where the source is seen as having a vested interest in the conclusion. Much of the same applies where drawing a conclusion would insult the audience's intelligence.

In the case of message appeal Delozier cites six alternative approaches – fear, distraction, participation, emotion *versus* rational, aggression arousal, and humour. Of these the most controversial are the use of fear appeals and distraction methods. Much criticism has been levelled against advertisements for consumer products which suggest that non-possession will lead to loss of status or social unacceptability (e.g. deodorants), while the use of fear is widely supported in health and safety advertising. Distraction is also criticised on the grounds that it diminishes/influences critical judgement concerning the prime subject of the communication, e.g. the expense-account lunch or the use association in consumer advertisements. Overall the evidence regarding the efficiency of different message appeals confirms that it is situation-specific and must be varied in light of the circumstances they are expected to encounter.

Some mention has already been made of the symbolic code in which a message is couched. Here the evidence is more clear cut and indicates that while choice of words can have an important bearing upon the interpretation of a message, non-verbal communications are often more important in conveying ideas and meaning than words alone. The validity of this is readily apparent in television commercials when sound and movement can be combined to enhance the impact of the purely verbal message to be put across.

At this juncture no reference will be made to the medium through which a message is conveyed to an audience, as this is discussed at some length in the next chapter.

THE ROLE OF COMMUNICATION IN THE MARKETING MIX

As a process marketing is firmly founded on the assumption of effective two-way communication – of consumer telling firms what they want and firms informing consumers what they have to sell. In this sense communication is central to everything the firm does and pervades all its activities. However, when we speak of marketing communications we do so in the more restricted sense of those functional activities which are collectively known as 'promotion' – advertising, personal selling, public relations and sales promotion. Each of these topics is treated at some length in the chapters which follow but before turning to these it will be useful to summarise the basic objectives of promotional strategy.

Martin Bell (*Marketing: Concepts and Strategy*, 2nd ed., Hughton Mifflin, 1972) rightly observes that each item on an exhaustive list of promotional objectives would need a chapter to itself and contents himself by selecting seven for specific mention:

1. Increase sales.
2. Maintain or improve market share.
3. Create or improve brand recognition, acceptance or insistence.
4. Create a favourable climate for future sales.
5. Inform and educate the market.
6. Create a competitive difference.
7. Improve promotional efficiency.

Clearly there is considerable overlap between these seven objectives but the distinction between them is important because emphasis upon any one will tend to lead to a different *promotional mix* being required. For example, creating a favourable climate for future sales is most appropriate for industrial products and consumer durables where there is a long repurchase cycle. Thus customers need to have the wisdom of their previous purchase confirmed in order to reduce post-purchase cognitive dissonance and will also respond favourably to advice on how to get the best out of their purchase. Conversely if one is seeking to win customers from other manufacturers, then one may be seeking to engender cognitive dissonance by suggesting the currently preferred brand is inferior to your own. To achieve these objectives it will often be necessary to use different messages and different channels – a requirement which will only be apparent if one has carefully defined the objective in advance.

Bell also cites five key conditions which favour the use of promotion in the marketing mix:

1. A favourable trend in demand.
2. Strong product differentiation.
3. Product qualities are hidden.
4. Emotional buying motives exist.
5. Adequate funds are available.

While a favourable trend in demand will usually result in a greater apparent return on one's promotional investment, it should not be overlooked that maintaining sales under conditions of stagnant or declining demand is equally and sometimes more important. Similarly, while the existence of strong product differentiation will allow clear distinctions to be drawn with competing products, it must also be remembered that the greater the departure from known and trusted concepts, the greater the intrinsic resistance to change. For these reasons it often happens that the most effective promotions are those which communicate hidden product qualities (purity, taste, durability, etc.) which can only be recognised in use, coupled with promotions which appeal to emotional buying motives. (As noted in my model of buying behaviour in Chapter 4, faced with a need to discriminate between two objectively similar competitive brands, the subjective/emotional factors may be trivial but determinant.) Finally, it is truism to extol the need for adequate funds but it is a factor which is often overlooked, as will be noted when discussing advertising appropriations in the next chapter.

SUMMARY

In this chapter we have reviewed some of the key concepts from communication theory in so far as they have a bearing upon the marketing function. In the nature of things such a review must be eclectic and readers are advised to consult the sources named for a fuller treatment of specific topics.

15 Advertising*

DEFINITIONS

Essentially advertising is a means of spreading information. This is too broad a description, however, to be useful as a definition, or to distinguish it from other forms of communication. The American Marketing Association has adopted the following as a definition: *Any paid form of non-personal presentation and promotion of ideas, goods or services by an identified sponsor.* This is certainly a very succinct statement and merits some elaboration. Firstly, advertising is paid for, it is a commercial transaction, and it is this which distinguishes it from publicity. It is non-personal in the sense that advertising messages, visual, spoken or written, are directed at a mass audience, and not directly at the individual as is the case in personal selling. Finally, advertisements are identifiable with their sponsor or originator, which is not always the case with publicity or propaganda.

The nature and role of sales promotion are dealt with in the next chapter, but it will be useful at this point to give the A.M.A.'s definition to avoid confusion with advertising*per se* in the meantime. *Sales promotion. Those marketing activities, other than personal selling, advertising and publicity, that stimulate consumer purchasing and dealer effectiveness, such as displays, shows and exhibitions, demonstrations, and various non-recurrent selling efforts not in the ordinary routine.*

*I am grateful to Boase Massimi Pollit Univas for their assistance in updating the factual content of this chapter.

OBJECTIVES

The ultimate purpose underlying all advertising is increased awareness. Many authors would also ally this with some form of statement concerning an increase in profit, but this is anticipating an end result applicable only to trading organisations, which is also attributable to a host of other factors (clearly, advertisements sponsored by government departments concerning road safety, or the health hazards of smoking, are not designed to increase profits).

Despite the problems inherent in measuring the effectiveness of advertising, which are the subject of a subsequent section of this chapter, it is only realistic to state that firms invest in advertising expenditures in the expectation of an improvement in profitability. If one examines the specific objectives which may motivate a particular advertising campaign, it is clear that an improvement in profit varies from a primary, to a very subsidiary, motive. An examination of the specific objectives listed by Matthews, Buzzell, Levitt and Frank (*Marketing: An Introductory Analysis*: McGraw-Hill, 1964) makes this clear.

1. To build primary demand.
2. To introduce a price deal.
3. To inform about a product's availability.
4. To build brand recognition or brand preference or brand insistence.
5. To inform about a new product's availability or features or price.
6. To help salesmen by building an awareness of a product among retailers.
7. To create a reputation for service, reliability or research strength.
8. To increase market share.
9. To modify existing product appeals and buying motives.
10. To increase frequency of use of a product.
11. To inform about new uses of a product.
12. To increase the number or quality of retail outlets.
13. To build the overall company image.
14. To effect immediate buying action.

15. To reach new areas or new segments of population within existing areas.
16. To develop overseas markets.

The above list is by no means exhaustive, but it does indicate that the aim underlying a campaign may be directed at a short-term increase in sales volume (price deals and other promotional offers), the development of a new market, an increased share of an existing market, or the building of a favourable attitude to the company as a whole (corporate advertising). The latter, like an increase in retail distribution, is a longterm objective for which it would be difficult to assess the actual return on the advertising investment.

Whatever the specific objective or purpose, it is generally agreed that its statement in explicit terms, is an essential prerequisite of a successful campaign. Similarly, it is also agreed that certain conditions are more favourable to successful advertising than others, for example an expanding market, or possession of a feature which differentiates the product from its competitors. This point will be returned to when discussing advertising strategy.

THE EVOLUTION OF ADVERTISING

It is often erroneously assumed that the advertising function is of recent origin, a point commented on by Henry Sampson in his *History of Advertising*, published in 1874: 'It is generally assumed – though the assumption has no ground for existence beyond that so common among us, that nothing exists of which we are ignorant – that advertisements are of comparatively modern origin.'

There is some evidence to suggest that the Romans practised advertising, but the earliest indication of its use in this country dates from the Middle Ages with the adoption of surnames indicative of a man's occupation, as opposed to some other distinguishing designation (Harrison = Harry's son). The producer's name is of equal importance today as a means of identifying the source of goods and services.

Signs represented the next stage in the evolution of advertising, acting as a visual expression of the tradesman's function as well as a means of locating the source of goods at a time when the numbering of houses was unknown. One can still see vestiges of the practice in the barber's pole, or the symbolic boot or glove.

The craft gilds of the Middle Ages disapproved of competition among their members, but were not averse to competition with one another in the adoption of distinctive liveries, or the sponsoring of mystery plays – an early form of institutional advertising! At the same time many gilds adopted trade marks as a means of identifying the producer, and as a guarantee of quality – the adoption of corporate symbols, as a more immediate means of recognising the firm's identity than the written word, is an interesting reversion to this practice.

Although Caxton had invented the hand press by the end of the fifteenth century, the use of the written word in advertising was limited by the low level of literacy, so confining written advertisements to the clergy. By Shakespeare's time posters had made their appearance, and the few remaining examples make it clear that advertising had assumed the function of fostering demand for new products as well as increasing demand for existing products.

Another important development at this time was the emergence of the pamphlet as an advertising medium, early examples of which disclose their sponsorship by companies bent on generating goodwill for their activities. (Later examples are more veiled as to their origin and, properly, should be considered as propaganda.) However, the seventeenth century was a period of unrest in England, resulting in government censorship which was to hinder the development of regular publications. From 1620 onwards a number of Mercuries, Gazettes, etc., made their appearance, but were mainly short-lived, and carried few advertisements.

The high cost of posters and handbills encouraged a number of publishers to experiment with the issue of free papers comprised solely of advertisements. Their success was limited, however, and posters and handbills continued as the main media until the early eighteenth century. An examination of the periodicals of the early 1700s, such as the *Tatler* and *Spectator*, reveals an increasing number of advertisements, but this growth was abruptly curtailed in 1712 by the imposition of a tax on both papers and advertisements. The first Stamp Act levied a tax of $\frac{1}{2}d$ per copy on publications and 12d per advertisement, supposedly to raise revenue but in fact intended to curtail a libellous and seditious press.

The effect of the tax was virtually immediate – the majority of unsubsidised papers ceased publication, and the legitimate businessman severely curtailed his use of advertising. On the other hand, the quacks and charlatans, with their enormous profit margins to fall back on, continued to advertise, and it is worth noting that the generally unsavoury nature of the advertising of this time was a direct consequence of government censorship and heavy taxation. Under the circumstances neither government control nor taxation would appear to be as effective as modern critics of advertising would have one believe.

The tax on advertisements was abolished in 1853, at a time ripe for the development of mass advertising as we know it today. Mass production was a reality, and channels of distribution were being developed to cope with the physical movement of goods, creating a need for mass communication to inform consumers of the choice available to them. This need was soon recognised by the forerunner of today's advertising agent – the space salesman. Initially space salesmen located customers for the media owners, receiving commission on the space they sold. Gradually the position changed, and the agent became a space-broker, or middleman, buying space wholesale from the media owner and reselling it retail, often at a profit of 25 per cent. The profits to be earned attracted competition and the agents found it necessary to offer incentives to advertisers to purchase space from them, in preference to their competitors. Thus the practice evolved of giving the advertiser free assistance in preparing his copy and later, as the number of publications increased, of selecting the media which would prove most effective in reaching the advertiser's potential customers. In essence this is the system which still obtains today, with the agent looking upon the advertiser as his client, while deriving most of his income from commissions paid by the media owner. (Many advertising agents now charge a service fee on smaller accounts, or where additional work is undertaken on behalf of the advertiser.)

THE STRUCTURE OF ADVERTISING

The above description outlining the evolution of advertising makes it clear that three separate parties are involved in the advertising process:

- The advertiser
- The advertising agent
- The media owners.

In market terms, advertisers constitute buyers and media owners sellers, and consequently they take considerable direct interest
in each other's activities. In many instances advertiser and media
owner will negotiate direct with one another, but beyond a certain
point the intervention of a third party becomes desirable, which
accounts for the existence of advertising agents.

From the advertiser's point of view the agency constitutes a
reservoir of skills which it would be difficult to duplicate in even
the largest company at an economic cost – for the smaller company
it would be impossible. Further, the discount on the purchase of
time and/or space, in the various media is usually restricted to
established and recognised advertising agencies, which enables the
agency to offer its services free of charge to the advertiser under
normal circumstances. From the media owner's point of view,
agencies act as wholesalers, bulking together a host of orders from
a variety of sources, thus reducing the area of contact between
buyer and seller to manageable proportions. In addition the agent
is familiar with the media owner's language and method of operation, and, in a sense, acts as an interpreter between the parties.
Both these factors create economies which the media owner considers justification for the payment of commission.

In the interests of clarity it will help if the role of the parties is
considered separately, before returning to an examination of their
interaction and interdependence in the development of an advertising campaign.

THE ADVERTISER'S VIEWPOINT

As was noted earlier, the justification for advertising from the
advertiser's point of view is that it increases profitability, even
though it is difficult to quantify precisely to what extent. (Mail
order is the only case where a sale can be directly credited to the
publication of an advertisement.) Advertising is but one variable

in the marketing mix, albeit an important one, and it is difficult to separate its contribution from that of the other mix elements. As was implied in the list of advertising goals in the section on 'Objectives', there are a number of ways in which advertising may increase the profitability of the firm (R. H. Colley lists 52 specific goals in *Defining Advertising Goals*: Association of National Advertisers, New York, 1961!) and these are stated more explicitly below:

1. To increase demand to the point where economies of scale are achieved. The larger the fixed costs of production, the greater the unit contribution once the break-even point has been reached – 'leverage'. The advertiser may wish initially to build primary demand for the product group as a whole, anticipating that he will benefit proportionally from the overall growth of the market. Once product acceptance has been achieved, advertisers usually concentrate on building brand recognition and loyalty. Colour television is a good example of this in that early advertisements for sets have tended to emphasise the benefits of colour as compared with black and white, i.e. selling colour rather than brand A, B or C. As the market becomes more competitive, advertisers concentrate on extolling the features of their product which differentiate it from that of other producers.

2. The building of a 'brand image' in a competitive, mature market has other benefits in addition to maintaining or improving the firm's competitive position. Brand recognition and brand loyalty relieve the producer of his dependence on the distributive channels. This is particularly true of convenience goods, but is also applicable to shopping goods where the manufacturer can place little reliance on either the ability or interest of the retailer to sell his specific product. Only where a retailer is a sole distributor can the producer rely on an equal and corresponding interest in the sale of his product.

3. Information gathering invariably precedes the purchase of a product to some degree and, clearly, the ready availability of such information in the form of advertisements reduces the prospective purchaser's dependence on personal selling. Personal selling is a cost to the producer, both directly, in the

payment of his sales force, and indirectly, through the margin he has to offer middlemen to perform the service on his behalf. The physical separation of producer and prospective buyer, coupled with competition, make advertising a more economic means of communication than personal contact in both the industrial and consumer selling field. Further, a good advertisement can go a long way to achieve the first two stages of the sales process – the creation of awareness and interest.

4. Most firms are subject to a fluctuating demand for their output, be it seasonal, cyclical or secular, and advertising can do much to minimise such fluctuations though its impact is greatest in the case of seasonal variations. Ice cream and soup are classic examples of building year-round demand for products formerly consumed during a particular season, through informing consumers of alternative uses by means of advertising.

5. Finally, it is maintained that advertising improves profitability in a less tangible way by creating goodwill for the firm as a whole and by improving the morale of its employees; everyone likes to work for a well-known firm.

ORGANISATION FOR ADVERTISING WITHIN THE FIRM

Recognising the enormous disparity in the size and nature of firms, it is clear that the formulation of generalisations about the nature of the advertising function within the firm is fraught with danger. At the same time, some description of the mythical 'average' firm is useful in that it provides a starting-point for an examination of actual practice in a company with which one is familiar by association, or through reading the practitioners' journals. This caveat should be continually borne in mind, however, in reading this section.

Whatever the specific objective behind the mounting of an advertising campaign, the maximum return on expenditure will only be achieved if the right information is conveyed to the right people in the right way. This is unlikely to be the case unless those responsible for the firm's advertising have a thorough understanding of:

(*a*) The nature of the market.
(*b*) The nature of the product.

(*c*) The nature of the channels of distribution.

(*d*) The nature of the channels of communication – the media available, and their characteristics.

The above list is in descending order of importance from the firm's viewpoint, and excludes reference to particular advertising skills, such as copy-writing, on the basis that these inputs are invariably supplied by the advertising agency. That this is so follows naturally from the media owners' practice of paying a discount (usually 15 per cent) on billings booked by accredited agencies. Agencies secure billings on the basis of the services offered to clients for the privilege of handling their accounts and, in turn, are evaluated and selected on the quality of the service they offer. Creative skills are limited in advertising, as in any other field, with the consequence that the available talent tends to gravitate to the firms offering the greatest rewards. These can be very considerable in the large agency (£8000 per annum upwards), which effectively ensures that the best creative talent is to be found in the agencies, and outside the salary structure of the average firm. As the services of agency personnel are 'free' to the advertiser there is little point in duplicating these skills within the firm. The critical factor is ability to communicate to the agency what the firm wishes to achieve, and what it has to

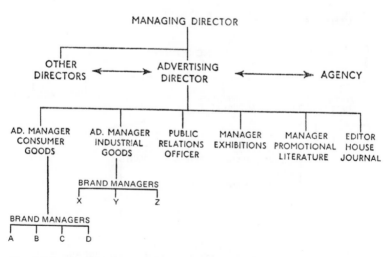

Fig. 15.1. Organisation chart for the advertising department of a large, diversified company

offer the consumer which differentiates it from its competitors. Essentially, therefore, the advertising manager's role is one of liaison and interpretation (i.e. explaining management's objective to the agency and vice versa).

In the large firm the percentage of revenue allocated to advertising may constitute a very large sum in absolute terms and necessitate the employment of a number of persons to manage it effectively. The organisation chart in Fig. 15.1 indicates the appointments that might typically be found in such a company – the actual number of staff employed in each section depending on the importance of advertising and promotion to the firm's marketing effort, and the financial resources allocated to it.

THE ADVERTISING AGENCY

The modern advertising agency of today has advanced a long way from the space salesman of a century ago, to the extent that some feel it would be more appropriate to call it a marketing agency.

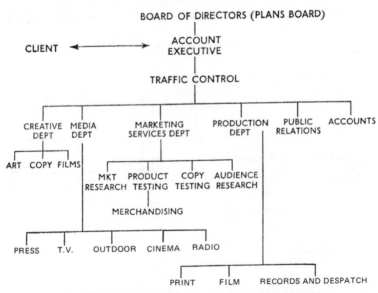

Fig. 15.2. Organisation chart for a large advertising agency

With increasing competition, advertising agents have extended the range of services available to clients, the scope of which is indicated in the organisation chart for a large agency in Fig. 15.2. Despite the apparent extent of the agency's expertise implied, it would be incorrect to assume that the agency could substitute for the firm's own marketing department. As was suggested in the preceding section, the advertiser might regard the agency as an extension of his own business, in that it would be uneconomical to duplicate its skills in terms of the creative aspects of advertising, but, at the same time, it would be foolish to delegate the whole marketing function to a third party specialising in only one aspect of it. It is a rule of agencies not to hold competing accounts, and for this reason alone it is unlikely that one could secure the services of an agency with the necessary experience to handle the total marketing of a specific product. It is also true that accounts change hands, so that one might be able to engage an agency with experience in the relevant product field, but this experience will invariably be limited to the advertising problems involved.

If one accepts that the agency is expert in the advertising function, it follows that it will only be able to perform effectively if it is given the full support and confidence of the advertiser. Much of the conflict which arises between advertiser and agent is the direct result of the former only giving the latter part of the information necessary to devise a successful campaign; it is the advertiser's responsibility to feed in the marketing inputs and data around which to build the campaign. While on the subject of the advertiser/agency relationship, it is appropriate to comment that there seems little evidence to suggest, that agencies 'wear out', in the sense of losing their creative touch, a belief which prompts some advertisers regularly to change agencies to avoid such an occurrence. Most of the firms which are well known for the quality of their advertising have enjoyed a long and unbroken association with their agency, which suggests that mutual confidence improves over time, as does the expertise of the agent in advertising a particular product.

AGENCY SELECTION

From the above comments it is clear that the selection of an advertising agent is not to be undertaken lightly, and the following is suggested as a structured approach to the problem. (This is based on the method adopted by Fine Fare when selecting an agency.)

1. Prepare a short-list of agencies that you think might be suitable. Details of agencies and their existing accounts can be obtained from the *Advertiser's Annual*. There is nothing to prevent you approaching an agency currently handling a competitor's account, but if they are prepared to drop the existing account to bid for yours, it is unlikely that you will achieve lasting success in this direction. Subjective information on agencies may be obtained from business acquaintances, or by asking media owners to identify the agency responsible for advertisements which you admire.

2. Construct a check-list of the factors on which you intend to base your decision and assign each a weight commensurate with the importance which you attach to each, e.g.:

   Creativity (i.e. ability to develop a distinctive/novel approach) –10
   Previous experience in the product field – 8
   Ability to undertake *ad hoc* research – 6, etc., etc.

3. Draw up a questionnaire to:
   (*a*) Elicit the agency's grasp of the problems inherent in marketing your product, and its approach for dealing with them.
   (*b*) Provide a basis around which to build a 'Presentation' – i.e. an outline for a campaign.

4. Approach the agencies on the short-list and ask them if they are interested in competing for the account. (Some indication should be given of the annual appropriation to be allocated to advertising.) Once the news gets around that you are looking for an agency it is quite likely that several agencies not on the short-list will ask if they may make a presentation. One should resist the temptation to expand the field, if the initial selection was undertaken thoroughly, as it will only serve to confuse the issue, unless there is some very valid reason, e.g.

an agency thought to be unavailable having severed its connection with a competitor.

5. Rate the completed questionnaires in line with the previously determined weights.

6. Convene a selection board from the company's executives, e.g. Managing Director, Marketing Director, Advertising Manager, and rate the presentations made as for the questionnaires. (To avoid difficulty in resolving the final outcome it is recommended that both the weights and rating scale be given a large spread, i.e. instead of rating from 1 to 5 use an interval of 5; Worst 5... Best 25.)

THE MEDIA

The third party to the advertising process is the media owners, and the aim of the following section is to review briefly the salient characteristics of the media available. Before proceeding to this review it will be helpful to outline a check-list as a basis for assessing the value of the various media. In common with most other similar lists appearing elsewhere, the outline given below is based on Hobson's *Selection of Advertising Media*, published by Business Publications on behalf of the I.P.A.

An evaluation of an advertising medium requires consideration of four major factors:

1. The character of the medium.
2. The atmosphere of the medium.
3. The coverage of the medium.
4. The cost of the medium.

Two further factors which should be taken into account are the size and position of the advertisement.

Character. The character of a medium may be largely determined on an objective and factual basis through consideration of the following:

(a) The geographical coverage of the medium, e.g. national, regional, local.

(*b*) The socio-economic composition of the audience.

(*c*) Composition of the audience by age and sex groupings.

(*d*) The medium's physical characteristics – visual, oral, standard of reproduction, availability of colour, possibility of movement, etc.

(*e*) Frequency of publication. Allied to this is the duration of interest in the medium – most daily papers are thrown away the same day, while magazines may be kept for several weeks and read by a number of people. The frequency of publication also has a direct effect on the booking of time or space, i.e. the timing of the appearance of an advertisement.

(*f*) The power to reach special groups – this is closely related to (*b*) and (*c*) above, e.g. *Punch* or the *Financial Times*, *Vogue*, etc., preselect a particular type of audience and so are especially suited to selling to this segment of the population. Further, the association of a product with a medium may give that product favourable connotations by transferring confidence in the publication to items advertised therein, e.g. *Good Housekeeping*.

Atmosphere. The atmosphere of a medium is difficult to define in that it is based on a subjective evaluation of its content, presentation, etc. A broad distinction may be drawn between acceptable and intrusive media, in that the latter create impact through intrusion and irrelevance to context, e.g. television commercials, whereas many magazines are purchased as much for their advertisements as their other content. The concept will become clearer when related to individual media.

Coverage. The essential criterion on which coverage is judged is the actual number of persons exposed to the medium, in the sense of being made aware of its content. For example, the number of people who actually see a poster is considerably less than the number that have the opportunity to see it; on the other hand, the readership of a magazine may well exceed ten times its actual circulation.

Cost. For purposes of comparison the cost of publishing an advertisement is usually expressed in terms of 'cost per thousand', which is arrived at by dividing the cost of publication by the audience in thousands. The difficulty in ensuring comparability in the measurement of audience size in terms of coverage, as defined above, makes this a rough measure at best, and media planners are actively seeking more sophisticated measures of cost effectiveness.

Advertising expenditure by media for the past 5 years is indicated in Table 15.1.

Size. The effect of increased size or duration of an advertisement is to increase effective coverage, but on a progressively diminishing scale. Larger advertisements enable the advertiser to make more selling points, or to create greater impact when properly used. It is also contended that 'bigness', of itself, creates confidence and prestige.

TABLE 15.1. *Total advertising by media*

	1972		1973		1974		1975		1976	
	(£m.)	*(%)*	*(£m.)*	*(%)*	*(£m.)*	*(%)*	*(£m.)*	*(%)*	*(£m.)*	*(%)*
National newspapers	130	18.4	160	18.3	161	17.8	162	16.8	197	16.6
Regional	188	26.5	256	29.3	273	30.4	282	29.2	328	27.6
Magazines and periodicals	60	8.5	72	8.2	71	7.9	79	8.2	92	7.7
Trade and technical	61	8.6	73	8.4	80	8.9	86	8.9	103	8.7
Directories	15	2.1	17	1.9	16	1.8	20	2.1	31	2.6
Press production costs	44	6.2	46	5.3	48	5.3	49	5.1	58	4.9
Total press	498	70.3	624	71.4	649	72.1	678	70.3	809	68.1
Television	176	24.9	210	24.0	203	22.6	236	24.4	307	25.8
Poster and transport	26	3.7	31	3.5	34	3.8	35	3.6	43	3.6
Cinema	7	1.0	7	0.8	8	0.9	7	0.7	8	0.7
Radio	1	0.1	2	0.2	6	0.7	11	1.1	21	1.8
Total	708	100	874	100	900	100	967	100	1188	100

Position. Detailed studies of the positioning of advertisements within a medium have shown that certain 'slots' consistently achieve greater coverage than other positions. Further, certain positions can be very useful in isolating a particular segment of the general audience. (Timing has the same effect for broadcast messages on radio and television.)

The national press

(The intention of these synopses is to give the reader an overview of the various media – detailed and up-to-date information may be obtained from *British Rate and Data (BRAD)*.)

The importance of the national press as an advertising medium has been gradually eroded since the transmission of the first television commercial in September 1955. The diversion of advertising revenues to the latter medium has increased competition between the national dailies to the point where several are in financial trouble such that a recent report on the industry by the Economic Intelligence Unit stated that unless the publishers adopted a more realistic approach to economic selling prices there was a strong possibility of their following the *News Chronical* into oblivion. (The E.I.U. suggested that an economic selling price would probably be about twice the present cover cost.) A further cause of the decline in the national dailies' popularity is thought to be the conservative editorial attitude to change. As a contrast to this general attitude, Lord Thomson's treatment of *The Times* is a clear indication of the benefits which marketing of the product can achieve in terms of building up circulation.

Following Hobson's 'check-list', the salient characteristics of the national press may be summarised as:

Character. Newspapers are bought largely for their news value and so are singularly appropriate for announcing new products and new developments of existing products. Because of their frequency of publication they are also well suited to 'opportunity' markets, e.g. advertising anti-freeze during a sudden cold spell, such-and-such a race was won on X tyres, Y petrol, Z oil, etc., etc. Despite their short life, newspapers have a high attention value and it is estimated that an 11 × 3 advertisement (i.e. 11 inches long by 3 columns wide) is seen by one-third of the readers. Further, the adverstisements in the national press are more likely to be seen by the retailer (also true of T.V. commercials) than are those appearing in magazines, and so have an indirect effect on the distributive channels.

In addition to their news content newspapers are also bought for the regular features they carry, and certain days have been developed to cater to specific reader interests, e.g. Thursday and Friday for grocery products, as the majority of grocery purchases are made on Friday and Saturday; mail order advertisements on Saturday and Sunday, to coincide with the week-end letter-writing peak, etc.

As their name implies, the national papers have national coverage. Their regional strength varies, however, and up-to-date data should be sought from *BRAD* or JICNARS (Joint Industry Committee for National Readership Surveys).

Atmosphere. In general terms this may be summarised as a sense of urgency and importance coupled, to a varying degree, with a certain authority. Most people read a newspaper which confirms their own view of the world and so is regarded as a high credibility source (i.e. the content is accepted at face value). To a certain extent, the authority of the factual content is transferred to the advertisements and may be regarded as 'assistance to selling' under the heading of 'Character'.

Quantity/Coverage. At the time of writing the circulation of the best-known national dailies was:

Daily Mirror – 3,905,258
The Sun – 3,883,189
Daily Express – 2,338,809
Daily Mail – 1,900,246
Daily Telegraph – 1,326,236
The Guardian – 267,417
The Times – 290,770
Financial Times – 178,408

Clearly, an evaluation based solely on the number of copies bought would be an inadequate guide to the suitability of a particular paper for a particular advertisement, and these 'raw' data must be related to the demographic composition of the audience *vis-à-vis* the consumer profile of the product or service in question. (This is a useful rule-of-thumb guide to media selection – i.e. define the demographic characteristics of the target consumers, and then select the medium whicn offers the closest match to this profile.)

Cost. Most newspaper advertising rates are based on a charge per standard column centimetre (S.C.C.) – i.e. one column wide by one centimetre deep. The actual column width varies, as does the cost, from paper to paper. In general, the cost per thousand tends to be roughly equivalent, but once again reference should be made to *BRAD* for exact and up-to-date information. Charges also vary within each paper depending on the actual position of the advertisement – see 'Position' below.

Size. As a general rule, readership does not increase with the size of the advertisement in a directly proportional manner. Despite diminishing returns, the consensus of opinion favours larger advertisements because of the greater impact which they achieve and because readers 'select' advertisements to a certain extent, i.e. there is a tendency to notice those of direct interest to the reader. This means that a series of small advertisements, costing the same as a single large advertisement, may be seen many times by the same people, but pass unnoticed by those with a latent demand – it is unlikely that a full-page advertisement will pass unnoted by these potential customers in the same way.

Position. The location of advertisements within the medium is at the discretion of the advertising manager, who, naturally, attempts to satisfy as many clients as possible. Owing to the demand for certain positions, however, it has been found both simpler and more lucrative to charge special rates for these favoured positions. It is clear that certain pages preselect a particular segment of the readership owing to the nature of the features on that page, e.g. the women's and sports pages. It follows that if one is advertising a product which has a particular appeal to a segment of the readership, there is a greater probability of it coming to their attention if it is located on a page that caters to that interest.

The actual position within the printed media may be defined by one of the following, largely self-explanatory, terms:

Top, centre, bottom.
Inside, i.e. towards the fold, or outside.
Next matter, i.e. next to editorial content.
Under matter, next and under matter.
Island position, i.e. matter on at least three sides.
Solus, on its own, no other advertisements appearing on the same page.
Semi-solus, only one other advertisement on the same page.

Research evidence on the value of such positions is inconclusive, but media planners contend that better results are obtained from some positions than others. For example it is contended that as the eye is accustomed to starting at the top of a piece of printed matter there is a greater possibility of catching the reader's attention if the advertisement is on the upper half of the page. Intuitively one is inclined to agree with observations of this type until adequate research either confirms, or infirms the hypothesis.

The regional press

At the time of writing there were 48 morning, 71 evening and 1798 weekly papers published on a regional basis in the United Kingdom. In many respects the characteristics of the regional press are similar to those of the national dailies already described, and this summary will be confined to noting certain differences, and the major advantages and disadvantages of local papers as an advertising medium.

First, local papers have the advantage that they achieve concentrated coverage of a limited area, and so are likely to achieve a greater density of readership than a national paper. Because of the 'local' content they also tend to receive closer scrutiny, but against this must be set the greater authority of the national paper.

Second, regional papers are ideally suited to developing regional markets based on local preferences – an examination of consumption patterns on a regional basis soon indicates that the British population is far from homogeneous in this respect.

Third, the limited circulation of the regional and local paper makes them a good medium for copy testing (i.e. running different versions of an advertisement in order to measure their relative effectiveness as a basis for final selection). The lower circulations of these papers also makes them more economical, although the C.P.T. rate may be comparable to, or even greater than, those of the nationals.

Fourth, and this also applies to the national papers to a lesser degree, the frequency of publication permits the development of a theme by instalments, or early repetition if desired to 'stiffen up' a campaign.

Finally, evening and weekly papers have the advantage over morning daily papers that they are taken *into* the home, and so are likely to be seen by more members of the household at greater leisure.

The major disadvantages associated with both regional and national papers are:

(*a*) The poor quality newsprint does not permit a very high standard of reproduction – this may be improved by colour printing 'inserts' on a glazed paper that will accept a smaller screen size than ordinary newsprint, e.g. *Daily Express.*

(*b*) News dates rapidly, so most papers are scanned rapidly on the day of issue and discarded, i.e. a newspaper advertisement is virtually a 'one-shot' attempt at attracting the public's attention and so will usually require a number of repetitions if it is to be seen by the majority of the paper's readers.

Sunday newspapers

J. D. Hughes of Hobson, Bates & Partners wrote of this group: 'The British Sunday press is a unique phenomenon. No other country possesses anything remotely like it. It is, moreover, a phenomenon rooted deeply in the habits and behaviour of the people it serves' (*Advertiser's Weekly*, 21 Oct 1966). When one considers that the *News of the World* alone has a readership of 32 per cent of the United Kingdom *adult population*, one begins to appreciate how deeply ingrained is the Sunday newspaper habit.

Unlike daily papers, which tend to be scanned, the Sunday paper is perused at leisure and so achieves greater attention value. The actual composition of the readership varies from paper to paper, and the serious student should consult the JICNARS for a detailed breakdown on both a national and regional basis.

A second feature of the 'quality' Sunday papers (*Sunday Times, Sunday Telegraph* and *Observer*) which differentiates them from most of the dailies is the colour magazine, which largely overcomes the criticism of low standards of reproduction associated with newspapers in general (*The Daily Telegraph* now publishes the magazine originally associated with the *Sunday Telegraph*).

Magazines

The major factor which differentiates a magazine from a newspaper is that the former preselects its readership through the nature of its content. A second distinguishing feature is that they are read at leisure.

Magazines, as a group, may be further subdivided into categories, and media planners have adopted the following classification:

1. General magazines – so designated because of their general appeal, as contrasted with:
2. Specialist magazines, which cater for the readership with clearly defined and specific interest – e.g. doctors, philatelists.
3. The retail trade press. This subdivision is justified because of the medium's importance in 'selling-in' a product prior to the start of a campaign aimed at the consumer.

General magazines. This category may be further subdivided into those which have a predominantly male or female readership, as compared with those which appeal to both sexes. For example *Woman* has a predominantly female readership, *Autocar* male, *Radio Times* male and female. Overall, the characteristics of the general magazine are so diverse that one should properly attempt to rate each separately by reference to the check-list. At the same time there are a number of points which justify generalisation, namely:

Character
    Read at leisure.
    Preselect their audience by the content e.g. *Popular Gardening, Homemaker, Punch.*

Better standards of reproduction than newspapers.

Longer duration of interest – e.g. of the ultimate readership of a woman's weekly, 60 per cent see it within two weeks of publication, 30 per cent in the next two weeks, and the remaining 10 per cent over a period of six months or longer.

Readership may be ten to fifteen times circulation.

The lower frequency of publication necessitates booking of space well in advance, i.e. less flexible in this respect than newspapers.

Atmosphere

More stable than that of the newspaper, which is affected by the news it carries.

Higher standards of reproduction convey a greater sense of luxury than is possible with a newspaper, particularly where colour is used.

Coverage/Cost

Difficult to estimate on a comparative basis owing to the variation in page size, on which rates are based, and of readership. Overall, the C.P.T. is higher than that for the national or regional press, and ranges from about £0.44 – in the mass circulation broadcasting publications, to around £1.07 – in the glossy fashion magazines. This higher cost is offset by the greater intrinsic worth of the advertisements to the reader, which ensures a higher 'page traffic', i.e. number of readers per page expressed as a proportion of the total readership.

Specialist magazines. Detailed information on specialist magazines is more limited than in the case of the general magazine, largely because so few of them are included in the National Readership Survey. In addition to the above generalised comments, one may add that the magazines in this category are even more selective in their readership appeal. Further, the advertising content is often of equal interest to the editorial content, e.g. collectors' magazines listing objects for sale, technical magazines detailing new products and product improvements. With the exception of direct mail, the specialist magazine offers the greatest opportunity of reaching a highly specific audience.

Retail trade magazines. The need to ensure adequate distribution and availability of a product prior to the opening of a campaign directed at the ultimate consumer is advanced as the main reason for using this medium. Some media planners are sceptical as to its value, owing to the generally low level of readership – around 25 per cent – which is compounded by the sheer volume of advertisements, thus making the actual possibility of any particular advertisement being seen correspondingly small. It is also argued that the smaller retailer, at whom much of the effort is directed in the anticipation that it will reduce the amount of direct selling required, is an ordinary mortal who reads newspapers, watches T.V., etc., and that advertisements in these media are more likely to be seen and carry greater authority. In the light of these arguments it is clear that each case should be considered on its merits, and that particular attention should be given to position within the medium.

A review of print media would not be complete without some reference to controlled circulation papers and annuals and directories.

There has been a considerable growth in controlled circulation papers in recent years, particularly in the trade, technical and professional fields. Papers or magazines with a controlled circulation are not sold but are distributed free of charge to persons with a known interest in the magazine's editorial content. As with all other media, space is sold on the basis of the medium's ability to reach an audience which in this instance is closely defined. Many of the these publications claim virtually total coverage of the predefined audience. This assertion should be treated with circumspection, but it is indisputable that some achieve spectacular results.

Annuals and directories may be subdivided into four categories:

1. Annual special numbers – these are published by the parent publication, usually a magazine or newspaper, as a completely separate entity, i.e. they are not a 'special issue'. Example: *Country Life Annual.*
2. Annual consumer reference books. Examples: *Whitaker's Almanack, Daily Mail Year Book, Pears Cyclopaedia.*
3. Trade, technical and professional diaries, buyer's guides, year books. These usually contain a mass of information

which the practitioner may require at a moment's notice. Example: *Electrical Trade Directory*.
4. Annual street directories and shopper's guides. (Telephone directories might be considered to come within this category, especially the classified directories or 'Yellow Pages'.)

Obviously the greatest disadvantage associated with this medium is the low flexibility that is a concomitant of annual publication. Against this may be set low cost – *AdWeekly* published a 'case history' of Automat some years ago which demonstrated how this company had concentrated its limited advertising appropriation in trade directories and, through careful positioning and repetition, achieved excellent results (25 Aug 1967).

Television
Television advertising is the most recent development in the field of advertising media and, as inferred when reviewing the national press, its impact has been enormous. In terms of expenditures, T.V. is second only to the press as a whole, and its growth in recent years has consistently exceeded that of all other media. The importance of the medium is reflected in the publication of books devoted solely to the subject of commercial television, and the serious student should refer to these sources for a detailed description. Limitations of time and space dictate that the barest outline can be developed in this context.

Character. Above all commercial television is a mass medium: it can be received in over 90 per cent of all British homes. On an average evening over 50 per cent of these homes will be tuned in to a commercial television station and, in the course of a day, an average of 2.9 hours of commercial transmissions will be received by the 93 per cent of households capable of tuning in. Although, in theory, it would be possible to reach all these households simultaneously with a single advertisement, few advertisers would in fact attempt this as coverage is subdivided among twelve contractors, each of whom is responsible for a geographical region in the country, namely:

Associated Television Ltd	Midlands
Anglia Television Ltd	East of England
Border Television Ltd	The Borders and Isle of Man
Granada Television Ltd	Lancashire
Harlech Television Ltd	Wales and West of England
London Weekend Television Ltd	London – weekends
Stags Television Ltd	Central and N.E. Scotland
Southern Television Ltd	South of England
Thames Television Ltd	London – weekdays
Trident Television	North-East England and Yorkshire
Ulster Television Ltd	Northern Ireland
Westward Television Ltd	South-West England

Thus, while national coverage is possible, most advertisers tend to advertise selectively on a regional basis. This trend is encouraged by the contractors, who on the one hand stress the purchasing behaviour which differentiates the consumers within their area from those in other areas, thus making a case for regional marketing, while on the other hand they publish statistics that demonstrate that their audience is an accurate reflection of the national audience and so suitable for a national campaign. If a note of scepticism is detected, the reader should consult some of the commercial television contractors' own publicity material to see how it is possible to substantiate essentially opposing claims from the same basic data. (This tendency is most marked in the case of those companies offering test marketing facilities, where a representative sample is a desirable prerequisite – it is difficult to accept that the inhabitants of central Scotland are identical with those of Kent and Sussex, or vice versa!)

With such a large potential audience, it follows that commercial television reaches all socio-economic groups. As might be expected, there is a slight bias towards the lower social groups, to larger families and to housewives, but as these constitute the mass market for consumer goods, this has clear advantages for the marketers of such products.

The great advantage of television over all other media, with the exception of the cinema, is its ability to combine sound, vision and movement. This combination permits the use of advertisements that demonstrate the product and its advantages, which, most would agree, is far more effective than a written or static visual representation. The sole ingredient lacking until recently has been the availability of colour. However, after a very slow start in 1968 sales reached 505,000 sets in 1970 double that projected, 920,000 in 1971, over 1.75 million in 1972, and in 1973 were well in excess of 2 million sets per annum. In 1978 56 per cent of all T.V. owners had colour sets.

Commercial television channels operate seven days a week, mainly between the hours of noon and midnight, with the result that the composition of the audience varies according to the time segment selected: e.g. programmes for housewives in the afternoon, children's programmes from 4 to 6 p.m., 'family programmes' 6–9 p.m., adult programmes from 9 p.m. onwards. The composition of the audience also varies from day to day, and once again the student is referred to *BRAD* or the publications of the Joint Industry Committee for Television Advertising Research (JICTAR) for a detailed break-down.

Television commercials themselves vary from 7-second 'spots' through multiples of 15 seconds to a normal maximum of 2 minutes. In practice, few advertisements exceed 60 seconds and most are in the 15-, 30- and 60-second bracket. A readily observed feature of television commercials which is infrequently commented on is the fact that the advertisements are concentrated into a series of 'natural breaks'. To the author's knowledge research has yet to be undertaken on the effect that this has on the viewer. Some media planners have commented adversely, however, to the effect that viewers must find it difficult to assimilate a fairly large number of advertisements within a short space of time. (An examination of peak loadings, in terms of water and electricity consumption, might lead one to believe that in fact the majority of viewers avoid the problem by attending to their toilet and making cups of tea during such breaks!)

Atmosphere. It is often claimed that a major advantage of television is that it is viewed in the home, in a relaxed atmosphere, when the audience is more receptive than is normally the case when exposed to advertising messages. Against this one must set the disadvantage that the injection of advertising into a programme is both intrusive and irrelevant. While attention may be concentrated on the programme itself, the popularity of the first and last 'spots' in the break would seem to indicate that media planners recognise that attention may wander once it is realised that a break has started, and only returns in anticipation of the commencement of the programme.

The more successful television advertisers, judged on the basis of their sales results, appear to have recognised both the intrusive and irrelevant aspects of commercials, and to have made a virtue out of necessity by issuing advertisements that superficially appear to have both these characteristics. Judging by the adverse comments directed at a margarine that gave one delusions of grandeur, one should be surprised to learn that at a time when margarine sales were in a decline the only brand showing an absolute increase in sales happened to be the one with the 'stupid' commercial.

Coverage/cost. With fifteen contractors, each with its own rate structure that varies both in terms of the time of day and the day of the week, little of general use can be said.

Position in terms of television commercials refers both to the time segment and the position within the segment.

Size is measured in terms of the duration of the commercial.

Commercial radio

Until the autumn of 1973 the only commercial radio transmissions which could be received in this country were those of Radio Luxemburg. However in October 1973 Capital Radio came on the air as the first of approximately sixty local commercial radio stations authorised for the country as a whole. A second London station, London Broadcasting, came on the air shortly afterwards, while the third, Radio Clyde, started transmissions on New Year's Day 1974. There are at the present nineteen local radio stations and the whole I.L.R. network has an average weekly reach of 49 per cent of the total adult population.

Outdoor advertising

(The 'check-list' approach will not be used for the remaining media – the student may like to formulate his own.) Outdoor advertising is often thought of as consisting solely of the poster medium. This ignores transportation advertising, illuminated signs and several lesser media which properly fall into this category.

As with the press and the cinema, the advent of commercial television resulted in outdoor advertising having to reappraise its role as an advertising medium. It was realised that television had become the prime medium for the advertising of a wide range of mass consumption goods which had formerly depended far more on press, poster and cinema. There are still instances in which outdoor advertising may be used as the prime medium, but in the majority of cases outdoor advertising is sold as a complement to a television campaign on the grounds that it serves as a reminder at, or near, the actual point of sale. This fact is supplemented by a gradual increase in audience size due to increased personal mobility.

The main outdoor medium is the poster, which suffers from three main disadvantages. First, to ensure that its message is conveyed quickly and concisely it can only accommodate a short copy story. Second, posters are not seen in the context of other matter of editorial or entertainment value. Finally, production costs are relatively high, as are maintenance costs. Offsetting this are a number of advantages.

It has been estimated that over 90 per cent of the population goes out of doors in the course of a week and thus has an 'opportunity to see' a poster. Actual poster sighting will obviously be considerably less than this but, unlike most other media, an accurate predictive model has been developed which enables the prospective advertiser to determine in advance the type of campaign he will have to mount to reach an audience of a given size. (See Mills & Rockley's Studies and the I.P.A. Audience Measurement Study 1964.) Second, poster advertising offers greater geographic flexibility than virtually any other medium; one may use a single site in a specific locality, cover all or part of a town, or all or part of the country. Third, the cost of poster advertising is relatively low, so that an advertiser with a limited appropriation can mount both an extensive and prolonged campaign for an amount that would make little impact on television when ranged against the large budgets of the major television advertisers. (This is not to say that posters will have more impact than a television commercial as such, but rather that impact is relative such that a limited television campaign would tend to be completely dominated by that of a major advertiser on the medium.) Fourth, posters can make full use of colour and achieve high standards of reproduction.

The size of a poster is given as a multiple of a standard 'sheet' measuring 30 by 20 inches, the standard poster being 16 sheet, or 10 feet by 6 feet 8 inches. Other sizes are 32 sheet – 10 feet by 13 feet 4 inches, 48 sheet – 10 by 20 feet, and 96 sheet, or 'Supersites', measuring 10 feet by 40 feet. The actual cost of a poster site varies depending upon its location, and no useful generalisation may be made. The poster industry offers advertisers various ways of mounting a poster campaign. From 'Line by line' where the contractor offers individual sites to build up a specific display to suit particular marketing objectives, the use of 'pre-selected target audience campaigns' (P.S.C.) which are market-tailored pre-selected displays offered by British Posters Ltd, and 'key plans' which are specially built displays offered by Independent Poster Sales Ltd. Full details are published in *BRAD* and representative costs for a key plan campaign or selected supersite campaign are given in the following tables (pp. 303–4).

TABLE 15.2. *Key plan campaigns*

Key plan region	No. of 4/16 sheets	Total cost per month (£)
London (inc. Outer region)	700	10,325
Southern	130	2,025
Anglia	85	1,145
Midlands	225	3,035
Wales, West and South-west	225	3,035
Yorkshire	225	3,035
Granada and Border	300	4,050
Tyne Tees	125	1,685
Scotland	110	1,485
Total	2,125	29,820*

*Subject to 6 per cent National Combination Discount providing all areas are taken.

TABLE 15.3. *Super heavyweight housewife campaign*

| | No. of 16/4 sheets | Rate per month (£) | | |
		A	AA	AAA
London	1,385	16,270	20,315	21,925
Midlands	920	9,470	11,835	12,785
South	520	5,350	6,690	7,225
East	220	2,150	2,685	2,900
Wales and West	495	4,830	6,050	6,525
North-west	1,040	10,155	12,700	13,720
Yorkshire	675	6,590	8,240	8,900
North-east	365	3,560	4,455	4,810
Scotland	515	5,025	6,290	6,790
Ulster	—	—	—	—
National	6,135	63,400	79,260	85,580*

*Subject to 5 per cent all Area Combination Discount.
Rate A　　= Jan, Feb, Mar.
Rate AA　= Apr, Aug, Sep, Dec.
Rate AAA = May, June, July, Oct, Nov.

Approximate costs of a poster campaign utilising 16-sheet posters for a three-month period (May–July) to back up a television campaign would be:

National – £155,460
London – £42,285
Midlands – £24,315
Lancashire – £26,250
Scotland – £12,930
Harlech – £12,360
Tyne Tees and Yorkshire – £26,070

Transportation advertising is a familiar aspect of our everyday lives which should not be overlooked when considering media selection. The general points made with regard to posters apply equally to transportation advertising, so that further description will be confined to a review of the sites available and the approximate costs associated with them.

Road transport sites
    Essentially these sites are to be found on and in buses.

Site	Approximate size	Cost per month (on annual basis)
		£
Target – a circular space on the corner of the bus	19-inch diameter	1.05
Fronts (double)	various	3.05
Rears – Upper (double)	20″ × 30″	3.05
– Lower	48″ × 20″	3.05
Sides	17′6″ × 21½″	5.05
Sides – illuminated	17′6″ × 21½″	14.95
Interior bulkheads	11″ × 11″	0.85
Interior panels – illuminated	26″ × 8″	1.50

Rail transport sites (London Underground)

Site	Approximate size	Cost per month (on annual basis)
		£
Carriage card – Underground	24″ × 11″	0.90
Stations – Double crown (per 100)	20″ × 30″	1.75
– Quad crown (per 100)	30″ × 40″	3.50
– 4-sheet	40″ × 60″	12.00
– 16-sheet	80″ × 120″	13.00
– Escalator cards	16½″ × 22½″	8.00
Van sites		
Van fronts	150 cm × 50 cm	1.50
Van side	225 cm × 105 cm	1.25

The cinema

The impact of television on the cinema is readily apparent in any major town where former sites have been converted into Bingo halls, warehouses or simply pulled down to make way for re-development. Although many may regret the passing of the local cinema and retain nostalgic memories of a 9*d* seat in the stalls, there can be no doubt that the competition of television has forced the cinema industry to undertake a massive face-lift. Cinema operators have realised that if they are to persuade customers to leave the comfort of their own fireside, and the hypnotic attraction of the 'box', they must make cinema-going an event. Despite the closure of many cinemas, many of which were themselves a mute reminder of the days of music-hall, there can be no doubt that the improvement and rebuilding programmes have greatly improved the standards of comfort offered to patrons. At the same time the

TABLE 15.4. *Cinema audience composition*

	% *audience*	% *population*
By sex:		
Male	57	57
Female	43	39
By age:		
15 – 24	34	86
25 – 34	26	68
35 – 44	17	56
45 – 54	12	39
55 – 64	7	22
65 +		
15 – 34	60	77
By social class:		
AB	19	58
C1	26	55
C2	33	50
DE	22	35

film producers have concentrated on the competitive advantages which they possess, and which cannot be duplicated on the small screen – size and colour. The box office success of the James Bond films, and films like *The Godfather* or *A Bridge Too Far* testify that the formula is a good one.

An examination of the composition of the cinema audience provides an interesting insight for the media planner.

Clearly, the Screen Advertisers Association's claim that it is the medium for reaching 'young adults' is justified by these statistics; it is further strengthened by data that indicate that on average this group makes twenty visits a year. This audience is of particular interest to the manufacturers of both semi-luxury goods, such as cosmetics, and consumer durables, appealing to single persons with high discretionary spending power, engaged couples and young marrieds.

Television can still offer a lower cost per thousand for the same audience but lacks the high attention value of a captive audience, viewing under ideal conditions over which the advertiser, not the viewer, has control, e.g. sound volume, quality of picture.

An indication of the cost of using the cinema for an advertising campaign may be judged from Tables 15.4 and 15.5.

Advertisements are normally of 15, 30, 60 and 120 seconds in length. Actual rates vary by cinema and may be obtained from the Screen Advertising Association's master list of cinemas.

Although the cost per 1,000 of using the cinemas is greater than for television the Screen Advertisers Association justifies this on the grounds that the cinema possesses undeniable qualitative advantages, particularly the combined impact of colour, sound, and the big-screen presentation upon a captive audience.

Direct mail

The great advantage of direct mail, by comparison with all other media, is its selectivity. Postal delivery is possible in every part of the country – a potential which enables the advertiser to reach a small, closely identified audience with a precision that could not possibly be duplicated by any other medium.

In the author's opinion direct mail is grossly underrated as an advertising medium, probably because of the dangers inherent in generalising from the particular. The common belief that the reci-

TABLE 15.5. *Cinemas, number and cost by ITV areas (one week in all cinemas)*

	No. of cinemas	30-second £	60-second £
London	433	4163	6604
Midland	224	1714	2719
Lancashire	261	1727	2745
Yorkshire	116	1180	1875
Central Scotland	95	812	1289
Wales and West	180	1106	1754
Southern	172	1189	1887
North-east	73	569	904
Anglia	92	606	962
Ulster	29	151	252
South-west	67	399	633
Border	22	116	185
North-east Scotland	42	234	372
Channel Isles	6	70	112
TOTAL (excluding overlap)	1525	12,412	19,708

Source: Screen Advertisers Association (1977).
Note: Rate for 90 and 120 seconds are pro rata to the 60-second rate. Cinemas can be bought individually for a minimum period of one week.

pients of a direct mailing 'shot' immediately consign it to the waste-paper basket without a glance is not borne out by a recent American survey, which showed that approximately two-thirds do read the advertisement, and that more thn 30 per cent subsequently made a purchase of the item advertised. Similar findings are reported by the British Market Research Bureau in its *Direct Mail Summary of Research.*

Direct mailing lists may be compiled by the advertiser himself from customer records, or from the same basic sources used by the direct mail house – classified telephone directories, trade directories, etc. Where it is intended to mount a campaign designed to increase one's market or to enter a new market, the cost would be disproportionate by comparison with the cost of 'buying' a list from a specialist direct mail house. (Lists are rarely sold as such – the rate quoted is for a mailing using the direct mail company's list.)

As with other aspects of advertising, the employment of an agency is to be recommended owing to the specialisation which they can bring to bear on the advertiser's problem. Those direct mail shots which do finish up in the waste bin most frequently do so because of either incorrect identification of a 'prospect' or poor copy and layout. A good agency will not be guilty of either of these faults.

On average a direct mailing will cost £0.10–0.15 per item, which, when it is considered that three mailings is considered a desirable target to aim at, makes a campaign of any size an expensive undertaking. Against this must be set the precision with which potential customers may be reached by comparison with the lower costs of the 'buck shot' approach of the other media. A further advantage of direct mail is that its effectiveness can be measured directly, which, as a later section will show, is not the easiest of things to achieve.

An off-shoot of direct mail is door-to-door distribution of advertising material. Several companies offer this service for the distribution of samples, coupons and leaflets, utilising the services of part-time employees under the control and supervision of a full-time area supervisor, e.g. Vernon's Distributors. Rates vary, depending upon the nature of the material to be distributed, and the frequency, i.e. every house, every tenth house, etc.

CAMPAIGN PLANNING

An excellent and inexpensive treatment of this subject is to be found in Olaf Ellefsen's *Campaign Planning* published by Business Publications on behalf of the I.P.A., and the student should consult this source for a fuller treatment than is possible here.

Earlier in the chapter a number of advertising objectives were stated, and it was noted that the determination of such an objective was an essential prerequisite to the formulation of a campaign plan. Assuming that management has given its advertising agency a clear statement of what it wishes to achieve, it then becomes the agency's responsibility to devise a campaign that will maximise the return on the appropriation allocated. As was inferred when discussing the agency/client relationship, the preparation of a campaign plan will require close co-operation between the parties. This will become clear if one considers the stages leading up to the introduction of a new product.

The first stage in the process is the recognition of a business opportunity. Once this has been identified, the marketer will undertake marketing research as a basis for quantifying the nature and extent of this opportunity. As a result of such research a consumer profile will be drawn up stating the demographic characteristics of the potential consumer, the geographical location of the market, the frequency and method of purchase, etc.

Armed with this 'blueprint' of the intended consumer, the next stage in the process is the development of a product to satisfy the demand represented by recognition of the original opportunity. Once developed, the product will be tested. It is at this stage that the agency should be brought in. Given the consumer profile, the nature of the product and a statement of the features which differentiate it from competitors' offerings, the proposed channels of distribution and intended price bracket, the agency will be in a position to suggest an appropriate name and package. The continued growth of self-service retailing, described in Chapter 8. demands that very careful attention be paid to the latter two factors (name and package), as recognition at the point of sale is a vital stimulus to purchase. For these reasons alone the advertiser will want to feature both the brand name and pack in his advertising. If concept and product testing have been carried out the comments of the respondents should also be made available to the agency, as they invariably provide leads as to the copy platform to be adopted. A good example of this was Johnson's Wax in the United States. When housewives were asked to list the most important properties of a floor polish, the majority gave considerable weight to the polish's ability to resist scuffing. Although 'scuffing' was not a word in common currency, the panel housewives had independently selected it as the most descriptive. When Johnson introduced their new brand it was advertised as the 'non-scuff' polish and achieved immediate success – it was just what housewives were looking for!

A further reason for bringing in the agency at this time is to discuss the method of launching the product – test market, regional or national launch – and the timing, from selling in to the channels of distribution to the product's appearance in the retail outlet. On the basis of all this information, the agency will draw up a plan for submission to the advertiser comprising two major elements – the copy platform and the media schedule

The copy platform is the theme around which the campaign is based, e.g. 'It's the real thing. Coke', while the media schedule lists the media in which the advertisements are to be published with details of size, timing, frequency and cost. The advertising literature is full of advice on the selection of U.S.P.s (unique selling points), E.B.T.s (emotional buying triggers) and the like, but for an insight into the preparation and execution of advertising campaigns the student is strongly recommended to read one, or all, of the following books: David Ogilvy, *Confessions of an Advertising Man*: a highly readable and somewhat unconventional description of how Ogilvy became one of America's top advertising men, packed with information and advice for the aspiring advertising agent; Rosser Reeves, *Reality in Advertising*: a short but highly concentrated coverage of do's and don't's in advertising, full of actual examples of advertising campaigns; Martin Mayer, *Madison Avenue*: a colourful and interesting description of what goes on at the heart of the U.S. agency business, a little dated now but still worth reading.

SETTING THE ADVERTISING APPROPRIATION

The decision of how much to spend on advertising and other promotional activities is one of the more difficult budgeting problems that management is called upon to make. As will become clear in the next part of this chapter, the measurement of advertising effectiveness is, to say the least, difficult. In the absence of a directly measureable relationship between the volume of advertising and the overall profitability of the firm, the majority of managements have adopted one, or a combination, of the following 'rule-of-thumb' approaches.

Fixed percentage of sales. Under this method management allocates a percentage of either past or anticipated sales to advertising.

A B.I.M. *Survey of Manufacturers' Marketing Costs* (Information Summary No. 111) published in 1964 indicates that there is a considerable variation in the percentage allocated to advertising, even within an industry, which, in turn, is a reflection of the different competitive strategies adopted by marketers. In this context it is noteworthy that total exenditures on advertising have remained a virtually constant percentage of the G.N.P. in most advanced economies during this century as may be seen by reference to the following table.

TABLE 15.6. *Total media advertising expenditure*

	£ million	% of Gross National Product
1952	123	0.9
1956	197	1.1
1961	338	1.4
1962	348	1.4
1963	371	1.4
1964	416	1.4
1965	435	1.4
1966	447	1.4
1967	458	1.3
1968	503	1.4
1969	544	1.4
1970	554	1.3
1971	591	1.2

Adoption of this policy may be justified on the grounds that it is rational to allocate a fixed proportion of sales revenue to advertising in the absence of a model which permits a prediction of variation in sales volume in response to variations in the volume of advertising. On the other hand, it ignores the fact that a decline in sales volume will result in a contraction of the advertising appropriation at the very time when increased advertising may be the stimulus necessary to halt the decline or reverse the trend.

In the case of companies operating in markets with an inelastic demand, the policy helps stabilise the competitive situation, always providing that it is a commonly accepted practice. Certain oligopolistic industries appear to exhibit this characteristic – the knowledge that increased advertising will not result in an increase in primary demand dissuades individual firms from attempting to improve their market share through increased advertising owing to the strong competitive response which it is bound to provoke. (This tendency was also noted with regard to the use of price reductions as a competitive weapon, unless the instigator had a clear cost advantage over his competitors.)

The 'me-too' approach. The adoption of this 'policy' was implied above, and constitutes the adoption of a level of advertising which corresponds to that of one's competitors. This is a purely defensive and negative reaction. Clearly, the firm is interested in what its competitors are doing as a guide to the policies it should adopt, but it also follows that if the firm is to improve its competitive position it must pursue policies that will enable the consumer to distinguish it from the competition and perceive it as superior.

What we can afford. This method tends to relegate expenditures on advertising to the bottom rung of the corporate budget ladder. It implies that whatever remains after meeting operating costs, dividend payments, etc., will be spent on advertising. As with the fixed percentage of sales method, the most likely outcome is that as sales fall the unit contribution will decline to the point where no advertising can be afforded at all. Conversely, as sales rise an increasing amount will become available and the possibility of wasteful expenditures will become a reality.

The 'task' approach. In the absence of a normative model of the relationship between various levels of advertising and profitability, this method is to be preferred to any of the above practices. The first step in this method is the definition of a clear objective. Given the objective, one can prepare a campaign plan that would achieve this goal. An examination of the costs of mounting such a campaign may indicate that it is beyond the company's available resources. Within this constraint, the plan may be modified by closely evaluating each of its component parts and dispensing with the least essential. Obviously the end result will be a lesser objective than originally laid down, but it will be a realistic statement of what the firm can hope to accomplish related to current resources.

The B.I.M. Survey *Marketing Organisation in British Industry* (Information Summary 148) indicated that the respondents used the following basis for determining their advertising appropriations.

	%
Proportion of expected future sales	39
Analysis of needs or objectives	19
Proportion of past sales	11
Proportion of profit	7
Historical expenditure	2
As much as can be afforded	1

THE MEASUREMENT OF ADVERTISING EFFECTIVENESS

When discussing media selection, frequent reference was made to *BRAD* and the I.P.A. Readership Surveys as a source of information on audience composition. Head counting is a long-established practice that yields sound demographic data. A measure of audience size is of interest to the advertiser but, ultimately, he is much more concerned with the effectiveness of his advertising, i.e. he wants a measure of the results of exposure to advertising. Five basic methods have been evolved to measure advertising effectiveness and these are reviewed below.

The measurement of awareness. Awareness is defined as 'knowledge about a company or its product without reference to the source of knowledge'. As, by definition, awareness tests do not relate knowledge to source they provide only a rough and ready guide to advertising effectiveness, and are usually undertaken as a preliminary to further tests. In the case of a new product it may be possible to isolate the source of awareness, but this is virtually impossible in the case of an established brand.

Actual measurement is obtained by asking respondents:

(*a*) Straight dichotomous questions, e.g. 'Have you ever heard of the XYZ company?'

Yes . . . No . . .

(*b*) An open-ended question, e.g. 'Do you know of any companies that make a detergent with a blue whitener?'

(*c*) Check-list questions with rating scales, e.g. 'How familiar are you with the XYZ company?'

> Very familiar . . .
> Know something about . . .
> Know very little about them . . .
> Never heard of . . .

Low cost and speed are cited as the major advantages of this method.

The measurement of recall. Recall – what people can remember about advertising messages – is the most frequently used measure of advertising effectiveness, on the basis that if the message has left a memorable impression it has fulfilled its communicative function. If the advertising objective is to communicate information then the method is appropriate, but in many instances the objective is to promote action, e.g. mail-order advertisements. Recall is also a useful measure when copy testing.

Recall studies are capable of measuring several dimensions of advertising effectiveness. At the lowest level they consist of the respondent's describing the basic theme of an advertisement, and progress through association of the correct theme with the product advertised, measures of comprehension, credibility and conviction, to significance.

Essentially, the method employed is to ask the respondent to reconstruct what he or she can remember having seen or heard advertised, either unaided – unaided recall – or with a varying degree of assistance to direct the respondent's thinking along particular lines – aided recall. Aided recall is generally preferred, as few people will spontaneously recall past events without some stimulus, in which case the researcher must guard against bias arising from too much assistance, or false answers resulting from guessing. Gallup and Robinson conduct regular surveys of recall, and attempt to minimise bias by first establishing that the respondent has read the issue being tested by showing him the cover, and then asking him to establish knowledge of its content. Once the respondent has demonstrated familiarity with the test issue, he is then asked to reconstruct his memory of the advertisements without opening the magazine. The final stage is to show the respondent brand names, advertisement logotypes, etc., and after telling him that some did not appear in the issue in question, ask him to identify those he remembers. A sample of 400 is used, the interviews are recorded verbatim and, after editing, are compiled into an index of recall – the 'proved name registration'. A P.N.R. is calculated for the medium as a whole, for the product group and for the specific brand. Although it is difficult to assign an absolute value to a P.N.R., it provides a useful guide to the advertiser in that he can measure his advertisement's performance against that of all other advertisers in the magazine and that of his immediate competitors. Further, over a period of time he can determine whether the impact of his advertising is increasing, declining or static.

A hybrid test which incorporates both aided and unaided recall is 'working along the time line'. For example you ask a respondent to describe what he did yesterday evening, anticipating that he will recall an event which involved consumption of a product in which you are interested. If the product group is mentioned, e.g. 'I washed, cleaned my teeth and went to bed,' you might ask the name of the brand of soap or toothpaste and lead into further questions related to these products. If the product group is not mentioned then the interviewer will ask directly 'Did you clean your teeth?', etc.

Three problems are inherent in all recall studies:

1. Respondent confusion, due to either confusing the advertisement and its sponsor – Kellogg's Puffed Wheat – or identifying advertisements correctly from recollections of previous campaigns.
2. Recall of advertising messages in the interview situation is not the same as recall at the point of sale (a strong argument for both poster advertising and P.O.S. display), nor does it indicate an intention to buy.
3. The ever-present danger of misinterpretation of the results.

For the two latter reasons recall investigations are often combined with:

Attitude surveys. A favourable attitude towards a company or its product nearly always precedes a decision to buy, even if this favourable predisposition is at the preconscious level, i.e. a consumer picks up a product on impulse without consciously identifying the motivation to purchase.

Attitude measurement may consist of a general assessment or be restricted to various dimensions of a specific brand – acceptance, preference or insistence – of either one's own or one's competitor's product. Unfortunately, it is difficult to construct a true measure of a person's attitudes, and several techniques are frequently used in combination to permit cross-checking. The more common methods are:

(a) Direct questions of the 'Do you like X?' type, followed by a request to explain why you do, or do not, like X. Direct questions suffer from their inability to distinguish between varying degrees of intensity of feeling. Rating scales provide a partial solution and are amenable to rapid analysis, but suffer from the disadvantage that the choice of phrases which are precise, yet universally understood, is extremely difficult; that, however large, the scale may still not permit a truly accurate expression of intensity of feeling; that intermediate positions are capable of varying interpretations, e.g. 'What is your attitude to Widgets?'

Favourable . . .
Mixed . . .
Indifferent . . .
Unfavourable . . .

Alternatively, one might use the scale: Excellent, 4, 3, 2, Poor, or even a seven- or ten-point scale.

(b) A second method is to ask the respondent to complete a checklist by indicating the most appropriate answer/description of those assigned to each question. By undertaking a preliminary survey it is usually possible to design questions that will cover the attributes which consumers, as opposed to advertisers, think important.

(c) A semantic differential test, in which a respondent indicates where a brand or company stands on a scale of paired opposites, either descriptive adjectives or phrases, e.g. reliable–unreliable.

(b) Partially structured interviews, in which the interviewer memorises the points to be covered and 'discusses' the subject with the respondent, rather than posing formal questions from a questionnaire. The lack of trained interviewers, the length of the interview and difficulties of interpretation severely limit the use of this method.

Attitude related to usage is usually considered a more significant measure of advertising effectiveness than attitude on its own, and it is usual to obtain a measure of usage as a basis for a comparison of attitudes.

Psychological measurement. The three techniques described above are designed to measure a respondent's reaction to advertising at the conscious or preconscious level. Psychological techniques are designed to probe deeper and reach to the subconscious mind. At this level the respondent is unaware of the reasons which result in certain expressed patterns of behaviour, although if asked, he will usually advance an acceptable and rational reason. As most advertising messages are directed at large audiences, the peculiarities of the individual are of little or no consequence unless they are common to a large number of individuals. It is to determine basic motivation that advertising researchers, among others, use psychological methods where direct questioning might lead to rationalisation or evasion.

Psychological techniques have limitations which require great care in their execution and interpretation, and it must be recognised that the results will be qualitative not quantitative. As noted above in regard to partially structured depth interviews, the lack of suitably qualified interviewers usually restricts the use of these techniques to small samples from which it is difficult to make acceptable projections of consumer behaviour.

The most frequently used method is the unstructured depth interview of from one to three hours, in which interviewer and respondent talk about a specific subject in the belief that if the respondent is kept talking about the same thing long enough some of his unconscious attitudes will begin to emerge.

A popular variation of the depth interview is the focused or directed group interview, in which a skilled interviewer leads a group of six to twelve people in an unstructured discussion that relates to the product and/or its advertising.

Other projective techniques used include thematic apperception tests, picture probes, narrative probes, sentence completion tests and word association tests.

Sort and count. Many advertisements contain an invitation to interested parties to write in to the advertiser for further information, free samples, etc. By sorting and counting the requests generated by such advertisements the advertiser can obtain much useful information at low cost.

Despite the potential bias due to respondent self-selection, this method does give valuable information in relative terms of the pulling power of different media, of different copy platforms and advertisement make-up, and of different sizes and positions within the media. The advertisements are usually keyed, i.e. given a coding, to assist identification, either by including the code in the address, e.g. Dept DM7 for an edition of the *Daily Mail*, or by requiring the respondent to clip the coupon on which the information is similarly recorded.

As mentioned by Ogilvy (in *Confessions of an Advertising Man*), direct mail advertisers have a continuous feedback of the pulling power of their advertisements, which supports his suggestion that those selling through more conventional channels might do well to adopt some of the former's advertising practices, e.g. use of long copy.

Others. Under this heading are a number of techniques which attempt to measure a causal relationship between advertising and measurable indicators of the firm's performance such as increased distribution (on the premise that if retailers are asked for goods not in stock they will seek supplies) or sales volume. The 'dealer playback' technique also deserves mention, and has been used by Black & Decker in a competition designed to increase sales push at the retail level. (Company representatives visit stores selling the goods in question, express an interest in them, and note the number of selling points suggested in their recent advertising that the salesman advances as a reason for purchase.)

LABORATORY TECHNIQUES FOR PRE-TESTING
ADVERTISEMENTS

A number of techniques have been developed to try and obtain an objective measure of people's response to advertisements, which interviewing methods are unable to elicit owing to an inability to verbalise or a tendency to rationalise. The use of the instruments listed below is based on the knowledge that emotional arousal in a human being results in various responses which are under the control of the autonomic nervous system and thus largely independent of conscious control. These responses include increases in pulse and respiration rates, erection of hair follicles, changes in pupil size and electrical brain pulses, perspiration rates, etc. As each person reacts to different stimuli to a varying degree, ideally one should measure all responses simultaneously, but this is clearly impossible under normal conditions. As such it is necessary to select the method(s) which provide the most reliable results in monitoring reactions to the specific variable under test with the minimum disturbance to the subject. The most frequently used are:

(a) *The psycho-galvanometer.* This instrument measures changes in the activity of the sweat glands via electrodes attached by suction to the subject's hands. Prior to exposing the subject to the test advertisements the basal level must be established for control purposes and care taken to maintain a constant temperature throughout the test. The highest reading recorded indicates maximum arousal.

(b) *The eye observation camera* is used to measure pupil dilation. As light also affects the pupil, care must be taken to ensure that both control and test material are of the same luminosity. The material to be tested is back-projected into a closed box while the camera records the pupil dilation over a period of time. The greatest change occurs with the highest level of arousal. The camera may also be used to measure the subject's blink rate – the higher the rate the greater the arousal. Blinking is partly under conscious control, and is also affected by humidity, irritation and fatigue, all of which must be controlled if an accurate measure is to be obtained.

(*c*) *The tachistoscope* is an instrument used for exposing material for controlled periods of time ranging from $\frac{1}{100}$ of a second to several seconds. Its main use is in measuring the impact of an advertisement by determining either the point at which its features are registered (noting and legibility studies) or its visual impact (what is communicated) when exposed for only a brief period. As individual 'thresholds' vary, a norm must first be established for each subject.

(*d*) *The eye-movement camera* tracks the movement of the eye over an advertisement by filming a point of light projected on to the eyeball. The track indicates the order and degree of attention given to the features of the advertisement.

All the above methods are subject to criticism on the grounds that they are unrealistic as a result of the laboratory situation; that only a limited number of respondents may be tested (owing to the high cost of the test and data processing equipment required), and these may not be representative; that no indication of the direction of the response is given, so that respondents have to be questioned as to their feelings, which reintroduces subjectivity into the test, i.e. a marked reaction may be due to either repulsion or attraction.

In mitigation, any test is better than no test if it helps in establishing whether or not advertisements are communicating their basic point to the subject. Further, it is only through experimentation that satisfactory techniques for measuring advertising effectiveness will be evolved.

ADVERTISING CASE HISTORY: QUAKER SUGAR PUFFS

The following case history is published by the kind permission of the advertiser, Quaker Oats Limited and the advertising agency, Boase Massimi Pollitt Univas. It concerns the development of a new advertising campaign for Sugar Puffs and the subsequent assessment of advertising effectiveness.

Background
Quaker Oats Limited appointed a new advertising agency, Boase Massimi Pollitt Univas in the summer of 1976. The brand, Sugar

Puffs, was at that time suffering a disturbing rate of volume decline (25 per cent p.a.). Before advertising could be developed there was thus a requirement to understand the underlying reasons for the poor brand performance.

The breakfast-cereal market

The market for breakfast cereals in the United Kingdom can be seen as four discrete segments. These are the 'staples' sector (Corn Flakes, Weetabix, Shredded Wheat, etc.), which constituted around 55 per cent of volume of the market by the summer of 1976, the 'hot' sector (Porridge and Instant Porridge), which constituted around 19 per cent of the market by volume, the 'health' sector (Special K, Alpen, All Bran, etc.) at around 12 per cent and the 'children's' sector (Rice Krispies, Frosties, Sugar Puffs, etc.) at around 14 per cent by volume.

Over the four years to 1976 these market shares had been very stable, except for a sudden decline in the 'children's' sector share from the summer of 1975, when it was holding a 17 per cent volume share.

Thus the total 'children's' sector of the market was losing share, accounting for some of Sugar Puff's decline. More worrying, however, was the fact that Sugar Puffs was losing its share of the declining children's sector volume share.

The reason for both these declines was the same. Between the summer of 1975 and the summer of 1976 wage inflation was overtaken by price inflation, so that the housewife was felt to be facing a shrinking housekeeping budget in real terms. This was reflected in the decline of premium brands in many markets.

The children's sector of the breakfast-cereal market was not only more expensive (on a price per pound basis) than the rest of the market but was perceived as particularly poor value for money owing to the indulgent nature of the constituent brands. Additionally Sugar Puffs was known to have a non-nourishing image, and so was perceived as worse value for money than competing brands.

The role of advertising

Before discussing the role of advertising it is important to refer to the nature of the purchase cycle for Sugar Puffs. Qualitative research indicated that a purchase will be initiated by a request from a child which requires endorsement from the mother on the basis of value for money and perceived nourishment in order for the purchase to be made. The brand is then taken into the home and the child must consume the whole packet (in competition with the three to five brands commonly in stock in the larder) before a repurchase is made. Repurchase may be automatic, or more typically it may be in response to a further request from the child.

Both mothers and their children are important for the maintenance of the brand franchise. Consequently there were three potential roles for advertising:

1. To counteract the poor value for money/poor nourishment image of Sugar Puffs among mothers (this was in fact the previous advertising strategy).
2. To increase child interest and involvement in Sugar Puffs and thus the intensity of child request and speed of consumption from the larder.
3. To do both.

In fact the third alternative was adopted since it was apparent from the purchase cycle that failure to accomplish either of the first two alternatives may have resulted in a block in the purchase cycle.

Media strategy
In order to accomplish the advertising objectives listed above television was adopted as the major medium. This was essentially a consequence of the characteristics of the medium noted earlier in this chapter, but also because it offered the opportunity to reach both mothers and children individually and together.

Creative strategy
The creative strategy was threefold:

1. To provide advertising that is of interest/amusing to children.
2. To communicate to children that Sugar Puffs are the most exciting/best-tasting breakfast cereal.
3. To reassure mothers that Sugar Puffs are a nourishing breakfast for their children through reference to the ingredients of whole, natural wheat and honey and to communicate this through a vehicle which is liked by mothers because their children like it.

Creative development
A campaign based on the Honey Monster advertising vehicle was
written, was subjected to qualitative research by showing rough
animated versions of the proposed commercials in group discussions and was modified in the light of the research results. The first
burst of advertising was transmitted during August and September
1976.

Advertising assessment
Both quantitative and qualitative research have provided
extremely satisfactory results. The advertising appears to be performing consistently with the defined objectives.

Shortly after the advertising started Sugar Puffs' volume sales
started to increase. However, the sales response attributable to the
advertising is difficult to determine because of the interaction of
the mix variables. However, a multivariate analysis was used to
separate the contribution to sales of the variables and the findings
would suggest that the advertising had made a significant contribution to the brand's volume growth.

ECONOMIC AND ETHICAL ASPECTS OF ADVERTISING

The above review of advertising has concentrated on the practical
aspects of the subject in so far as they affect the marketer. At the
same time one must be aware that advertising is frequently the
subject of criticism, and the aim of this section is to summarise the
arguments both for and against. In view of the author's interest in
marketing it follows that he has a favourable attitude towards
advertising, and the reader is warned that this treatment is bound
to be somewhat subjective.

The economic argument. Essentially the question is 'Is advertising productive in the economic sense, i.e. does it maximise satisfaction through the utilisation of scarce resources?' The cliché 'It pays
to advertise' is tacit recognition of the fact that advertising
improves the profitability of the advertiser, but this is not to say
that it necessarily makes any real contribution to the welfare of the
community as a whole.

From the economist's point of view, the acid test of any
economic activity is the utility of the output of that activity, which

is measured by the extent to which it satisfies wants. For the economist the difficulty of accepting that advertising creates utility in this sense is both semantic and conceptual. The economist would argue that rather than satisfy existing wants the advertiser seeks to create wants for something that is already available. Advertisers would probably argue that you cannot create wants – you can only create better ways of satisfying existing wants, and that consumers derive satisfaction from advertised goods is undeniable. Similarly, to argue that advertising persuades people to consume things they do not want is to deny one of the basic assumptions of the economist – that, by and large, people are rational in their purchasing behaviour.

Many economists draw a distinction between 'informative' and 'combative' advertising, following the definition of Alfred Marshall in his book *Industry and Trade*, published in 1919. The distinction was further elaborated in the March 1928 issue of the *Economic Journal* (Braithwaite), where it was claimed that advertising which contains information may be regarded as a true selling expense, whereas advertising designed to stimulate demand is non-essential and largely unproductive. In the April 1962 issue of the same journal, Samuel Courtauld was to assert '. . . most competitive advertising is a costly national extravagance'.

It would seem, therefore, that the critics concede the value of informative advertising as a means of making the consumer aware of the existence of goods and services and their basic properties, but that they consider combative or persuasive advertising to be a wasteful use of resources. It is difficult to see how the distinction can be maintained., since an advertisement for a new product may be justified as informative in that it makes consumers aware of the existence and characteristics of this product, but combative in that it seeks to persuade consumers to buy the new product in preference to a previously available substitute.

All advertisements contain some information, and it is a fruitless exercise to try and evaluate their individual utility in any precise manner as the informative/persuasive distinction will depend entirely on the existing state of knowledge of each individual member of the audience.

Partial recognition of this fact has diverted many economists, and other critics of advertising, to accept that 'persuasive' advertising can be beneficial, providing that it results in lower prices.

Unfortunately, this distinction ignores that price stability is the same as a price reduction under conditions of inflation, and that a consistent improvement in quality may represent the equivalent of a price reduction in that it increases consumer satisfaction for the same nominal money outlay.

To summarise, the case against advertising may be stated as:

1. Advertising leads to higher prices by conditioning demand and so leads to distortion of the productive machine, e.g. maize may cost only £0.01 per pound, but when converted into branded cornflakes it retails at about £0.40 per pound.
2. Advertising leads to non-price competition, e.g. the use of promotions. This creates diseconomies due to difficulties associated with the accurate measurement of demand, and results in a high proportion of product failures.
3. It is an unreliable guide as to value and satisfaction.
4. It leads to oligopoly and monopoly.
5. It is a waste of national resources.

Proponents of advertising would argue that:

1. Advertised goods are cheaper because:
   (a) Advertising brings about economies in 'true' selling costs, e.g. by reducing the need for direct selling, encouraging the development of self-service, etc.
   (b) It raises the scale of production, helps to stabilise output and promotes standardisation.
   (c) Competition ensures that the benefits of these economies will be passed on to the consumer.

2. Advertised goods are better goods because:
   (a) The identification of the product with the manufacturer through branding constitutes a guarantee of quality which must be maintained if the manufacturer is to secure repeat purchases from users.
   (b) To maintain market share manufacturers must constantly strive to improve their product to meet, or exceed, the claims of competing products.

3. Branded and advertised goods create a freedom of consumer choice that was unknown when the same articles were sold from bulk.

4. Advertising improves the standard of living by making new developments quickly available to the public and, by stimulating demand, creates investment, production and employment opportunities.

The ethical argument. Advertising is indicted on ethical grounds on the basis that it encourages the development of materialism. F. P. Bishop, in his book *The Ethics of Advertising*, defines materialism as ' . . . an acquisitive ideology in which the satisfaction of material desires is held up as the sole or principal end for the individual or group'.

In the creation of a materialistic society advertising is charged with deliberately concentrating on those motives that are least desirable in man and of least value to society. One can be shown innumerable advertisements that appeal to one or more of the 'seven deadly sins', or that play on the emotion most easily stimulated in the human animal – fear. Fear of being left out, of being socially unacceptable, or of being considered socially inferior in some way or other, e.g. dull, lifeless hair; B.O.; halitosis; X washes whiter – and it shows.

Advertising is further indicted in that it sets out to eliminate non-conformity and discourage originality in thought, word and deed. Admass leaves no room for reason, and cultivates the herd instinct.

Finally, in the words of A. S. J. Baster in *Advertising Reconsidered* (1935), 'The major part of informative advertising is and always has been a campaign of exaggeration, half-truths, intended ambiguities, direct lies, and general deception' (quoted by Bishop).

Most marketers would readily agree that the acquisition of material things is a means to an end and not an end in itself, but would also argue that man has free will and therefore the right to decide for himself what level of material consumption he will seek to attain. Religion and philosophy offer us a wide range of alternatives from which to choose a set of principles that will constitute a 'good life'. Whereas mere possessions are unlikely to result in satisfaction in the total sense, it is also true that a certain level of material goods is essential to the maintenance of life. Over and above these essentials, the desired level of material possessions will depend on the society of which we are a member, our education and income.

It is also appropriate to point out that it is only in this century that the possibility of a reasonable standard of living for all members of society has been achieved, and this, as yet, only in advanced economies. Earlier civilisations were largely based on the sweated labour of the masses and only the aristocracy could afford the luxury of philosophising about the 'good life' – only in the next world was it conceivable that all might share in the material comforts enjoyed by the few. (It is an interesting reflection on middle-class morality that the demand for labour-saving kitchen equipment only really got off the ground in this country with the passing of personal servants following the creation of alternative opportunities for female employment in the Second World War.)

Present-day 'welfare economics', designed to remove 'poverty in the midst of plenty', have grown out of the belief that we are now capable of producing sufficient to permit an adequate standard of living for all, and that the major problem is a more equitable distribution of output. At the same time, experience of a full employment policy in the post-war period has taught us that in the absence of adequate demand, production is frustrated and both human and physical resources lie idle. Many would argue that restriction of demand in recent years has mainly resulted from government policies designed to curb inflation, rather than from the inability of the productive machine to create goods in demand. It is my opinion that the inflationary trend is largely the result of a lack of demand.

In the case of the average consumer, the material possessions which constitute the good life are limited to a relatively small number of goods and services. There is a latent demand for many other goods and services, but their utility is less than the effort necessary to earn sufficient to pay for them owing to the disincentive of increasingly punitive levels of taxation. Consequently there is no incentive to work more effectively and improve productivity, an attitude which is compounded by the Government's provision of a range of social services that caters for virtually all of life's emergencies.

Both government and management have been singularly ineffective in explaining the real benefits that will accrue from
increased productivity, and the working man resists measures to
achieve this in the belief that he may be making himself redundant.
The possibility of redeploying labour into new industries creating
new products to satisfy existing wants is overlooked. On the other
hand if the consumer could be made to want dish-washing
machines, colour television, electric tooth brushes or any other
similar but 'non-essential' item, this might provide sufficient incentive to call forth the increase in productivity that is so urgently
required.

In a sense, therefore, materialism and an acquisitive society are
necessary if we are to maintain and improve the quality of life for
both ourselves and those less fortunate in the developing
economies. The more wealth we create domestically, the greater
will be our ability to help others.

The other argument for the retention of advertising is that it
helps preserve freedom of speech and freedom of choice. Modern
media are dependent upon advertising revenues for their continued existence. On their existence largely rests the continued
freedom of speech for, as noted when discussing the evolution of
advertising, one of the first acts of a dictatorship is to secure control of the means of mass communication.

16 Sales Promotion

INTRODUCTION

The discussion in the previous chapter was concerned solely with media advertising, or what is sometimes known as 'above-the-line' expenditure. The balance of advertising expenditure 'below-the line' is on sales promotion and has assumed growing importance in recent years, to the extent that it accounts for over 50 per cent of all advertising expenditure in the United Kingdom as it does in the United States.

In a book of this type it is impossible to do justice to all sectors of marketing activity, and in any event the selection of material must mirror the author's preferences and prejudices. But in the case of the subject of sales promotion the dilemma of what to include and what to exclude is compounded by the availability of an excellent handbook, *A Guide to Consumer Promotions*, 2nd ed., by A. Morgan (Ogilvy, Benson & Mather, 1976). While the introduction of this handbook states that it is not comprehensive, its scope goes far beyond that to be found in most textbooks, and it would be wasteful to offer a watered-down version here. Ogilvy, Benson & Mather have kindly consented to the reproduction of extracts from their publication. These comprise a substantial part of this chapter and greatly extend the material which appeared in earlier editions.

OBJECTIVES

The basic objective underlying all promotions is an increase in sales. This aim may be further subdivided, in terms of the time dimension, by devising strategies designed at achieving either short- or long-term gains. Hopefully, both aims will be achieved, but the immediate objective will condition the strategy and the promotional tools employed.

Although display advertising can be very effective in making consumers aware of the existence of a product, inertia frequently prevents consumer sampling and some additional incentive is required to persuade non-users to try it. Promotions are designed to provide this incentive. Consumers invariably view trial of a new product as containing a risk element – perceived risk – yet without trial there is no possibility of repeat purchases. A product may be totally new, in the sense that it has never previously been offered for sale, or new in the sense that the individual has no previous experience of it. A different strategy will apply to each of these situations.

In the case of a totally new product the initial campaign will seek to obtain the widest possible trial and will employ a combination of methods, e.g. coupons, free samples, in-store trial, banded offers, etc. Where the brand is already established and has a known brand share, the promoter will adopt a more selective approach and concentrate on those segments of the market with the lowest usage rates. A totally new offering will also merit a more prolonged campaign to encourage repurchase; this would not be justified for an established brand because of the cost of 'subsidising' users who would have bought the product without a promotion. Against this element of subsidy must be set the fact that a 'bonus' helps maintain brand loyalty in the face of one's competitors' promotions.

In highly competitive markets, where product differentiation is difficult, if not impossible, such as detergents, breakfast cereals, etc., promotions are frequently employed to secure short-term increases in sales in the knowledge that once the promotion is finished the new buyers will revert to their former brand, or a competitive brand which is running a promotion. Clearly, promotions of this type are subject to criticism on the grounds that they are combative and do nothing to increase primary demand, and it is argued that the consumer would be better served by a permanent price reduction. From an industry viewpoint there is some truth in the argument, but from the position of the individual firm there is little incentive in adopting such a policy. Faced with an inelastic demand all firms would follow suit and reduce price, but would still be faced with the need to continue promotional activity to protect their individual brand shares. If it is assumed that the manufacturer would protect his profit margin, one is drawn to the inescapable conclusion that such a price reduction would eventually lead to an overall decline in product quality.

DETERMINATION OF THE APPROPRIATION

A distinct advantage of promotions as compared with display advertising is that the former is capable of reasonably accurate costing in terms of a desired result whereas the latter is speculative.

In setting the appropriation a two-stage approach is possible. The first stage requires the quantification of only two variables, which are reasonably accessible to the company – sampling cost and the additional contribution arising from the sale of a marginal unit. The second stage requires the determination of three further, and less accessible, facts – the conversion rate from sampling to regular usage, frequency of purchase among regular users, number of purchases by those sampled who do not adopt the product and become regular users.

The sampling cost can usually be calculated in advance and comprises two elements – the distribution cost and the value of the sample or coupon. Where the promotion consists of a coupon redeemable on purchase of the item being promoted, the value of the unit discount must be adjusted in line with the anticipated redemption rate to arrive at a total cost – previous experience usually provides a reliable estimate of this rate.

The growth of the promotions business has resulted in the setting up of firms which specialise in all its aspects, several of which are wholly owned subsidiaries of agencies like Young & Rubicam, J. Walter Thompson and L.P.E. These companies are well qualified to advise on all aspects of promotions, and will provide estimates of redemption rates with a reasonable degree of accuracy. Many companies like Donnelly Marketforce Limited also publish rate lists for door-to-door distribution of samples and/or coupons. The basic cost of the service in 1978 was £3.50 plus 50p. for warehousing and dispersal per thousand households covered. Marketforce claim to be able to reach 90 per cent of all households in Great Britain and offer a number of different schedules based on major TV areas, as shown in Table 16.1.

Once the sampling area has been defined and the nature of the offer decided, it is a relatively simple matter to calculate the redemption rate/sales volume which will ensure break-even in the short term. In order to allow for the long-term potential of a promotion an estimate must be made of the three second-stage variables referred to above. Conversion rates, like redemption rates, may be estimated with reasonable accuracy on the basis of past experience. The same is true of the percentage of those who will make subsequent purchases without becoming 'brand adopters'. (Many large companies undertake continuous market research which enables them to predict at an early stage in the life of a promotion exactly how repurchase patterns will develop.) Product usage is also quite well documented, both by independent firms like Nielsen and by the larger agencies and manufacturers. Armed with this data it is possible, with a little educated guess-

TABLE 16.1. *Households: Marketforce schedules by TV area*

TV area	'Extended'	'Full'	'Standard'	'Urban'
London	4,163,000	3,974,000	2,676,000	2,005,000
Southern	1,186,000	989,000	669,000	123,000
Midlands	2,476,000	2,168,000	1,478,000	1,142,000
Anglia	762,000	479,000	319,000	—
Harlech	1,017,000	918,000	635,000	250,000
Westward	322,000	302,000	194,000	—
Lancashire	2,334,000	2,242,000	1,530,000	1,044,000
Yorkshire	1,835,000	1,539,000	1,043,000	688,000
Tyne Tees	894,000	814,000	545,000	348,000
Border	137,000	67,000	47,000	—
Central Scotland	1,351,000	1,117,000	780,000	400,000
Grampian	186,000	93,000	84,000	—
National	16,663,000	14,746,000	10,000,000	6,000,000

Note: All Marketforce distribution schedules exclude 'E' type property.

work, to formulate an acceptable forecast of the long-term benefits.

PROMOTIONS IN CURRENT USAGE

As every consumer is aware there is a bewildering array of promotional offers available. A short review of these is given below.

Free samples. Of all the promotions this method offers the greatest chance of getting a consumer to actually try the product. At the same time it is the most expensive, and its usage is invariably restricted to brands with potential annual sales of several million pounds. (On a door-to-door basis the cost could well be in the region of £10 per 1000 households!) A number of companies seek to reduce sampling cost by co-operating in a joint promotion of non-competing products on similar lines to the gift pack given to mothers of first babies.

Off-price labels. In terms of consumer acceptability the label featuring X*p* off the regular price is the most popular promotion. It is also popular with retailers as it involves none of the diseconomies associated with coupon redemption and also provides the opportunity to feature a price reduction in their local advertising.

The actual extent of the price reduction is an important determinant of the level of sampling, and careful thought, and preferably testing, must be given to the selection of a discount. As discussed in the chapter on pricing, some prices have the apparent effect of being perceived as less than they really are, and it is these which have the greatest impact on impulse purchases. Obviously, if sales volume can be increased sufficiently the firm may be able to both even out seasonal fluctuations and make a profit.

A price reduction is a short-term strategy, however, and the simplest for one's competitors to duplicate. For these reasons it is avoided by companies that are sensitive to a price war wherever possible, e.g. the petrol companies, until Jet and others pre-empted a sufficient market share through price cutting to make a general price reduction necessary on the part of the 'Big Five' to protect their market share.

Banded offers. This type of promotion takes two forms:

(*a*) The use of an existing and well-known brand to 'carry' a free sample of another non-competing product. Both products may be produced by the same firm, e.g. soap and toothpaste, which has the dual advantage of increasing sales of the carrying brand while securing trial of the carried brand, or complementary products of different producers e.g. instant coffee and sugar.

(*b*) Two-for-the-price-of-one.

Premium offers. There are three main varieties of premium offer:

1. *The free gift.* This may be contained in the package – plastic animals in breakfast cereals – attached to it – a plastic rose, tea-towels, etc. – given out at the checkout to those purchasing the item carrying the offer – bowls, china, waste-paper baskets, etc. In some instances the offer will be the pack itself, as is the case with instant coffee packed in storage jars. A common feature of these promotions is that they encourage a collecting habit and so achieve extended trial as the consumer builds up the collection.

2. *The free, sendaway premium.* This type of promotion offers a free gift in exchange for proof of purchase of the product. This approach has greater appeal to the retailer than those promotions which require him to stock 'giveaways', especially as the promotion usually involves point of sale material that builds store traffic and stimulates impulse purchases. From the promoter's angle an added advantage is that many people buy the product intending to send off for the premium but in fact never do.

3. *Self-liquidating premiums.* These differ from the other type of premium in that the consumer has to send both money and proof of purchase to obtain the offer. The advantage to the consumer is that he secures merchandise, often carrying a leading brand name, at a significant discount on its normal retail price. The promoter benefits in that, as the name suggests, the offer pays for itself. If combined with a collecting habit, offers of this kind may run for years ensuring long-term usage, e.g. Kellogg's silverware offer.

Competitions. Like all other promotions these are no newcomers to the marketing scene (Lever Brothers were spending £1 million a year on promotions at the turn of the century), but they have attracted more than their usual share of attention of late as a result of tangling with the betting and gaming laws. Interest in competitions is considerable owing to the attraction of a very large prize, together with a sufficient number of consolation prizes on an area basis to encourage people to continue to try their luck. (Petfood's Big Name Bingo, which crossed with the law, pulled in approximately half a million entries.)

TABLE 16.2 *Estimates of expenditure (£m.)*

	1974	1975	1976
Price reductions	350	425	660
Money-off coupons	7.5	12	22
Extra quantity	2.5	3	3
Banded packs	1.0	3	3
Stamps	100	110	130
Gift coupons	7.5	8	9
Free gifts	1.5	1.0	1.5
Free mail-in premiums	6	7	10
Self-liquidating premiums	6	3	4
Competitions	2.5	3.5	4
Samples	5	3	3
Display material	50	65	85
Trade press support	1	1	1
Consumer media support	75	185	240
Sponsorship	12.5	15	20
Product sales force and trade incentives	15	23	30
	645.5	867.5	1225.5
Display advertising	672	753	820

Source: *Annual Review of Shopping and Promotion Intelligence*, Harris, International Marketing, Kingswell, Health Street, Hampstead, London NW3.

Personality promotions. As with the door-to-door distribution of samples, this type of promotion is limited to the big brands with large advertising appropriations. The method employed is to offer a prize if the housewife has the advertised product in her home when the personality (Egg-chick, Ajax Superman, etc.) calls, provided that she can answer a simple question. Including in-store displays, leaflet distribution, etc., but excluding display advertising, this type of promotion can cost in excess of £200,000

An estimate of expenditure on the different types of promotion is contained in Table 16.2.

From the above description of the major types of promotions, it is clear that there is a wide choice of alternatives. Ogilvy, Benson & Mather offer both general and specific advice on how to evaluate these, and the following sections are reprinted from their handbook. It should be stressed that the section on sampling has been chosen for illustrative purposes only and all the other major alternatives are given the same detailed treatment.

HOW TO DECIDE WHETHER TO RUN A PROMOTION AND WHICH PROMOTION TO CHOOSE*

Introduction

Consumer promotions are not a panacea. They have, unfortunately, become fashionable. A belief has developed that they are *the* modern marketing technique. This is nonsense. Consumer promotions are just one part of the marketing mix, not a substitute for it. If a promotion is run it will normally work better as a part of the whole, fitting in with the advertising, product development, packaging, trade incentives and salesmen's incentives as a logical development of the marketing strategy.

In particular, it must be made clear that 'promotions' and 'advertising' are complementary techniques, not substitutes for each other. There is a growing body of evidence that companies who switch their marketing expenditure exclusively 'below-the-line' make temporary gains in volume at the expense of perma-

---

*The extract quoted (pp. 337–48) is reproduced by kind permission of Messrs Ogilvy, Benson & Mather.

nently undermining their brand-image and the loyalty of their most regular buyers.

A well-designed promotion can help solve certain specific marketing problems, and together with the rest of the marketing mix help to achieve a marketing objective. Therefore, before discussing whether to mount a promotion at all, and certainly before selecting the type of promotion, the *marketing objectives* of the brand must have been agreed, specific *marketing targets* set, and the *problems* to be overcome identified.

This assumes that the following information is available:

(*a*) Who is the target market for the brand.
(*b*) Why they use the product and how.
(*c*) How frequently it is bought and where.
(*d*) Who are its main competitors.
(*e*) How the consumer rates the brand compared with its competitors.

If these facts are not known then what is needed is not a promotion but basic research into the brand to determine its problems and market positioning.

How to decide whether to run a promotion

(*a*) Determine, in order of priority, the problems facing the brand.
(*b*) Determine the money available to solve the problems.
(*c*) List and cost all the possible alternative solutions to the problems: e.g. more advertising, consumer promotions, pricing strategy, product change, etc.
(*d*) Estimate (or guesstimate) the effectiveness of each solution.
(*e*) If the answers to (c) and (d) suggest that a promotion is the most efficient answer to the brand's problem and if the answer to (b) shows there is enough money for a successful promotion then a promotion is indicated.
(*f*) It does not make sense to run a promotion simply because a competitor is running one unless this has caused problems for your brand which a promotion would solve. If the problems

confronting your brand, at that time, would not be solved by a promotion, then it would be a costly mistake to allow your competitor's action to stampede you into panic action. His problems or his perception of his problems may be quite different from those confronting your brand.

Which promotion to choose?

(*a*) The one most likely to solve the brand's problem successfully, within the available budget.
(*b*) You can help to decide this by looking up your problems in the chart [in the next section].
(*c*) Then for each promotion listed as likely to help, look up the separate section on that type of promotion.
(*d*) Look initially at the sub-sections on

     (i)   Advantages
     (ii) Disadvantages
     (iii) Essentials for success
     (iv) Points to look out for
     (v)   How much will it cost?

(*e*) Does the promotion offer an incentive to the market target, from their point of view?
(*f*) Consider the impact of the promotion on the image of the product. An expensive, high-quality product, should have an expensive, high-quality promotion.
(*g*) Consider whether the consumer has any problems which the promotion could solve: e.g. if a product is messy to use, it may be worth considering a free spreader or spatula.
(*h*) Promotions are tactical tools. There is no formula for picking the correct one. They will usually be better if they are designed in the context of the individual brand's consumers, its market and its trade practices.
(*i*) Because of this need for bespoke designing it is usually better not to copy other companies' promotions but to think ideas out from scratch.

PROBLEMS AND AN INDICATION OF THE CONSUMER PROMO-
TIONS MOST LIKELY TO HELP IN SOLVING THEM

These are suggestions, not hard and fast rules. Altering the design
of a promotion may make it a suitable solution for other problems.
The nature of the product, the company and the trade will also
affect the best solution to any problem.

	Promotions *which may help*
(*a*) To get consumer trial of new or existing product	Free with-, in- or on- pack premium Money-off voucher Money-off offer Sampling Proprietary promotions
(*b*) To obtain repeat purchasing	Any premium offer of a collectable item (free or 'self-liquidating promotion') Competition Free mail-in Free continuous mail-in (coupons) Money-off voucher promotion' 'Self-liquidating promotion'
(*c*) To obtain long-term consumer loyalty	Continuous 'self- liquidating promotion' (coupons) Trading stamps
(*d*) To increase frequency or quantity of consumer purchase in the short run	Competition Free on-, with-pack premium Free mail-in Household stock reward scheme (personality promotion)

In-store self-liquidator
Money-off offer (includ-
ing banded packs)
Shop-floor promotions
Tailor-made promotions

(*e*) To move high stocks out of
stores

Competiton
Free with-pack
Free mail-in
Shop-floor promotions
Tailor-made promotions

(*f*) To get consumers to visit
your premises

Free gifts
Money-off voucher
Shop-floor promotions
Tailor-made promotions
Trading stamps
Proprietary promotions

(*g*) *To get increased distribution.* This will call for trade and
salesmen's incentives primarily although a consumer promotion may be necessary to 'pull the product through'. However the choice of consumer promotion will really depend
on other problems facing the brand at the time.

(*h*) *To obtain increased stock levels/stocking in depth.* As with
the increased distribution this calls for trade and salesmen's
incentives. The choice of a consumer promotion to 'pull the
product through' will depend on other problems facing the
brand at the time.

(*i*) *To obtain information on consumer product usage.* This is a
research, not a promotional problem.

POINTS WHICH MAY ARISE IN CONNECTION WITH ANY PROMO-
TION

Legal clearance
The number of U.K. Statutes with which marketing activity has to
comply has proliferated in the last decade. Key Acts are quoted
throughout this document. . . The EEC is developing a body of
Directives towards harmonisation of the laws of member countries, which include 'misleading advertising', 'premium offers' and

'informative labelling' among other marketing topics. These could affect planning for the long-term, or a continuing promotion.

In addition there are several voluntary codes of practice . . . . Most important is the British Code of Sales Promotion Practice (CAP Committee 1977). Compliance with this code reduces but does not eliminate the risk of illegality.

For multinational operations, also consult the series of Codes by the International Chamber of Commerce.

It is important to check for Copyright. Similarity to a previous promotion by another company might give rise to a claim of 'passing off' or breach of copyright (apart from causing confusion among consumers and retailers!). If an outside agency is involved it should be made quite clear whether or not any work done by the agency is their copyright.

Claimed value of premium items or gifts or prizes
These must comply with the provisions of the 'Trade Descriptions Act 1968'. It is also wise to check whether a prize or premium is on public sale and at what price. It is advisable to be aware of the practices deemed acceptable and unacceptable by the Office of Fair Trading in their Consultative Document on 'Bargain Offer Claims' (1975). While no legislation is in prospect, it offers guidelines for any promotion in which the price of the product is modified temporarily or where some other product is offered in connection with it.

The EEC is developing legislation on 'unit pricing' whereby both the price of the pack and of the relevant unit (pound, kilogram, litre etc) must be quoted. This will also apply to price modifications.

The printing of any promotion offer on the pack
The following problems arise:

(a) Ensuring adequate supplies have reached direct and indirect outlets by the time advertising breaks (IPA regulations).

(b) The Advertising Standards Authority requires that details of the closing date and of any limitations on an offer (e.g. 'while stocks last') must appear on the outside of the pack or label.

(*c*) While the special pack is on offer, the retailer may put away 'Normal' merchandise which may have deteriorated when it is returned to the shelves.

The sending of items or literature by post

(*a*) There are restrictions of overall size, weight and nature of items that can be sent by post.
(*b*) The GPO will not pay compensation for the loss of items with a monetary value, unless sent by registered mail. (Postal regulations concerning paper money introduced 3/10/66.)
(*c*) Substantial discounts are available for bulk postage if some regional pre-sorting is done.
(*d*) Care should be taken that goods sent by mail to adults should not fall into the hands of children.

Promotions advertised on TV
There are ITCA rulings:

(*a*) That such promotions must be available to all consumers whether viewers or not.
(*b*) That if a promotion is limited to certain sizes or packs, this must be made clear in the advertisement.

Promotions aimed at offering prizes to children
Promoters should take extra care that the promotion accords with the letter and spirit of the laws and guidelines. There are specific and stringent ITCA rulings relating to:

(*a*) Exaggerated claims and trade puffery, such as the use of the word 'free' or 'free with'.
(*b*) Promotions on a product whose brand choice cannot normally be considered to be a child's prerogative, e.g. floor polish, soap.
(*c*) Promotions where the premium, gift or reward is dependent upon collecting a number of items.
(*d*) In the case of children under 16, entry forms should require the consent of a parent or guardian (particularly where a prize or gift is a holiday, a pet, or goods to the value of £50 or more).

Company administration
Check that there is provision in salesmen's order forms, accounting procedure etc, for special packs sold alongside normal packs.

Check that any liabilities incurred by the promotion are adequately covered by your insurance or that of the promotion company concerned.

Check that all advertising and promotional material include closure dates and adequate descriptions of the rules of the promotion.

Check that all liabilities to *tax* are included when budgeting the costs of a promotion. Even when an item is given away 'free', the promoter may be liable to VAT on its value. Consult the VAT General Guide, or the Customs and Excise.

SAMPLING

Definition
The consumer is either:
  (*a*) given some of the product free; or
  (*b*) allowed to use the product freely during a given period.

The size of the product give-away may vary from a taste or spray to a full-sized pack.

The samples can be distributed in a number of ways:
  (*a*) Given by a demonstrator in a store. These are usually used instantly, e.g. a tasting of food or drink, a spray of perfume, a cigarette to smoke.
  (*b*) Given away with another product.
  (*c*) Distributed in some medium, e.g. a shampoo sachet in a magazine.
  (*d*) Delivered door-to-door.
  (*e*) Sent on application from the consumer.
  (*f*) Given to visitors to some specific location, e.g. hotels, exhibitions, showrooms, race tracks, etc.
  (*g*) Where the consumer is invited to use the product freely, e.g. a car or a televison set, then the 'sample' is delivered, by arrangement, to the home or place of business.

Advantages
The advantage to the consumer is immediate and obvious (this does not apply if the consumer has to apply for the sample).

The consumer has to make no effort, is involved in no expense (again except in the case where he has to apply for it).

Mass sampling is by far the quickest way of obtaining widespread consumer trial.

Demonstrates to the consumer, the product's qualities, and the manufacturer's faith in his product.

Creates excitement.

Disadvantages

This is very expensive.

Considerable administration is involved in distributing the samples.

The special costs of trial-sized packs can be as expensive as a normal pack.

The product needs to have an advantage, or difference, that the consumer can perceive.

It will not increase usage by existing consumers.

Essentials for success

A good product.

Efficient distribution, especially in:

(*a*) getting the samples to the potential market
(*b*) preventing samples going astray.

Where the sample is left with the consumer, it should be of sufficient size for the consumer both to appreciate the product's qualities and to form the habit of using the product. Consumers show disproportionately more gratitude for a 'full-size' sample.

Trade co-operation. This is very important. If the nature of the product makes a large sample necessary it may be necessary to persuade the trade that you are not depriving them of the profit they could have made selling the product.

A product that regular users are likely to buy frequently.

Advertising support.

Good distribution for the product so that consumers who are persuaded by the sample have the maximum opportunity to buy.

That consumers are informed where they can obtain further supplies of the product.

While not essential the conversion rate to product usage will be increased, if the consumer is given a money incentive to make the first purchase. Thus if the sample is distributed in a store the consumer's attention can be drawn to a money-off offer. If the sample is distributed away from the store or shop the sample should be accompanied by a money-off coupon or voucher.

Decisions that have to be taken

What size sample to distribute? This will depend on:
  (*a*) The nature and value of the product.
  (*b*) Consumer usage, e.g. do not give consumers a year's supply preferably sample the size you most want them to buy.
  (*c*) How apparent is, the difference or advantage e.g. can it be discerned on the first try or bite of the product?
  (*d*) The method of distribution to be used, e.g. you cannot put a pound pack inside a magazine; retailers prefer in-store samples to be small
  (*e*) The cost of special sample packaging.
  (*f*) The promotional budget.

How to distribute the sample. This will depend on:
  (*a*) The size of the sample.
  (*b*) The nature of the product, e.g. is it breakable?
  (*c*) The market target. If it's not a mass market product there is no point in distributing door-to-door.
  (*d*) The possibilities for sample misuse.
  (*e*) The promotional budget.
  (*f*) The promotional objects.

How research can help
It could help to determine the most efficient sample size, e.g. how little of the product is needed to convert the consumer to the product (but see also [third para.] under Disadvantages). There could, however, be a security problem here with a new product.
  Subsequently, in measuring conversion rate to the product and in planning further operations.

Points to watch/problems which may arise
In connection with any form of sampling operation. That there is adequate check on samples at all stages of distribution
  That the packaging of the sample will stand up to its method of distribution. It is advisable to check this in action. The standard

pack may encounter much rougher treatment in a distributor's sack than in a standard outer moved by a forklift truck.

That any quotation received for distribution has been made with knowledge of both the weight and dimensions of the sample.

That there is no chance of the sample tainting other products or of being tainted by them.

See also . . . 'Points which may arise in connection with any promotion'.

Sampling in stores and shops. That all details are fully discussed and agreed with the store in advance, e.g.

(*a*) Dates.
(*b*) Amount of space.
(*c*) Location of space.
(*d*) Hours the demonstrator will work. It can cause conflict if these are markedly different from store staff.
(*e*) Any necessary equipment, e.g. electrical socket.

That demonstrators are subject to adequate supervison and spot checks.
That adequate provisions are made for demonstrators to have clean overalls, etc. under all circumstances.
That if food is being sampled to eat, all food hygiene rules are strictly observed.

Samples given away with another product. That the market target for the two products is similar.

That the products are non-competitive.
See also 'Free on-pack premiums'.

Samples distributed in a Press medium. That there are no disputes between media owners and their distributors that will interfere with sample distribution.

Samples distributed door-to-door. Medicinal samples may not be distributed door-to-door.

Both the Board of Trade and C.A.P. require manufacturers to exercise care in putting samples through letter boxes. Complaints have been made of products dangerous to children or dogs and where there is any danger of this C.A.P. recommend personal handing over of the sample instead of distribution through the letter box.

That a sample intended to go through a letter box can go through the average letter box and that instructions cover premises with no letter boxes.

That a household sample is sufficient for a household, If it is something desired and there is not enough to go round you may cause ill-will and the market target may never even see the sample.

How much will it cost?
The following list includes some of the main costs likely to be incurred:

(*a*) Cost of sample contents.
(*b*) Sample packaging.
(*c*) Distribution.
(*d*) Advertising.
(*e*) Display material.
(*f*) Merchandising force.
(*g*) Supporting trade and salesmen incentives.

Suggestions for further reading
Christopher, M., *Marketing Below the Line* (Allen & Unwin, 1972)
Darkin, T., *Sales Promotion Handbook* (Gower Press, 1974)
Ferrée, H. (ed.), *Handbook of Consumer Sales Promotion* (Kluwer-Harrap, 1975)
Hodgson, P., 'Sales Promotion Research: A Plea for more Research Investment', *Journal of Market Research Society*, vol. 19, no. 1, Jan 1977
Hodgson, P., 'What Happened to Sales Promotion Research?', *Marketing*, Apr 1977
Morgan, A., *Glossary of Sales Promotion Terms* (Admap, 1971)
Spillard, P., *Sales Promotion: Its Place in Marketing Strategy* (Business Books, 1975)
Ward, J., *A Guide to Sales Promotion* (I.P.A., 1976)(The Thomson Medals and Awards for Advertising Research.) (Thomson Organisation, 1969).

17 Personal Selling and Merchandising

Despite the importance of advertising and sales promotion in disseminating information and stimulating interest in products and services, there are many circumstances where personal contact is necessary to effect a sale. Of necessity most advertising is generalised, and so cannot answer all the consumer's information needs; it cannot elaborate upon specific points perceived as significant by the individual, nor can it resolve doubts as to suitability in a particular context. Further, there can be no guarantee that the potential user's media habits will expose him to advertisements for a given product, or that if he does see the advertisement he will perceive it as relevant.

The function of personal selling is to provide the specific inputs which advertising, or non-personal selling, cannot offer at the individual level. It should be remembered that advertising and personal selling are complementary activities, and that their relative importance will vary depending upon the nature of the product and the buying behaviour associated with it. Many theorists stress the nature of the product as a determinant of the appropriate promotional mix and are collectively identified as the 'Characteristics of Goods School'. Members of this school would argue that advertising will be dominant in the case of small simple and frequently purchased items of low unit value, while personal selling is appropriate to high-priced, technically complex products which are bought infrequently.

Although useful, this approach is oversimplified, for the user's perception of any given product defies classification into convenient categories, such that a 'convenience' good may be perceived as a 'shopping' good and vice versa, depending upon the individual's frame of reference. The importance of allowing for the behavioural dimensions of perception is implicit in the different promotional strategies adopted by firms selling near-perfect substitutes in the economic sense, e.g. Avon sells cosmetics door-to-door, Estee Lauder products are available in less than 150 outlets, Yardley and Coty are available in some 7000 department stores and chemist's shops, while Miner's brands are sold through variety chains and supermarkets. There are no hard-and-fast rules which dictate the adoption of a given promotional strategy for a product.

THE EVOLUTION OF THE SALESMAN

Although our stereotype of a salesman probably owes more to the music-hall comedian than to reality, there can be no doubt that selling has long occupied a relatively low position in our social and economic hierarchy. Fortunately, there are signs that this state of affairs is slowly changing and that selling is increasingly regarded as a profession rather than a trade. Several factors may be distinguished as contributing to this change and the resultant increase in the flow of better qualified recruits, namely:

1. 'Salesman' applies equally to all persons engaged at all levels of selling, from the retail sales clerk to the negotiator of multi-million-pound contracts. In that the former greatly outnumber the latter, selling tends to be identified with the functions performed by retailers rather than with manufacturer's salesman. However, increased labour costs have led to wide-scale reduction in personal selling at the retail level and have thus brought more sophisticated sales functions into sharper focus, i.e. an emphasis on creative selling as opposed to mere order-taking.
2. The pressures of international competition have made it clear that the manufacturer can no longer leave his product to 'speak for itself' – effective selling and promotion are essential.
3. Increased product complexity, and more sophisticated buyers demand high-calibre salesmen. The scarcity of such personnel has boosted salary levels above those offered in many other occupations, improving selling's economic status and attracting in better-qualified recruits.

Collectively, these factors have made a career in sales more respectable, and resulted in a better understanding of the sales function.

THE SALESMAN'S ROLE

In view of the possible variations in product and market characteristics it is virtually impossible to formulate a single definition of the salesman's role.

Where a user/consumer has previous experience of a product the salesman is often a passive 'order-taker' whose function is to price the product specified, take payment and effect delivery, e.g. 2 lb of potatoes, a packet of Whizzo, 50 tons of cold-reduced mild steel sheet. Such a situation is very different from the case where the potential buyer has no previous experience of the product and is actively seeking information, and different again from the situation where the consumer has only an ill-defined or latent demand for a product to fill a given need. In the latter situations the salesman becomes an 'order-maker' and plays an active role in the purchasing decision.

Although there is more than an element of truth in the generalisation that retailers are order-takers, whereas manufacturers' salesmen are order-makers, no such clear-cut distinction exists in reality. Many manufacturers have become sensitive to the important influence which the retail sales assistant can have on the purchasing decision, and have installed their own employees in leased departments or provided training for their customers' staff. Similarly, the high cost of personal selling has persuaded many manufacturers to adopt standardised reorder procedures and to eliminate unnecessary or uneconomic sales calls. Alternatively, less experienced personnel are assigned to perform routine functions, leaving the salesman free to devote more time to missionary and developmental selling.

Although emotional factors undoubtedly influence both industrial and consumer purchasing decisions at all levels it is felt that there is a tendency to overemphasise these and, consequently, to overstress the salesman's role as a 'persuader'. In everyday speech, 'persuasion' is often used to suggest that a person has been, or can be, induced to act against his better judgement – this is certainly the context in which Vance Packard views 'The Hidden Persuaders' of advertising. In reality it is doubted if consumers are persuaded by spurious arguments as frequently as Packard suggests, and the salesman's role might be more usefully viewed as a problem-solving activity in which facts and arguments are used to justify the selection of a given product to satisfy a specific want. The salesman's skill lies in his ability to perceive the attributes which the 'prospect' considers important, and to structure his presentation so that his product's suitability along those dimensions is adequately conveyed to the potential customer. Thus, the car salesman will emphasise performance to his male customers, and finish and trim to his female customers – if he is a good car salesman he will also realise that the middle-aged bank clerk's concept of peformance is rather different from that of the junior account executive and so on. (There is more than a grain of truth in the old adage 'Let the customer tell you what he wants and then sell it to him', i.e. given the wealth of detail which you could give the customer, concentrate on the points in which he expresses interest.)

THE ECONOMICS OF PERSONAL SELLING

A recurring theme of this book is that the well-managed firm will seek to develop strategies that will enable it to achieve certain predetermined objectives. Fundamental to the firm's ability to achieve its stated aims is the need to earn profits, so that the adoption of policies, and the strategies by which they will be implemented, will revolve largely around cost/revenue considerations. This point has already been stressed at some length elsewhere but it is particularly relevant in the context of personal selling.

In absolute terms personal selling is the most expensive method whereby the producer can establish contact with the potential consumer. Relatively, however, it is often the least expensive method owing to the higher conversion factor achieved by direct selling *vis-à-vis* the use of middlemen or other promotional efforts. Whether the manufacturer should employ his own sales force, how big it should be, and how he should deploy it to maximum effect are questions which may only be resolved through a full evaluation of the alternatives. Although it is possible to quantify many of the parameters, no single prescriptive formula is available, but a number of steps can be offered as the basis for structuring such an evaluation.

1. The company should state its sales target for the coming year and for the next five years or so.
2. The promotional budget should be reviewed in the light of the sales target to ascertain whether the proposed expenditures will be sufficient to generate the desired sales volume – see 'The "task" approach' in Chapter 15.
3. Personal and non-personal selling are complementary activities and should not be segregated when determining the size of the promotional budget, i.e. management should decide how much it is willing to spend on all promotion, before attempting to allocate it to specific promotional efforts.
4. The optimum mix of personal and non-personal promotional efforts will vary by product, firm, industry and market, and is subject to change over time, therefore the total budget should be allocated roughly in accordance with the relative importance attached to each.
5. The adequacy of the sales budget may be evaluated by reference to past sales data or, if the firm has no previous experience of direct selling, by reference to the industry/product data published by trade associations, the B.I.M., the trade press, etc. A rough and ready guide is to substitute such data into the formula:

$$\text{Sales} = \frac{\text{Sales budget}}{\text{Average cost per call}} \times \text{Average sales per call}$$

In the absence of hard data, the firm would have to rely upon its own subjective estimates of likely events, and could easily test a large number of alternatives by running a simulation on a computer.

Once a field sales force is in existence, a continual process of adjustment is necessary to maximise its productivity. Ideally, salesmen should be used to point where the marginal cost of making a sales call is equivalent to the marginal revenue which it generates. In practice, adoption of this principle is rarely feasible because of the high fixed costs associated with the addition of an 'incremental' salesman, unless payment is on a straight commission basis.

DEPLOYING THE FIELD SALES FORCE

Optimum deployment of the sales force is an ever-present problem for the sales manager. Essentially this problem has three dimensions:

(a) The geographical dispersion of potential customers.
(b) The nature of the company's product mix.
(c) The buying needs of customers.

The geographical dispersion of customers imposes a major constraint on sales force productivity in that time spent travelling between customers is largely wasted. The amount of travelling time will vary considerably depending upon a number of factors but, on average, it is estimated that salesmen only spend 40 per cent of their time actually in contact with customers. Clearly a major objective must be to minimise the spatial distribution of accounts, which suggests that the sales force should be organised on a territorial basis.

However, such an organisational structure may conflict with the essential requirement that a salesman know his product. For the single product company, or the company with a limited range of closely related products, this may not create any problems, but as product line diversity and/or complexity increase, so product specialisation becomes progressively more essential. In the steel industry it would be impossible for any individual to be completely familiar with all products, and specialists are required for the sale of tinplate, mild steel sheet and plate, electrical steels, billets and bars, etc.

In turn, product knowledge must be backed by an understanding of the buying needs and practices of different customer groupings. Thus the detergent manufacturer's salesman will find it necessary to adopt a very different approach when selling to a major grocery chain as opposed the small independent outlet. Similarly, it will be necessary to use a very different strategy when selling to industrial users.

There is no simple rule which dictates that the manufacturer should organise his sales force on a territory, product or market basis and, in fact, many companies have adopted a composite structure. Many of the arguments examined when discussing product and market management in Chapter 5 are equally applicable in this context, but it is important to recognise that the internal organisation of the marketing department on either product or market lines does not automatically require that the sales force be organised in the same way. For obvious reasons of economy most sales forces are organised on a territorial basis, but within these boundaries salesmen may specialise on either a product or customer needs basis. The role of the product or market manager is to supply the salesman with detailed information of the most appropriate marketing inputs, such that several product managers may brief a single salesman on the 'best' tactics to be used in respect of each of their different products. Similarly, the market manager will lay down the nature of the selling approach most suited to the particular customer grouping for which he is responsible.

At the territory level a number of techniques have been evolved in recent years to improve sales efficiency. The sales call pattern is in the nature of a 'transportation problem' in the language of operations research, and is capable of at least partial solution through the use of linear programming techniques. In order to permit analysis it is necessary to adopt a number of simplifying assumptions, e.g. the relationship between time spent with buyer and size of order, the value of new account development or 'prospecting', etc., and it is clear that no true optimum solution is possible. None the less, the discipline of developing empirically valid generalisations is in itself worth while as it can lead to valuable insights into the more effective deployment of the field sales force.

SELLING SITUATIONS CLASSIFIED

One of the central themes of this chapter is that selling situations vary across a number of dimensions and that one must be careful to distinguish between them. At the same time there are sufficient similarities to permit the identification of a number of situations in which a particular kind or type of selling will be appropriate. It will be useful, therefore, to outline the basis characteristics of each as a first step towards identifying the sales situation facing the company and the necessary sales inputs to cope with it effectively.

One of the more recent investigations into sales management practice was that undertaken by Dr Derek Newton of the Harvard Business School, a preliminary report of which was published in the *Harvard Business Review* ('Get the Most out of Your Field Sales Force', XLVIII V (Sept–Oct 1969) 130–43).

Although this research was primarily concerned with performance and turnover, a secondary finding was that ' . . . one can effectively isolate four basic styles of selling that cut across industry boundaries to a large degree . . . '. These four styles are characterised as:

1. Trade selling.
2. Missionary selling.
3. Technical selling.
4. New-business selling.

Although there is nothing new in identifying selling styles and attaching labels to them, this classification is preferred by the author in that it offers the broadest level of categorisation consistent with utility. In summary the characteristics of the four styles are:

Trade selling
  (a) Major aim to build sales volume by providing customers with promotional assistance, i.e. selling *through*, e.g. food, textiles and wholesaling.
  (b) Personal selling subsidiary to non-personal activities.
  (c) Low-pressure selling, with an emphasis on continuity and a thorough understanding of customer practice.

Missionary selling
  (a) Primary aim is to build sales volume by providing direct customers with personal selling assistance, i.e. to persuade ultimate users/consumers to buy from the company's immediate customers.
  (b) Most typical of firms selling to distributors for resale.
  (c) Low pressure but requires energetic, articulate men capable of making a large number of calls in order to cover all the potential users, e.g. medical representatives.

Technical selling

(a) Primary responsibility is to increase sales to present customers through the provision of technical advice and assistance.

(b) Requires an ability to identify, analyse and solve customer problems, and so places a premium on technical and product knowledge.

(c) Continuity is an important factor in building up buyer confidence and goodwill.

New-business selling

(a) Primary aim is to secure new customers.

(b) The high level of rejection of new product propositions favours the employment of mature, experienced salesmen who can take an objective view of 'failure' and have a wider range of techniques to deal with buying objections.

THE RECRUITMENT, SELECTION AND TRAINING OF SALESMEN

Attributes of the successful salesman

Given the possible variations in the role which salesmen are called upon to play in different selling situations, it would be surprising to find that potentially successful salesmen may be identified by the presence, or absence, of a stereotyped set of personality variables. On the other hand, the high costs of selection and training make it essential that wastage through salesmen turnover be minimised, and have prompted the construction of innumerable check-lists which purport to identify the attributes of a successful salesman. The majority of such lists emphasise factors such as 'intelligent, extrovert, energetic, self-confident', etc., and a number of selection tests have been devised to measure such characteristics.

Collectively these lists, and the associated tests, presume the existence of a stereotype the validity of which is doubted by the author. This doubt would appear to be supported by the findings of Samuel N. Stevens, who has summarised '. . . the major conclusions which social scientists have reached in regard to social and psychological characteristics of salesmen . . .' as follows:

1. There is no significant relationship between intelligence test scores and sales success.

2. No significant relationship has been found between independent measures of personality traits and sales success.
3. No correlation exists between age and sales success.
4. There is no correlation between measurable character traits and sales success.
5. There is no significant correlation between level of education and sales success.
6. No significant correlation exists between level of sales activity and sales success among individual salesmen.
7. Each of the above factors has significance when studied in relation to all of the others in individual salesmen.
8. Such study as that indicated in point 7 above can provide a useful tool for selection and development.
9. Salesmen are more likely to succeed when chosen with regard to the kinds of customers they will deal with than in terms of the types of products sold.
10. Salesmen differ from non-salesmen in four important ways

   * Salesmen are persuasive rather than critical.
   * Salesmen are intuitive rather than analytical.
   * Salesmen have higher average energy levels (expressed in activity).
   * Salesmen are more strongly motivated by the desire for prestige, power, and material gain than by a service ideal or the need for security.

11. Salesmen's interests cluster around a dominantly persuasive common core.

('The Application of Social Science Findings to Selling and the Salesman', *Aspects of Modern Marketing* (A.M.A. Management Report no. 15, American Management Association, New York, 1958) pp. 85–94.)

Recruitment

As noted in point 7, factors 1–6 have no individual significance and their collective importance will vary depending upon the selling task to be performed – point 9. If this is so, then it follows that firms should develop their own selection procedures based on a job specification appropriate to their own sales policies and objectives. Such a job specification is vital to efficient recruitment and selection.

Most sales positions are advertised in the classified columns of the major newspapers and trade journals, and media representatives frequently quote the number of applications received by advertisers as an indication of their publication's 'pulling power'. Such statements would seem to confuse volume with quality, and usually indicate that the advertisement has failed in its function as a screening device. On occasion a loosely worded advertisement is a useful guide to the calibre of people who are actively seeking new jobs – as a means of securing applicants for a specific post it is both a wasteful and 'sloppy' approach. (A leading firm of management consultants once informed the author that they had received over 800 applications for a sales manager's post requiring previous experience with a highly specialised product. As there could not have been more than fifty people with such experience, either the consultant was 'fishing' for applicants to fill other vacancies, or he didn't know his job. In either case he was wasting his client's time and money.)

Most job advertisements require applicants to submit details of their previous experience and other evidence to indicate their potential suitability for the post. Where the job specification is fairly loose or the employer intends to give recruits extensive training, standardised application forms greatly assist the preparation of a short-list as they ensure that all applicants supply information considered important by the prospective employer.

Selection

Once a short-list has been prepared, the final selection of candidates usually involves some combination of tests and interviews. If a job specification has been prepared the purpose of the selection procedure will be to identify the applicant who most closely matches the job profile. In the absence of a job specification selection is likely to be overly subjective.

Although many factors will be common to all sales positions, and permit the use of structured interviews, the relative importance of these factors will vary depending upon the precise nature of the selling job to be performed. To deal with this problem and permit the development of standardised selection procedures, it is recommended that some form of factor rating be employed, similar to that described in connection with the screening of new product ideas.

In recent years an increasing number of firms have adopted some form of psychological testing in addition to the traditional personal interview. Such tests are seen as a cross-check on both interviewer bias and respondent consistency, and fall into four main categories:

Aptitude
Interest
Mental ability
Personality.

Tests of this kind conform more with the American than with the British ethic and are most frequently used in companies with strong links with the United States, e.g. Esso, Procter & Gamble, Mars.

Criticism of psychological tests is not based solely on cultural differences, however, and a number of American marketers are equally as sceptical as their more conservative British counterparts. For example, David Mayer and Herbert Greenberg ('What Makes a Good Salesman?', *Harvard Business Review*, XLII (July–Aug 1964) 119–25) discern four reasons which appear to account for the failure of aptitude tests:

1. Tests confuse interest with ability.
2. It is possible to fake answers and give the response the interviewer is looking for.
3. Tests favour conformity not individual creativity.
4. Tests concentrate on personality traits in isolation and fail to measure the person as a whole.

However, psychological testing techniques are becoming increasingly sophisticated and it is anticipated that they will come into wider use in the future.

Training
The function of the selection procedures described above is to recruit candidates who are potentially suited to the company's

selling tasks. Often the firm will use previous experience as a selection criterion, although a B.I.M. survey indicated that only forty of the seventy-five respondents stipulated that this was essential. (This survey, *Methods of Selecting and Training Salesmen* (Information Summary 87, 1966) provides useful background data but is based on too small a sample to permit valid generalisation.) Even where the new recruit has previous experience it is unlikely that this is directly relevant to the products, markets and administrative procedures particular to his new employer, and some training will be necessary.

The objective of training is to make the salesman more effective *as judged by the firm's criteria.* As is evident from the distinction drawn earlier between trade, missionary, technical and new-business selling, sales volume is only one criterion, and may be totally inappropriate in some circumstances. Although the need for training is clearly greatest in the case of new, inexperienced recruits it should be looked upon as a continuing process. Over time products, channels and markets change, and the well-managed firm will adjust its policies accordingly – continuation training is fundamental to the effective implementation of such changes in policy.

The length, content and cost of the sales training programme varies enormously between companies, but all seek to cover two main areas – knowledge and skills. Knowledge is concerned with the acquisition of facts and will normally include coverage of:

The company – its history, structure, policies and procedures.
The product(s) – composition, manufacture, performance and usage.
The market – size, structure, composition, buying behaviour, etc.

Skills may be subdivided into two categories – technical and behavioural. Technical skills cover training in techniques appropriate to various stages of the buying process such as securing interviews, opening the interview, overcoming objections and the 'close'. If the product can be demonstrated this would also be considered a technical skill.

Behavioural skills are concerned with the development of empathy between buyer and seller. They are difficult both to define and to acquire, and are usually described in texts on salesmanship under titles such as 'How to be a good listener', 'How to excite curiosity', etc.

SALESMAN COMPENSATION

Selling is a function which lends itself to some kind of payment by results in the majority of cases. If it is borne in mind that every incentive has a corresponding disincentive, then it follows that one must determine which incentive is most appropriate to a given selling situation.

Surveys into the remuneration of salesmen by the Tack organisation and the B.I.M. indicate that about 18 per cent of salesmen are paid a straight salary, with no bonus or incentive, while the remaining 82 per cent all receive some form of financial incentive. Every method has its advantages and disadvantages and these may be summarised as:

Salary only
- (*a*) The salesman's income is based on his overall performance and not subject to fluctuations beyond his control, e.g. the impact of a credit squeeze or marked seasonality of demand.
- (*b*) The method is fairest where the salesman is engaged in missionary selling or required to spend much of his time providing technical services.
- (*c*) Where there are variations in territory potential it prevents friction between salesmen, and gives flexibility in sales and journey planning.
- (*d*) It simplifies payment and avoids complications in the salary structure of the company as a whole.

As suggested, each of these advantages has a built-in disincentive:

- (*a*) Sales effort will not be maximised when most needed.
- (*b*) The quality of the services rendered will affect sales volume and so should be measured in just the same way.
- (*c*) Territories should be designed so that they have the same potential to encourage salesmen to compete with one another.

(*d*) If incentives are properly designed they will ensure that all members of the company receive a reward proportionate to their contribution.

Salary and commission
This is the most frequently used method on the grounds that:

(*a*) The salary provides a basic income while the commission provides the incentive to extra effort to achieve a better standard of living.

(*b*) Variable commissions on different products ensure that salesmen give them the degree of attention desired.

Commission only
In practice this method is found very infrequently – Tack reports 5.5 per cent, B.I.M. nil – as it has little attraction to any but the most confident of salesmen. From the employer's point of view it has the great attraction that payment is directly related to the results achieved, but it can also create considerable friction among other employees owing to the very high earnings which can be achieved by a good salesman.

Bonus schemes
Bonuses may be paid in addition to commission, either as an individual or group incentive, as a reward for sustained effort or the achievement of a predesignated target, or where a purely quantitative assessment would not adequately reflect performance, e.g. reduced sales on a falling market when such sales still represent an increase in market share.

EVALUATION OF SALESMEN

In the preceding section little reference was made to the methods used in evaluating salesmen's performance, on which most remuneration schemes are based. Once again it is necessary to reiterate that the relevant criteria will depend upon the company's own sales policies and objectives but, in general, performance will be measured in both quantitative and qualitative terms. Quantitative criteria include:

Sales volume.
Number of orders secured.
Number of sales calls made.
Number of service calls made.
Expenses incurred.
Territory contribution to profit.

Among the qualitative criteria in common use are:

Degree of product knowledge.
Quality of sales presentation.
Rating on personality traits such as initiative, judgement, etc.
Self-organisation, i.e. use of time, handling of correspondence, reports, etc.
Customer relationships.

Once the relevant criteria have been selected, some basis for evaluation must be chosen. Methods based on past performance, or involving a comparison of salesmen, suffer from the disadvantage that present conditions may differ markedly from those obtaining in the past, and that sales territories, and hence salesmen, are rarely, if every directly comparable. To overcome these difficulties many companies prefer to measure performance against pre-scribed standards, e.g. actual sales versus forecast, number of new accounts secured versus target, expenses incurred versus budgeted expense, etc.

MERCHANDISING

In the chapter on retailing reference was made to the transference of some of the 'traditional' retailing functions to the manufacturer intent upon securing greater control over the marketing of his output. Subsequently, the role of packaging, advertising and sales promotion were examined in the context of generating, demand for particular goods and services. It now remains to consider mer-chandising as an extension of the selling process whereby the man-ufacturer seeks to ensure that the retailer sells his products as quickly and as profitably as possible.

From the manufacturer's point of view the retail outlet provides the ready availability and convenience which are so expensive to achieve by direct selling methods. Once the retailer has taken delivery of goods from the manufacturer they become his property until he can effect their resale to ultimate consumers, and it follows that until he is able to achieve this he will have neither space nor capital with which to purchase further supplies from the producer. Clearly, any assistance which the manufacturer can give the retailer to stimulate demand and encourage purchase will be to their mutual advantage – this is the role of merchandising.

To maximise sales volume the sales force must ensure that its products are in the right place at the right time, in order to translate potential demand for them into effective demand. The right place means not only the outlets with the highest turnover or largest clientele but also the right place within the outlet to achieve the maximum impact on the prospective purchaser. Given the cost of a salesman's time, plus the cost of point-of-sale display material, it is obvious that merchandising efforts must be concentrated on the larger outlets which promise the greatest potential return. Within outlets, research has shown that certain locations are to be preferred. Thus in self-service outlets the best positions have been found to be:

1. At the end of gondolas facing the main traffic flow. (A gondola is a shelving unit on the main floor area which subdivides this area into a series of aisles.)
2. At eye level on the shelves around the sides of the shop. Impact can be further improved by siting the product immediately prior to the area normally set aside for display of the product group.
3. In dump displays in the main traffic aisles as these tend to cause congestion and focus attention on them.
4. Immediately next to the checkout – here again congestion creates a 'captive' audience.

In shops which still retain counter service the preferred positions are:

1. On the counter itself. If this is extensive, then next to the till or scales.

2. At eye level behind the counter.
3. In a dispenser placed in front of the counter.
4. Next to a complementary product, e.g. cream next to tins of fruit.

Timing is also an important factor underlying successful merchandising. Research indicates that the majority of purchases are made at the week-end and so emphasises the need to ensure adequate display at this time. Similarly, seasonal products such as mincemeat, Easter eggs and the like must be put on display in plenty of time, as must goods which are to be the subject of heavy promotion.

The major pitfall to be avoided by the salesman is that of becoming a merchandiser first and a salesman second. The salesman's role is to instruct retailers in the use of proven techniques to stimulate demand at the point of sale, and it is undesirable that he should become involved in routine activities associated with stocking shelves and putting goods on display. The salesman's job is to ensure that his products are given sound merchandising and a fair share of the favoured sites, and the normal call frequency precludes his devoting much time to in-store promotion.

In view of the heavy demands on the salesman's time, many firms now employ personnel whose sole function is to assist the retailer with the creation of effective store displays. Much merchandising is purely mechanical and so can be performed by part-time or less highly paid employees than is the case when salesman are required to do their own merchandising. In view of the desirability of achieving maximum impact simultaneously over a wide area at the commencement of an advertising campaign, several independent television companies now offer additional sales and merchandising support to supplement the advertiser's own efforts. Most of the televison contractors offer such a service representative of which is that of Associated Television. The A.T.V. retail sales force can operate in any retail field and quotations are prepared on an estimate of the total calls required to be made related to the cost of making an effective call. An effective call is where an interview is achieved and the sales proposition made to an individual in the retail outlet with the power to make the decision. Costs of this service at the time of writing were

Selling-in	£59 per girl/week
Merchandising	£55 per girl/week
Cash & Carry/in store demonstration and sampling	£35 per girl/week

These costs are inclusive of sales management, field supervision, A.T.V. uniform and briefing facilities at the A.T.V. Centre, Birmingham.

The following table provides a useful basis for an *ad hoc* estimate of the cost of any particular operation:

Outlet type	*Estimated number of calls per day*
Selected grocery	15
Comb canvass grocers	20
Chemists	10
Hardware	10
Selected grocery Multiple/merchandising	8
Confectioners/tobacconists	20
Sampling only grocery/ Tobacconists/confectioners	25

Expenditures on point-of-sale display material alone were estimated at £55 million per annum in 1966 (*Advertiser's Weekly*, 27 Jan 1967) and have doubtless increased considerably since that time. The magnitude of these expenditures, coupled with the recent formation of an 'Institute of Point-of-Sale Advertising', would seem to indicate that merchandising will play an increasing role in the sale of consumer goods in the future.

Suggestions for further reading
Rathmel, John M. (ed.), *Salesmanship Selected Readings* (Richard D. Irwin Inc., 1969)
Smallbone, Douglas, *An Introduction to Sales Management* (Staples Press, 1968)
Wotruba, Thomas R., and Olsen, Robert (eds.), *Reading in Sales Management* (Holt, Rinehart & Winston Inc. 1971)

Part Five

Marketing in Practice

18 Marketing and Economic Growth

INTRODUCTION

Throughout the 1970s growing concern has been expressed about the materialistic basis of Western society. This concern has taken many forms, from the publication of reasoned analyses of the likely consequences of unconstrained consumption – such as the Club of Rome's *Limits to Growth* – through moderate movements to preserve the 'quality of life', to strident denunciations of marketing as a deliberate attempt to mislead and exploit consumers. Elsewhere (*Marketing in Adversity*, Macmillan, 1976, and 'Marketing under Attack', in *Marketing: Theory and Practice*, Macmillan, 1976) I have examined these trends in some detail, but in the present context it will be helpful to review the broad arguments in order to support the basic thesis that economic growth is a necessary condition for improving standards of living and that marketing has a vital role to play in optimising the growth process.

THE NATURE OF ECONOMIC GROWTH

For those who subscribe to Lord Kelvin's dictum that measurement is a prerequisite to knowledge, it must be a matter of some surprise that serious efforts to measure growth postdate the Second World War. An explanation of this delay is to be found in H. V. Hodson's *The Diseconomies of Growth*, (Pan/Ballantine,

*Many of the ideas contained in this chapter were first aired in the Samuel Achinivu Okorie Memorial Lecture given at the University of Nigeria, 1977.

1972) and I draw heavily on this source in the following discussion.

Hodson suggests that 'The conceptual study of economic growth by economists in the Western tradition is quite remarkably recent' and cites J. M. Keynes's *General Theory of Employment, Interest and Money* (1936) as the watershed between the largely descriptive or at best static analysis of the classical economists and the dynamic analysis of the business cycle and economic growth which followed Keynes's identification of the role of expectations in moulding consumption behaviour. Of course, this is not to say that earlier generations of economists had not recognised the importance of growth – only that they had failed to see any pressing need to explore and explain its nature. (In fact we can discern a very interesting parallel between this situation and the formal statement of the marketing concept and attempts to develop adequate theory to explain what marketing is and how it works. We will return to this similarity later.) At this juncture it will suffice to say that to earlier generations the desirability of generating a surplus from economic activity was as self-evident as the need to exchange surpluses in order to increase utility. As I have noted earlier, in *The Wealth of Nations* Adam Smith makes very little reference to consumption – in his view, and presumably that of his contemporaries, predecessors and successors, 'Consumption is the sole end and purpose of production.' That said, the problem is how to create a sufficient volume of production to match an apparently ever-growing and insatiable demand for consumption goods. In addressing this issue Smith failed to develop a theoretical analysis of growth, and the same is equally true of Marshall over a century later.

In Hodson's opinion this failure was largely due to the classical economists' mechanistic view of the economy 'as a machine ticking over well or ill, faster or more slowly, rather than as an organism constantly in motion and growing as it moved'. Similarly, while Keynes provided the breakthrough which was to permit the evolution of a dynamic theory and a conceptualisation of growth, he did not achieve this himself, for his preoccupation was with the creation of stability and equilibrium so necessary to a world in the grip of a major depression. It is understandable that these problems should have been central to economic thinking during the 1930s and it took the changes brought about by the Second World War to initiate a change in emphasis and direction.

Among these changes may be identified the increased role of

central government in the direction and control of the Western market economies, the people's acceptance of government responsibility to assume this role, and the need to make good the losses of the war itself. In addition full employment became a primary objective of political and economic endeavour. Clearly, if one is to achieve such ambitious objectives, then it is necessary to identify the present status of the economy and the means of expanding it. The former was fairly readily achieved, for war-time controls had required and resulted in detailed statistical records. These were to provide the raw material for the theories of economic growth which were to emerge in the 1950s.

Among the many theories of growth which have been postulated are those which hold that it is investment-led, others that it is export-led, while still others claim that growth is demand-led. As we shall see, it is this latter school which is most closely identified with modern marketing practice. However, each of these and many other theories has its proponents and detractors and there is no single agreed theory of growth. It is perhaps surprising, therefore, that a consensus does exist concerning the measurement of growth. Thus, as Hodson comments, 'Economic growth, a very complex notion, has come to mean, for the vast majority of those who use the term, no more nor less than Gross National Product (or of G.N.P. per head).'

Of course, G.N.P. is a very crude indicator, a sort of lowest common denominator, but as long as those who use it compute it in a consistent manner then it provides a convenient starting-point for analysising changes within and between economies. However, it is no more than a starting-point, for despite its general acceptance and apparent validity as an accurate statistic G.N.P. is a crude, aggregated measure and can tell us little if anything about the real standard of living, let alone the quality of life enjoyed by a country and its people. As we shall see later, it is arguments about quality as opposed to quantity which lie at the heart of the criticisms of growth. Be this as it may it will be useful to accept that a country's economic performance is generally judged in terms of the increase in its G.N.P., for, or so the argument runs, if the Gross National Product is expanding (in real terms of course), then there is more to go around, so the welfare of the individual must be increasing too.

An immediate, obvious, and very important qualification is that

the numbers participating in the share-out do not change significantly, *and herein lies the basic problem.* History underlines that the
almost automatic response to a marginal improvement in living
standards is an increase in population which has the effect of
reducing the *per capita* increase in gross product. As Hodson
notes:

> It is one of the daunting dilemmas of this aspect of human life on
> the globe today that the more rapid the rise in population in a
> poor country, the more growth it needs to keep its standards
> even where they are, yet the less the means of growth it is likely
> to have, because a first charge on any surplus output (above
> consumption for its existing numbers together with maintenance
> of its existing capital) is levied by consumption for the increment
> of population.

We must therefore be careful to use G.N.P. *per capita* when
making our comparisons, and to adjust it for inflation – a particularly important adjustment at the present time.

But surely this is getting far too technical and detracts from the
thrust of the argument, namely that if the Gross National Product
adjusted for population and inflation is growing, then there is
more for everyone, so everyone must be better off. Critics of the
cult of economic growth would disagree on at least two major
counts.

In the first case G.N.P. does not allow for the deduction of
waste, deterioration and replacement of capital and physical
resources – in other words the N.N.P. (or Net National Product).
Second, even if agreement could be secured on the means of
adjusting the G.N.P. to a *net* figure, it seems unlikely that adequate compensation would be allowed for the use of finite natural
resources.

The first is essentially a technical point and can be allowed for
provided that we can agree upon the appropriate allowance or
deduction to be made for depreciation, etc. This, however, is a
major caveat and emphasises the problem of securing agreement
on the second point – that of allowing adequate compensation for
the use of finite natural resources. Clearly both require the exercise of value judgements and this is bound to differ according to
one's present status and standard of living. It is not without signifi-

cance that many of the most vocal critics of growth are persons enjoying a high level of personal consumption who would be little affected by a reduction in overall growth provided that they were able to maintain their existing standards. As an aside one might question whether this is a reasonable assumption, for the redistribution of wealth and a more equal distribution of national income is the declared objective of many economies. If this is to occur in a stagnant, no-growth situation, then it is obvious that the poor can only improve their standard of living by reducing that of the rich.

In a book called *In Defence of Economic Growth* (Cape, 1974) Wilfred Beckerman sums up the basic issue succinctly when he observes that 'The growth problem is a problem of how resources should be allocated over time.' Economists, and we hope politicians too, are concerned primarily with maximising welfare, which may be seen as comprising two elements – the level of consumption and the equality of its distribution. In addressing the problem of how to maximise welfare it is of the utmost importance that we consider the time dimension, for it is apparent that future consumption is highly dependent upon present consumption, in the sense that investment in new plant and equipment, in research and development, in education, etc. requires us to accept a lower level of current consumption in order to reap greater benefits (or welfare) in the future. It follows, as Beckerman pointed out, that 'the essential point is that it is *consumption* over some relevant time period which should be maximised, not the growth rate'.

To be correct we should recognise that what we are seeking is *optimum* growth, which we can define as the growth rate at which the sacrifice of present consumption necessary to promote future growth is just balanced by the extra future consumption this will generate.

In assessing what is an optimum growth rate we are again faced with the intractable problem identified earlier – namely, that 'optimum' is a subjective concept and will be perceived differently by different pressure groups. Thus influential critics like Galbraith have suggested that mankind keeps on raising the definition of optimum instead of being satisfied with what it has got. If we regard the United States as the pacemaker, in that its citizens enjoy the highest standard of living in the world, we can see immediately that standards there have increased significantly in the past decade – for the rest of us trying to catch up we are faced with an ever-receding frontier. And so we come to the crux of the controversy, for it is marketing which is case in the role of villain in the piece. In *The Affluent Society* (Penguin, 1974) Galbraith comments:

> As a society becomes increasingly affluent, wants are increasingly created by the process by which they are satisfied. This may operate passively. Increases in consumption, the counterpart of increases in production, act by suggestion or emulation to create wants. Or producers may proceed actively to create wants through advertising and salesmanship. Wants then come to depend on output.

In the same vein Professor Harry Johnson of Chicago made the following observation in his *Money, Trade and Economic Growth*, 2nd ed. (Allen & Unwin, 1961): 'The fact that wants are created and not original with the individual, raises a fundamental philosophical problem, whether the satisfaction of wants created by those who satisfy them can be regarded as social gain.' It would appear, then, that while growth is essential to ensure an improved standard of living, for most of us the marketing function is in some way responsible for exaggerating consumption needs to the point where the level of growth necessary to sustain such consumption is beyond the optimum and becomes wasteful.

To test the validity of this claim one must first define the nature of marketing and answer the question 'What is marketing?'

WHAT IS MARKETING?

As we saw in Chapter 1, marketing is an enigma. At the same time it is both simple and complex, straightforward and intricate, a philosophy or state of mind and a dynamic business function; it is new and it is as old as time itself. Cynically we might observe that it is exactly what you want it to be, and thereby everything or nothing. In attempting to resolve this paradox the views expressed must be those of the author, though they clearly owe much to the influence and thinking of others. Similarly, the reader must perforce draw his own conclusions concerning the boundaries and parameters of marketing. Fundamentally, however, it is felt to be of little consequence whether the listener thinks or agrees that the concept and processes discussed in this chapter are the province of marketing or some other discipline or orientation. What is important is the credibility and conviction which can be attached to them.

While the science of economics is founded essentially upon analysis of the interaction of supply and demand and the causes and consequences of this interaction – one might say the issues of what will be produced and how – so the art of politics is concerned mainly with who will receive what share of the resultant output. In the eyes of marketers this may be restated somewhat as follows. The economic problem is to maximise the satisfaction arising from the consumption of scarce resources. Accordingly we are concerned with consumer satisfaction, and the best judge of such satisfaction is the individual consumer. This must be so, for satisfaction is a subjective concept that varies between individuals and even within individuals over time. We are therefore concerned with consumer sovereignty founded upon the basic proposition that supply must be a function of demand.

In essence, therefore, the marketing concept is concerned with exchange relationships in which the parties to the exchange are seeking to maximise their personal satisfaction. This proposition is fundamental to the discipline of economics but goes beyond it in its emphasis upon the subjective rather than the so-called rational or objective measurement of satisfaction. The importance of this distinction is made clear by Lawrence Abbott in his book *Quality and Competition* (New York: Columbia U.P., 1955), in which he asserts that 'what people really desire are not products but satisfying experiences'. He then goes on to say that 'what is considered satisfying is a matter for individual decision: it varies according to one's tastes, standards, beliefs and objectives – and these vary greatly, depending on individual personality and cultural environment. Here is a foundation for a theory of choice broad enough to embrace Asiatic as well as Eastern cultures, non-conformists as well as slaves to convention. Epicureans, Stoics, Cynics, roisterers, religious fanatics, dullards and intellectual giants alike'. To put it another way, we are claiming that marketing is concerned with the establishment of mutually satisfying exchange relationships in which the judgements as to what is satisfying depends upon the perception of the parties to the exchange.

But the marketing concept goes beyond recognition of the fact that the parties to an exchange enter into such an exchange out of self-interest (in which each is seeking to maximise his personal satisfaction). The marketing concept stresses that the desired satisfaction of one party should be the motivating force or catalyst behind an exchange, and this party is the consumer, *not* the supplier. In fact we are positing a theory of choice founded on consumer sovereignty.

In our modern sophisticated societies it has become necessary to develop a marketing function to bridge the gap which has developed between the two parties to an exchange – producer and consumer, or buyer and seller, or supplier and user – and has grown up as a result of task specialisation, the division of labour and the application of technology to the production function.

In the days of a simple barter economy we may safely assume that the two parties to an exchange at least get what they bargained for. To this extent the exchange must have been mutually satisfying, though one can understand how the different values placed upon different goods might necessitate multiple exchanges in order to convert the homogeneous output of one product or service into a variety of desired outputs and services produced by other suppliers. Clearly the development of a medium of exchange greatly facilitates such transactions and encourages the development of formal places of exchange, which become known as 'markets'. Initially the development of markets does not necessarily lead to the separation of producer and consumer, but over time a new class of intermediary begins to emerge whose function is to bring together the outputs of the producers of a related group of products, concentrate these at a point of sale and enter into transactions for the exchange of title to these goods with prospective consumers. It is not difficult to see how economic growth and development leads to an increasing separation between producer and consumer and the development of more and more sophisticated mechanisms for facilitating exchanges between them.

Clearly this separation is not new, and may be traced back to long before major economic changes such as those precipitated by the industrial revolution. On the other hand, it is only in this century, and many would say in the second half of this century, that the balance between supply and demand has reached a point where producers have once again to take the sort of interest in their relationship with a consumer which is inimical to a barter relationship. Thus in the modern advanced industrial economy we have arrived at the point where the basic capacity to produce exceeds the basic propensity to consume. In fact this situation has existed for many decades but the impact has been greatly reduced by population growth and increased international trade. However, since the mid-1950s population growth in the advanced economies has tended to slow down, while technological innovation has accelerated, so continuing the growth in our capacity to produce.

Given the attitudes to work which prevail in industrial economies, most governmemts have seen it as desirable to maintain full employment and therefore to encourage increased consumption to absorb the output of this employment. Thus two basic trends may be identified. The first of these is demand stimulation, which has led to the rediscovery of the marketing concept and the development of a sophisticated marketing function to enable its implementation. The second is the redistribution of the working population into less productive or even non-productive (unemployed) activities.

THE DEVELOPMENT OF THE MARKETING FUNCTION

With rare and localised exception the history of mankind has been one of scarcity. Not until recent times, and even now only on a limited scale, has it been possible to do much more than satisfy the basic physiological needs of people. Thus the provision and acquisition of food, shelter and clothing have been major preoccupations of the majority, with only a small and privileged minority able to develop and satisfy demands for higher-order needs concerned with leisure, recreation, the arts, etc. In such circumstances the basic choice tends to rest between having and not having, rather than selecting between alternative means of satisfying different needs. Under these conditions the nature of demand tends to be simple and basic and the producer will maximise satisfaction by producing the largest possible output at the lowest possible unit cost.

Such an approach has been characterised as production orientated and is immortalised in Henry Ford's dictum that 'You can have any colour of car so long as it is black'. In other words Henry Ford recognised that the basic need which he was satisfying was for a cheap form of personal transportation. Only when this basic demand had been satisfied did consumers become more sophisticated and begin to look for ways of differentiating one motor-car from another, and so express a preference for differentiated motor-cars, including the provision of different colours. Henry Ford has frequently been criticised as an arch example of the old-fashioned production orientation in which the emphasis was laid upon product standardisation in order to achieve the lowest possible unit cost through pursuit of the economies of scale of large-scale production. Such criticism tends to ignore the fact that when Henry Ford first produced the Model T he was exactly in tune with the needs of his market, and that his failing, if such it was, was in not seeing that the basic demand for cars had become saturated and that the demand needed to be stimulated through the provision of a differentiated product. It also ignores the fact that without a sophisticated distribution, sales, promotional and service system all the production in the world would be of little use in the sense of 'creating' consumer satisfaction.

From the foregoing comments it is clear that consumer demand must not be regarded as a homogeneous and unchanging entity. In fact it is just the reverse – it is heterogeneous and dynamic, and it is these factors which decree that one must not only establish the dimensions of consumer needs before setting out to satisfy them but that one must also anticipate change and adjust one's output to respond to these changes. However, inertia or resistance to change is an endemic human condition. In the short run it may appear to work but in the long run it is inevitably doomed to failure, and retribution is invariably more immediate and final in the case of goods and services (as opposed to ideas, political systems, etc.), for consumers can easily switch or withhold the money votes on which suppliers depend for their existence. Herein, then, lies the essential difference between the marketing orientation, with its emphasis upon the future, and the production and/or sales orientations, with their emphasis upon the past and present, which results in attempt to mould demand to match the existing and often obsolescent supply.

If one accepts the proposition advanced by Lawrence Abbott,

quoted earlier, namely that satisfaction is particular to the individual, then it would seem fairly logical that if we wish to maximise consumer satisfaction we must first establish what it is that consumers want. It also seems fairly obvious that perhaps the easiest way to establish what it is that people want is to ask them. Hence, while basic demands may be so obvious as not to require specification, the recognition that all consumers are not alike demands that we try and classify the nature of similarities and differences between individuals in order that we may identify aggregations or segments of sufficient size to warrant the production of a specialised product. Thus in the 1920s and 1930s increasing attention was given to the development of one of the basic elements of the marketing function – marketing research. At the same time producers were also faced with the need to sell what they could make, and this led to a transitional period between the so-called 'production orientation' and the present 'marketing orientation'. In the transitional period the emphasis has to be on sales and promotion, in order to enable the producer to dispose of the products which his existing capital investment has been designed to produce. In the short term this is an operational necessity, for unless the investor can capitalise his existing investment he will be unable to generate funds to invest in the new plant and equipment designed to satisfy the new needs of his customers, as identified by and through marketing research.

With increasing affluence the consumer spends less of his disposable income upon the basic goods and services for which demand is fairly predictable, and is left with an increasing amount of discretionary purchasing power to spend (or save) in accordance with his or her own personal preferences. In consequence we can discern two basic tendencies – on the part of producers an increased awareness of the need to establish the precise nature of consumer preference, and on the part of consumers a desire to satisfy higher-order needs. Many of these higher-order needs fall into the category of personal services, and so the two trends coalesce with producers seeking to get closer to their consumers in order to establish a closer personal relationship, while consumers seek to extend the satisfaction gained through the consumption of physical goods by increasing their consumption of services, which, by definition, requires a high level of personal contact.

In the opinion of marketers recognition of the need to establish closer contact with the consumer predicates the adoption of a marketing approach, which may be summarised as consisting of the following basic steps:

1. Identification of a need which can be satisfied profitably within the constraints and opportunities represented by the potential supplier's portfolio of resources, and which is consistent with the organisation's declared objectives.
2. Definition of a particular segment (or segments) of the total demand which offers the best match with the producer's supply capabilities (the target audience).
3. Development of a specific product or service tailored to the particular requirements of the target audience.
4. Preparation of a marketing plan specifying the strategy to be followed in bringing the new offering to the attention of the target audience in a way which will differentiate it from competitive alternatives. (The main elements of such a plan will comprise pricing, promotion, selling, and distribution policies.)
5. Execution of the plan.
6. Monitoring of the results and adjustment as necessary to achieve the predetermined objectives.

Collectively these activities constitute the objectives of marketing strategy, and encompass the responsibility of marketing management.

MARKETING AND ECONOMIC GROWTH

Now that we have stipulated the nature of economic growth, and recapitulated on the nature of marketing, it is possible to spell out why marketing has a role to play in both advanced economies, where it has been accused of creating conspicuous consumption, and developing countries, where many point to the scarcity of basic commodities as evidence that it is production not marketing that is needed.

Let me deal first with the advanced economies. While marketing is often identified with materialism it is important to recognise that this is not the same as proving that marketing is a materialistic business philosophy. It is probably nearer the truth to assert that, as a business philosophy, marketing is neutral and that overtones of materialism merely mirror society's preoccupation with improving the standard of living. In turn, this laudable objective became embroiled with a perceived need to maintain a high level of employment; and employment results in increased production of goods. Obviously, if such increased supplies are not consumed, the process becomes sterile so we get into a vicious circle of stimulating consumption to increase demand and maintain employment opportunities. If we are not careful we lose sight of our real objective of improving human welfare and begin to confuse the means (growth) with the end (a better standard of living). The standard of living is concerned primarily with the quality of life and, while an increase in the quantity of goods and services may be an essential part of that quality, the two are not synonymous. In fact in advanced countries it would seem that beyond a certain point the consumption of physical goods is subject to diminishing returns and may reduce the quality of life due to environmental pollution, creation of stress, loss of leisure and recreational opportunities, etc.

It seems to me both ironical and paradoxical, assuming that marketing is so powerful in persuading people to consume more against their own interests, that no one suggests that these same skills and techniques cannot be used in the interest of conservation and moderation. In fact they can, and I predict that this will increasingly be the case. Thus in post-industrial society marketing will have a crucial role to play in identifying the satisfactions which people are seeking, for, as we have seen, the central economic problem is that of maximising satisfaction from the consumption of scarce resources. Where marketers tend to differ from economists is in the emphasis they give to measuring individual consumer preferences as the basis for resource allocation – in other words they give greater attention to the subjective and qualitative dimensions of demand than is common with economists.

As has been pointed out to me on numerous occasions on visits to developing economies, their problem is seen very differently. Supply deficiency or scarcity is seen as the fundamental problem and marketing is regarded as superfluous when there is such an obvious imbalance between supply and demand. Such a viewpoint is perfectly valid if you think marketing is a sort of sophisticated selling and concerned solely with demand stimulation by means of advertising, promotion and packaging.

To recapitulate, economies are conerned with maximising the satisfaction gained from the consumption of scarce resources. It is the satisfaction of individual consumers we are concerned with, and it would be paternalistic, not to say presumptuous, to assume that any single person is able to specify just what gives people the greatest satisfaction without asking them. To point to the fact that the available supply is consumed is not to prove that we are maximising satisfaction – it only goes to prove that something is better than nothing. My need for shoes is stronger than my need for brown shoes. If you only produce black shoes which I do not particularly like, they are still preferable to no shoes at all, but you are not maximising my satisfaction. Certainly you are not going to motivate me to work harder to own two pairs of shoes I do not like. (In passing it should be mentioned that one of the reasons why marketing is now practised in Soviet countries is that they had an awful lot of black shoes no one would buy!)

In a thoughtful analysis of the relevance of marketing to developing countries Fred Austen ('The Relevance of Marketing to Developing Countries', Paper presented to the Marketing Education Group of the United Kingdom, North Region Workshop, 1978) discusses the following ten areas which he considers to be characteristic features of developing countries:

1. *Segmented.* In Western countries considerable skill and ingenuity is displayed in dividing homogeneous groups by social purchasing-power grouping, consumer attitudes, etc. In developing countries no such ingenuity is necessary. Peasants and townsmen, rich and poor, are clearly separated. Even a medium-sized country like Nigeria has not merely three main religious groups but 200 different tribes, each with its own tradition and language.

2. *Fast-changing.* The cries of woe from the beggars for foreign aid disguise the fact that growth in national income is commonly as fast as in England during the heyday of the industrial revolution and the change in balance between town and country is taking place at a staggering rate. Places like Katmandu, Dar-es-Salaam and Jakarta are not only now enormous by any standard but are growing at an alarming rate.

3. *Badly administered.* Fast growth, plus major, often frequent, political changes, combined with little administrative tradition and ambitious concepts of state control, have almost univerally overstretched the administration. The prevailing tribal and family loyalties are a further important cause which lead administrators and executives to have priorities out of line with good practice or optimum effectiveness.

4. *Low general purchasing power.* Not only are the countries poor, with general money incomes usually well under £250 p. a. per head, and in many countries well under £100 p.a. per head, but much of the work is absorbed in subsistence farming, of food purchase. The well-off, who have purchasing power high even by our standards, contribute comparatively little to the move towards Western or Soviet, styles of market economy. The rich in developing countries, like Adam Smith's feudal barons, spend a disparately high proportion of income on servants, imported luxuries or purpose-made articles, none of which are generators of low-cost, mass-market structures.

5. *High military expenditure.* A reflection of insecurity – and the influence of military leaders – is shown by the staggering expenditure on defence. George Dalton, in *Economic Systems and Society* (Penguin, 1974), looked at developing countries, defined somewhat more broadly than we have, and quotes 1970 figures of 200 billion dollars, compared with 168 billion dollars for education and half that for public health, with rates of growth (1961–70) of 8 per cent, nearly four times the growth rate in developed countries, and often well over 10 per cent of G.N.P. Looked at slightly differently, according to figures quoted by Dalton developing countries spent twenty times on armaments of what they received in aid.

6. *State dominated.* Almost regardless of political complexion the state plays a greater role in the economy than in developed nations. Partly this is due to balance-of-payments problems, partly due to ideology, partly to the absence of an existing management and commercial infrastructure. Normally the economy is geared to a five-year plan, handsomely printed but indifferently executed. Restriction of imports is particularly common. Foreign capital aid normally operates through state channels.

7. *Monopolistic.* In most products monopoly or oligopoly is the rule and competition the exception. This largely follows from the common import restrictions, small fragmented markets and the associated problem complex.

8. *Poor infrastructure.* Both social items, such as roads, hospitals, schools, sewers, postal and telephone services, and also private networks in the transport, finance and media fields are deficient, causing a completely different pattern of requirements and opportunities.

9. *Vulnerable exports.* In general developing countries are dependent on a few products. Characteristically one primary product will be 55–85 per cent of total exports (Tyagunenko, *Industrialisation of Developing Countries*, Moscow, Progress Publishers, 1973) and apart from the recent rises in commodity prices (petrol, cocoa, coffee, tea especially) the long-range terms of trade appear to be moving against developing nations (see *Terms of Trade Policy for Primary Commodities*, Commonwealth Secretariat, 1975). This can largely be attributed to the fact that the goods produced by developing countries stayed the same, while the markets changed and the more sophisticated countries changed products and product mixes in line with market valuations. It also reflects the fact that the sharpest discrimination was by developing countries against other developing states. Tyagunenko quotes revealing figures which show that from 1955 to 1971 trade with the developed Western countries and Soviet bloc countries rose by 2–3 per cent for each bloc (as a percentage of the total), which was balanced by a 5 per cent drop in the already small (about a quarter of the trade) with other developing countries. Incidentally the same figures show how insignificant the proportion of trade with the Eastern bloc is when compared with the massive (about three-quarters) proportion of commerce with capitalist countries.

10. *Inadequately documented.* British marketers envy the information commonly available in the United States, while industrial marketers similarly respect the published consumer data, but differences between our fields are as nothing when compared with most developing countries. Even where there is a superficial veneer of sophistication in the presentation of figures, they are nearly always out of date, generally ineffectively collected

and frequently deliberately tailored. It must be appreciated that with the differences in culture it is often almost impossible to get urban, numerate patriates who can still communicate with the predominantly rural peasant population. Beyond this, in a subsistence economy with a population which is largely illiterate, worried about tax implications and with no general traditions as to the integrity of information and the importance of figures, one cannot expect good primary statistics, or find gathering secondary statistics easy.

To overcome the barriers to economic growth implicit in these features of developing countries, Austen argues that 'It is clearly vital, therefore, that the management process at organisation level, as opposed to governmental planning level, which optimises and predicts the relationship of inputs to outputs over time, i.e. "Marketing", should play an increasingly significant role' an assertion which echoes the sentiments of such well-known authors as Galbraith, Drucker and McCarthy.

Consider what Drucker had to say as far back as 1958 ('Marketing and Economic Development', *Journal of Marketing*, Jan 1958, pp. 252–9):

> My thesis is very briefly as follows, Marketing occupies a critical role in respect to the development of such 'growth' [i.e. underdeveloped] areas. Indeed, marketing is the most important 'multiplier' of such development. It is in itself in every one of these areas the least developed, the most backward part of the economic system. Its development, above all others, makes possible economic integration and the fullest utilisation of whatever assets and productive capacity an economy already possesses. It mobilises latent economic energy.

In the first instance most would agree with Kindleberger (*Economic Development*, McGraw-Hill, 1958) that whether markets stimulate development or vice versa, distribution systems tend to be neglected and are the source of considerable inefficiency. It follows that improvements in physical distribution are likely to have a high pay-off and help break the vicious circle so typical of the developing economy, where surpluses are small or non-existent, leaving little or nothing for investment to provide the necessary stimulus to growth. Allied with developments in physical distribution it is also clear that efficient retail practice has a significant contribution to make in optimising the satisfaction derived from the available supply. Austen cites a study by Slater which showed that ten years after supermarkets were introduced into Puerto Rico they accounted for 40 per cent of all food sales in San Juan and offered lower prices than traditional small outlets. In a similar vein several studies in Latin America have claimed that mass retailing methods used by Sears, Roebuck have been an important contributor to economic growth.

However, marketing can perhaps make the greatest impact by ensuring that scarce resources are channelled into those products which offer the greatest consumer satisfaction. Unfortunately in economies where scarcity is endemic it is often difficult to persuade managers that an ability to sell everything they can make is not necessarily the same as maximising satisfaction. A simple case history will help make the point.

In Nigeria soft drinks such as coke, lemonade and orangeade are extremely popular and often difficult to obtain. A survey by marketing students at the University of Nigeria in Enugu showed that although the major bottling company was able to sell all its output, customers were not entirely satisfied with the product mix, which emphasised coke and contained relatively small proportions of orange and lemon flavours. It appeared that consumers had a very strong preference for orange and deliveries were consumed immediately; lemon ranked second, but it was only after both orange and lemon were sold out that coke became acceptable as third best, but still preferable to no soft drink at all. Because demand exceeds supply the manager assumed that all was well and paid little attention to new firms being set up concentrating mainly on orange and lemon flavours. In ignoring this potential competition he clearly had forgotten that some years previously coke had built up its sales in preference to beer, which had now lost its dominant place in the beverage market.

The moral is as clear in developing economies as it is in developed ones – an understanding of consumer needs is fundamental to long-run business success, and therefore to optimising the allocation of scarce resources. In turn it is clear that the scarcer resources are, the greater the need to optimise the return from them, so that even where growth is restrained voluntarily marketing practices and techniques have a major role to play in ensuring the greatest possible return in terms of consumer satisfaction.

By improving the efficiency of the marketing function we improve profitability, and increased profitability means a larger surplus to invest in expanding production facilities. In other words marketing productivity is an essential contributor to reducing and solving the scarcity problem.

To conclude, it seems to me that the marketing concept is universal to all stages of economic development and to ignore it is to slow down the optimum rate of growth as I have defined it – put another way, neglect of the marketing concept wastes scarce resources. When it comes to application of the concept then it is clear that different marketing functions are more relevant in some situations than in others. In developing countries one needs market research as an essential input to planning future development; one needs greatly improved distribution to ensure that the limited goods available are put into consumption in the most efficient manner possible; one needs greater control over distribution to eliminate distortion of the price mechanism through diversion into a black-market operation. One has proportionately a much lesser need for promotional and selling activities than is the case in advanced economies, where supply and demand are much closer to equilibrium. However, these differences do not deny the relevance of marketing, merely a better understanding of its application.

19 International Marketing

Over the past decade, the chronic imbalance in the United Kingdom balance of payments has focused attention on the need to increase sales of goods and services to other countries in order to pay for those items which we wish to buy from them. In fact, the cost of physical imports has exceeded the value of exported products for well over a century, but this discrepancy was little cause for alarm so long as income from foreign investment, and the sale of services such as shipping, banking and insurance made good the difference. For a variety of reasons, however, the income from the so-called invisible exports has failed to keep pace with the growing expenditures on physical imports and has resulted in the overall deficit referred to above.

Elimination of this deficit may be approached in one, or both, of two ways:

(a) We can reduce expenditures by cutting back on imports, foreign travel, the maintenance of overseas bases and foreign aid, etc.
(b) We can increase revenues by exporting more goods, selling more services, encouraging foreign investment, attracting more foreign visitors, etc.

Government policy has laid varying degrees of emphasis on all of these alternatives, but it is clear that there is only limited scope for reducing expenditures if we are to maintain and improve our standard of living. In that the latter is a fundamental aim of our economy it follows that the main thrust must be to increase revenues, which, in turn, is the *raison d'être* of international marketing.

INTERNATIONAL MARKETING *VERSUS* EXPORTING

The term 'international marketing' is preferred to the more conventional 'exporting' for a variety of reasons. First, exporting usually connotes the sale of physical goods in foreign markets. Second, the study of exporting tends to concentrate on procedures such as transportation, insurance, credit, foreign legislation and the like. Third, exporting generally excludes alternative strategies such as the setting up of foreign subsidiaries, and fourth, although our second major source of foreign revenue is tourism it has little to do with the sale of physical goods in foreign countries.

By contrast, international marketing is concerned with all marketing activities undertaken on an international scale, and so includes consideration of the cultural and behavioural aspects of foreign markets, the sale of services and the operation of overseas subsidiaries.

As with industrial marketing, there is a tendency to present exporting as different from other marketing activities and, therefore, to isolate it from the mainstream of marketing thought and practice. A leading marketing theorist, Robert Bartels, has explored the validity of this point of view and has concluded that:

(*a*) Marketing is a process of twofold character: technical and social.

(*b*) Marketing technology, i.e. '. . . the application of principles, rules, or knowledge relating to the non-human elements of marketing', has universal validity and potentially universal applicability.

(*c*) 'The applicability of marketing technology is dependent upon circumstances of the environments in which it is applied', i.e. cultural and societal factors condition the technical factors.

(*d*) There are wide differences in cultural and societal factors between countries and, therefore, in marketing practice. Despite these differences 'the *relationships* between marketing practice and environment are susceptible to generalisations in analysis termed "comparative marketing" '. Thus, although the marketer may expect both differences and similarities between foreign and domestic markets, 'both are embraced within a consistent body of marketing theory'.

('Are Domestic and International Marketing Dissimilar?', *Journal of Marketing*, XXXII (July 1968) 56–61.)

If these conclusions are accepted, then it follows that no useful purpose is to be served by segregating exporting from the mainstream of marketing practice, and that marketing in foreign environments should be approached in exactly the same way as marketing at home. Clearly the marketer must be sensitive to cultural and behavioural differences, but this is equally true of the domestic market.

THE GROWTH OF INTERNATIONAL MARKETING

Of necessity, Britain has long been involved in foreign trade in order to make good her limited endowment of land and raw materials. During the middle of the last century we had a virtual monopoly of international trade, but since that time our share has declined continuously. In large degree this decline has been due to the enormous expansion in international trade, for in absolute terms our total trade today is many times greater than it was during the last century. Several factors may be distinguished as having contributed to this growth, including:

(*a*) Nationalistic policies, emphasising self-sufficiency, have yielded to the logic of the theory of comparative advantage, i.e. that countries will maximise their growth by specialising in those activities with the greatest marginal product, and exchanging excess supplies for the surplus output of other specialised economies. The creation of international trading communities is an implicit recognition of this, e.g. E.E.C., EFTA, LAFTA (Latin America Free Trade Association), etc.

(*b*) Politically, it has been realised that the removal of trade barriers will not only stimulate the growth of economies but will also lead to cultural exchange and the easing of international tension.

(*c*) The 'population explosion' has created new mass markets and expanded the demand for all types of goods and services.

(*d*) Developments in communications and transportation have opened up hitherto inaccessible markets.

(*e*) The removal of trade barriers has intensified competition in formerly protected markets, and encouraged domestic manufacturers to develop new products and to look farther afield for markets in which to sell them.

FACTORS WHICH PREDISPOSE THE FIRM TO ENTER INTERNATIONAL MARKETS

Fundamentally, entry into any new market, domestic or foreign, is undertaken to increase overall profitability. In turn, the decision to enter the international market may arise from any combination of a number of factors, among which may be distinguished:

1. Loss of domestic market share due to increased competition. Whereas a price reduction in the home market might be suicidal, the firm using a contribution approach may be able to increase total profits by selling at a lower price in foreign markets. (This strategy is often precluded by the existence of anti-dumping agreements.)
2. Loss of domestic market share due to product obsolescence. In many cases products made obsolete by the introduction of more sophisticated substitutes are still appropriate to less advanced countries, e.g. oil lamps.
3. Saturation of the domestic markets precluding the attainment of scale economies. Unlike the previous points, which presume the existence of excess capacity, this situation suggests that an increase in market size will permit the firm to expand its production and reduce average cost. In turn, this will permit the firm to expand its domestic market, as well as compete more effectively overseas.
4. The provision of incentives. Incentives to enter international markets are of both the 'push' and 'pull' variety, and invariably originate at government level. International agreements such as GATT (General Agreement on Tariffs and Trade) frequently exclude the provision of direct subsidies to exporters, but there are a number of ways in which a government can provide indirect support. The

Appropriation Accounts, 1971/72 indicate that the Department of Trade and Industry (Export Promotion) expended £6,313,000 on such activities.

In addition to the information and promotional support represented by these expenditures, the exporter can also call upon other departments such as those of the D.T.I. for specialised help, can insure against loss through the Export Credits Guarantee Department, and receive preferential tax treatment for expenses incurred.

'Pull' incentives are those offered by foreign governments to encourage entry into their national market. Originally, such incentives included import licences and tax relief on profits, but these are less common now. Most developing economies wish to develop domestic industry, in order to create employment opportunities, as well as wishing to conserve foreign exchange. Consequently, pull incentives are now largely designed to attract foreign firms to establish subsidiaries, rather than to attract the importation of finished goods.

5. Probably the strongest incentive of all, however, is the existence of potential demand backed by purchasing power. Essentially, such market opportunities are of three types:

Type 1. One can offer an equivalent product at a lower price.

Type 2. One can offer a better product at a competitive price.

Type 3. Once can offer a product which is not available in the foreign market.

In view of the high labour costs/low productivity of many of our industries, few type 1 markets are open to British exporters and attention is largely concentrated on type 2 and type 3 situations.

Over the years many traditional British exports have built up a reputation for quality, soundly based on product superiority, e.g. woollens, speciality cotton textiles, china, machine tools, etc. Unfortunately, complacency and poor marketing have allowed competitors to pre-empt many type 2 markets, although personal experience of the American consumer goods markets suggests that these markets are not irretrievably lost, as many British products of unrivalled quality could be sold at twice their domestic price and still undercut the Japanese imports which predominate.

Type 3 markets offer the greatest profit opportunity of all, but are the least common. Further, the small size of the domestic market, and insular thinking, frequently delay the development of technological innovations, allowing other countries to overtake us, e.g. the Hovercraft. Hopefully, entry into the E.E.C. will encourage the adoption of more aggressive, and less risk-averse, R. and D. and marketing policies which will fully exploit our inventive genius.

THE LOCATION OF MARKET OPPORTUNITY

In general, the identification of foreign market opportunities will result from systematic marketing research of the type described in Chapter 9. In the particular, however, it is usually necessary to modify this approach for a number of reasons:

(*a*) Most companies are seeking a market for an existing product with which they have had considerable domestic experience, i.e. one is seeking to match needs with a product, rather than develop a product to satisfy identified but unfilled needs.

(*b*) Few companies or executives have any 'feel' for foreign markets, which tend to be totally unknown quantitites in a way which the home market can never be. Some might argue that this is an advantage in that it demands a fuller and more scientific analysis, with less dependence on subjective, judgemental opinions.

(*c*) Few countries possess the wealth of published data available for use in domestic desk research, making precise quantification difficult.

(*d*) Field research using survey methods is frequently precluded because of language difficulties, the non-availability of trained personnel, cost, etc.

(*e*) There are literally dozens of countries which might represent a potential market, and some form of screening procedure is essential to reduce the list to manageable proportions.

In the latter context the development of comparative marketing as an area of study offers considerable hope in that it is concerned with 'The identification and analysis of common factors and differences in marketing concepts, systems and techniques among various societies, including nations' (David Carson, 'Comparative Marketing – A New–Old Aid', *Harvard Business Review* (May–June 1967)). As the title of Carson's article suggests, comparative analysis is a long-established technique, but it is only in the past decade that it has become the subject of formal study in the marketing context. As a result of these studies a number of formal classificatory systems have been, or are in the course of being, developed which take into account economic, geographic and human factors. Although none of these systems has yet been accepted as definitive, reference to any or all of them should permit early elimination of countries which are clearly unsuited as potential markets for a given product or service. Similarly, a study of the differences and common factors between countries should sensitise the marketer to their relative importance when formulating a marketing strategy.

SOURCES OF INFORMATION

In the nature of things, the classificatory systems being developed by comparative marketing theorists are based largely on generalisations, and should be regarded as a screening device. Once a short list of potential markets has been decided upon, the researcher must seek out more detailed data. A number of sources are available to assist him in this task, some of which have already been quoted in Chapter 9. These may be supplemented by reference to:

The Department of Trade and Industry.
Chambers of Commerce
Commercial Officers of the Diplomatic Service
Export Councils
Federation of British Industries
Institute of Directors
Institute of Marketing
National Association of British Manufacturers
Trade Associations
The Foreign Departments of the major banks, etc., etc.

(The D.T.I. publishes a wide selection of free publications which are available on request and contain full details of sources of information, export services available, etc.)

Many of the sources quoted can provide first-hand information on specific opportunities, as well as advising on the procedure to be followed, and the pitfalls to be avoided, when entering specific markets.

FIELD RESEARCH

Although it is generally true that few countries have market research organisations capable of undertaking field research, this certainly does not apply to the advanced, affluent economies which represent the best potential markets for British goods. On the other hand few companies are prepared to make a large-scale entry into a foreign market, and so baulk at the expenditure that an extensive survey would involve. Consequently, many would-be exporters confine their field research to a 'fact-finding' tour in which they solicit the opinions of informed sources, the quality of which varies enormously. Owing to the uncertainties associated with entry into a foreign market, as opposed to risks which are quantifiable, many marketers prefer to enlist the support of a third party in the country concerned, i.e. an indirect approach, which is usually regarded as a substitute for field research.

DIRECT *VERSUS* INDIRECT EXPORTING

Direct exporting is essentially direct selling in a foreign market, and thus requires the firm to take full responsibility for establishing contact with potential customers. Indirect exporting occurs when the exporter employs the services of middlemen to look after the distribution, and often the complete marketing, of the product.

Channel policy is a technical aspect of marketing, and the general principles discussed in Chapter 13 and elsewhere are equally applicable to foreign and domestic markets. Thus, the same considerations of cost versus control should be evaluated in the context of direct versus indirect exporting. The decision to export direct will almost always necessitate the establishment of sales offices and the appointment of full-time employees to staff them, although other functions, such as physical distribution and advertising, may be delegated to agents, Supporters of the direct approach argue that the setting up of branch offices and the employment of salesmen are reassuring to potential buyers as they represent a definite commitment to the market, as well as giving the marketer direct control over elements such as price, credit policy, after-sales service, etc.

In the case of technically complex industrial goods, with a small, clearly defined potential market, the direct approach is probably to be preferred. However, where the product is simple, largely undifferentiated and aimed at a mass market, most manufacturers prefer to use middlemen and test the market before committing themselves to an extensive sales and distribution network. As in the home market, middlemen fall into two main categories – merchants or wholesalers who purchase goods outright for resale, and agents who act on the manufacturer's behalf in return for a fee or commission on sales. The same problems of control discussed earlier have to be discounted against the economics of using middlemen, although it is probably true to say that the middleman's contacts in a foreign country are more valuable to the manufacturer than they are in a domestic market.

OTHER ALTERNATIVES

Broadly speaking, three other alternatives are open to the firm which wishes to operate on an international scale:

1. It can license a foreign company to manufacture to its specification, e.g. Pilkington has licensed Corning Glass to manufacture float glass in the United States.
2. It can undertake a joint venture with another company, e.g. Gerber's alliance with Corn Products.
3. It can set up a subsidiary company.

Licensing has several factors to recommend it:

(*a*) It avoids the risk of expropriation of assets by the 'host' country, already familiar to many British companies with subsidiaries overseas.

(*b*) It avoids direct competition with the licensee on his home ground. (Obviously, the licensee must have the same skills and resources as the licensor or there would be no point in taking up the licence.)

(*c*) It allows the capital resources that would be tied up in increased capacity, at home or abroad, to be deployed in other profitable opportunities. In the absence of the necessary capital resources, it permits the earning of increased profits which would otherwise be unattainable.

(*d*) It enables the product to be produced at a competitive price, which might not be possible if it were to be exported as a finished good, e.g. float glass is both bulky and fragile and transportation costs would probably price it out of every foreign market where it is currently produced under licence.

(*e*) Licensing avoids import tariffs and restrictions, and minimises the possibility of loss due to a change in trade policy.

(*f*) It avoids the risks of product failure.

The major disadvantage to licensing is that the royalties are invariably less than the normal profits which would be earned if the product were manufactured and sold by the licensor.

Joint ventures require a greater commitment by the firm than is necessary in the case of licensing, but if successful, offer greater rewards for the risks assumed. An alliance with a well-established foreign distributor or manufacturer smoothes the exporter's entry into the market, but can lead to bitter conflict over policy and practice, cf. the Concorde.

The establishment of a foreign subsidiary exposes one to all the risks which licensing minimises. Tax incentives are often offset by requirements that nationals of the foreign country hold a majority of the shares in the subsidiary, in which case it becomes a joint venture. It is also probably true to say that such incentives are directly proportionate to the risks.

In politically stable countries, however, the wholly owned subsidiary frequently offers the greatest potential – a factor which tends to be overlooked by restrictions on overseas investment. Economies of local production can be reinforced by the parent's technical, financial and marketing expertise and resources. Past experience would seem to suggest that the parent should avoid keeping too tight a rein on its subsidiary, and should be prepared to appoint foreign managers and delegate authority for all but major policy decisions to them. Long established European companies active in international markets would appear to have accepted this principle, but American firms have only lately begun to come round to this point of view, after some fairly costly attempts to retain full control at 'head office'.

Space limitations preclude fuller analysis of international marketing, for which the reader must refer to specialised texts on the subject. It is worth reiterating, however, that such texts rest on the same marketing principles as have been discussed in this book, so that their major contribution lies in the descriptive content rather than in their treatment of marketing technology.

Suggestion for further reading

Duguid, Andrew, and Jacques, Elliott, *Case Studies in Export Organisation* (H.M.S.O., 1971)

Livingstone, J. M., *International Marketing Management* (Macmillan, 1976)

20 Planning for Marketing

Planning is a pervasive human activity by which we seek to exercise some degree of control over the future. As a process it will vary enormously depending upon a number of variables, foremost among which will be the complexity of the activity and the degree of uncertainty concerning the future situation in which the activity will take place. Fundamentally, however, all planning seeks to arrive at a present decision concerning future action – the more complex the activity and the more uncertain the future, the greater the need for formal, systematic planning procedures. The purpose of this chapter is to provide a brief synthesis of the separate treatment given the marketing environment and the various mix elements, and to indicate how the marketer can integrate all these considerations into a marketing plan.

THE CONCEPT OF CORPORATE STRATEGY

Some reference has already been made to the concept of corporate strategy, as, for example, when discussing new product development, but some elaboration is necessary here. Like comparative marketing, corporate strategy is an old concept in a new and revitalised form. Probably the most important distinction between strategy as practised by earlier generations of entrepreneurs and today's professional managers is that the latter consciously and explicitly state their aims and objectives and develop plans designed to achieve them.

In his book *Strategy and Structure* (Massachusetts Institute of Technology Press, 1962), Alfred D. Chandler defines corporate strategy as 'The determination of the basic long-term goals and objectives of an enterprise, and the adoption of courses of action and the allocation of resources necessary for carrying out these goals'.

This definition suggests three distinct phases in the strategic process:

Appreciation
Plan
Implementation.

Each of these stages is capable of further subdivision, and Kotler (in *Marketing Management*) offers the following progression:

Diagnosis: where is the company now, and why?
Prognosis: where is the company headed?
Objectives: where should the company be headed?
Strategy: what is the best way to get there?
Tactics: what specific actions should be undertaken, by whom, and when?
Control: what measures should be watched to indicate whether the company is succeeding?

Similarly, the Marketing Science Institute (see Patrick J. Robinson and David J. Luck, *Promotional Decision Making Practice and Theory:* Marketing Science Institute series, McGraw-Hill, 1964) has developed a model called APACS (Adaptive Planning and Control Sequence) which recognises the following stages:

Step 1. Define problem and set objectives.
Step 2. Appraise overall situation.
Step 3. Determine the tasks to be accomplished and identify the means to achieving these aims.
Step 4. Identify alternative plans and mixes.
Step 5. Estimate the expected results arising from implementation of the alternative plans.
Step 6. Managerial review and decision.
Step 7. Feedback of results and postaudit.
Step 8. Adapt programme if required.

In turn, each of these models is capable of further subdivision, but the basic three-stage model will serve our purposes here.

APPRECIATION: THE MARKETING AUDIT

In accounting practice the purpose of an audit is to investigate systematically the firm's financial records and practices at regular intervals. To be valid it must be comprehensive, objective and critical, in the sense that it should compare actual practice with accepted theoretical standards and principles. To be useful it should also be prescriptive and indicate how the firm may improve on its current performance. The marketing audit should seek to attain the same ends for the marketing function.

In practice this is usually achieved through continuous marketing research, supplemented by special *ad hoc* studies as and when necessary. This research frequently provides the data base for the firm's forecasts on which plans and strategies are based. Usually such forecasts will be prepared in detail for the immediate and more certain future – the short-range forecast – and in outline only for the more distant and uncertain future periods. What actually constitutes short and long range varies from industry to industry, but a useful and generally accepted rule of thumb is that short range is anything from one to five years and that long range is anything in excess of five years.

PLANNING

At this stage in the process it is important to distinguish clearly between the environmental constraints within which the firm must operate and those activities over which it can exercise control. It is also important to recognise that in the long run all fixed constraints are variable in some degree – thus in the short term management must accept the exising distributive network, in the long term it can modify it through its own action, just as it can develop new markets and shape the nature of competition. However, in time the environment will change too owing to technological innovation and competitive activity, and the firm must seek to develop objectives which are sufficiently well defined to require commitment, yet flexible enough to permit a change in emphasis and direction as the situation evolves. 'Servicing the travelling public' is a good example of an overall long-term objective which meets these criteria. In the short term, the skill lies in developing strategies which make the best use of available resources in moving the firm from where it is to where it wants to be.

IMPLEMENTATION

In essence a strategy is a broad statement of the means to be employed in achieving a given objective, while the actual methods used constitute the tactics. Thus, a firm's strategy might be based on skimming the cream off the market, which suggests that the appropriate tactics would be:

High product quality
Distinctive design and packaging
High price
Selective distribution
Direct sale
Extensive after-sales service
Low pressure advertising, etc.

At the risk of overstating the obvious, the success of a given strategy depends upon the co-ordination of the tactics into an integrated, complementary and cohesive whole. There is a finite number of alternative strategies open to the firm and, in a given market, it is usual to find several competing firms pursuing the same basic strategy simultaneously. If this is so, then observed variations in performance must arise out of the quality of the plan, or statement of tactics, and its execution. Factors such as motivation and morale have an important bearing on the execution of a plan, but also tend to be a function of the plan's quality and credibility.

THE PREPARATION OF A MARKETING PLAN

If the author has segmented the textbook market correctly, many readers will be preparing for examinations, such as those set by the Institute of Marketing, which require the student to analyse a case study and prepare a written marketing plan. Hopefully, the following outline will help the student in preparing such an analysis:

Analysis of the situation: appreciation. There is little point in restating the descriptive content of a case as the objective of an appreciation is to define the central issue. This is probably best achieved by a systematic analysis of the available material in terms of :

(*a*) What business is the company in and what are the salient features of this business?
(*b*) What is the firm's goal, explicit or implied?
(*c*) What resources has the company – Productive
                                           – Technical
                                           – Financial
                                           – Marketing?
(*d*) What policies, explicit or otherwise, has it adopted in respect of these resources?
(*e*) Is there a single strategic variable which dominates all others – if so, what is it?
(*f*) Has the firm any special skill or distinctive competence?

In analysing the case (or problem, in real life), one should seek to isolate those areas which bear directly upon both the immediate problem and the more general problem of which it is symptomatic. Once these areas have been defined they should be ranked in some rough order of importance and analysed in detail. For example, if a major issue is the nature of the product itself, one should list all the advantages and disadvantages which one can think of to permit an overall conclusion to be drawn. Similarly with all other issues. The conclusions drawn from the separate analysis of the relevant issues should then be summarised and stated as the basis upon which the plan has been based. This statement should also make explicit any assumptions which have been made, together with the reasons which support their adoption.

The marketing plan. This must be realistic in the light of the analysis described in the appreciation, and should commence by stating the overall objective or aim. If the student feels that the company's stated aims are incapable of attainment he must be able to present a very convincing argument as to why, and how, they should be changed. Thus the statement of the long-term aim must be supported by an exposition of all those factors which will affect the company's ability to achieve its objective, paying particular attention to environmental changes and changing consumer needs.

Following the statement of the long-term aim, the plan should state the short-term objective and the specific policies to be adopted to achieve it. In the interests of both clarity and coverage of all salient factors, some form of outline should be used similar to that given below.

1. Short-term aim, e.g. to increase market share by 5 per cent.
2. Forecast of market conditions for the period of the plan.
3. Statement of further marketing research to be undertaken to provide feedback on performance and to be used in the preparation of future marketing plans.
4. Statement of product policy.
5. Statement of pricing policy.
6. Statement of packaging policy.
7. Statement of distribution policy.
8. Statement of advertising and sales promotion policy.
9. Statement of sales policy.
10. Budget statement with explanation of how it is to be used for control purposes.
11. Outline of how plan is to be financed.
12. Timing for implementation of various policies.

Clearly, the amount of detail will vary considerably depending upon the central issue identified in the appreciation, and the data available. It should be remembered, however, that the overall marketing plan cannot be expected to go into the same detail as would be expected of, say, the media plan, but it should provide the skeleton around which such plans can be prepared by the various functional specialists. In an examination context, the main intention is to discover whether the candidate has acquired a sufficient understanding of theoretical principles, and these should always be outlined, even though case data is not available for purposes of exemplification. For example, if the case concerns a convenience good the student may consider sales promotion relevant, even though it is not specifically referred to, and so might suggest the use of a banded offer designed to increase consumer sampling, achieve increased consumer and retail inventories, etc.

Finally, the impact of a marketing plan will be lost if it lacks clarity of expression, no matter how logical the sequence or how sophisticated the analysis. To this end, the student must practise expressing himself clearly and concisely in order to convey the maximum information in the least number of words.

MARKETING ARITHMETIC

On first acquantance one of the more confusing aspects of marketing is the basic financial data associated with selling – mark-up, discounts, and stock-turn – and that necessary to monitor the financial health of the marketing function – standard costing, budgetary control and ratio analysis. While these factors, and the latter particularly, are more properly the province of a financial text a brief overview is essential to underline their relevance to marketing and encourage more detailed study. (It is appreciated that many students will be pursuing a broadly based course which includes a study of accounting and finance. Such students should regard the next few pages as basic revision material.) Each of the topics identified is the subject of separate treatment in the following pages.

Mark-up
This is the amount which a firm adds to its cost of goods in order to arrive at its selling price, i.e.

$$SP = C + M$$

Where SP = selling price, C = cost of goods, and M = mark-up or margin.

The mark-up, or margin as it is sometimes termed, is intended to cover *selling, general* and *administrative* expenses ('S.G.A.' in some accounting texts and case studies) as well as a percentage for profit. The convention which frequently causes confusion is that mark-up is usually expressed as a percentage of selling price rather than cost, probably due to sellers working backwards from a going market price, as would be essential under conditions of perfect competition. That is, one accepts the market price, deducts the desired profit, assesses the S.G.A. associated with the anticipated volume of sales and deducts this, and is left with the amount for which the product will have to be made. If this amount is less than actual cost, one will have to accept a lower profit, or even a loss, or decide not to produce, while if it is greater an above-average profit becomes possible.

Four basic calculations are frequently called for in connection with margins/mark-ups and these are as follows:

1. Determination of selling price when costs and percentage mark-ups are given. Since the selling price always equals 100 per cent we can substitute the data given into a simple formula to arrive at the retail price, i.e.

$$C + M = SP$$
$$C = SP - M$$

Thus if cost = £100 and the mark-up = 25 per cent then

$$£100 = SP - 25\%$$
$$= 100\% - 25\%$$
$$= 75\%$$
$$\therefore £SP = \frac{£C}{100\% - M}$$
$$= \frac{£100}{75\%}$$
$$= £133.33$$

2. To find the margin given cost and selling price, using the same figures as above, we have:

$$C + M = SP$$
$$M = SP - C$$
$$M = £133.33 - £100$$
$$M = £33.33$$

This may be expressed as a percentage of the selling price:

$$M = \frac{£33.3}{£100}$$
$$= 33.33\%$$

3. To convert a margin based on selling price to one based on

cost. Here the formula is

$$\% \text{ margin on cost} = \frac{\% \text{ margin on selling price}}{100\% - \% \text{ margin on selling price}}$$

$$= \frac{33.3}{100 - 33.3}$$

$$= 50\%$$

4. To convert a margin based on cost to one based on selling price:

% margin on selling price

$$= \frac{\% \text{ margin on cost}}{100\% + \% \text{margin on cost}}$$

$$= \frac{50}{100 + 50}^*$$

$$= 33.3\%$$

Discounts

The calculation of discounts is a constant source of confusion due to the fact that a discount is always expressed as a percentage of the *reduced* price and not the original retail selling price. For example, a 25 per cent discount on £100 is in fact £20 and not £25, i.e.

$$\text{discount} = \frac{\text{amount of discount}}{\text{original price} - \text{discount}}$$

$$= \frac{20}{80} \text{ (i.e. } 100 - 20)$$

$$= 25\%$$

(*Note:* in American texts/case studies/discounts are often termed 'mark-downs'.)

Stock-turn

As the term suggests, the stock-turn is the number of times the stock 'turns over' during a given period and gives a useful indicator of how a particular type of outlet is performing. Clearly the rate of stock-turn will vary enormously according to the nature of the goods sold, being fastest in fresh foods and slowest in durables such as furniture or luxuries such as jewellery, cameras, etc. There is usually a direct relationship between the margins which manufacturers anticipate in recommending a retail selling price and the stock-turn of the average outlet. It follows that more efficient outlets (i.e. those with lower operating costs) will earn higher net profits if they maintain margins and achieve average stock-turn. However, in recent years many retailers have pursued a more aggressive strategy designed to increase market share, and thereby long-term profitability, by offering discounts and increasing stock-turn.

To compute stock-turn one must divide net sales for the period by the average inventory (at selling price) for the same period. Average inventory is simply:

$$\frac{\text{opening stock} + \text{closing stock}}{2}$$

while net sales is total sales less any returns or allowances.

STANDARD COSTING AND BUDGETARY CONTROL

Tradititionally the accounting function concerned itself solely with recording the historical performance of an organisation. It is for this reason that many people seek to differentiate between the major business functions by characterising accounting as an orientation to the past. By the same token production is seen as being preoccupied with the present – a 'present orientation' – and marketing is conceived of as a 'future orientation', with an emphasis upon the planning and control of future activities. Nowadays such a simplistic distinction would be very far from the truth, for all business functions are conscious of the need for forward planning and the need to control operations so as to achieve the desired outcome. Standard costing and budgetary control have been developed for just this purpose.

In his excellent introduction to the subject, *Costing: A Management Approach* (Pan Management Series, 1974), A. H. Taylor expresses the view that defining standard costs as predetermined costs or yardsticks fails adequately to 'convey the fundamental change in viewpoint of costing which occurs when a standard costing system is instituted in place of an historical costing system'. Taylor goes on to say:

> The standard cost is what the cost of an operation or service ought to be under given conditions and subject to given conventions of costing. It is thus a notional amount which depends entirely on the conditions predicated. It is this notional amount which is treated as the value of the stock and the cost of the goods sold.
>
> The conditions associated with a standard cost are essentially a standard of efficiency and a level of activity. Using material as an example, the standard material cost of a product implies the purchase of the required quantity of material at an economic price and in economic lots. This in turn implies the existence of a production plan and a storing policy. All the standards inherent in the elements of cost which comprise a product cost or the cost of an operation are interdependent. To carry the argument to the extreme, it could be said that the standard costs derive from the corporate plan.

Put another way, using standard costs is very similar in principle to the economist's use of *ceteris paribus*: it enables one to predict outcomes due to the interaction between factors under consideration given no change in all the other factors which might influence that interaction. In this sense standard costs do act as yardsticks, for they enable management to ascertain whether the business is performing as planned according to the predetermined conditions necessary for that achievement – conditions which it is management's responsibility to create. Any departure or *variance* from the standard will immediately warn management of a difference between planned and actual which will enable it to analyse the nature of the variance and the possibility of rectifying it. Of course, all variances are not negative, though this is most often the case in periods of inflation when costs are often rising in an unpredictable manner which cannot be accommodated when setting the standard cost. However, when positive variances do occur it is equally important that management be aware of the fact so that they may capitalise on an opportunity if such exists, e.g. a seasonal fall in raw material prices.

It must also be emphasised that conformity with the standard should not be accepted at face value, for it may well conceal countervailing trends – for example, a fall in cost due to greater machine efficiency counterbalanced by increased labour or material costs. Thus to use a standard costing system as one of management by exception could be dangerous. Its major benefits lie in its requirement that one should plan future operations, i.e. prepare a budget, identify the conditions necessary for the successful execution of the plan, the creation of such conditions and the comparison of actual and planned performance as the basis for controlling activities (hence 'budgetary control').

To cite Taylor again:

The merits of a standard costing system may be summarised as follows:
1. Information is provided for managerial control through the comparison of actual expenditure against standard expenditure.
2. The analysis of variances between actual expenditure and standard expenditure saves managerial time, because the managers need only give their attention to those operations where substantial variances occur.
3. Stable and, presumably, sound figures of cost are provided to assist price determination.
4. Stable values are assigned to stock and work in progress, thus eliminating . . . anomalies . . . and assisting in the production of a true and fair view of profit and a reliable trend of profitability.

For a discussion of the anomalies mentioned, of costing principles and their managerial use the reader is referred to the original source.

RATIO ANALYSIS

In most countries trading organisations are required to publish an annual statement of their financial affairs – most usually a balance-sheet, which summarises the financial position, and a profit-and-loss account, which is a statement of income and expenditure. The manner in which companies choose to publish these financial statements varies enormously, from the elaborate and extensive documents put out by large public companies to the minimum required by law characteristic of most private firms. However, even this minimal information can provide an analyst with a great deal of insight into the strengths and weaknesses of an organisation and the purpose of this section is to indicate a small number of ratios which can enable such an evaluation to be made. (Such analysis is particularly important for students preparing for formal examinations using the 'case method' (see Chapter 21), as most cases contain financial statements. Only if you are able to interpret these can you decide whether or not they are relevant to the marketing problem you have been asked to solve.)

In *The Meaning of Company Accounts* (Gower Press, 1971) Walter Reid and D. R. Myddelton group the more common ratios under three headings:

Investment measures

(a) Return on equity $= \dfrac{\text{Profit after tax}}{\text{Shareholders' funds}}$

(b) Earnings per share $= \dfrac{\text{Profit after tax}}{\text{Number of shares issued}}$

(c) Price/earnings ratio $= \dfrac{\text{Market price per share}}{\text{Earnings per share}}$

(d) Dividend yield $= \dfrac{\text{Dividend per share}}{\text{Market price per share}}$

(e) Dividend cover $= \dfrac{\text{Earnings per share}}{\text{Dividend per share}}$

Measures of performance

(f) Return on net assets $= \dfrac{\text{Earnings before interest and tax}}{\text{Net assets}}$

(g) Profit margin $= \dfrac{\text{Earnings before interest and tax}}{\text{Sales}}$

(h) Asset turnover $= \dfrac{\text{Sales}}{\text{Net assets}}$

Measures of financial status
   Solvency

(*i*) Debt ratio $\quad = \dfrac{\text{Long-term debt}}{\text{Capital employed}}$

(*j*) Interest cover $\quad = \dfrac{\text{Earnings before interest and tax}}{\text{Interest}}$

Liquidity

(*k*) Current ratio $\quad = \dfrac{\text{Current assets}}{\text{Current liabilities}}$

(*l*) Acid test $\quad = \dfrac{\text{Liquid assets}}{\text{Current liabilities}}$

The purpose of all the foregoing ratios is to enable an analyst to conduct a spot check on the financial health of an organisation in much the same way that a doctor takes one's pulse, temperature, blood pressure, etc. Diagnostically ratios are used in combination so that a satisfactory outcome for one test is not sufficient to guarantee that all the others will yield the same result. Accordingly it is necessary to work systematically through a series of tests before a clean bill of health can be issued. Which series of tests if most appropriate will vary according to one's viewpoint, but in general all analysts will wish to consider *liquidity, solvency* and *performance*, with less importance attached to investment measures *per se*. (For a discussion of how to interpret ratios one should consult Reid and Myddelton, *The Meaning of Company Accounts* or B. K. R. Watts *Business and Financial Management*, 3rd ed. (M & E Handbooks, 1978) ch. x.)

21 The Written Analysis of Cases

While case studies are usually employed as the focus for a classroom discussion, they are being used increasingly as the basis for a written assignment. This is particularly so where the case method of instruction is followed in a formal course of study when the written analysis of a case is frequently adopted as the appropriate means of examination. Similarly, case studies often provide excellent material for examining students who have pursued a more conventional programme of instruction by means of lectures and tutorials. For these reasons it will be useful to consider the objectives of a written analysis and suggest some approaches to the execution of such an exercise. (It goes without saying that the following observations apply equally to case analysis, where a formal, written analysis is not required.)

OBJECTIVES

Despite the fact that most European teachers tend to spend more time upon the discussion of an individual case study than their North American counterparts, it is still rare for such an extended consideration to cover all the issues contained in a given situation. Certainly, if the case study is used as a catalyst for encouraging an exchange of ideas between students, it is unlikely that spontaneous contributions will occur in the logical or odered manner one would expect in a formal lecture. Indeed, one suspects that if the case leader succeeds in eliciting a structured analysis, then it can only be at the expense of ruthlessly discouraging digressions and diversions, some of which inevitably would prove both stimulating and illuminating. Clearly the latter approach would eliminate much of the interest and involvement engendered by a lively debate in open forum, which is one of the strengths of the case method.

However, it is generally recognised that while case discussion has a vital role to play in management education, it possesses deficiencies which can best be remedied by alternative teaching methods. As implied above, case discussions frequently lack the cogency and impact which can be achieved by marshalling one's thoughts in a logical sequence, as well as neglecting issues of possible relevance and importance. Further, at the individual level discussion can result in a superficial treatment as students soon learn that their fellows have often not undertaken a rigorous analysis, and so will not challenge apparently complex analyses of data, while the case leader may not have opportunity. A similar danger exists in that the student can struggle through by 'debating' the points made by others, or simply by preparing a detailed analysis of one issue which is regarded as his 'contribution'.

The basic objective of the written analysis is to eliminate these deficiencies while developing skills in:

 (*a*) problem definition
 (*b*) analysis
 (*c*) presentation

We consider each of these in turn.

PROBLEM DEFINITION

There is wide support for the view that problem definition is the most critical and most difficult step in problem-solving. This view is generally predicated on the grounds that while problem definition is invariably cited as the first stage in problem analysis, in fact it only becomes possible after an extensive consideration of a wide range of other issues. Consider two popular statements of the normative approach to problem-solving.

First, there is the Adaptive Planning and Control Sequence (APACS) proposed by Robinson and Luck which we introduced in the previous chapter and which comprises eight steps:

 Step 1 Define problem and set objectives
 Step 2 Appraise overall situation
 Step 3 Determine the tasks to be accomplished and identify the means to achieving these aims

Step 4   Identify alternative plans and mixes
Step 5   Estimate the expected results arising from implementation of the alternative plans
Step 6   Managerial review and decision
Step 7   Feedback of results and post audit
Step 8   Adapt programme if required

Second, there is the operational approach to research suggested by Ferber and Verdoorn (*Research Methods in Economics and Business*, Collier-Macmillan, 1962) with six stages:

1. Formulating the problem
2. Development of working hypotheses
3. Planning the study
4. Collecting and processing the data
5. Analysis and interpretation
6. Presentation of results

While the second model may appear rather different from the first, in fact they both cover the same basic elements. Similarly, both convey the impression of an orderly sequence stemming from the identification and statement of a problem, though steps 7 and 8 in the APACS model suggest that feedback and revision of the intial problem definition do not take place.

In reality we feel that feedback and adjustment of the original problem statement will be a major feature of the whole problem-solving process. This is not to suggest that no problem is ever solved, but rather than the depth analysis of one issue will inevitably raise questions concerning related but previously unconsidered issues. Given the dynamic nature of the business environment it would be surprising if this were not the case. However, we make this point solely to reinforce the fact that the steps in the problem-analysis model are neither discrete nor necessarily sequential and, having given this warning, we will immediately find it simpler to treat them as if they were both.

In simple terms we can distinguish two alternative scenarios for the case analyst:

(*a*) he is given a case study and a problem statement, or
(*b*) he is given a case study with no indication of the specific problem to be addressed.

The first alternative is typical of the examination situation and also encompasses certain cases in which the opening or closing paragraphs contain a statement of the problem as perceived by the case writer or a character in the case itself. Such a situation corresponds well with the circumstance where an organisation has identified the existence of a problem and wishes to brief a consultant (internal or external) to analyse and solve it. The second alternative is much more open-ended and usually adopted by teachers where they wish their students to decide whether in fact a problem exists at all. A real-world parallel of this approach might be the study of an industry, market or company by a financial analyst. Fundamentally the case analyst is well advised to treat both situations in the same way.

If given a brief, then it is necessary to establish that it does reflect the real issue to be investigated rather than a symptom or effect of the real problem. Similarly, it is essential to eliminate any possible ambiguities in the problem statement or brief and to define any terms capable of differing interpretations. Equally it is of vital importance to establish the precise parameters of the topic – how long is 'the short term', 'the long term', 'the future', what firms are to be taken as comprising 'the textile industry', what is understood by 'competition' – immediate and direct competition from firms producing similar products or services, or is it intended to include competition from substitute products? Clearly exactly the same points need to be taken into account when preparing a brief of one's own.

Naturally the above is a counsel of perfection. If, for example, one knew that declining sales were directly and solely attributable to a specific cause, then, as claimed earlier, the problem is largely resolved, for one can focus all one's efforts upon eliminating or avoiding that cause. While pedants will argue that such elimination or avoidance is itself a problem requiring resolution, it is believed that it will usually be a relatively trivial one. If, for example, one is certain that declining sales are the result of product inferiority due to the absence of an ingredient or feature present in a competing product, it would seem that all that needs to be decided is

(*a*) Do we wish to increase our sales to their former level?

(*b*) If yes, can we improve our product at a cost which will enable us to sell them at a price and volume which will earn us a satisfactory profit (including issues of complementarity, goodwill, etc.)?

(c) If the answer to (b) is 'no', then clearly we must revise our original position.

On the other hand, if the problem has been incorrectly identified and the decline in demand has resulted from other causes, then treating the wrong symptoms (product composition) is unlikely to have much effect. Of course, if one could survive long enough it might permit problem-solving by elimination!

Essentially we are arguing that it would probably be more accurate to define the first stage in problem analysis as 'setting up a working problem definition' in much the same way as the scientist sets up a null hypothesis. In this way we acknowledge that problems exist because of imperfect information and uncertainty – it would be surprising if the acquisition of more information did not help to reduce uncertainty and so permit more exact problem formulation. How, then, should we set about acquiring more and better information?

ANALYSIS

Armed with a working problem definition and a declared objective the analyst is well placed to commence formal investigation. At this juncture it is well to accept that while one may be embarking upon a voyage of discovery many other explorers have done the same and much can be learned from their experience. In other words there is a body of knowledge and experience concerning problem-solving which is relevant to the solution of any particular problem. While several different approaches have been proposed (and we will only discuss our own preferred method) all are agreed on the fundamental point that a structured procedure is to be preferred. This claim does not deny the utility of unstructured methods such as brainstorming, lateral thinking or the like but would suggest that these are techniques to be used in particular circumstances and especially where a structured analysis has revealed deficiencies which cannot be remedied by more formal methods. Further, the more complex the problem, the more necessary is a detailed and structured approach to its solution. Thus where the nature of the problem is very well understood, as, for example, launching a space probe or landing an aircraft, it is usual to develop a check-list of all the steps to be taken in the sequence in which they are to be taken, and to follow this unswervingly unless there are indications to the contrary. Even in the latter case, for example a pilot observes an obstruction on the runway just prior to touch-down, alternative procedures are also likely to be highly specific.

Of course, business problems are far less amenable to the highly structured analytic method characteristic of the sciences, and appropriate to science-based activities, e.g. flying and aerodynamics, largely because business is an activity arising from the interaction of people who are far less predictable in their behaviour patterns than are materials. However, experience would seem to suggest that human behavioural patterns are perhaps more open to observation and prediction than has generally been appreciated. If this is so, then an ability to predict how a person or organisation would react under a specified set of circumstances must help reduce the uncertainty faced by decision-makers and so reduce the need to exercise judgement. Unfortunately it often appears that many decision-makers confuse the amount of judgement they exercise with the quality of the decisions made. While it is true that the true exercise of judgement is the function and responsibility of the decision-maker, none but a fool would seek to substitute uncertain judgement for fact or known risk where the alternatives can be completely specified and probabilities attached to their occurrence (as in life insurance). None the less it seems that this is just the error to which so many would-be decision-makers fall prey – they cannot be bothered with the labour, much of it boring, repetitive and trivial, necessary for a rigorous analysis and so flee into the exercise of 'judgement'.

From the above comments it is clear that I am proposing at least two steps to formal analysis, namely:

1. The identification and measurement of all facts which impinge upon the problems.
2. The application of judgement to the uncertain areas which are the residual remaining following the factural analysis.

The first step is frequently described as a 'management audit' and is usually sub-divided into two parts – internal and external.

THE INTERNAL AUDIT

The purpose of the internal audit is to develop a comprehensive list of the organisation's resources, together with an assessment of their relative importance *vis-à-vis* each other. As suggested in Chapter 5 this audit should encompass all of the following:

1. *Physical resources*

   Land – as a source of raw materials
       – as a location for manufacturing and distributive activities

   Buildings – general purpose or specific, i.e. designed for light engineering, assembly, storage, etc., or for heavy manufacturing requiring special foundations, services, etc.

   Availability of and access to – power supplies, drainage and waste disposal
                                 – transportation: road, rail, canal, port facilities, etc.

   Plant and equipment – general purpose, e.g. lathe, press
                       – specific, e.g. steel rolling mill, foundry, etc.

2. *Technical resources.* Essentially these reside in the technical expertise of the firm's employees, together with the possession of patents, licences or highly specialised equipment.

3. *Financial resources.* These comprise the liquid assets in the firm's balance-sheet, the ability to secure loans against fixed assets and the ability to raise capital in the market on the basis of past and anticipated future performance. They also comprise the skill of the firm's financial management.

4. *Purchasing resources.* Managerial expertise backed by a special advantage enjoyed by the firm by virtue of its size or connections, e.g. reciprocal trading agreements.

5. *Labour resources.* The skills, experience and adaptability of the work-force.

6. *Marketing resources.* The degree of consumer/user acceptance or 'franchise' developed through past performance.
Access to and degree of control over distribution; the
specialised skills and experiences of personnel.

While such an audit should provide a good summary of the
nature and extent of the company's assets, together with an indication of the relative importance of the major business functions, its
value can only be realised by comparison with similar data for
companies with which it is competing. To obtain this one must
carry out an external audit.

THE EXTERNAL AUDIT

An assessment of the environment in which the company has to
operate should be carried out at two levels. First, one should
appraise the overall economic climate and seek to establish
whether it is growing, static or declining and for what apparent
reasons. Second, within this broad framework one should evaluate
the industry/market in which the company is competing. Our own
preferred approach to this stage of the analysis is to use the
framework developed by the well-known management consultants
McKinsey & Co.

The basis of the McKinsey approach is to sub-divide the business system into a series of sub-systems, as indicated in Fig. 21.1.
Starting with raw material extraction the analysis proceeds by
examining each major sub-system in turn in order to establish the
interrelationship and interdependence between them in terms of:

(*a*) The degree of *competition* within and between each sub-
system, e.g. raw material extraction might be in the hands of
only one or a few producers to that conditions are
oligopolistic while retail distribution could be characterised
by thousands of small sellers none of whom could influence

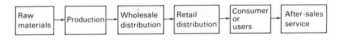

Fig. 21.1 The business system

the market. Clearly the latter circumstances describe perfect competition, and both sets of conditions apply in the oil industry. Thus in establishing the nature of competiton one should measure:

  (i)   the number of competitors;
  (ii) their profitability;
  (iii) their degree of integration;
  (iv) their cost structure;
  (v)   the existence and nature of any barriers to entry, e.g. technological, size of investment in production and/or marketing.

(b) Where, in the total system, *value* is *added* by the activities of members of the production, distribution, or servicing sub-systems. For example, a significant proportion of turnover in many consumer-durable industries is accounted for by after-sales servicing and the efficiency of this sector may have a radical influence upon the market shares of individual suppliers, as well as on industry profitability.

(c) The location of *economic leverage* in the system. Does this arise from being a fully integrated producer, or can one exercise leverage by avoiding the extensive fixed investment implicit in vertical integration and concentrating on only one sub-system?

(d) Where is the system's *marketing leverage?* Usually this is associated with control of a scarce resource which might be an essential raw material, a patent on a process, control of a distribution channel, a brand name ('Hoover', 'Elastoplast') or some other type of consumer franchise.

Once the analyst has established the major characteristics of the production, distribution and servicing sub-systems his next task must be a thorough documentation of the consumer or user. Such documentation requires one to supply answers to the five basic questions which underlie all market research – who, what, where, when, and how.

  1. *Who* buys in terms of demographic and socio-economic criteria such as age, sex, income, education, occupation, marital status, etc. (for consumers), or status, authority, functional specialisation, etc. (for users)? Who *consumes?* (Com-

pare consumption and purchase of breakfast cereals; of hand tools in a factory; etc.)

2. *What* do people buy in terms of variety, design, quality, performance and price characteristics?
3. *Where* do people buy? In specialist outlets, in general purpose outlets, by mail or telephone from a catalogue, in the home or on their premises, i.e. how important is direct selling through representatives versus indirect selling via the media?
4. *When* do people buy? Are purchases seasonal, regular, irregular, associated with another activity, etc?
5. *How* do people buy? Impulsively, after considerable deliberation, in large quantities, small quantities, from multiple sources or a single source, etc?

A sixth and equally important question is 'Why?' Unlike our other five questions one cannot usually supply a definitive and factual answer. However, when one considers that consumers (or users) do not buy products, as such, but rather the satisfactions yielded by the product, then even a partial understanding of the satisfactions looked for will go a long way towards explaining actual behaviour in the market-place.

At this juncture one should have developed a good understanding of both the company and the environment in which it is operating. It now remains to combine the two threads of the analysis in order to isolate the company's particular strengths and weaknesses in terms of the environmental threats and opportunities. An indication of the sort of questions appropriate to such a comparison is given in Fig. 21.2., which is taken from McKinsey's model.

Thus far we have proceeded as if information were freely available and also as if it were of a known value. Rarely will these conditions be satisfied; in fact the most frequently voiced complaint of case students is 'lack of information'. Accordingly we turn now to consider this.

THE QUANTITY AND QUALITY OF INFORMATION

It is tautologous to point out that certainty exists where there is perfect information, from which it is a simple step to deduce that problems exist because of the absence of perfect information.

WHERE IN SYSTEM ARE COMPANY'S MEASURABLE STRENGTHS AND WEAKNESSES?

(How company compares with competition — today and future)

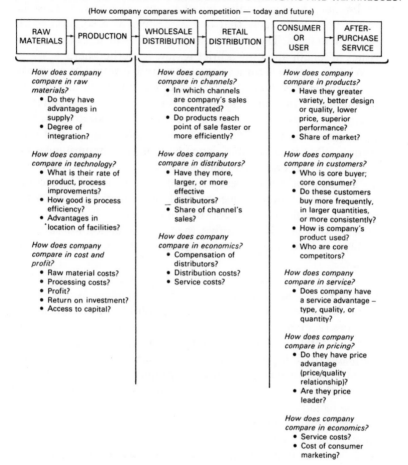

RAW MATERIALS → PRODUCTION → WHOLESALE DISTRIBUTION → RETAIL DISTRIBUTION → CONSUMER OR USER → AFTER-PURCHASE SERVICE

How does company compare in raw materials?
- Do they have advantages in supply?
- Degree of integration?

How does company compare in technology?
- What is their rate of product, process improvements?
- How good is process efficiency?
- Advantages in location of facilities?

How does company compare in cost and profit?
- Raw material costs?
- Processing costs?
- Profit?
- Return on investment?
- Access to capital?

How does company compare in channels?
- In which channels are company's sales concentrated?
- Do products reach point of sale faster or more efficiently?

How does company compare in distributors?
- Have they more, larger, or more effective distributors?
- Share of channel's sales?

How does company compare in economics?
- Compensation of distributors?
- Distribution costs?
- Service costs?

How does company compare in products?
- Have they greater variety, better design or quality, lower price, superior performance?
- Share of market?

How does company compare in customers?
- Who is core buyer; core consumer?
- Do these customers buy more frequently, in larger quantities, or more consistently?
- How is company's product used?
- Who are core competitors?

How does company compare in service?
- Does company have a service advantage – type, quality, or quantity?

How does company compare in pricing?
- Do they have price advantage (price/quality relationship)?
- Are they price leader?

How does company compare in economics?
- Service costs?
- Cost of consumer marketing?

Fig. 21.2. Company's measurable strengths and weaknesses

It is for this reason that we have stressed the methodical collection of as much information as possible as an essential prerequisite to problem-solving. However, in this task we are faced with three major difficulties – data are frequently incomplete, second much information is presented in the form of opinion, or, third may only be inferred from the apparent relationship between facts or events. It follows that a major job of the analyst is to screen all the available evidence for accuracy, validity and reliability as a preliminary to determining whether any relationships exist between acceptable facts that are suggestive of a solution to the problem in hand. There are many textbooks which deal with these issues at length and only a brief review is merited here.

While complete accuracy constitutes truth it would be erroneous to infer that less than complete accuracy is untruth and thereby unacceptable. In a business context it is rare that one requires the degree of precision necessary in the scientific laboratory, or even the engineering workshop, and a reasonable estimate will often suffice. What is reasonable depends upon the circumstances and may vary by several percentage points around the true value, e.g. an estimate of market size. Essentially the need for accuracy depends upon how sensitive the final outcome of one's analysis is to changes in the value of constituent elements – if the end-result appears to be largely insensitive, then approximation will suffice; if highly sensitive, then the more accurate the point estimate the better.

A good example of this is provided by a feasibility study of the suitability of a Scottish mountain for development as a ski slope. While access to the slope, nature of the uplift facilities and back-up facilities (car parks, toilets, cafes, etc.), price to be charged, growth trends in total demands, etc., all have a bearing upon the decision, estimates of all these parameters are relatively unimportant compared with the value of the critical or limiting factor – the prevailing weather conditions. In the event analysis revealed that when one deducted the number of days when it would not be possible to ski due to high winds or poor visibility from the total days on which snow could be guaranteed, the residue was so small as to make it quite obvious that a commercial venture was impractical almost regardless of the values one attached to any of the other parameters.

The mark of a good analyst is an ability to isolate the critical factors and then focus all available resources in eliciting the most accurate information available concerning them. When using data from published sources one must distinguish between the credibility to be attached to government statistics gathered by census and estimates extrapolated from samples by trade associations, consultants and those with a vested interest in the interpretation of the data they convey. One must be conscious of recency and assess how delay in publishing data may affect its current validity. One must also be sensitive to changes in the collection and recording of data over time and satisfy oneself as to the comparability of such data.

Such strictures are all very well when dealing with information from published sources, but how does one deal with opinion and hearsay? Much information in case studies falls into the latter category and is often conflicting in its indication of the true state of affairs. A classic example of this is to be found in the Barnstaple case study, in which three executive managers responsible for the finance, production and sales functions each attribute the company's declining fortunes to a different cause. However, by carefully adducing factual data in the case, or inferences which may be drawn from *these data* with a very high degree of confidence, it can be clearly demonstrated that only one manager's opinion is acceptable. Herein lies a key skill of the analyst – an ability to pick out relevant pieces of information, while discarding those which only serve to confuse an issue, and link them together to demonstrate a functional relationship.

It is possible to distinguish three different levels of analysis in this sorting and synthesising process – deduction, inference and the formulation of assumptions. A deduction is made when one derives a logically necessary conclusion about a specific case from perfect information concerning the general case – for example, all retailers of cars operate on a 20 per cent gross margin; the *XYZ* company is a retailer of cars: *deduction* – the *XYZ* company operates on a 20 per cent gross margin.

The status of an inference is less clear cut than is that of a deduction. An inference may be defined as the interpretation placed upon evidence by an observer, from which it follows that the quality of an inference may range from excellent, i.e. a very high probability that it reflects reality, to very poor. Assuming, however, that the correct inference is drawn, then the distinction rests in the fact that there is always an element of uncertainty associated with an inference while there is none with a deduction. However, by linking logical deductions with reasonable inferences one can proceed a long way towards the solution of a problem.

The need for assumptions only arises where there is an absence of evidence necessary to link other information which seems to bear upon the problem. Assumptions may be of two kinds – working assumptions and critical assumptions. Working assumptions are those necessary to move an argument along and provide links in the chain of reasoning, but unlike critical assumptions they are not vital to the final decision. In every case an assumption should only be made as a last resort when it is obvious that other information is not available. When setting out an assumption, and especially a critical assumption, it is important to state clearly the evidence considered in deriving one's assumption, the reasons for selecting and rejecting particular points, and the precise form of the final assumption made. Only by careful attention to these factors will the analyst be able to communicate the thought processes leading to his conclusion; without them his argument will be open to criticism and lack conviction.

From the foregoing it is obvious that *both* the drawing of inferences *and* the formulation of assumptions demand the exercise of judgement, and this is the proper role for its application. In all other cases a strictly formal and factual approach should be followed.

PRESENTATION

Skill in problem definition and analysis is of little consequence if the analyst is unable to communicate his findings to others. There are several good books on report writing including:

Gallagher, William J., *Report Writing for Management* (Addison-Wesley, 1969) Mitchell, John, *How to Write Reports* (Fontana, 1974).

and the student should consult these for detailed guidance on how to set about writing a report. However, in doing so it will become apparent that even the textbook writers are not in complete agreement and Gallagher and Mitchell suggest different formats for writing management reports. My own preference is for the Gallagher sequence, namely:

    Summary
      Purpose
      Scope
      Conclusion(s)
      Recommendations

Introduction
Body
Appendix

However, for a Written Analysis of Cases (WAC) the Mitchell approach may be more appropriate:

Statement of the problem
Factors causing the problem
The effects of the problem
Examination of possible solutions and their implications
Conclusions
Recommendations
Appendices

Whichever method is preferred two final words of warning seem appropriate. First, the student can assume that the examiner is familiar with the case and so should avoid the regurgitation of descriptive material unless it is introduced for a specific purpose. Second, facts seldom, if ever, speak for themselves.

22 The Changing Face of Marketing

INTRODUCTION

When preparing the second edition of this book the majority of revisions were concerned with updating the factual content and few changes of substance were made, with the exception of the inclusion of the present chapter. In this edition several substantial additions have been made along the lines set out in the Preface to the Third Edition and there is a correspondingly lesser need to modify the substance of this chapter.

In retrospect it is both surprising and satisfying that the major trends identified in 1974 have tended to dominate the 1970s and look like maintaining their influence into the 1980s and beyond. As a consequence only two changes have been made to this chapter. First, we include a list of legislative measures designated to protect consumers which indicate the extent to which government and public policy have become involved with, and responded to, the consumerist movement. Second, we have reviewed our prognostications for the 1970s and extended our look ahead into the 1980s.

In Chapter 18 we took a broad look at marketing and economic growth and some of the expressions of concern about 'the quality of life', 'maintenance of the environmental and ecological balance', 'conservation', and so on. Collectively all these concerns tend to be lumped together as 'consumerism' and clearly have major implications for the practice of marketing. This was the first major trend we identified in 1974 and some of its features are reviewed in the pages that follow.

Consumerism represents a major environmental change to

which marketing must respond but the other major change has originated in marketing itself and so is influencing the environment rather than responding to it. This change is summarised in the definition of marketing used by Philip Kotler in the second edition of his book. Its significance will be heightened if we cite first his original definition, namely: 'Marketing is the analysing, organising, planning and controlling of the firm's customer impinging resources, policies and activities with the view to satisfying the needs and wants of chosen customer groups at a profit.'

Contrast this with that proposed in 1972:

'*Marketing* is the set of human activities directed at facilitating and consummating exchanges.'

This definition demands that we extend our view of marketing from that of technology, which has been the majority view hitherto, to one of marketing as a social process. The implications of such a change comprise the second major theme of this chapter.

CONSUMERISM

In the first chapter of this book we examined the nature of the marketing concept and suggested that a somewhat simple statement of it might be:

' "If economies are comprised of people, and we are endeavouring to allocate scarce resources in order to maximise satisfaction, then it is the satisfaction of people which we are aiming at. This being so it is essential that we determine first what people want and then allocate our resources accordingly." In other words, we must determine the nature and strength of demand and create supplies of goods and services to satisfy these demands.' (p. 28)

Further, we suggested that free market economies largely permit the evolution of consumer sovereignty by allowing consumers to express their preferences as between goods and services through the daily casting of their money 'votes'.

It would be naïve to suggest that any such system is or ever could be perfect. None the less, market economies and the marketing philosophy rest upon the same fundamental proposition that consumer preferences will determine the allocation of available inputs to the creation of the most desired outputs.

So much for marketing. What is consumerism?

The term 'consumerism' first came into currency in the last decade when it was applied to a number of issues which had first attracted serious concern in the 1950s. Vance Packard was one of the first to use the expression in relation to these concerns foremost among which were planned obsolescence (see *The Waste Makers*), declining quality, and the absence of satisfactory after-sales service, particularly in saturated mass consumption markets for convenience goods. This connotation was gradually extended as the 1960s progressed. In 1962 Rachel Carson's *Silent Spring* drew attention to the impact which pollution of the environment was having upon plant and animal life. In 1962 President Kennedy addressed his first consumer message to Congress in which he stated four basic consumer rights:

1. *The Right to Safety* – to be protected against the marketing of goods which are hazardous to health or life.
2. *The Right to be Informed* – to be protected against fraudulent, deceitful or grossly misleading information, advertising, labeling or other practices, and to be given the facts needed to make an informed choice.
3. *The Right to Choose* – to be assured, wherever possible, access to a variety of products and services at competitive prices and in those industries in which Government regulations are substituted, an assurance of satisfactory quality and service at fair prices.
4. *The Right to be Heard* – to be assured that consumer interests will receive full and sympathetic consideration in the formulation of Government policy and fair expeditious treatment in its administrative tribunals.

(Quoted by Senator Warren G. Magnuson, 'Consumerism and the Emerging Goals of a New Society' in Gaedeke, Ralph M., and Etcheson, Warren W. (eds.), *Consumerism* (Canfield Press, San Francisco, 1972).)

Still later in the decade (1966) Ralph Nader was to publish *Unsafe at Any Speed*, a book which might well have gone unremarked had it not been for General Motors' attempts to discredit Nader which resulted in their losing a lawsuit brought by him. The publicity attendant upon the trial focused intense attention upon the standard of car manufacture and resulted in Nader himself being cast in the role of consumer champion.

It was from these grass roots that the consumerist movement developed to the proportions it has now achieved when scarcely a day goes by without the publication of some book or article on the subject, or statement by some or other government department. In fact we now have a Minister of Consumer Affairs and an extensive body of new legislation whose existence is directly attributable to the impetus generated by the movement. It is not anticipated that there will be any lessening in this interest which, in the longer term, will concentrate upon two basic areas: (*a*) the more equitable treatment of consumers through the provision of choice and information, reinforced by legislation where necessary, and (*b*) protection of the physical environment or conservation.

RECENT CONSUMER LEGISLATION

In recent years there has been a spate of legislation designed to protect consumers when they go shopping. A very useful pamphlet *Fair Deal* was published in 1976 (H.M.S.O.) under the aegis of the Office of Fair Trading and the Central Office of Information and the following synopses of the more important Acts are taken from this source. However, readers are also commended to obtain their own copy of this free publication as it contains much useful information, including details of existing codes of practice, informative labels and the names and addresses of consumer bodies and trade and professional organisations that give advice to consumers.

Sale of Goods Act – as amended by the Supply of Goods (Implied Terms) Act 1973
These Acts are concerned with your rights in civil law. When you buy something in a shop you enter into a legally binding contract with that shop. Once the shopkeeper has accepted your offer to buy he takes on obligation under the above Acts which are part of his bargain. These obligations include:

1. The shopkeeper undertakes that the goods he has sold you are of merchantable quality. If, for instance, you find a hole in a blanket when you unpack it, you are entitled to return it. The same if you buy a washing machine which, when plugged in, refuses to function.

2. The goods must be fit for the purpose for which goods of that kind are normally used: a bucket mustn't leak. Furthermore, if you ask for goods to perform a specific job, perhaps a glue to mend broken china, then the goods supplied must serve that specific purpose.
3. The goods must meet the description applied to them. If, for instance, you buy a blanket described as blue it shouldn't turn out to be pink.

If any of these obligations are not met then the retailer has broken the contract and you may be entitled to return the goods and ask for your money back. . . . If you prefer, you can accept a repair or an exchange. Some retailers will offer you a credit note as compensation. You are not obliged to accept a credit note for faulty goods; but if you do so you may find it difficult to get your money back later if you don't find anything else you want in the shop, *as you would no longer have the original article to prove it was faulty!*

These rights cannot be taken away from you and don't depend on any guarantee, which may be given with the goods. But if there is a guarantee, sign it and send it off – it can't limit your rights against the retailer but it may give you extra ones.

Don't be fobbed off by a shopkeeper telling you that faulty goods are the manufacturer's responsibility and must be returned to him. This isn't true. If the goods are faulty it is the *seller's* responsibility to put things right. If necessary, you can take him to court to make him do so. . . . You will *not* be entitled to a refund if you examined the goods before you bought them and should have seen if they were faulty, or if faults were pointed out to you. And you will not be entitled to a refund on the grounds that goods are not fit for a purpose if you didn't rely on the seller's skill or judgement – for instance, if he said that the glue you were buying might not mend broken china. Nor will you be entitled to a refund if the seller told you he was not expert enough to know whether or not the glue would mend china.

But you must watch the following points: these rules about merchantable quality and fitness for purpose apply *only when you buy from somebody in the normal course of his business*, so be particularly careful if you buy from a private seller.

Be especially careful when buying goods secondhand because there are no special laws to cover secondhand purchases – but the general rules about the sale of goods apply as they do to new goods. Normally, if you buy something secondhand you must be prepared to acquire its faults as well as its virtues. But if a trader tells you something untrue about the secondhand goods you are buying – such as 'This TV set is only two years old' when in fact it is six years old – you could return it and ask for your money back; or you could go and discuss it with your local trading standards officer because there may be a case for prosecution under the Trade Descriptions Act. Having someone with you as a witness is a good idea when you buy a major item secondhand just in case a dispute arises later. Other points to remember when buying goods are:

If you *order* goods which are not in stock you may give a specific date by which the goods are required. If the goods do not arrive by that date you have the right to say that you no longer want them and to ask for your money back.

If you do not specify a date by which the goods must be delivered, the seller should still deliver them within a reasonable time. If you think that a reasonable time has passed, and you are not prepared to wait any longer, contact the seller again and state clearly that if you haven't received the goods by a certain date (say, within 14 days) you will no longer require them and you will want your money back. (*Note:* In either situation, if you agree to wait longer you will have forfeited your right to cancel the purchase during that period.)

Secondly, remember that goods are not always bought in shops. They can be ordered from a catalogue or through a newspaper advertisement (mail order), or bought from a street trader, doorstep seller, or at a selling party in a private home. Providing you are dealing with a trader (and not a private seller) you have the same protection under the Sale of Goods Act as you have with ordinary sales. *But*, make sure you keep a note of names and addresses – otherwise, some traders could be difficult to trace.

Lastly, remember that a shopkeeper doesn't have to sell you an article. It is up to him either to accept or refuse your offer to buy. But, if the article has a price on it and he agrees to sell it to you, he mustn't charge more than the price shown. If he does, he can be prosecuted under the Trade Descriptions Act. More about this and other Acts below.

Unsolicited Goods and Services Act 1971

The main way this Act affects the general public is to make it an offence for traders to demand payment for goods (such as records, books, Christmas cards) which people have not ordered. If you receive goods which you did not ask for and you do not agree to keep them, the sender can take them back during the six months after you have received them. If you have not agreed to keep or to send back the goods they become your property after six months. You can then use them, sell them, or otherwise dispose of them as if they had been a gift.

You can, if you like, cut short the six months' period by writing to the sender giving your name and address and stating that the goods were unsolicited. If the sender then fails to collect them within 30 days they become your property. But in either case you must give the sender reasonable access to collect them. Anyone who demands payment for unsolicited goods can be fined. Corresponding legislation in Northern Ireland is the Unsolicited Goods and Services Act (Northern Ireland) 1976.

Trade Descriptions Act 1968

This Act makes it a criminal offence for a trader to describe inaccurately the *goods* he is selling or the *services* he is offering, and he can be fined or imprisoned. This applies to many different kinds of descriptions – where goods are made, who made them how they work, and so on. If a trader tells you 'This pan has a non-stick coating', 'Your hotel is one kilometre from the beach', then these statements must be true. If not he has committed a criminal offence. A spoken false description is just as much an offence as a written one. (If he does *not* say something, don't draw your own conclusions; always ask.)

In the case of textile products special regulations are in force which require that such goods *must* have the fibre content marked on them.

Where services are concerned, a trader commits an offence only if he knows the description of the service he is providing is wrong, or if he doesn't care whether it is true or not.

Under this Act some kinds of false price reductions or 'markdowns' are also an offence. If a shopkeeper simply crosses out £2.55 on the price ticket and adds £2.10 as the new price he must have sold the goods at the higher price for at least 28 consecutive days in the last six months. If not, he must make this clear on the label – for instance 'last week's price £2.55; now £2.10'. It is also an offence to suggest that the price of goods is less than it really is.

The local authority trading standards or consumer protection people enforce this law and the Act gives them powers to enter premises, inspect and seize goods. So if you think the law is being broken you should let your local authority trading standards people know. They may decide to prosecute. If a conviction is obtained, courts in England and Wales can award compensation to people who have suffered because of the offence. In less serious cases the matter may be dealt with by an advisory officer who may help you to get compensation for any difficulties or disappointments you have suffered. In either case, the local authority can take steps to prevent other people from being deceived. If you want to prepare your own individual complaint against the trader you can do so.

Weights and Measures Act 1963
Nowadays many goods – particularly groceries – are pre-packed instead of being weighed out for you at the time you buy. This Act makes it a criminal offence if the weight, or some other indication of quantity, is not marked, for most items, on the packet, tin, or bottle. Such items as meat, fish, cheese, and sausages which in recent years have become more frequently pre-packed for display on supermarket shelves, must either have their weight marked on the packet, or the weight must be made known before purchase. Certain goods must only be sold in what are called 'prescribed quantities' – e.g., milk can only be sold in measures of $\frac{1}{3}$-pint, $\frac{1}{2}$-pint, or multiples of $\frac{1}{2}$-pint.

The Act is being amended gradually to permit metric prescribed quantities. This means that pre-packed foods like breakfast cereals, salt, sugar, are now being sold more frequently in weights like 500 g instead of 1 lb, or 1 kg instead of 2 lb. The new packs are clearly marked METRIC PACK, and the imperial weight is marked as well. Not all pre-packed goods must be marked; for example, everyone recognizes a one-pint milk bottle when they see one. And there are also exceptions in the case of small packets. The Act also makes it an offence to give short weight or inadequate quantity, and to mark goods with a wrong indication of their amount,. Traders who do not conform with the Act can be prosecuted and fined. Your local authority is responsible for seeing that these laws are carried out and that traders' weights, measures and scales are accurate. In Northern Ireland, the Department of Commerce enforces the Weights and Measures Act (Northern Ireland) 1967.

Food and Drugs Act 1955
This Act makes it an offence to sell unfit food, or to describe food falsely, or to mislead people about its nature, substance, or quality, including the nutritional value. Regulations cover food hygiene, wherever food is sold; food labelling (name of the contents, list of ingredients, and address of labeller or packer for use in complaints): and food composition (such as how much meat is in a sausage, control of food additives, contaminants, etc.). Local authorities are responsible for enforcing these regulations. Scotland is covered by the Food and Drugs (Scotland) Act 1956 and Northern Ireland by the Food and Drugs Act (Northern Ireland) 1958.

Consumer Protection Act 1961
This Act gives the Secretary of State for Prices and Consumer Protection powers to make regulations for any type of goods to prevent or reduce the risk of death or personal injury. For example, regulations have been made about domestic electrical equipment, wiring colour codes, toys, oil heaters, guards on heating appliances, carry-cot stands, cooking utensils, pencils and crayons, and the flammability of children's nightdresses. It is a criminal offence to sell goods which do not comply with these regulations, which are enforced by local authority trading standards departments. In Northern Ireland, the Department of Commerce has similar powers under the Consumer Protection Act (Northern Ireland) 1965.

Prices Act 1974
This Act enables the government to subsidise food and to regulate the price of food and other household necessities. Shopkeepers may be required to mark prices on goods (including unit prices) and display price ranges in their shops showing the price at which

goods are commonly sold. Unit pricing is a means of helping the customer to compare prices of different-sized packs where goods are not packaged in standard weights or volumes. For example, shopkeepers are required to display the price per lb of packets of bacon rashers, and similarly to indicate the price per lb if the rashers are sold loose. A notice about price ranges would enable shoppers to compare the prices charged at one shop with the range of prices generally charged.

Consumer Credit Act 1974

This is the most far-reaching reform of consumer credit law ever undertaken in this country and when fully implemented it will give you much greater protection than you have had in credit and hire transactions before. The Act controls the activities of not only creditors but also brokers, owners of hired equipment, debt collectors, debt counsellors and adjusters, and credit reference agencies. They need to be licensed by the Director General of Fair Trading who will also superintend the working of the Act.

'Truth in lending' is the main aim of the Act and once the various regulations have been made, people will be given much more information about their credit or hire transactions than at present.

THE CONSUMERISM–MARKETING INTERFACE

Oversimplified as they may be, the foregoing statements on the nature of marketing and consumerism reflect a fundamental paradox for while they are invariably seen as being in conflict both activities possess the same basic objective – consumer satisfaction. A still more fundamental paradox is that while everybody is in favour of consumer protection there is still a need for it.

At various points in the text reference has been made to particular issues where consumerists and marketers appear to be at cross-purposes with each other. Among those which the reader may wish to explore in greater depth are the following.

1. *Product Policy*   — issues of Quality
                                  Brand proliferation
                                  Planned obsolescence
                                  After-sales service

2.	*Pricing Practices*	— Recommended prices and Price-off promotions Unit pricing
3.	*'Truth in Advertising'*	— By category of product — By media
4.	*Pollution*	— By product, e.g. motor-cars, enzyme detergents — By packaging – non-returnable containers; non bio-degradable materials
5.	*'Truth in Lending'*	— Statement of true costs of borrowing

In considering these and similar salient issues it would be unreasonable to follow the practice favoured in certain quarters of ascribing all the blame to private industry. We must accept that existing institutions have succeeded very well in terms of their aims and objectives as originally stated. Because society now questions the desirability of continued and rapid economic growth due to excesses derived from its past pursuit, society is not entitled to belabour those organisations which previously enacted its collective will. A more constructive attitude recognises that the emergence of the marketing concept reflects an awareness of the side-effects of mass production and mass consumption, and that enlightened self-interest will predispose business to vary its response to consumer needs as these change. In a far from perfect world we cannot expect all firms to be equally responsive to these changed needs, and so will have to resort to legislation to ensure compliance with certain minimum standards. In the long run, however, we see no reason to believe that the greatest success will not continue to accrue to the firms most sensitive to their markets' needs.

CONSUMERISM – THREAT OR OPPORTUNITY?

Because of the manner in which many consumer concerns have been expressed, many firms have tended to react defensively. In consequence of this defensive reaction there is a growing tendency in certain quarters to regard the consumerist movement as a threat to business. It would be more constructive to regard it as an opportunity.

One particularly salient feature of consumerism is that it is both overt and vocal, which is a marked contrast with most market situations where considerable time, effort and money has to be expended upon eliciting consumer attitudes and opinions. In other words, expressions of consumer concern clearly indicate the wishes of at least a sizable segment of particular markets and reduce the need for research activity. More astute companies have already perceived this opportunity. Consider the following examples.

Increased concern over pollution and the quality of the environment has enabled many firms to cash in on devices for monitoring, reducing, alleviating, or avoiding pollution. Thus firms have developed instruments to measure the nature and extent of pollutants discharged into the air and water and clearly this market will grow as states seek to enforce laws against pollution and firms try to ensure that they comply with such laws. Having detected the existence of pollutants then a need arises to remove or mitigate their effect resulting in a demand for sewage and effluent treatment, water purification, air filtration plants and so on. Similarly, alternative solutions are required as in the case of the internal combustion engine, or fossil fuel sources of energy.

At a lesser level, firms can cash in on explicit anxieties such as the need for more informative labelling by providing it, of non-returnable containers by making them returnable, of packaging waste by making it capable of re-use through recycling. Similarly the express demand for after-sales service represents considerable scope for creative marketing – if leasing television sets is possible why not other household consumer durables?

The foregoing examples are very limited but, hopefully, they indicate the scope for constructive and positive responses rather than defensive and negative ones. The same comment applies equally to the extension and application of marketing ideas and methods into the non-business sector which topic is the second basic theme of this chapter.

MARKETING AS A SOCIAL PROCESS

Probably the first influential statement of a need to re-examine the scope of marketing was contained in a seminal article by Philip Kotler and Sidney J. Levy ('Broadening the Concept of Marketing', *Journal of Marketing*, vol. 33, Jan 1969). In the opening paragraphs the authors review briefly the traditional emphasis on the marketing of products in a business context and go on to assert: 'It is the authors contention that marketing is a pervasive societal activity that goes considerably beyond the selling of toothpaste, soap, and steel.'

In essence the argument that marketing is a pervasive societal activity is predicated on the observation that as man's productive capability has grown so he has been able to devote more of his energies to social activities and that in order to do so he has had to develop organisations other than business firms. In reality, many non-business organisations have a longer history than the now dominant business firms, e.g. the Church, universities, government departments, hospitals, etc. However, the very forces which were to lead to an emphasis on marketing, namely the ability to create supplies in excess of basic consumption needs (see Chapter 1), were also necessary to permit such non-business organisations to realise their potential. Thus, only when we can release human and physical resources from the treadmill of satisfying the basic needs of food and shelter can we turn our attention to the satisfaction of higher needs such as education, the Arts, health, and social welfare. Further we require new forms of social organisation to cope with enfranchisement of the whole population, i.e. political societies, the need for organised labour to be able to express its view, i.e. the trade unions, and so on.

As Kotler and Levy point out, all these social organisations perform the classic business functions. Finance is necessary to pay for the organisation's operations and a personnel function is necessary to ensure that people are available to discharge such operations. A production function is necessary to organise the most economic use of inputs to achieve the desired level of outputs. Purchasing is necessary to acquire these inputs and presumably marketing is required to dispose of them. If the marketing function has not been particularly conspicuous, however, we should not be surprised for, as we have seen in earlier chapters, the need for such a function has only just become apparent in the case of physical goods.

But, given the exponential acceleration which has characterised all spheres of human endeavour throughout history we may anticipate a rapid diffusion of the marketing concept through non-business organisations within the next few years. To determine *how* the marketing concept may be applied we must first identify those ideas which have appeared generally useful in marketing other goods and services. We have already argued when discussing the marketing of industrial goods (Chapter 7) that in our opinion there is no fundamental difference in principle as compared with the marketing of consumer goods. This I believe is equally true of the marketing of services whether they emanate from profit or non-profit organisations.

In the same spirit Kotler and Levy suggest that a useful basic approach is to think in terms of three fundamental constructs or ideas – products, consumers, and tools.

First, products. All organisations produce a product although in the interests of definitional clarity we frequently prefer to differentiate as between categories of products. Thus in Chapter 3 we offered specific definitions for categories of consumer and industrial goods. To these may be added services which are intangible, such as insurance and banking, although they may confer a tangible benefit such as health and welfare services. Such services may be offered by private or public organisations which may or may not have a profit motive. Evidence of the marketing of such services is most marked in the case of those private firms such as banks which are profit-orientated and least evident in the case of public sector welfare services. To these easily recognised categories Kotler and Levy add persons, organisations and ideas, while in a more elaborate statement ('Beyond Marketing: The Furthering Concept', *California Management Review* (Winter 1969), vol. XII, no. 2) they add 'places'. In the case of these latter categories a limited marketing activity may be noted in the past but it has largely concentrated on public relations type activity supported by a limited amount of paid promotion. Clearly, there is considerable scope for the use of other elements of the marketing mix, expecially in the field of marketing research, to better define consumer needs. This observation leads naturally to consideration of the second basic construct.

In a limited sense consumers are viewed solely as those persons or organisations which consume the output of another organisation. In the wider concept 'consumers' includes at least three other groups with a direct interest in any given organisation. First, there are persons responsible for the control of the organisation. These may be shareholders in a company or those nominated by them (directors), they may be the trustees of a private foundation, or the elected ministers who control our government departments and so on. The second category is comprised of persons/organisation which take a *direct* interest, and the third of those with a passive or *indirect* interest. Examples of the former are, say, consumer organisations or government departments in the case of business firms, former students and local and central government in the case of a university; while the latter category conveniently encompasses all those who might be influenced by or wish to influence the organisation at some future time.

The third construct is that of the tools of marketing. Among these we may distinguish the four 'p's' of product, price, place (distribution) and promotional policy, each of which has an important role in marketing the output of any type of organisation. We have already stressed that change is symptomatic of the world in which we live – accordingly all organisations must continually reappraise and update their 'product' in order to best satisfy changing needs. Pricing has an important role to play although it frequently seems to be ignored in the provision of many public services. It is difficult for the individual citizen to decide whether the collective taxes we pay are being allocated to the ends we most desire except in a very gross way. Certainly it is impossible in the particular to determine whether we are getting value for money and the suppliers often seem insensitive to the concept of cost-benefit. Indications of changing attitudes in the latter area are to be seen in the concept of contract research in which the researcher is required to produce results in line with a prearranged budget and the suggestion that individuals be given 'tickets' which they can exchange for, say, education. In the present social climate it seems unlikely that the latter idea will gain support but its currency does imply that the consumers of such services would like a more effective way of demonstrating their wishes other than at general elections. (The reader may care to reconsider the analogy between money and political votes at p. 431.) Equally some of the dangers of monopoly power which we monitor so closely in the private sector merit more attention for they appear to exist in the pricing and quality decisions of many public services.

In the case of distribution and promotion there is also scope for the application of marketing techniques, although perhaps somewhat less than in the product and price areas. Distribution still merits attention, however, in that in many cases it appears to be dictated by the convenience of the supplier rather than the consumer. Similarly, some of the promotional techniques already in use would no doubt benefit from comparison with the sophisitication typical of the promotion of consumer goods.

Essentially, therefore, we are arguing that the philosophy and techniques which have apparently worked so much to the advantage of private profit-oriented organisations are equally relevant and meaningful to all other forms of organisation. Three things must be appreciated, however. First, one must not strain the analogy between business and non-business organisations too far and so try to force the latter to fit patterns which have proved successful in the former context but which may be wholly inappropriate to non-business organisations. Second, success in marketing depends upon commitment – mere lip-service to the concept and changing the sales function's title is insufficient. (See, for example, B. Charles Ames, 'Trappings *vs*. Substance in Industrial Marketing', *Harvard Business Review*, July–Aug 1970.) Finally, success depends upon matching skills with opportunities (see Chapter 20).

Collectively, these three caveats indicate that the greatest benefit is likely to accrue where one attempts a transfer of basic ideas from the traditional content of marketing physical products rather than promote the wholesale adoption of particular marketing techniques. An example will help make our meaning clear.

PRODUCT LIFE-CYCLE AS AN AID TO IMPROVED PERFORMANCE

Some reference to the concept of the product life-cycle (P.L.C.) has already been made in Chapter 10 where it was suggested that because of its consistent nature one might use changes in the direction of sales trends as a predictive device. Classically the product life-cycle is represented as having four basic phases as represented in Fig. 22.1 overleaf.

If the stylised P.L.C. shown reflects reality then clearly the change in the inflection of the curve at *A* heralds rapid exponential growth, at *B* a levelling off of demand, at *C* a diminution that suggests either product rejuvenation or replacement. Although the utility of the P.L.C. concept is occasionally challenged by sceptical

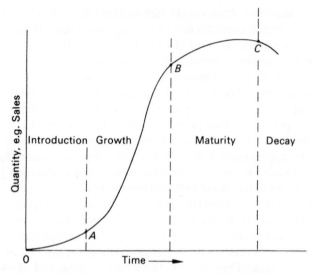

Fig. 22.1. Stages in the product life-cycle

practitioners their criticisms tend to reflect their own failure to understand its meaning, and to the rather naïve assumption that all products will exhibit perfectly symmetrical S-shaped curves. In fact, consideration of a number of other areas reveals that some form of exponential function (represented graphically by a cumulative S-shaped curve) is typical of the manner in which objects or ideas spread or diffuse through populations of 'adopters'. Elsewhere (*Marketing New Industrial Products*, Macmillan), I have argued that the consistent and pervasive nature of the diffusion process approximates a law of nature and reflects an underlying process such that if one can initiate diffusion it will proceed to some extent automatically thereafter due to the 'bandwagon' or 'contagion' effect.

In the context of new-product marketing we find that success is usually defined in terms of achieving a predetermined sales target within a specified time period. It follows that the sooner one can achieve an initial sale the sooner diffusion will commence. In essence the logic is that proof of a sale adds conviction to the selling process, while word-of-mouth recommendation or pure visibility, e.g. a new car at the kerbside, will accelerate awareness of the new product's existence and so improve the probability of further purchases.

Put very simply then, success or failure is highly dependent upon the speed with which we can achieve initial sales and the lesson to be learned from the concept is that effort to pre-identify 'early adopters' is essential to long-run success. In the particular, however, it is impossible to be highly specific about the specific characteristics of early adopters in different contexts and situations as has been demonstrated by the lack of correlation between the findings of various research studies. Such a lack of correlation does not invalidate the utility of the concept – it merely emphasises the need for persons well versed in their own product – market interface (however we define 'product' and 'market') to apply their experience and knowledge in seeing how such a basic idea can be of use to them.

Although these comments have been made about a particular concept it is believed that examination of other ideas, approaches, and techniques which enjoy currency in the marketing of goods will reveal opportunities for transfer into a broader interpretation of marketing as a social process. We may also anticipate that with increasing maturity the somewhat miscellaneous ragbag of borrowings from other disciplines and fields of study will be combined with current marketing thought into a more cohesive whole deserving the title marketing theory.

TRENDS IN THE 1970s AND 1980s

Writing in 1974 three additional trends were selected for particular attention, as follows.

First, in the 1970s we must anticipate much greater attention being devoted to Peter Drucker's 'Dark Continent' – distribution. As pointed out by Drucker, distributive costs are a major element in total cost, any reduction in which will have a marked impact on profitability. Furthermore, control of the channels of distribution, direct or indirect, confers considerable marketing leverage – a fact which traditional manufacturers, wholesalers, and retailers have only recently come to appreciate, as the cold winds of competition have made themselves felt. Thus, while manufacturers endeavour to integrate forward into retailing, retailers will continue their efforts to integrate backward into manufacturing, while wholesalers try to integrate in both directions. In that such moves are likely to be initiated by companies with above-average managerial skills, we forcast acute competition, particularly in the area of acquisitions and mergers, with many long-established but traditionally oriented firms going under.

Second, the current interest in mathematical models as an aid to problem-solving at both the tactical, or 'mix element', and strategic levels is foreseen as accelerating in parallel with the increase in computer installations, particularly those with a time-sharing capability. The availability of time-sharing where an executive can access a major computer from a remote terminal, possibily located in his own office, has resulted in the development of a number of 'canned' conversational programmes into which the user may input his own data. One such programme which has received considerable publicity is SPRINTER I, developed by Glen Urban at M.I.T. for evaluating new-product development proposals. In addition to the tactical aspects of marketing such as new-product development, media selection, pricing, etc., which are most amenable to quantification and, therefore, to the development and use of computer models, simulation on the computer also holds out considerable promise for the marketing strategist. Further, the computer offers scope for considerable improvement in information-handling which should improve the quality of strategic decision-making.

Finally, we perceive a trend to increasingly selective product–market definition and an abandonment of the shotgun, mass-market approach. With increased competition, the pin-pointing of specific market segments will command greater attention, as will the development of differentiated products to meet the needs of such segments, while the computer offers the means to cope with the complexities implicit in such a competitive strategy.

Taken together, these trends seem to reflect a move away from the acquisitive society in which physical possessions conferred a purely material satisfaction of their own. With growing affluence such possessions are more often seen as a means to an end and not an end in themselves. Cars are desirable because they provide personal mobility and access to leisure and recreation activities, prepared convenience foods are not a luxury but a means of freeing the housewife from the tyranny of the kitchen so that she can spend more time with her family and friends, and so on. In turn, growing affluence and leisure create a growing demand for services coupled with an increased awareness of social and environmental problems such as pollution and urban decay. In the coming decade it is the firms which recognise the opportunities inherent in these trends which will prosper.

With the benefit of hindsight it is clear that all three predictions anticipated a more rapid rate of change than actually materialised. It is true, as we saw in Chapter 2, that there has been a move to greater concentration, but the distribution function itself is still very largely neglected. There are some indications of greater interest in logistics and physical distribution managment and these can only gather momentum as we progress into the 1980s.

In regard to the use of mathematical modelling and computer simulation we were clearly more optimistic than events have justified. A possible explanation is that while we possess the computational power we lack adequate theoretical understanding of marketing transactions to permit the statement of operational models. There is a clear need for much greater effort to be devoted to theory development, with perhaps less attention to statistical manipulation. That said, it is also clear that increasing use will be made of electronic devices in improving the efficiency of day-to-day marketing activities.

A case in point is the introduction of article numbering whereby individual articles are given a unique code which can be read by a scanner at the check-out point. The check-out scanner is linked to the store's own computer, which automatically prices the article and adjust the stock-level figures. Several advantages are immediately apparent: there is a saving in handling costs as items do not have to be priced separately; the customer gets a detailed printout showing the description and price of each item; automatic re-ordering systems can be operated enabling the store to reduce its buffer stock, and consequently its capital tied up in stock; the check-out is speedier than current manual systems. Of course, the degree to which stores pass on the potential benefits to their customers has yet to be seen but there can be no doubt that article numbering will greatly improve retailing efficiency.

But while these trends will continue in the 1980s perhaps the most important developments will occur in four main areas:

1. The interface between marketing and public policy, with the choice between self-regulation from within and imposed regulation from without becoming more acute.
2. The growing importance of services in advanced economies

and the transfer of product marketing techniques and practices into the service sector accompanied by 'demarketing' of physical consumption goods.

3. An increased emphasis upon the transferability of the marketing concept and marketing concept and marketing practice into the not-for-profit sector.

4. A growing recognition of the benefits of marketing in centrally planned and developing economies.

While these are only predictions, of one thing we can be certain, the 1980s will continue to offer excitement, challenge and opportunity for marketers.

Review Questions and Problems

Many of the following questions are taken from papers set for the Certificate and Diploma examinations of the Institute of Marketing (coded I.M.) and are reproduced by permission. Questions coded U.S. are taken from papers set for the Degree of B.A. in Marketing at the University of Strathclyde.

Chapter 1
1. Why is there no single, generally accepted definition of marketing? Should there be such a definition? If so, what developments are necessary to permit its statement?
2. What is the 'marketing concept'? Is it solely applicable to firms selling goods and services, or is it a 'philosophy' which can be usefully adopted by all formal organisations?
3. Why is it that marketing has only recently become an issue of central concern to producers/sellers of goods and services?
4. What do you understand by the phrase 'accelerating change'? What factors underly this phenomenon? Will they continue to apply in the future?
5. What is the 'marketing mix'? How useful is the concept to practitioners? In what respects?
6. Marketing: art or science? Discuss.
7. 'The marketing concept is applicable to all business organisations irrespective of their size or the nature of the goods or services marketed.' Give reasons for agreeing, or disagreeing, with this view. (I.M.)
8. How would you counter the view that marketing exists only as a loose collection of techniques practised by specialists? (I.M.)

9. What contribution can comparative data on world markets, marketing structures and behaviour, make to the generation of theory in marketing? (U.S.)
10. Industry in general, and marketing practice in particular, would reap great benefits from the availability of fully developed and reliable marketing theories. Discuss. (U.S.)
11. Since we cannot observe demand curves, there is little need for the marketing manager to be acquainted with economic concepts. Critically appraise this statement. (I.M.)

Chapter 2
1. It is said that oligopolies could not be created except by means of heavy consumer advertising. The advertisers maintain that the security created by this relatively stable situation gives protection and time to embark on product development and improvement. Discuss this statement in relation to the detergent market. (U.S.)
2. What are the advantages and disadvantages of industries which are dominated by a few large-scale companies manufacturing similar, but differentiated products? (I.M.)
3. What does the Government mean when it refers to its 'industrial strategy'? Say whether you think the strategy is viable and describe, using examples, the effect it has had on the structure of U.K. industry. (I.M.)
4. What relationship is there between oligopoly and the concept of product differentiation? (I.M.)
5. To what extent do you accept the statement that much so-called planned obsolescence is actually the working out of competitive and technological factors, both signifiying a dynamic economy? (U.S.)

Chapter 3
1. Complete the following 'shopping list' of needs and wants:

Need	*Want*
Bread	. . .
. . .	P.G. Tips
Meat	. . .
. . .	Omo

Cooking fat	. . .
. . .	Blue Band
Floor cleaner	. . .
. . .	Birds Eye Frozen Peas
Heat	. . .

2. What factors would you consider *most* important in forecasting the demand for:

   Automatic washing machines
   Classical records
   Colour television
   Enzyme detergents
   Fluoride toothpaste
   Frozen dinners
   Package tours?

3. Which 'personality theory' do you subscribe to? Why?
4. What utility has reference group theory for the practising marketer?
5. How is Maslow's 'hierarchy of needs' reflected in the nature of consumer demand?
5. How is Maslow's 'hierarchy of needs' reflected in the nature of consumer demand?
6. One of the most difficult decisions any marketing executive has to take concerns the determination of those consumer characteristics which can be used to segment a market in the best possible way. What are the particular difficulties he has to face? (I.M.)
7. The IPA socio-economic grading of the population should be of fundamental importance to the practitioners of marketing. To what extent is it so, and how accurate are the results obtained from its use? (I.M.)
8. Why has product differentiation superseded price as the major dimension of competitive activity in consumer goods markets?
9. Discuss the advantages/disadvantages of:

   (*a*) Individual brands,
   (*b*) Family brands.

10. Account for the widespread development of private branding in recent years.
11. How useful is the classification of goods described in the text? Suggest an alternative classificatory system.
12. How, and on what grounds, would you classify the following products:

    (*a*) Branded pain remedies, butter, detergents, frozen peas, matches, petrol, shirts, stockings?
    (*b*) Cement, lathes, lubricants, sulphuric acid, transistors, wood pulp?

13. Describe the problems confronting the marketing executive when he sets out to discover what the consumer wants. (I.M.)
14. Clearly explain what you understand by the term 'demand'. In what sense can a knowledge of this economic concept have practical application? (I.M.)
15. Demand is made up of two elements, the ability to buy and the willingness to buy. Discuss the advantages to be gained from studying the effects of both elements separately. (U.S.)

Chapter 4

1. Attitudes have a central role in the development of behavioural patterns. Consider the use of attitude studies as a guide to the marketing practitioner. (U.S.)
2. Consider the value of the life-style concept as an approach to market segmentation. (U.S.)
3. The main alternative to problem-solving behaviour is habitual behaviour. Discuss the application of these patterns of behaviour to the market-place. (U.S.)
4. Measures of social class have been both valuable and misleading as an aid to market segmentation. Discuss the use of social class, and the possibilities offered by the addition of complementary psychographic techniques. (U.S.)
5. Should the marketer assume that organisational buying decisions are always based upon rational/economic considerations? (U.S.)

6. What do you understand by the term 'learning'? Briefly outline any one learning theory and discuss its relevance to an understanding of consumer behaviour. (I.M.)
7. Maslow's theory of motivation postulates five general types of needs. Define these needs and explain with examples how their economic importance can be exploited by advertising. (I.M.)
8. Culture has a pervasive influence on consumption patterns. Discuss the implications of cultural factors in new product diffusion. (U.S.)

Chapter 5
1. Distinguish the salient differences between the functional and product forms of organisational structure. Under what circumstances is each to be preferred?
2. What is the 'product manager concept'? Name five firms which have adopted this concept. (See the classified ads for clues!)
3. How does the concept of market management differ from product management? When is the former organisational structure to be preferred?
4. What distinguishes the marketing oriented firm from those which have not adopted the marketing concept?
5. Using published data, e.g. annual reports, articles in the trade press, etc., and/or personal knowedge/experience, summarise the corporate resources of a major manufacturing company. Based on your summary, what recommendations would you make to the firm's top management concerning its future strategy, i.e. on what markets/products should it concentrate its efforts?
6. Discuss the proposition that the position of the marketing department in the total organisation is particularly difficult because of the types of conflicts which tend to occur between the logic of customer satisfaction and the cost minimisation logic pursued by other departments. (U.S.)
7. The system of organising marketing divisions around the job of the brand manager, or product manager, has recently been widely criticised. What criticisms of this system would you expect to be valid in practice, and what opportunities does

this system offer for more effective marketing management? (I.M.)

8. The marketing function is so central to the company's continued success that it requires to be carefully controlled by those in charge of the company. Outline a comprehensive system of such controls on marketing to ensure top management retain the responsibility with which they are charged. (U.S.)

9. Indicate the types of conflict which might arise in a firm employing sales, marketing and product managers and the ways in which these might be organisationally resolved. (I.M.)

10. Write a job description for a product manager in either:

   (*a*) a typical company making products for industry
   (*b*) a typical consumer goods company. (I.M.)

11. In what ways would the Marketing Manager of a large company be able to do a more effective job, if he were appointed to the Board as Marketing Director? How would his responsibilities change? (I.M.)

12. It should be possible to assess the extent of a company's commitment to marketing by looking at its organisation chart. Discuss. (I.M.)

Chapter 6

1. Discuss the efforts of producers/users of primary commodities to stabilise markets by agreeing upon quotas, price, etc. What are the advantages/disadvantages of such agreements?

2. How valid is the argument that farm size will remain small in order to attain the yields sufficient to satisfy the demands of a rapidly expanding population?

3. What factors account for the erratic short-term price fluctuations in markets for agricultural products?

4. What are the essential features of:

   (*a*) Spot transactions?
   (*b*) Futures contracts?

5. Distinguish between agents, brokers and merchants.

6. What advantages/disadvantages have processed foodstuffs over fresh produce, and how has this affected consumer purchasing patterns?
7. Discuss the pros and cons of agricultural marketing boards in the United Kingdom.

Chapter 7

1. There are no fundamental differences between the marketing of industrial and consumer goods. Comment.
2. What basic distributive alternatives are open to the manufacturers of industrial goods? Which do you consider most appropriate to the sale of:

> Basic chemicals
> Computers
> Electronic components
> Machine tools
> Office supplies
> Plastic pipe?

Why?

3. Describe the economist's concept of concentration ratios. How useful is this concept to the marketer – industrial or consumer? In what way?
4. What functions do wholesalers perform? Does performance of these functions add value to the product, or merely add to its final cost without adding to its value?
5. It is frequently contended that industrial buying is an essentially rational process whereas consumer purchasing is not. State your reasons for agreeing/diagreeing with this statement.
6. Does the industrial market merit special consideration or is it merely a particular application of general marketing principles? (U.S.)
7. Do we understand enough about how buyers and sellers interact in industrial markets to be able to predict industrial buying (or selling) behaviour? If yes, discuss; if no, why not? (U.S.)
8. In industrial marketing there is normally a much closer link

between the information-gathering and promotional sides of marketing than is found in consumer goods marketing. Discuss. (I.M.)

9. Evaluate the usefulness of models of the industrial buying process (like Robinson and Faris's buygrid framework) in industrial marketing decisions. (U.S.)

Chapter 8

1. There is considerable variation in the retail mark-up on a bar of soap, a household electrical appliance, a suite of furniture and a diamond ring. As all retailers perform the same basic functions why should this be so?

2. In what ways do retailers provide consumers with product information?

3. How well does McNair's concept of the 'wheel of retailing' fit post-war changes in retail distribution in the United Kingdom?

4. What is a 'voluntary chain'? To what do they owe their existence, and what role do you expect them to play in future?

5. What basic distribution alternatives are open to the manufacturers of consumer goods, and what are the major advantages/disadvantages associated with each?

6. Evaluate the factors for and against the establishment of out-of-town shopping centres.

7. The last decade has witnessed an ever-increasing concentration of power into the hands of a reducing number of multiple retailers. Discuss the main ways in which manufacturers have attempted to meet this challenge, indicating what degrees of success have been achieved. (U.S.)

8. Account for the predominance of direct manufacturer-to-user channels in the marketing of capital goods in comparison to the almost pervasive use of some type of middleman in the marketing of consumer goods. What factors determine the choice of channel in each sector? (U.S.)

9. Outline the principles involved in the development of the hypermarket, and show how the conditions in Europe favoured their application in the 1960s. (U.S.)

10. Mail-order marketing has been particularly successful during recent years. How has advertising helped this growth? Your

answer should outline the various methods of mail-order operation and use of media. (I.M.)

11. Examine the factors which, since 1945, have principally affected the development of retailing. (U.S.)

12. What methods have been used to measure and compare efficiency between different retail organisational types? Comment on the usefulness of the methods. (U.S.)

Chapter 9

1. What factors, and what sources, would you take into account in preparing a forecast of the potential market for:

   (*a*) A new 'snack' food?
   (*b*) Frozen T.V. dinners?
   (*c*) A combined refrigerator/freezer unit with a capacity of 14 cubic feet?
   (*d*) Computer time sharing services?
   (*e*) Industrial catering equipment?

   Make whatever assumptions you like about the 'product', but state them clearly.

2. Under what circumstances would you consider a non-probability sample a useful and valid market research technique? What disadvantages do you associate with such samples?

3. Compile a short questionnaire:

   (*a*) For sampling the opinion of industrial users on the benefits of containerisation.
   (*b*) To elicit the opinions of housewives about freeze-dried coffee. You should stipulate how the questionnaires are to be administered and to whom.

4. What is market segmentation? What variables would you use in segmenting the market for:

   (*a*) Detergents?
   (*b*) Fractional horse power electric motors?
   (*c*) Motor cars?
   (*d*) Vacuum cleaners?

5. Provide an explanation of the following methods of structur-

ing samples for market research surveys:

(*a*) systematic sampling,
(*b*) cluster sampling,
(*c*) area sampling, and
(*d*) quota sampling.

In each case, give an example of a marketing situation in which the particular method could be most effectively employed. (I.M.)

6. Formulate the main rules to be kept in mind when designing a questionnaire. How important is question order in securing a satisfactory response? (I.M.)

7. Describe the main guidelines to be followed when framing market research questionnaires to be administered by interviewers to a large sample of respondents. (I.M.)

8. Qualitative research is often criticised as producing results subject to the bias of the investigator. How far do you think this is dangerous, and what compensating advantages do you see in the qualitative approach? (U.S.)

9. Give a definition of an 'attitude', and discuss the difficulties of providing such a definition. Why do marketing researchers concern themselves with attitude measurements? (U.S.)

10. Users of a motorway service area on leaving are to be interviewed to find out, among other things, whether their decision to shop at that particular service area was dependent on their immediate need for petrol or refreshment, the distance or time since their last stop (and where that was), or on other factors.
   Draft a section of a face-to-face questionnaire designed to establish which of these was or were most influential, and which facilities the respondent in person has used in the current visit. Do not show any punched card column allocation, or any introductory section. (U.S.)

11. (*a*) Describe the nature and source of the statistical information provided in the United Kingdom Department of Employment Gazette. (10 marks)
   (*b*) Describe two sources, other than government departments of any country, from which you would expect to obtain statistical information and indicate the nature of the information available. (10 marks) (I.M.)

12. It has been said that the art of management consists of 'taking account simultaneously of the inner workings of the firm and its interaction with external forces'. Describe the contribution of marketing research to the understanding of these external forces. (U.S.)

Chapter 10

1. Why is the firm's product policy of such central importance to its continued growth and development? Describe a declining firm or industry, and suggest how it might improve its fortunes by adopting a macro view of its markets.
2. Describe how the product life-cycle concept might be of operational use to the marketer.
3. Suggest a system for classifying 'new' products. What are the parameters on which your classification rests, and how were they selected?
4. What advantages do you perceive in being (*a*) a leader, (*b*) a follower, in terms of product innovations?
5. Design a rating table for evaluating new product ideas, specifying the industry in which the table is to be used.
6. How would you product test:

   (*a*) An instant soup mix?
   (*b*) A new plastic resin?
   (*c*) A new model car?

7. Summarise the advantages/disadvantages of test marketing.
8. Is the fact that intuition and judgement are important factors in the development of new products a valid argument against the use of formal sequential procedures in this area? (U.S.)
9. Distinguish between product and market testing. Explain the contributions and limitations of each in both the consumer and the industrial goods field. (U.S.)
10. Is it possible to reconcile grocery manufacturing companies' continuous introduction of new products with a supermarket policy of variety reduction? (I.M.)
11. Define 'product policy'. What is the role in product strategy of the product life-cycle? Under what circumstances would it be advisable to try to arrest a declining sales curve? Discuss the alternatives to attempting to arrest such a decline. (I.M.)

12. Explain the significance and implications of the timing of a new product launch. (I.M.)
13. What scope is there, in your view, for the successful introduction of strict management control and evaluation procedures in the area of product planning and new product development? (U.S.)
14. Outline the major 'steps' in the new product evolutionary cycle, and assess the extent to which these are amenable to systematic organisation, management and control. (U.S.)
15. Comment on the value of a systematic approach to new product development. Can such development be planned ? (U.S.)
16. Discuss the benefits that accrue to a company in setting up a system of regular, detailed product marketing plans. (U.S.)

Chapter 11

1. What considerations would you take into account in selecting the basic packaging material, e.g. tinplate, glass, etc., for the following items (stipulate the material to be used and the reasons for your choice in rank order of importance, i.e. cost, strength, etc.):

   Breakfast cereal
   Jam
   Hand cream – (*a*) standard quality
             – (*b*) de luxe quality
   Frozen vegetables
   Chocolates
   Panty-hose
   Men's shirts
   Instant coffee
   Salt
   Shampoo.

2. A well-known book on packaging is entitled *The Silent Salesman*. Discuss.
3. Summarise the consumer's requirements of a satisfactory pack; the retailer's requirements.
4. Select any three well-known consumer products and analyse packaging's contribution to their marketing.

5. What contribution can motivation research make to the packaging decision? Quote specific examples to illustrate your answer.
6. Account for the increased importance of packaging as an element in the marketing mix of a typical fast-moving consumer good in recent years. (U.S.)
7. Packaging plays a major part in the promotion of branded products. Discuss this contribution in the light of growing dissatisfaction from conservationists and consumerist interests throughout the world. (I.M.)
8. Write an essay on the social psychology of colour in packaging and sales promotion. (I.M.)

Chapter 12
1. How valid do you consider the reasons offered to explain the relatively low rating of the importance of price policy in the Udell study? Why? What alternative explanations can you think of?
2. Summarise the major factors that should be taken into account in developing a price policy.
3. Discuss the advantages/disadvantages of each of the price 'formulas' discussed in the text.
4. Under what circumstances would you recommend (*a*) a 'skimming' approach, (*b*) a 'penetration' policy? Identify a current example of each and document the reasons which you believe prompted its selection.
5. Discuss the importance of price as an 'indicator of quality'.
6. What relevance have the concepts of the product life cycle and market segmentation for pricing policy?
7. Describe three ways in which product pricing policy can be used as a means of creative marketing. (I.M.)
8. Explain the statement that optimal pricing policies should be based upon a combination of contribution analysis techniques and a marketing-oriented view of customers. (U.S.)
9. Describe the uses of break-even analysis as a tool of effective marketing management. (I.M.)
10. Explain and comment on the view that optimal price is that price which best serves the central aims of the business. (U.S.)

11. What have recent studies revealed about the effect of price differentials on consumers' perceptions of product quality? (I.M.)
12. Under the existing Price Code, what freedom does the marketer retain to manipulate prices to optimise long-term net profit? (I.M.)
13. In *How British Industry Prices*, the authors found that 63 per cent of the firms investigated used the Absorption (full) costing approach to establish the cost and selling prices of their products.

    (*a*) What are the problems which can arise when this method is used to calculate the selling price?
    (*b*) Discuss the use of marginal (direct) costing and indicate how this method can be particularly important during a period of depressed economic conditions.

    Illustrate your answer with simple numerical examples. (U.S.)
14. Consider the differences of emphasis placed upon 'price' by economists and marketers. Does the recent decision of Tesco to drop trading stamps and to use price cuts as an alternative marketing tool indicate that the economist's views are correct? (U.S.)
15. A surprisingly large number of companies relegate price policy to a secondary role in the planning of their marketing strategy. What factors might cause a company to act in this way? (U.S.)

Chapter 13
1. Rank the 'essential distributive functions' cited in the text in order of importance for each of the following:

   (*a*) Steel stockholder.
   (*b*) Primary commodity wholesaler – (i)   perishable goods.
                                        – (ii) non-perishable goods.
   (*c*) Packaged-food wholesaler.
   (*d*) 'Main' car dealer.

2. Which distribution policy do you consider most appropriate

to the sale of the following products:

Car accessories
Car tyres
Ethical pharmaceuticals
Household cleaning materials
Luxury cosmetics
Transfer presses?

Stipulate the assumptions underlying your selection of a given policy and cite actual examples wherever possible.
3. Discuss the impact of vertical integration on the structure of traditional distribution channels.
4. Selection of a distribution policy invariably demands a compromise between cost and control. Discuss.
5. Evaluate the possible effect of mail order, automatic vending and door-to-door selling on retail distribution in the coming decade.
6. How can a manufacturer evaluate the following choices in the construction of a marketing/distribution system:

   (*a*) Own retail sales force and direct delivery with own transport system.
   (*b*) Own retail sales force and commercial warehousing/delivery service.
   (*c*) Wholesale salesmen and own transport system delivering to wholesalers only.
   (*d*) Any other combination.   (U.S.)
7. Describe the variables which affect the design of distribution channels and comment on their relative importance. (U.S.)
8. What are the possible sources of innovation in distribution, describing some you are familiar with, and comment on the process of adoption or of rejection. (U.S.)
9. Describe the variables which affect the choice of distribution channels by a manufacturing firm. (U.S.)
10. Fundamentally the (marketing) channel decision requires resolution of the often conflicting forces of cost and control. Discuss. (U.S.)
11. Argue the case for managing the physical distribution of a company's products as an aspect of its marketing strategy. (I.M.)

12. What problems are inherent in producing a definition of the term 'channel of distribution'? (U.S.)
13. What do you understand by the total distribution cost concept? Outline the scope of the constituent centres involved and relate the importance of an understanding of the concept to the marketing manager. (I.M.)

Chapter 14
1. It has been suggested that the major thrust of consumer protection activities should be concentrated on the provision of information. Can this be justified? (U.S.)
2. Sandage and Fryburger's 'model' of how advertising is thought to work is based on four stages: exposure/perception/integration/action. Describe what takes place at the *integration* stage. (U.S.)
3. How might the characteristics of the 'message' itself affect the success or failure of an advertisment? Discuss with specific examples. (U.S.)
4. With regard to the source of a communication, what factors can provoke attitude change in the recipient? What alternatives to attitude change are open to the recipient? (I.M.)
5. Do we really know how advertising works? What theories have been advanced that might help you to explain matters to a person who asks such a question? (I.M.)

Chapter 15
1. Your company is considering changing its advertising agency. How would you undertake the selection of a replacement?
2. Analyse the following publications, using the 'check-list' described in the text: *Punch, T.V. Times, Vogue, Financial Times, Woman.*
3. Discuss the merits of the cinema as an advertising medium.
4. Develop an outline campaign plan for *either* frozen concentrated orange juice *or* off-peak travel on British Railways, assuming an annual budget of £500,000.

5. What are the economic arguments for and against advertising? Which do you find more convincing? Why?
6. How would you determine the advertising budget for a new household detergent with an expected sales volume of £5 million, a recommended retail price of £0.50, and a gross margin of 25 per cent? Distinguish between above- and below-the-line expenditures.
7. What problems do you associate with the derivation of a measure of advertising effectiveness?
8. What are the objectives of sales promotion? What type of promotion would you use:

   (a) When launching a new consumer product?
   (b) During the growth phase?
   (c) When the product has reached maturity?

9. Evaluate each of the following statements:

   (a) Advertising costs the consumer millions of pounds every year. If advertising were eliminated, prices could be reduced and everybody would benefit.
   (b) Most advertising is a social waste because it merely diverts demand from one firm to another.
   (c) Advertising is of no value to the consumer because it consists of doubtful claims of small differences between similar products.   (U.S.)

10. 'We believe in advertising; it is an essential factor in the economics of modern industry.' Discuss. (I.M.)
11. State your views on the purpose and value of sales promotion and merchandising schemes, ranging from contests to premium offers, as additions or alternatives to conventional advertising. What effect are they likely to have on brand loyalty? (I.M.)
12. 'People in advertising are parasites. They contribute nothing to the real wealth of the community.' These sentences occur in a letter in your local newspaper. Write a reply, putting the case for advertising and advertising agencies. (I.M.)
13. Summarise and evaluate any five different methods by which a national advertiser can determine the annual advertising appropriation. (I.M.)

14. 'It is not possible to make a realistic test of the effectiveness of a (television) commercial in a laboratory situation in advance of real-life exposure' (Alan Hedges). Explain. (U.S.)

15. What are the main print media? What are the main electronic media? List each. Take one media group from each category and describe its advantages and limitations. (U.S.)

16. Repetition is the key to advertising success. Evaluate the values and limitations of a repetitive campaign. (U.S.)

17. The Stimulus–Response Theory, as applied to advertising, stresses the importance of frequency and recency of exposure to advertisements by target audiences. Explain why this theory cannot by itself offer a satisfactory explanation of the influence of advertising on consumer buying behaviour. (I.M.)

18. What social benefits, if any, do the community derive from creative/display advertising? Explain your opinion with examples. (U.S.)

19. 'Personal influence is seven times more effective than magazine or newspaper advertising in the persuasion of women to switch brands of household products' (Katz and Lazarsfeld). How can this factor be employed in media planning? (U.S.)

20. Explain the advantages and disadvantages of exhibitions and trade fairs for the industrial advertiser. (U.S.)

21. Write a headline and 50–60 words of copy for a quarter page ad for a teenage magazine selling a two-week desert tour of Morocco by minibus. Describe or draw the illustration if you want to use one. (U.S.)

22. The economist Alfred Marshall (1922) drew a distinction between 'constructive' advertising and 'combative' advertising. Can such a distinction usefully be made? Discuss with examples. (U.S.)

23. Describe the main functions of a full-service advertising agency. Explain how advertising agencies are remunerated. Discuss the viability of alternatives to the advertising agency system. (U.S.)

24. Discuss three methods used in setting an advertising budget for a particular product, discussing their advantages and disadvantages. (U.S.)

Chapter 16

1. 'Unlike Advertising, there are no accurate national expenditure figures available for Sales Promotion, because many companies are undertaking such promotion without realising that they are doing so.' Explain this statement and outline some of the major uses of Sales Promotion. (U.S.)
2. From some situation in your experience, illustrate the role of 'below-the-line' sales promotion as part of the overall promotional campaign. Show how the 'below-the-line' component integrated with and contributed to the success of the total. (I.M.)
3. Define 'selling-out' and 'selling-in'. Show how a well-designed promotional campaign keeps the two elements in balance. (I.M.)
4. It is often suggested that the main role of 'below-the-line' expenditures for sales promotion is to encourage the marketer's and dealer's sales people. Give examples of such promotional activities, some of which would tend to support and others to refute this view. (I.M.)
5. In deciding on the promotional mix for a particular range of products, what circumstances would tend to favour special emphasis on:

   (*a*) dealer incentives
   (*b*) sales force activity, and
   (*c*) sampling. (I.M.)

Chapter 17

1. Direct selling is the most expensive method of establishing contact with the potential customer. Under what circumstances is this expense justified?
2. Distinguish the essential differences between trade, missionary, technical and new-business selling. What 'type' of salesman do you consider to be best suited to each?
3. Compare and contrast the various methods of salesman compensation discussed in the text. Which would you select in each of the following situations? Why?

   (*a*) Sale of capital equipment.
   (*b*) Sale of industrial lubricants.

    (*c*) Door-to-door selling of cosmetics, encyclopedias, etc.
    (*d*) Sale of packaged goods to independent retail outlets.

4. Account for the recent emphasis given to merchandising.
5. What is systems selling? What advantages does it have over the traditional product specialisation approach?
6. Critically examine the alternative methods of compensating salesmen. (U.S.)
7. 'There is something of the salesman in every good buyer. However, very few salesmen would ever make good buyers.' Discuss this view. (U.S.)
8. How should a sales manager determine the size of his sales force? (I.M.)
9. What do you think is the ideal way in which to recruit and select salesmen? (I.M.)
10. Show how a knowledge of interaction and influence processes in personal selling can contribute to an enhancement of sales-force productivity. (U.S.)
11. To what extent are psychological tests of value in the selection of salesmen? (I.M.)
12. What are the main factors which sales managers should bear in mind when evaluating the performance of their sales forces? Give your views on the extent to which remuneration of salesmen should be related to their performance. (I.M.)

Chapter 18

1. There continues to be emphasis on growth as the central corporate aim of most business organisations. Discuss the reasons for the importance of the growth concept, and consider the alternative of zero growth as a practical possibility. (U.S.)
2. What preconditions besides economic growth would you consider essential for the development of large-scale retailing? Provide illustrations of lack of development attributable to their absence. (U.S.)
3. How are the less developed countries assisted by the industrialised nations in pursuing economic development? (I.M.)
4. In what ways could the more widespread application of marketing techniques aid a country's economy? (I.M.)

Chapter 19

1. There is a considerable controversy over the validity of the argument that marketing should be 'tailored' to meet the needs of different national markets when there are significant cost savings to be achieved from the adoption of a standardised multi-national approach. Discuss.

2. How would you set about estimating the export potential for:

    (*a*) Fork-lift trucks?
    (*b*) Knitwear?
    (*c*) Atomic reactors?
    (*d*) China tea sets?

3. What other alternatives are open to the would-be exporter in addition to direct and indirect sale? What advantages/disadvantages do you associate with these alternatives?

4. Select a major United Kingdom export market, e.g. Australia, Germany, the United States, and make a comparative analysis of the salient points of similarity and difference between it and the domestic United Kingdom market. Indicate how you would use your analysis to identify broad marketing opportunities.

5. 'Market orientation is an ideal, not a practical reality, so far as the Export Manager is concerned.' Do you agree? (U.S.)

6. Submit a comprehensive brief for your market research agency instructing them on the investigation of an overseas market with which you have no previous experience of dealing. (I.M.)

7. As Director of Marketing in a company manufacturing footwear, what kinds of research would you consider it necessary to undertake to provide an assurance of successful sales in the E.E.C. countries? (I.M.)

8. How are the eating habits of the typical United Kingdom family likely to be altered by Common Market entry? (I.M.)

9. Describe the main reasons for differences in the marketing approach to different national markets for some group of products with which you are familiar. (I.M.)

10. What is meant by a 'multinational company' and under what constraints do multinationals now operate? (I.M.)

11. As an overseas marketing manager for a vacuum-cleaner manufacturers, compare and contrast some of the differences

you would anticipate in carrying out marketing research in: (*a*) the United States, and (*b*) Sri Lanka. (U.S.)

12. How can the study of comparative marketing contribute to solving the multinational firm's problems in devising product/market strategies? (U.S.)

13. To what extent can an overseas marketing manager apply the marketing concept? (U.S.)

14. The export of goods is being replaced by the export of 'know-how'. Discuss. (U.S.)

15. Discuss the advantages and disadvantages of a common universal advertising policy as against letting such policies evolve separately for each market. (U.S.)

16. Is there any real justification for treating international marketing as a separate issue from marketing in general? (I.M.)

17. The market strategy of the American Multinationals in the 1950s was to move away from exporting to local production: now the strategy has been reversed. Comment. (U.S.)

18. Is it possible to reconcile the ideals of market orientation and segmentation with the tendency of international companies to produce standard products for different national markets? Discuss. (U.S.)

Chapter 20

1. 'Management's sensitivity to strategy should be proportionate to the instability of the environment of the firm.' Explain this statement and emphasise in your answer the major characteristics of strategic change, and the problems to be encountered by the firm committing itself to such change. (U.S.)

2. What would be the main headings in an annual marketing plan? Select one of these headings and show the detail with which it would be concerned, explaining how the content of your detailed section of the plan would be related to the whole. (I.M.)

3. While the marketing planner is the central figure in drawing up the annual product plan, other departments in the company will make important contributions to the final plan. Discuss. (U.S.)

4. Describe how a marketing audit might be conducted in a

firm, and evaluate the contribution of such auditing to overall marketing control. (U.S.)

5. Assess the impact on marketing tactics and strategies of changes in roles within the family during the last 20 years. (I.M.)

6. Leading businessmen have been quoted as relying to a large extent on the regular submission and analysis of financial ratios from the trading companies under their control. Why do you think they regard such measures of control as so important? (I.M.)

7. What is the function of a Marketing Plan and how does it relate to the Corporate Long-Range Plan of an organisation? (I.M.)

8. Explain the purpose and application of any *six* of the commonly used financial ratios relating to the operation of a business. (I.M.)

9. 'Every major industry was once a growth industry' (Theodore Levitt). Discuss. (U.S.)

Chapter 22

1. 'As the general rate of change in society accelerates, the conomics of permanence are being replaced by the economics of impermanence.' (Toffler.) Is there any evidence to suggest that the above statement is an accurate description of the way in which United Kingdom society is developing? What effects would such a change have upon marketing and, in particular, upon the marketing of consumer goods? (U.S.)

2. Write a critique of the concept of metamarketing, showing the extent to which you believe marketing ideals can legitimately be extended beyond business products and services. (U.S.)

3. It has been argued that a continued expansion of output will create intolerable ecological problems. Do market-oriented firms therefore perform a social disservice by encouraging more purchases? Give reasons for your answer. (U.S.)

4. A recent Government publication described the main social trends in the United Kingdom during the last decade. Identify these trends and comment on those of particular significance in marketing. (I.M.)

5. What need is there, in your view, for a British counterpart of Ralph Nader? (I.M.)
6. A major problem in the development of a consumer-orientated economy is defining the relative roles of government and business in ensuring consumer satisfaction. Evaluate the response of business to the consumerist challenge. (U.S.)
7. Advertising is often used to add subjective values to products (e.g. cosmetic, soft drinks). This practice is widely regarded as socially undesirable. Discuss this proposition. (U.S.)
8. Consumerism has arisen because management has been guilty of one-way communication with the buyer; it is not listening to what is being said in reply. Discuss. (U.S.)
9. Has consumerism become a casualty to inflation? (I.M.)
10. Consumer sovereignty is the myth of the contemporary market-place. Discuss the role of this concept in the development of a realistic consumerist philosophy. (U.S.)
11. Consumerism is a phenomenon of the post-war years, and is a fact of life for many companies. How is it likely to affect the work of:

    (*a*) the Marketing Department, and
    (*b*) the Production Department

    of a company marketing consumer durables? (I.M.)
12. What do you understand by the term 'social marketing'? What is the relationship between social marketing and consumerism? (I.M.)
13. Describe the factors leading to the growth of consumerism in the 1960s and 1970s and consider how adequately the present U.K. consumerist structure and philosophy meets the demands that arise from these factors. (U.S.)
14. Waste – in excess production of undesirable goods, in unnecessary packaging, in squandering precious resources – in an inevitable outcome of marketing freedom. Discuss, suggesting constraints and controls if you feel they are necessary. (U.S.)

Supplementary Reading List

It is clear that an introductory text can do no more than outline basic principles and provide an overview of the subject matter as a whole. The purpose of this reading list is to suggest sources which the author believes will prove useful in supplementing the material covered in this book. In turn, many of the references contain bibliographies, or cite other sources, which should prove useful in pursuing an in-depth study of a particular topic. Many of the sources cited have been 'carried over' from earlier editions and may now appear to be dated. This is not believed to be the case – relatively few new books have been introduced which offer new perspectives or insights beyond those contained in what have come to be regarded as basic texts. However, the list is by no means exhaustive and students should consult the reading list published by the various examining bodies as well as those issued by their own tutors.

MAGAZINES, PERIODICALS, ETC.

To keep abreast of current developments, and update factual data, at least some of the following publications should be consulted on a regular basis:

Admap
Advertiser's Weekly
European Business
European Journal of Marketing
Financial Times

Harvard Business Review
Journal of Marketing (U.S.A.)
Journal of Marketing Research (U.S.A.)
Journal of the Market Rearch Society
Management Decision
Management Today
Marketing
Quarterly Review of Marketing
Sunday Times Business News
Advertising Quarterly
The Economist.

GENERAL TEXTS

Many general texts have appeared in several editions and students should seek to obtain the most recent.

Bell, M., *Marketing: Concepts and Strategy*, 2nd ed. (Houghton Mifflin, 1972).

Boyd, H. W. and Massey, W. F., *Marketing Management* (Harcourt, Brace, Jovanovich, 1972).

Frey, A. W. (ed.), *Marketing Handbook*, 2nd ed. (Ronald Press, 1965).

Kotler, Philip, *Marketing Management*, 3rd ed. (Prentice-Hall, 1976).

McCarthy, E. J., *Basic Marketing*, 6th ed. (Irwin, 1978).

PART ONE

Baker, Michael, J. (ed.), *Marketing: Theory and Practice* (Macmillan, 1976).

Enis, B. and Cox, D., *Marketing Classics,* 3rd ed. (Allyn & Bacon, 1977).

Halbert, Michael, *The Meaning and Sources of Marketing Theory* (McGraw-Hill, 1965).

Howard, John A., *Marketing: Executive and Buyer Behaviour* (Columbia University Press, 1963).

Robinson, P. J., and Luck, D. J., *Promotional Decision-Making, Practice and Theory* (McGraw-Hill, 1964).

PART TWO

Day, Ralph L., *Marketing Models: Quantitative and Behavioural* (International Textbook Co., 1964).
Engel, J. F., Blackwell, R. D., and Kollatt, D. T., *Consumer Behavior*, 3rd ed. (The Dryden Press, 1978).
Howard, John A., *Marketing: Executive and Buyer Behaviour* (Columbia University Press, 1963).
Kassarjian, H. H., and Robertson, T. S., *Perspectives in Consumer Behaviour* (Scott Foresman, 1968).
Savage, Christopher I., and Small, John R., *Introduction to Managerial Economics* (Hutchinson, 1964).
Spencer, Milton H., *Managerial Economics*, 3rd ed. (Irwin, 1968).

PART THREE

In addition to the sources cited in the text, the following deal specifically with the subject of industrial marketing:

Alexander, Cross and Hill, *Industrial Marketing* (Irwin, 1967).
Baker, Michael J., *Marketing New Industrial Products* (Macmillan, 1975).
Fisher, L. W., *Industrial Marketing*, 2nd ed. (Business Books, 1976).
Hill, R. W. and Hillier, T. J., *Organisational Buying Behaviour* (Macmillan, 1977).
Williams, L. A., *Industrial Marketing Management and Controls* (Longmans, 1967).
Wilson, Aubrey (ed.), *The Marketing of Industrial Products* (Hutchinson, 1965).

PART FOUR

Marketing research
Adler, Max, *Marketing and Market Research* (Crosby Lockwood, 1967).
Crisp, Richard D., *Marketing Research* (McGraw-Hill, 1957).
Fitzroy, P. T., *Analytical Methods for Marketing Management* (McGraw-Hill, 1976).

Green, Paul E., and Tull, Donald S., *Research for Marketing Decisions*, 3rd ed. (Prentice-Hall, 1968).

Livingstone, J. M., *A Management Guide to Market Research* (Macmillan, 1977).

Smith, Brien and Stafford, *Readings in Marketing Information Systems* (Houghton Mifflin, 1968).

Stacey, Nicholas, and Wilson, Aubrey, *Industrial Marketing Research* (Hutchinson, 1963).

Wills, Gordon, *Marketing Through Research* (Pergamon Press, 1968).

Product policy

Baker, Michael J. and McTavish, R., *Product Policy and Management* (Macmillan, 1976).

Berg, Thomas, and Schuchman, Abe, *Product Strategy and Management* (Holt, Rinehart & Winston, 1963).

Gerlach, John T., and Wainwright, Charles Anthony, *Successful Management of New Products* (Hastings House, 1968).

Levitt, Theodore, *Innovation in Marketing* (McGraw-Hill, 1962).

MacDonald, Morgan B., Jr, *Appraising the Market for New Industrial Products* (National Industrial Conference Board, 1967).

Pessemier, Edgar A., *New Product Decisions* (McGraw-Hill, 1966).

Silk, Leonard, *The Research Revolution* (McGraw-Hill, 1960).

Stone, Merlin, *Product Planning* (Macmillan, 1976).

Pricing and price policy

Backman, Jules, *Price Practices and Price Policies* (Ronald Press, 1953).

Dean, Joel, *Managerial Economics* (Prentice-Hall, 1951).

Harper, Donald V., *Price Policy and Procedure* (Harcourt, Brace, 1966).

Livesey, F., *Pricing* (Macmillan, 1976).

Pricing: The Critical Decision (Management Report no. 66, American Management Association, 1961).

Pricing: Policies and Practices (National Industrial Conference Board, 1961).

Taylor, Bernard, and Wills, Gordon (eds.), *Pricing Strategy* (Staples Press, 1969).

Distribution policy

Bucklin, Louis P., *A Theory of Distribution Channel Structure* (Institute of Business and Economic Research, Berkeley, California, 1966).

Clewett, Richard M. (ed.), *Marketing Channels for Manufactured Products* (Irwin, 1954).

Stern, Louis W. (ed.), *Distribution Channels: Behavioural Dimensions* (Houghton Mifflin, 1969).

Advertising and sales promotion

The four texts sponsored by the Institute of Practitioners of Advertising (I.P.A.) provide a good introduction to this subject, namely:

Caplan, *Advertising: A General Introduction* (Business Publications).

Hobson, *The Selection of Advertising Media* (Business Publications).

Ellefsen, *Campaign Planning* (Business Publications).

Langdon-Davies, *Modern Advertising Law* (Business Publications).

Boyd, Harper W., and Levy, Sidney J., *Promotion: A Behavioural View* (Prentice-Hall, 1967).

Broadbent, S., *Spending Advertising Money*, 2nd ed. (Business Books, 1975).

Canon, T., *Advertising Research* (Intertext, 1973).

Corkindale, D. and Kennedy, S., *Measuring the Effect of Advertising* (Saxon House, 1975).

Delozier, W. M., *The Marketing Communication Process* (McGraw-Hill, 1976).

Gilligan, C. and Crowther, G., *Advertising Management* (Philip Allan, 1976).

Spillard, Peter, *Sales Promotion* 2nd ed. (Business Publications, 1977).

Personal selling

Battersby, Albert, *Sales Forecasting* (Cassell, 1968).

Hudson, C. L., *Professional Salesmanship* (Staples Press, 1967).

Robinson, Patrick J., and Stidsen, Bent, *Personal Selling in a Modern Perspective* (Allyn & Bacon, 1967).

The Field Sales Manager (American Management Association, 1960).

PART FIVE

International marketing
Comparative Analysis for International Marketing (Marketing Science Institute, Allyn & Bacon, 1967).
Deschampsneufs, Henry, *Marketing Overseas* (Pergamon Press, 1968).
Fayerweather, J., *International Marketing* (Prentice-Hall, 1964).
Hess, J. M., and Cateora, P. R., *International Marketing* (Irwin, 1966).
Leighton, D. S. R., *International Marketing: Text and Cases* (McGraw-Hill, 1966).
Livingstone, J. M., *The International Enterprise* (A.B.P. Ltd, 1975).
Livingstone, J. M., *International Marketing Management* (Macmillan, 1976).
Tookey, D., *Export Marketing Decisions* (Penguin, 1975).

Planning and case analysis
Adler, Lee (ed.), *Plotting Marketing Strategy* (Business Books, 1968).
Bingham, J. S. (ed.), *British Cases in Marketing* (Business Books, 1969).
Bursk, Edward C., and Chapman, John F. (eds.), *Modern Marketing Strategy* (Mentor, 1965).
Drucker, Peter F., *Managing for Results* (Pan Piper, 1964).
Giles, G. B., *Case Studies in Marketing*, 2nd ed. (Macdonald & Evans, 1968).
Kelley, Eugene J., *Marketing: Strategy and Functions* (Prentice-Hall, 1965).

Index